An Extraordinary Atlantic Life

An Extraordinary Atlantic Life

Sebastián Nicolás Calvo de la Puerta y O'Farrill, Marqués de Casa-Calvo

Gilbert C. Din

University of Louisiana at Lafayette Press
2016

ISBN 13 (paper): 978-1-935754-78-7

University of Louisiana at Lafayette Press
P.O. Box 43558
Lafayette, LA 70504-0831
http://ulpress.org

Printed on acid-free paper.

Library of Congress Cataloging-in-Publication Data
Names: Din, Gilbert C., author.
Title: An extraordinary Atlantic life : Sebastián Nicolás Calvo de la Puerta y O'Farrill, Marqués de Casa-Calvo / Gilbert C. Din.
Other titles: Sebastián Nicolás Calvo de la Puerta y O'Farrill, Marqués de Casa-Calvo
Description: Lafayette, LA : University of Louisiana at Lafayette Press, [2016] | Includes bibliographical references and index.
Identifiers: LCCN 2015049828 | ISBN 9781935754787
Subjects: LCSH: Casa Calvo, Sebastián Calvo de la Puerta y O'Farrill, marqués de, 1751-1820. | Louisiana--History--To 1803. | Governors--Louisiana--Biography. | Spaniards--Louisiana--Biography. | Spain. Ejército--Officers--Biography. | Spaniards--Cuba--Biography. | Cuba--History--To 1810.
Classification: LCC F372 .D55 2016 | DDC 976.3/01092--dc23
LC record available at http://lccn.loc.gov/2015049828

Contents

List of Illustrations

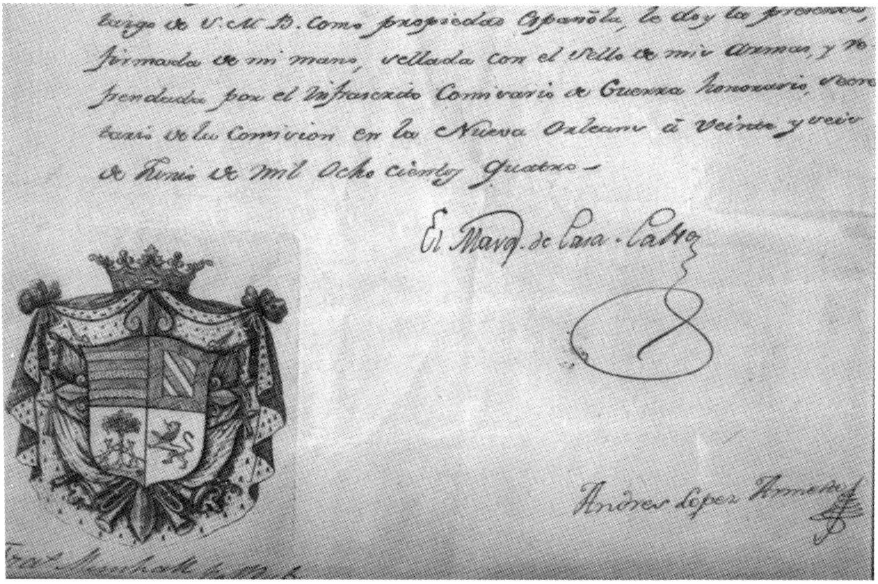
cargo de V.M.B. Como propiedad Española, le doy la presente,
firmada de mi mano, sellada con el sello de mis Armas, y re-
frendada por el Infrascrito Comisario de Guerra honorario, secre-
tario de la Comision en la Nueva Orleans a veinte y seis
de Junio de mil ocho cientos quatro —

El Marq. de Casa-Calvo

Andres Lopez Armesto

Casa-Calvo's signature on an official document
Courtesy of Jorge Auñón

Preface

Sebastián Nicolás Calvo de la Puerta y O'Farrill, who for much of his life was known as the Marqués de Casa-Calvo, has long been treated as no more than a marginal figure by Louisiana historians. Despite their limited attention to him, he has kindled more notice in the state than he has in his native Cuba, except for genealogists interested in his family, or in Europe where he spent nearly a quarter of a century. Nevertheless, even in Louisiana where students are given some exposure to its governors—he was an interim Spanish governor for two years—his name is seldom recognized.

As he was born in Cuba, the Atlantic Ocean played a formidable role in his life.[1] The family's presence on the island began with his sixteenth-century Spanish ancestor Martín Calvo de la Puerta's arrival at Havana nearly 180 years before Sebastián's birth in 1751. The city became the home town of all his New World ancestors. They descended in an uninterrupted masculine line from the first Calvo de la Puerta as they gradually added wealth and status to their economic holdings and social position. By the time Sebastián's father took hold of the family fortune, it had become one of the most significant on the island. Sebastián chose a career in the regular army unlike his two brothers who became planters first and militia officers second. Nevertheless, his father and later his mother willed him some properties upon their deaths that generated extra income for Sebastián. Although he felt an attachment to his birthplace, similar with other upper class Cubans he regarded himself a Spaniard in ethnicity if not in background. He

1. Jack P. Greene and Philip D. Morgan, eds., *Atlantic History: A Critical Appraisal* (Oxford: Oxford University Press, 2009). In their introductory essay, Greene and Morgan provide a lengthy examination of the development in Atlantic studies.

crossed the Atlantic several times and sailed through extensions of its waters—the Gulf of Mexico and the Caribbean—on a number of occasions. As knowledge, trade, travel, and inter-change throughout the Atlantic world intensified in the eighteenth century, it drew him and fellow inhabitants of all coastal regions closer together.

Much of what is presently known in the United States about Casa-Calvo—aristocrats loved being called by their titles—has come from scattered American sources, not from Spanish records. The writers of the prominent American documents, Thomas Jefferson, James Madison, and William C. C. Claiborne, among others, regarded him as an adversary and disparaged him at the same time they schemed to seize adjacent territory in the Mississippi Valley from the crumbling Spanish Empire. They typically alleged national security as the reason for gobbling up the eastern Spanish borderlands, not greed or imperialism, even when they knew that Spain no longer possessed the might to resist them. They denigrated Casa-Calvo as a corrupt official from a tyrannical government that blocked their way and failed to see him as a loyal servant who attempted to protect his government's possessions. Casa-Calvo played a limited role in countering Jefferson's contrived assertion that West Florida was part of the Louisiana Purchase, although the Cuban knew better because he had participated in its conquest from the British between 1779 and 1781, and indeed it was Great Britain, not France, that ceded it to Spain.

In 1803 Casa-Calvo was in New Orleans to take part in Louisiana's retrocession to France, which Napoleon Bonaparte had already sold to the United States. Early in 1804 while Casa-Calvo presided over Spain's evacuation from the province, he learned that ambitious American officials were engaging in power politics and demanding West Florida inasmuch as that required less effort than brute force to seize it. As long as Casa-Calvo was in Louisiana, the Americans were unsuccessful in their aspirations, not that he played a role in resisting them. But he came to grips with the American desire for more territory and tried to devise a plan to recover Louisiana.

More important, he surveyed the Sabine River and helped prove that French settlement had not penetrated into Texas, as Jefferson boisterously alleged. In this way, Casa-Calvo deserves some recognition in United States history, not as a foreign schemer engaged in nefarious chicanery and skullduggery, but as an able and loyal Spanish subject committed to protecting imperial territory.

An impartial assessment of Casa-Calvo has eluded the few American historians who have written tidbits about him inasmuch as no biography on him has heretofore appeared. Grace King, who wrote in the late nineteenth and early twentieth centuries and examined negligible documents about him, seemed captivated that a nobleman was governor of Louisiana. She wrote about him at the time of the retrocession,

> [He] was not such a man who would permit the outgoing monarchy to be put to shame by the incoming republic. Attended by a staff and a pompous guard, he gathered around him the most brilliant representatives of Spanish blood in society, with all of their connections and affiliations, and by a lavish expenditure of money, he turned his official mission into a triumphant apotheosis of his government in Louisiana.[2]

Her flamboyant account, however, erred in several ways, as only a paltry twelve-soldier guard from his regiment in Cuba attended to his security, and "the most brilliant representatives of Spanish blood" consisted of the "usual" good and bad Louisiana officials. It seems that in King's eyes, Casa-Calvo's refined behavior in New Orleans, his sugar estates in Cuba, and his extravagant entertainment expenditures helped cast him in a more radiant light.

Arthur P. Whitaker, who had an acquaintance with Louisiana documents, disparaged virtually all Spaniards in New Orleans in his 1934 book, *The Mississippi Question, 1795-1803: A Study in Trade, Politics, and Diplomacy*. He only faintly praised Casa-Calvo, belittling him and Juan Ventura Morales as "entitled to the slightest respect, and the respect due them is very slight." Whitaker did not inform his readers that the two officials were at odds with one another and differed enormously in personality. In imitation of King, he repeated that Louisiana

2. Grace Elizabeth King, *New Orleans, The Place and the People* (New York: Macmillan, 1895), 157.

Creoles esteemed Casa-Calvo as "an elegant gentleman," and added derisively that it alone constituted the "measure of his greatness." Whitaker personified Casa-Calvo with worn-out clichés as "a typical Spanish bureaucrat" who possessed the "graceful negligence of the office that gave him his livelihood." Although "unoriginal" and "unenergetic," he had the redeeming grace to keep subordinates at their posts to carry out government business, which in Whitaker's estimation gave him the appearance of possessing, at least in this regard, praiseworthy Anglo-Saxon traits.[3]

Whitaker repeated the vitriol of the New Orleans entrepreneur Daniel Clark Jr., who wrote in November 1799 that Casa-Calvo depended on the procrastinating government secretary Andrés López Armesto. Much the same information comes from a document written by the contemporary James Wilkinson and later quoted by historian Isaac Joslin Clark, which states,

> the marqués is entirely under the direction of his secretary [López Armesto]; that the latter is not capable of keeping a secret, and he would hardly learn of my [Wilkinson's] plan before communicating it unreservedly and in complete detail to his friend and comrade, the intendant [Juan Ventura Morales]. At the present the latter is on very intimate terms with Mr. Daniel Clark, and they are likewise associated in land speculations.[4]

Thus, Wilkinson, the commanding general of the western American army and a master of deception, in short order denigrated several Spanish officials—not that Morales deserved better; he did not. Wilkinson, however, erred significantly in linking Casa-Calvo to the foibles of the others. It is known that as interim governor he had initially relied on López Armesto because of his familiarity with the Spanish documentation, and Casa-Calvo had admitted to the captain

3. Arthur Preston Whitaker, *The Mississippi Question, 1795-1803: A Study in Trade, Politics, and Diplomacy* (repr. Gloucester, Mass: Peter Smith, 1962), all the short quotations are on p. 159.

4. Isaac Joslin Cox, "General Wilkinson and His Later Intrigues with the Spaniards," *American Historical Review* 19 (July 1914): 796.

general before departing Cuba of his limited acquaintance with Louisiana affairs. In appointing Casa-Calvo, the captain general trusted in his subordinate's ability to learn quickly once he arrived in Louisiana, which was precisely what he did.

After reaching New Orleans in September 1799, Casa-Calvo read the voluminous documents stored in the governor's archives to discover at first-hand the province's many problems. Clark, instead, alleged that the effete aristocrat "hates application to business, is fond of company and amusement, affects to be frank and open in his manner, but is full of the consequence derived from the possession of rank and riches."[5]

Whitaker, however, neglected to examine Clark's remarks carefully. Casa-Calvo was not a civilian "bureaucrat" but a high-ranking army officer; did not depend on his office for his livelihood since he was also a planter; and, in an age that loved military uniforms, dressed as the brigadier general he was at the time. Contrary to Whitaker's judgment, Governor Casa-Calvo's voluminous letters to and from officials in and outside the colony demonstrate the slew of matters that consumed his attention. Instead, Whitaker endorsed Clark's notion that Casa-Calvo "hated" government business and preferred to indulge in vacuous pastimes.[6] No doubt businessman Clark wanted the governor to divulge more of his thinking on issues then affecting the colony as he impatiently sought inside information about investment opportunities. Casa-Calvo, however, parried his delicate questions with empty talk, especially at social gatherings. Both Whitaker and Clark failed to perceive the smokescreen that Casa-Calvo cast on his innermost thoughts. He knew that Americans hungered to seize the Mississippi River and the colony, and some of their contemporaries prematurely regarded both as already theirs. They were notorious for smuggling and violating Spanish customs laws. In the late 1790s, the insecure Mississippi delta

5. Whitaker, *The Mississippi Question*, 159.

6. In a short article, Edna C. Sorber and Joseph Velo (a Casa-Calvo descendant), "A Sketch of the Marquis of Casa Calvo, Governor of Louisiana (1751-1820)," *Revista: Cuban Genealogical Society* 4 (July 1991): 1-6, try to correct errors about Casa-Calvo made earlier by assorted writers, including Whitaker and Pierre Clément de Laussat.

was filled with contentious issues and ambitious politicians. Casa-Calvo handled problems as well as he could, given the scarcity in soldiers, settlers, money, and other essentials needed to turn West Florida and Louisiana into formidable barriers to safeguard the precious mineral deposits in the viceroyalty of New Spain.

Among current historians who have written on Casa-Calvo is Jared William Bradley who published some essays on Spanish figures of Louisiana's late colonial period in his *Interim Appointment: W.C.C. Claiborne Letter Book, 1804-1805*, edited with Biographical Sketches. His essay on Casa-Calvo utilized predominantly American documents and books. Many of his sources came from Claiborne, the first American governor of the Louisiana Territory, who dealt with Casa-Calvo. Claiborne, a young and inexperienced Jeffersonian, tried with every letter he sent to Washington City to please the president and Secretary of State James Madison. But his relations with Casa-Calvo repeatedly hit snags as the Cuban official showed that he had learned over the years how to deal with high government and army officials in Madrid, Cuba, and Santo Domingo, and he irked the insecure Claiborne by lingering in New Orleans to finish the tasks given him to evacuate Louisiana of Spanish personnel and equipment and to determine the Louisiana-Texas boundary. In the end, Bradley provides a subjective depiction of his subject since his American-derived knowledge of events gave him a skewed perspective on the multifaceted Casa-Calvo.[7]

All that said, this study utilizes an abundance of information about Casa-Calvo drawn from sources outside Louisiana. Besides describing the rise of his Calvo de la Puerta ancestors and explaining the making of their fortune, it examines Sebastián's army career in Cuba, New Orleans, Santo Domingo, and Spain. His experiences during the American War for Independence, his formation of a regiment in Spain, and his return to Cuba shortly before the Haitian Revolution exploded are also discussed. He spent three years (1793-1796) in Spanish Santo Do-

7. Jared William Bradley, *Interim Appointment: W. C. C. Claiborne Letter Book, 1804-1805*, edited with Biographical Sketches (Baton Rouge: Louisiana State University Press, 2002), 484-94.

mingo and neighboring Saint-Domingue during the French war and after. Louisiana then saw him from 1799 to 1801 and again from 1803 to 1806. Lastly, he returned to Spain on a third occasion shortly before the French intervention (1808 to 1813) in the Iberian Peninsula. Because he sided with the Bonapartists, he fled into exile in France for the final years of his life. Many of these events about Casa-Calvo are little or totally unknown until now.[8]

Casa-Calvo lived in an extraordinary time. Revolutionary conflict filled the Atlantic world of the late eighteenth and early nineteenth centuries as inhabitants on both sides of the ocean had tired of the repressive conditions that had been imposed on them, and they now sought greater freedom. He, however, was a royal army officer and tried to preserve the status quo militarily on the western side of the Atlantic and later worked to obtain moderate economic changes from the Spanish monarchy on the eastern side. Therefore, he was by no means a revolutionary since he opposed radical alterations to society and government. These highlights form the basis of this study as it proposes to enlighten readers on Casa-Calvo's adventurous life and the troubled times in which he lived.

Several people helped me complete this study. First of all, Dr. Jorge Auñón Prieto Calvo de la Puerta, a Casa-Calvo descendant through his younger son Ignacio Calvo de la Puerta y Peñalver, provided me with information he uncovered about his ancestor and several illustrations. Among the illustrations is one that depicts two of Casa-Calvo's children, the only known image of persons belonging to the marqués's immediate family. An amateur genealogist and a retired dean of the College of Engineering at the University of Alabama in Huntsville, Auñón has traced his ancestry across nearly five centuries of Cuban history. I am likewise indebted to Professor Stephen Webre, of the History Department at Louisiana Tech University and a noted Latin

8. A sketch of Casa-Calvo's life that is somewhat more nuanced is José Montero de Pedro, Marqués de Casa Mena's *Españoles en Nueva Orleans y Luisiana* (Madrid: Talleres Prensa Española, 1979), 62-68. However, Montero de Pedro combines his sketch on Casa-Calvo with that of Manuel Juan de Salcedo and, consequently, it sometimes becomes confusing.

Americanist. He took time from his busy schedule to read an early draft of the manuscript, make helpful suggestions, and provide hard to find sources. Judge Morris Arnold of the United States Eighth Circuit Court and a renowned authority on colonial Arkansas, and Dr. John E. Harkins, former head of the History Department at Memphis University School, an earlier collaborator and well-informed on Spanish New Orleans and the Cabildo, also kindly read the manuscript. Also, I want to thank Mary Karnath Duhé and James Wilson for their work on producing this book. Finally, my son Alexander M. Din, a geographer and a Geospatial Information Systems specialist, helped me with the maps used in this book. I can say without reservation that all their input has enhanced the study.

1
Rise of the Calvo de la Puerta Family

In 1574 Martín Calvo de la Puerta arrived in Havana, Cuba, the first known member of his family to cross the Atlantic Ocean to the New World. He represented a transitional generation given that he and his ancestors were from the kingdom of Castile, and he became the progenitor of a new branch of the family in Cuba. Although his forebears' name does not reflect a Basque derivation, their origins in the region of Vizcaya in northern Spain confirm that fact. Possibly they had once lived in a Roman settlement called in Latin *Calvus*, meaning "exposed" or "uncovered." In time the word evolved into Castilian as Calvo, and the community's inhabitants often adopted it as a surname to designate where they lived. Centuries later, because of marriages, Martín's immediate predecessors added "de la Puerta" to note a new union in the family, and in this curious manner Calvo de la Puerta emerged as a single surname.[1]

In about the late fifteenth century, family members relocated from Vizcaya to Andalusia and more particularly to southwestern Spain, which two hundred and fifty years before had been the Moorish king-

1. Francisco Javier de Santa Cruz y Mallén (Conde de San Juan de Jaruco y de Santa Cruz de Mopox), in *Historia de familias cubanas*, 4 vols. (La Habana: Editoriales Hércules, 1943), 4: 104, states that Martín Calvo de la Puerta's paternal grandfather was Gonzalo Hernández Calvo and his maternal grandfather was Martín Juan de la Puerta. From these forebears' surname, Calvo de la Puerta emerged. Genealogical studies of the Calvo de la Puerta family, unfortunately, often provide contradictory information that confounds the reader.

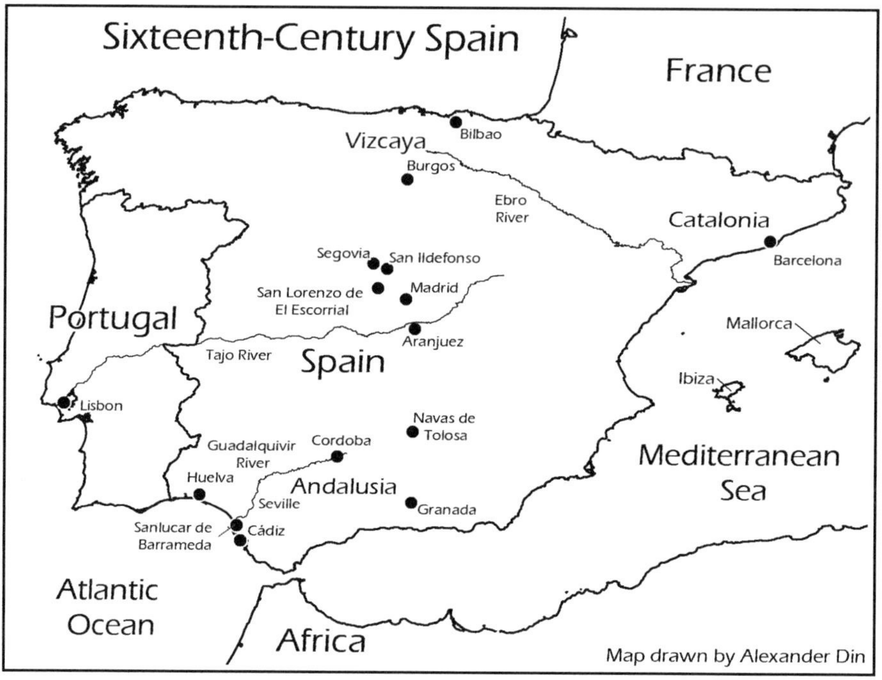

dom of Seville. They selected the small community or *villa* of Cumbres Mayores nestled amid rolling hills at the northern edge of today's Huelva province. About eighty-two miles south from Cumbres Mayores, the coastal river town of Huelva lies adjacent to the tiny port of Palos that is situated on the Río Tinto. And it was from Palos that Christopher Columbus departed in 1492 on his epoch-making voyage. His dramatic announcement of lands on the other side of the Atlantic Ocean and the resettlement of the Calvo de la Puerta family in Cumbres Mayores were probably connected because the discovery impacted Spain in countless ways.[2] Columbus's journey into the Atlantic had

2. Among the many works on Columbus, see Samuel Eliot Morison, *Admiral of the Ocean Sea: A Life of Christopher Columbus* (Boston: Little, Brown, and Company, 1942); *Christopher Columbus, Mariner* (Boston: New American Library, 1942), 21-32. Disagreeing with genealogists who claim that the Calvo de la Puerta family moved south in the early sixteenth century, Mallén, in *Historia de familias cubanas*, 4: 104, states that the family relocated to Andalusia in the fifteenth century.

been preceded during the fifteenth century by Portuguese and Spanish exploration and trade down the western seaboard of Africa and to the islands off its coast (the Canaries and the Cape Verdes) and off Portugal (the Madeiras and the Azores). It was truly an age of astonishing discoveries and alterations in Europe's Atlantic nations, especially Spain.[3]

Columbus's exhilarating news on his return after finding unknown lands coincided with the termination of the Christian reconquest of Moorish Spain. It generated enormous repercussions inasmuch as people from throughout the kingdom of Castile soon thronged southward to participate in the many economic, social, and military activities that sprang up. Drawn like metal to a magnet, they sought out opportunities in trade, diverse employment, and adventure. Seville, an inland port on the Guadalquivir River at fifty miles from the Atlantic and about eighty miles east of Cumbres Mayores, figured at the center of the activity. Its population swelled quickly and transformed it into the largest and most dynamic city in Spain, and it became the nerve center for Spain's many dealings with the transatlantic lands. Among the people who poured in but without the adventurous spirit to emigrate were merchants, traders, artisans, and free laborers of diverse abilities who were not tied to the feudal estates that dominated most rural sections of Castile. The sixteenth century emerged as an era of urban economic development and social flux in Andalusia and across the sea where prospects beckoned and success awaited the fortunate. Through the century, trade in Seville's bustling economy grew significantly, and nouveaux riche merchants often applied their earnings to purchase noble status from the impecunious crown and gain access to offices denied commoners. Even gifted artisans occasionally became merchants,

3. Alberto Veira, "Sugar Islands: The Sugar Economy of Madeira and the Canaries, 1450-1650," in *Tropical Babylons: Sugar and the Making of the Atlantic World, 1450-1650*, ed. Stuart B. Schwartz (Chapel Hill: University of North Carolina Press, 2004), 65. Among the many Italian, Portuguese, Flemish, French, and Spanish merchants involved in the Madeira sugar trade was a Francisco Calvo, who possibly was related to kin in Cumbres Mayores. The many new trade objectives discovered during fifteenth-century exploration are discussed in John K. Thornton, *Africa and Africans in the Making of the Atlantic World, 1400-1500* (Cambridge: Cambridge University Press, 1992).

and a rare few ascended to the lower nobility. All too often, however, the wealthiest merchants imitated the stifling example of the higher nobility and thrust their riches into status-bearing landholdings. While this investment strategy perhaps advanced their social standing, it perpetuated Castile's economic stagnation.[4]

In its own way, Cumbres Mayores, home of the Calvo de la Puerta family, reflected Iberian history. Defensive fortresses built in the Middle Ages on three adjacent hillcrests received names that described their relative elevation. The highest crest of Cumbres Mayores possibly had accommodated inhabitants since before the first millennia B.C. Over time, they endured the onslaught of numerous invaders—Iberian tribesmen, Celts, Carthaginians, Romans, Vandals (who left their name on Andalusia), Visigoths ("godo" survives today as a derogatory name for peninsular Spaniards in the Canary Islands), and Moors (al-Andalus was the name they used for their lands in what earlier had been Roman Hispania). The Moorish occupation of much of the Iberian Peninsula beginning in 711 A.D. gave rise to the Christian struggle to recover Muslim-held regions, an undertaking that consumed centuries. After the momentous victory at Navas de Tolosa on the northern edge of al-Andalus in 1212 by a large coalition of Christian crusaders, they poured south and claimed the kingdoms of Córdoba (1236), Jaén (1246), and Seville (1248) from the Moors. These conquests gave Castile dominion over western Andalusia, Spain's richest agricultural area, filled with vineyards, olive and citrus orchards, vegetable gardens, and fields that produced diverse foodstuffs for humans and animals. This verdant zone differed enormously from the mountain stronghold of eastern Andalusia, where the kingdom of Granada (today's provinces of Granada, Almería, and Málaga) resisted Christian warriors until1492. Western Andalusia's energetic towns, however, provided greater opportunities for enterprising youth than for their socially and economically stagnant feudal counterparts in other regions of Spain, where change arrived slowly or not at all. Soon similar oppor-

4. Ruth Pike, *Aristocrats and Traders: Sevillian Society in the Sixteenth Century* (Ithaca: Cornell University Press, 1972), 1-20, 170-92. Seville became the fourth largest city in Europe.

tunities opened up in the lands beyond the Atlantic. The year 1492 was also pivotal for Castile's religious unification through the forced conversion or expulsion of Jews and Columbus's discovery. The protracted reconquest, however, imposed entrenched systems and attitudes on the government, economy, society, and religion that the Spaniards transferred to the New World and where aspects of their ingrained effects lingered on for centuries.[5]

In the late fifteenth century, the Calvo de la Puerta family began its labors in businesses tied to agriculture in Cumbres Mayores. Martín, a member of the third generation of the now Andalusian family, was probably born in Cumbres Mayores and soon after baptized in its church on September 19, 1551. The region still carried the Moorish political designation of kingdom of Seville—that changed only in 1833, when it was divided into provinces that included Huelva.[6] As Martín matured, he developed an instinctive awareness, if not training, in commercial affairs that later contributed to his financial success in Havana. The region around the *villa* was devoted to animal husbandry and to the manufacture of olive oil and meat products, especially hams. At four hundred meters above sea level, the community was, and still is, modest and rural. It most likely supplied food to vessels engaged in the *carrera de Indias* (transatlantic trade) and to the expanding populations of Andalusian cities.[7]

5. Charles Julian Bishko, "The Spanish and Portuguese Reconquest, 1095-1492," in *The Fourteenth and Fifteenth Centuries*, vol. 3 of *A History of the Crusades*, ed. Harry W. Hazard (Madison: University of Wisconsin Press, 1975), 396-456; Rhea Marsh Smith, *Spain, A Modern History* (Ann Arbor: University of Michigan Press, 1965), 3-111; Donald E. Worcester and Wendell G. Schaeffer, *The Growth and Culture of Latin America* (New York: Oxford University Press, 1956), 12-13.

6. Conde de Vallellano, *Nobilario cubano: Las grandes familias isleñas* (Madrid: Francisco Beltrán, [1929]), 235. Martín Calvo de la Puerta's paternal and maternal grandfathers both rose in importance through their earnings in commerce.

7. Vallellano, *Nobilario cubano*, 1: 235, provides additional confusion. Citing *El Curioso Americano* (1910), 118, he states that the grandfather possibly was Martín Juan Calvo de la Puerta who married Leonor Sánchez; they had a child, Hernán Gómez de la Puerta, who was born in Seville. He, in turn, married Juana Hernández Gil, from a leading family in both Cumbres Mayores and Hinojales, a nearby town. From this

By the time of Martín's birth, Spanish conquests and possessions in the New World and Old had grown extensively. They included the major Caribbean islands and continental lands that stretched from New Spain (Mexico) in the north down to Central America and along the north and west coasts of South America as far south as Chile. In addition, the grandson and heir of the Catholic Kings (Queen Isabel of Castile and King Fernando of Aragon) was also heir to the Habsburg possessions in central Europe, and he succeeded first to the kingdoms of Castile and Aragon as Carlos I in 1516, and later was elected Holy Roman Emperor as Carlos V (as he was known in Spain) in 1519, which gave him suzerainty over widespread European lands. The acquisition of extensive domains, accomplished through strategic dynastic marriages and military conquests by the formidable *tercios* (legions) of the Castilian infantry, elevated Spain and the Spanish Habsburgs to global power and prominence.[8]

No doubt the Calvo de la Puerta family of Cumbres Mayores benefited from these historic developments. Andalusia's Atlantic ports at Cádiz, Sanlúcar de Barrameda at the mouth of the Guadalquivir River, and Huelva, along with the rest of Andalusia, became the region most closely associated with the New World colonies in economics and emigrants. Seville was designated in 1503 as the port of departure and return for all vessels involved with the new possessions, and it hummed briskly as newcomers from all social classes and occupations swarmed into the city and its expanding suburbs until skeptics dubbed it the "Great Babylon of Spain." Economic growth profited manufacturers and merchants and gave the impoverished employment and criminals victims to prey on.[9] Seville's busy trade radiated out to neighboring ports and to Europe's

---

marriage came Martín Calvo de la Puerta y Hernández who immigrated to Cuba.

8. John Lynch, *Spain under the Habsburgs*, 2 vols. (Oxford: Basil Blackwell, 1964), 1: 28-36. The military unit called the *tercio* combined infantry, artillery, and cavalry and is explained in Stanley G. Paine, *A History of Spain and Portugal*, 2 vols. (Madison: University of Wisconsin Press, 1973), 2: 249.

9. Pike, *Aristocrats and Traders*, 1-2, 99-153, 192-214; Mary Elizabeth Perry, *Crime and Society in Early Modern Seville* (Lebanon, N.H.:University Press of New England, 1980), discusses the many social classes from the nobility to the *gente de mal vivir*

Mediterranean and Atlantic coasts. Italian, French, Dutch, English, and Flemish merchants, among others, moved to Spain to arrange the sales of their national products for Castile and the new colonies and to purchase exotic colonial imports (tobacco, cacao, dyes, woods, and even animals). Foreign merchants also welcomed colonial silver and gold in payment for their goods, coinage that stimulated economies elsewhere in Europe but inflated commodity prices and ruined industries in Spain. The volume of the transatlantic trade rose steadily through the sixteenth century as Spanish conquests, settlements, and populations expanded. The *Casa de Contratación* (House of Trade) regulated commerce and was headquartered in Seville for two centuries before moving to the superior port facilities at Cádiz in 1717. Merchants, settlers, sailors, royal officials of assorted types, army personnel, priests and missionaries, and many other people of diverse occupations and talents (servants, slaves, criminals, and deserters) cluttered Seville as they sought passage on the ocean-crossing vessels. Over fifty thousand known men, women, and children, and possibly as many as 150,000 more uncounted, of all social conditions sailed to the new lands during the sixteenth century, with a preponderance choosing the richer and more settled colonies of New Spain and Peru as their final destinations.[10]

Possibly a special purpose drew the first Calvo de la Puerta to Cuba.

(lowlifes), among whom figured itinerant actors, puppeteers, palm-readers, beggars, soldiers, sailors, prostitutes of various classes, outlaws, and many more. See also Ruth Pike, "Sevillian Society in the Sixteenth Century: Slaves and Freedmen," *Hispanic American Historical Review* 47 (August 1967), 344-69.

10. Peter Boyd-Bowman, *Índice geobiográfico de cuarenta mil pobladores de América en el siglo XVI*, 2 vols. (Bogotá: Instituto Caro y Cuervo, 1964); Auke Pieter Jacobs, "Pasajeros y polizones: Algunas observaciones sobre la emigración española a las Indias durante el siglo XVI," *Revista de Indias* 172 (1983): 437-79; Peter Boyd-Bowman, "Patterns of Spanish Emigration to the Indies until 1600," *Hispanic American Historical Review* 56 (November 1976): 580-604. Guillermo Céspedes del Castillo, in *América Hispánica, 1498-1898*, (Barcelona: Editorial Labor, 1983), 180, 182, estimated that true Spanish emigration to the New World, including legal and illegal passengers in the sixteenth century, was closer to 200,000 people, with more from Andalusia than anywhere else. Lyle N. McAlister, in *Spain and Portugal in the New World, 1492-1700* (Minneapolis: University of Minnesota Press, 1984), 115-17, agrees.

New World lands, particularly undeveloped colonies like Cuba with its few settlers and absence of educational facilities, could not produce literate royal employees. Despite six decades of Spanish settlement by the time Martín arrived, the island's cultural development had been negligible. Spanish colonization began in 1511, when Gov. Diego Colón (Columbus), son of the Admiral, at Santo Domingo in Hispaniola (*Española*), the large island east of Cuba that the Spaniards first occupied, ordered Diego Velázquez to begin settlement. It was an immense task given that Cuba comprised about 44,000 square miles, was roughly 750 miles in length but averaged only 62.5 miles in width, and was divided almost equally between a flat or rolling topography and higher elevations that ranged from hills to mountains. The island is larger than Hispaniola by three times, Jamaica by nine times, and Puerto Rico by twelve times. A moderate subtropical climate, with temperatures varying from average lows of 70 to highs of 81 degrees Fahrenheit and seasonal rainfall, endowed the island with abundant vegetation. The worst features to life in Cuba, then as now, were the devastating hurricanes that periodically slammed into the island between June and November and coincided with its rainy season. Starting with a tiny Spanish male population, Cuba grew slowly in European settlers. Its first capital at Baracoa, on the eastern edge of the island that consisted of little more than hovels, quickly shifted west to better suited Santiago de Cuba on the southeastern coast, and finally in the 1550s to Havana on the northwest coast to take advantage of its unique harbor and location at the entrance to the Gulf of Mexico and the Gulf Stream that sped ships home to Spain. Life in the early colony was wretched with its few inhabitants, primitive dwellings, and exposure to foreign depredations. In 1538, Havana had at most seventy to eighty Spanish abodes, and the few other settlements across the island were even smaller in size.[11]

11. Louis A. Pérez Jr., *Cuba: Between Reform and Revolution* (New York: Oxford University Press, 1988), 26, 38; Roberto Segre, Mario Coyula, and Joseph L. Scarpaci, *Havana: Two Faces of the Antillean Metropolis* (Chichester, U.K.: John Wiley and Sons, 1997), 3; Francisco Figueras, *Cuba y su evolución colonial* (Havana: Imprenta Avisador Comercial, 1907), 23, 34-41; Hubert H. S. Aimes, in *A History of Slavery in Cuba, 1511 to 1868* (New York: Knickerbocher Press, 1907) 11n.

Cuba remained largely undeveloped when in 1574 Calvo de la Puerta first laid eyes on Havana. Although larger than Cumbres Mayores, Havana could not compare with Seville. Expeditions in the exciting first days of discovery and conquest had repeatedly drawn off restless adventurers who anxiously sought the financial security that Cuba lacked, a prime consideration of the New World's early Spaniards who funded their own expeditions. The island initially produced some gold, 100,000 pesos worth in 1517 alone, but the deposits soon played out. With no hope of striking it rich in Cuba, roughly 80 percent of the men not tied down departed on exploration parties, including one in late 1518 that headed toward Mexico under Hernán Cortés. With the discovery of the Aztecs, many more fortune-hunters streamed out of the islands eager to benefit from Mexico's riches. Departures for diverse mainland El Dorados persisted throughout the next half century. Only after the era of fabled bonanzas ended did Cuba's Spaniards increase in number while the island's indigenous tribes (Guanajatabey, Ciboney, and Taíno) died off from diseases.[12] In the first half century of Spanish domination white women on the island were virtually absent, and in the second half they never exceeded 10 percent of the European population. Their absence led Spanish men to turn to miscegenation that proceeded rapidly with dependent Native and African females. In time mestizas became preferred partners, and some of their offspring merged into the ranks of white society. The absence of censuses, however, leaves only crude estimates of the island's lethargic rise in Spanish people who remained far below twenty thousand in 1600. Cuba and the other Caribbean islands such as Hispaniola, all woefully deficient in the precious ores that initially attracted newcomers, had lapsed into

12. Noble David Cook, in *Born to Die: Disease and New World Conquest, 1492-1650* (Cambridge: Press Syndicate of the University of Cambridge, 1998), 17-18, indicated diseases such as histoplasmosis, tuberculosis, leishmaniasis, Chagas's disease, dysentery, intestinal worms, rickettaial fevers, salmonella and bacterial pathogens such as staphylococcus and streptococcus, and non-venereal treponema or an endemic syphilis were already present in the Western Hemisphere. In addition, Europeans introduced smallpox, measles, bubonic and pneumonic plagues, and typhus. Controversy surrounds whether they were also responsible for malaria and yellow fever.

the backwaters of empire by the mid-sixteenth century.[13]

The wealth the Spaniards found through the years in the Caribbean, Mexico, Peru, Colombia, and elsewhere, nevertheless, lured robust foreign predators to prey on the Spanish islands and homeward-bound treasure fleets. Their depredations burdened Cuba's governor, who bore numerous responsibilities in administering and defending the thinly populated island. He acquired military authority upon being given the title of captain general, and governors, who were military men, used that designation for its prestige.[14] Although the Spanish government tried to protect and develop the Caribbean islands, pirates in peacetime and enemy nations in wartime wrought havoc on their coastal communities. As early as the 1520s, predatory vessels from Europe's Atlantic nations harassed the islands to pick up easy loot. Attacks on Cuba from the 1530s included repeated raids on Santiago de Cuba and other settlements on the southeastern coast that developed first. The French inflicted their greatest harm when they sacked Santiago de Cuba in 1554 and put Havana to the torch the next year. In succeeding decades, English pirates John Hawkins and Francis Drake pillaged and laid waste to settlements throughout the Caribbean. Before the end

13. Jaime Suchlicki, *Cuba, From Columbus to Castro* (New York: Pergamon Press, 1986), 3-9; Franklin W. Knight, *The Caribbean: The Genesis of a Fragmented Nationalism*, 2nd ed. (New York: Oxford University Press, 1990), 38-41. Population estimates for Cuba vary widely. David Turnball, in *Travels in the West: Cuba, with notes of Porto Rico, and the Slave Trade* (London: Longman, Orne, Browne, Green, and Longmans, 1840), 234, placed the population as nearly 16,000 in 1580, with 10,000 living in the Havana district.), Aimes, *A History of Slavery,* 16, with incomplete figures puts Cuba's population as 6,974 in 1620, with Havana having 4,082 inhabitants. Jacobo de la Pezuela, in *Crónica de las Antillas* (Madrid: Rubio, Grilo y Vitturi, 1871), 82, estimated Cuba's inhabitants as not over 20,000 in 1610.

14. Suchlicki, *Cuba, From Columbus to Castro*, 22-23. Although technically part of the viceroyalty of New Spain, the governor of Cuba was independent in all respects. Foremost among his duties, he collected and spent revenues in the royal interest. In judicial matters, local courts determined most civil and criminal cases, and the Audiencia of Santo Domingo on the nearby island of Española (Hispaniola) heard those sent on appeal. In 1797, the audiencia relocated to Puerto Príncipe (Camagüey) in Cuba on the cession of the Santo Domingo colony to France by the Treaty of Basel two years before.

of the century, the Dutch followed suit and rained more destruction on Spanish communities. The crowning Dutch achievement was Piet Heyn's seizure of a treasure fleet off Matanzas on Cuba's north coast in 1628; its loss dealt Spanish finances a crushing blow since the nation had become dependent on New World riches, namely gold and silver.[15]

With foreign corsairs constantly preying on Spanish vessels, the Council of the Indies that assisted in the governance of the colonies introduced the convoy system in 1543 that provided armed escorts—war galleons—for the merchant ships that now sailed yearly. In his three voyages across the Atlantic, Martín Calvo de la Puerta traveled aboard vessels of the *flota* (fleet). In regulations issued by the Council of the Indies in 1561, two fleets departed annually from Seville, the first in April for Mexico that included a stop at the Canary Islands. It then sailed to Caribbean waters with stops in the Antilles before moving on to Veracruz. The second convoy left in August sailing to Cartagena de Indias (then in New Granada, which is today's Colombia) and to Nombre de Dios in the Isthmus of Panama. Some individual vessels broke off from the fleet to call at smaller Caribbean ports. They later reunited in Havana for the voyage home. The convoy system, however, had harmful consequences as it seriously limited commerce, inflated prices for European products, and contributed alarmingly to a foreign contraband trade that sprang up everywhere in the colonies. Cuban settlers as well as officials in out-of-the-way nooks welcomed the clandestine exchange and paid willingly with raw materials and agricultural products for the goods Spain could not provide. Despite this nuisance, Spanish trade rose steadily in the second half of the sixteenth century.[16]

15. Pérez, *Cuba*, 35; Worcester and Schaeffer, *Growth and Culture of Latin America*, 183-84; Irene A. Wright, "The Dutch and Cuba, 1609-1643," *Hispanic American Historical Review* IV, no. 4 (November 1921): 597-634. See also Clarence H. Haring, *The Buccaneers of the West Indies in the XVII Century* (New York: E. P. Dutton and Sons, 1910), and his *Trade and Navigation between Spain and the Indies in the Time of the Hapsburgs* (Cambridge, Mass.: Harvard University Press, 1918).

16. Alejandro de la Fuente, *Havana and the Atlantic in the Sixteenth-Century* (Chapel Hill: University of North Carolina Press, 2008), 11-50; Segre et al., *Havana*, 13. On explanations for the convoy system under the Habsburgs, see Haring, *Trade and Navigation*.

In another move about 1580, the Spanish government accepted the unfeasibility of defending every community in the Caribbean and adjoining mainland. It possessed neither the manpower nor the resources for such a Herculean task. Adopting the counsel of Pedro Menéndez de Avilés who advocated cost effective methods, the Spanish government limited fortifications and military forces to major ports such as Havana, Santiago de Cuba, San Juan de Puerto Rico, Santo Domingo, Veracruz, and Cartagena de Indias. Even St. Augustine, Florida, acquired a large fortress. Havana's fortifications thereafter were built and rebuilt several times to safeguard the port and city. Menéndez's decision, nevertheless, left multitudes of small towns exposed to pillaging and contraband traffic that flourished for decades to come. Before the sixteenth century concluded, the English and French tried to colonize regions Iberians had neglected, especially on the upper Atlantic coast of North America. Initial efforts, however, foundered until early in the next century when behind the onslaught of Dutch warships English, French, and Dutch settlements sprouted up along coastal North America. Simultaneously, the three nations began seizing the smaller islands that made up the Bahamas and Lesser Antilles.[17]

International rivalry imperiled Spanish colonies throughout the Caribbean when Martín Calvo de la Puerta landed in Havana in 1574. What adventures he had experienced by age twenty-three when he accepted the challenge of living on an imperial frontier are unknown, but surely a desire to explore unfamiliar lands and exploit financial prospects that were growing in Havana must have figured prominently in his decision. Possibly older siblings at home about whom nothing is known had staked claims on the family business, and Martín, as a *segundón* (a younger son who was not an heir to his father's property), needed to find his own way in life. Armed with an education his parents provided and perhaps with other work proficiencies, Martín cast his fortune on opportunities in the New World. Most likely arrangements on what he would do preceded his departure, and because few emigrants traveled alone, he accompanied a settler or an official on his

17. Knight, *The Caribbean*, 47-49.

journey. Once in Havana, he spent years as an apprentice acquiring the skills of a scribe and notary with the Pérez de Borroto family. Perhaps he had contacted them prior to his departure from Spain.[18] Francisco Pérez de Borroto and an unknown contingent of family members had left Seville in 1554, and several males among them became the scribes and notaries in both Havana and its municipal government. Their arrival approximated Havana's becoming the island's de facto capital. Certainly the presence of friends or employers in Cuba eased Martín's adjustment to his new surroundings.[19]

Calvo de la Puerta perhaps took funds with him to invest in economic opportunities or to live on until he earned an income. He may have achieved a degree of security relatively quickly. On December 24, 1578, his name, abbreviated to "Martín Calvo," appeared in a notarized sale in Havana of his eighteen-year-old African slave María for 215 ducats to Antonio Pérez, possibly a relative of the Pérez de Borroto clan and a pilot of the *carrera* (Indies fleet). Martín's ownership and sale of a valuable slave suggested that he was doing reasonably well, but the

18. General works on the Cabildo in Spanish America are John Preston Moore's two studies *The Cabildo in Peru under the Habsburgs: A Study in the Origins and Powers of the Town Council in the Viceroyalty of Peru, 1530-1700* (Durham, N.C.: Duke University Press, 1954), and *The Cabildo in Peru under the Bourbons: A Study in the Decline and Resurgence of Local Government in the Audiencia of Lima, 1700-1824* (Durham, NC: Duke University Press, 1966); and Constantino Bayle, *Los cabildos seculares en la América española* (Madrid: Sapientia, 1952). María Teresa de Rojas, in *Índice y extractos del Archivo de Protocolos de la Habana, 1578-1585*, 3 vols. (La Habana: Ucar, García y Companía, 1997), includes the notaries Juan Pérez de Borroto, Francisco Pérez de Borroto, and Gaspar Pérez de Borroto in Havana. The last person named sold his post as Cabildo scribe and notary to Martín Calvo de la Puerta. Ida Altman, in *Emigrants and Society: Extremadura and America in the Sixteenth Century* (Berkeley: University of California Press, 1989), 165-68, points out that people of all classes traveled either in families or with relatives, friends, servants, and employers. People journeying alone were the exception.

19. Francisco Pérez de Borroto was appointed *escribano de número* (an official scribe) of the city council of Havana; he was the son of Juan Pérez de Borroto of Havana. He seems to have left Seville for Havana in 1554. AGI, Pasajeros de Indias, leg. 3, Exped. 2383; this ítem is also in Catálogos de Pasajeros a Indias, vol. 3 (1539-1559), and listed under Francisco Pérez Borroto.

notarized record did not explain the reason for parting with María.[20]

Aside from this document, Martín's activities in Havana between 1574 and early 1583 are mostly obscure. It is known, nevertheless, that he learned the multiple duties of a scrivener, the operations and opportunities in Havana's *ayuntamiento* (municipal government), and how the local economy functioned. Perhaps he worked as a secretary or apprentice to Gaspar Pérez de Borroto, whose post he eventually purchased. Martín's noble birth held him in good stead in an age when bloodlines, family background, and social standing aided immeasurably in opening doors and attaining positions. Because his family originated in Vizcaya where all Basques claimed the rights of *hidalguía* (the lower nobility), he and his ancestors were above accusations of being *conversos* (converts or New Christians) and tainted with Jewish or Moorish ancestry. As time passed, the crown, or self-interested Old Christians who sought exclusive privileges and envied *converso* financial successes, demanded religious purity for employment, and insisted on *limpiezas de sangre* ("blood cleansings" literally, but meaning "inspections of one's genealogy"); discovery of forbidden ancestors disqualified aspirants from securing advantageous government offices, titles, rewards, and even marriage partners. After nine years in Havana and at age thirty-two, Martín headed home to obtain the instruments that would facilitate his rise in status and financial security.[21]

Upon arriving in Spain in 1583, Martín visited his family in Cumbres Mayores, where he shed light on life in Havana and learned about family deaths, births, and other significant events during his lengthy absence. Once his filial obligations terminated, he pursued the true purpose behind his return. On October 15, he testified in Cumbres Mayores before Juan Mateo Largo, an *alcalde ordinario* (a municipal magistrate for people without a *fuero* or special protection before the law that privileged members of the nobility, church, and army enjoyed). Martín easily verified his noble status, which for most people of his

20. Rojas, *Índice y extractos*, 1: 12; Mallén, *Historia de familias cubanas*, 4: 104.

21. Pike, *Aristocrats and Traders*, 99-100; Henry Kamen, *Spain, 1469-1714: A Century of Conflict* (London and New York: Longman, 1983).

station meant the untitled and tax-exempt lower nobility or hidalgos (*hijos de algo*, the "children of some possessions or social standing").[22]

In November Martín journeyed to Madrid to obtain other documents directly from the crown that would entitle him to hold office in Havana. Apart from seeking essential permits, his movements in Madrid are not known. Small when compared to Seville, the city was Spain's politico-administrative center and had little of the commerce, industry, and activity found in coastal ports. Many Castilian noblemen, who savored the proximity to the royal court for the offices, titles, and honors it dispensed, wintered in the city. Martín had purchased the post of scribe and notary from its holder in Havana and now sought royal confirmation of his skills and validation of his purchase. He accomplished these bureaucratic chores and secured the needed documents. A royal cédula dated November 29, 1583, issued to him at El Pardo, the royal residence outside Madrid, read: "By this means we give you Martín Calvo de la Puerta and to each one of your servants you take to that island [Cuba] to guard and defend your person two swords, two daggers, and one harquebus, and we order that you not be molested in any way." It was signed "Yo el Rey," who was Felipe II, the son of Carlos V.[23] Two servants accompanied Martín on his return to Havana.

Permission to leave Spain was soon followed with his appointment to the office he sought. On December 6, a royal cédula directed to Gabriel de Luján, the governor and captain general of Cuba, stated that the king "recommends him to employ (Calvo de la Puerta) in offices and responsibilities in the Royal Service commensurate with his social status and ability."[24] That was an important first step. A week later Martín obtained a clearer definition of what he sought. On December 13, the

22. Mallén, *Historia de familias cubanas*, 4: 105; Lynch, in *Spain under the Habsburgs*, 105-06, discusses the aspirations of sixteenth-century hidalgos.

23. Real Cédula, December 13, 1583, AGI, IG, leg. 2, f. 162; "Del Pasado-Por el Conde San Juan de Jaruco," (Francisco Xavier de Santa Cruz y Mallén), in *Diario de la Marina*, Havana, May 4, 1952.

24. Conde de Vallellano (Fernando Suárez de Tangil y de Angulo), *Nobilario cubano: Las grandes familias isleñas*, 2 vols. (Madrid: Francisco Beltrán, [1929]), 1:235-36; Mallén, *Historia de familias cubanas*, 4: 105.

king issued a royal dispatch appointing him to the office of scribe in the Havana Cabildo. His purchase of that office, his employment of bodyguards, and his journey to Spain in pursuit of documents denoted his acquisition of admirable means. Possibly, too, his bodyguards were either friends, townspeople from Cumbres Mayores, or relatives who also sought opportunities across the sea. At least one known kinsman relocated to Havana. After obtaining the needed documentation in Madrid, little is known about how Martín spent his remaining time in Spain. His visit lasted into the spring of 1584, before he bid his relatives and friends goodbye inasmuch as he would never see them again. He then traveled to Seville to arrange passage on that year's *flota*.[25]

By October he had arrived in Havana. While its early reputation was dismal inasmuch as the town's masses often lived in crowded, dirty, and makeshift hovels, it was growing in size as its designation of *villa* changed to *ciudad* or city in 1594. More important, it became a port for the war galleons and merchant ships to gather in prior to the voyage home, and they boosted its economic activities and inhabitants. When the fleets grew in size, they brought in thousands of passengers—sailors, soldiers, priests, civilian administrators, families, and other people who were overwhelmingly male. The passengers disembarked to spend several weeks ashore while provisions were gathered and vessels refitted. During those days, inns, eating establishments, taverns, laundries, shipyards, and numerous businesses of many kinds, including brothels, peaked in activity, and the money that poured into the city massively stimulated its financial well-being. The rest of year, however, until Havana increased in occupants and diversified its economy, the city relapsed into near somnolence. While both resident and transient criminals preyed on the vulnerable, a foreign seaborne attack posed a greater threat, and protection against that possibility required troops, artillery, defensive walls, and fortresses. Their augmentation, consequently, continued through the years.[26]

25. *Real provisión* to Martín Calvo de la Puerta, Madrid, December 13, 1583, AGI, IG, leg. 27, f. 28 verso, gave him the title of "notario de Indias"; Mallén, *Historia de familias cubanas*, 4: 105.

26. De la Fuente, *Havana and the Atlantic*, 51-80; John Edwin Fagg, *Cuba, Haiti,*

Amid the menace of corsairs in the Caribbean, on October 4, 1584, Martín presented to the governor and city council his credentials that consisted of his royal appointment as scribe and his purchase of Gaspar Pérez de Borroto's office. Once accomplished, he assumed his post.[27] His duties as a Cabildo scribe and notary provided him with a privileged position to learn about current and future economic and social activities in the city.

In a three-volume study that examined the notarial records in Havana between 1578 and 1585, María Teresa de Rojas has summarized the documents that notaries, including Calvo de la Puerta, copied and preserved. These records open a window into life during those tumultuous times. Among other things, they note that the city's structures consisted of more than hovels, and many were well-constructed buildings and private residences belonging to the affluent. Well-to-do Creoles (native-born whites) flaunted their wealth in homes, clothes, jewels, furniture, carriages, servants, horses, and fiestas.[28] Some of these males inundated the government with petitions for prestigious administrative jobs, honors, and military posts commensurate with their social standing. The documents also noted the prominent role religion played in the lives of city inhabitants, especially persons concerned with their souls in the afterlife. They paid obeisance to numerous saints and prayed for their intervention as the supplicants traveled down life's un-

and the Dominican Republic (Englewood Cliffs, N.J.: Prentice Hall, 1965), 18-19; Irene Wright, *Early History of Cuba, 1492-1586, written from original sources* (New York: Macmillan, 1916), 313, 346-70.

27. Vallellano, *Nobilario cubano*, 1: 236. Vallellano states that in 1585 Martín Calvo de la Puerta y Arrieta married Beátriz Pérez Borroto, who was born in Seville. They had four children: Beátriz Calvo de la Puerta y Pérez de Borroto, baptized April 22, 1596; María Calvo de la Puerta y Pérez de Borroto, with no date for her birth, baptism, or death; Catalina, who died on August 2, 1643; and Capt. Martín Calvo de la Puerta y Pérez de Borroto, baptized on October 14, 1598. Mallén, in *Historia de familias cubanas*, 4: 104-6, mentions seven children and provides minimal information on six of them. Several writers, however, list only four children.

28. Although the word Creole means any person born in the Western Hemisphere, it will be used here primarily to denote Spaniards.

certain road toward salvation. It was an age with limited life expectancy, especially for infants and children, and longevity eluded most adults beyond a few precious decades. Death, disease, and primitive medical knowledge reminded everyone daily of the frailty of life. Many people, especially the poor, frequently resorted to prayers, herbs, and *curanderos* (folk healers) to overcome mysterious afflictions. In this often sorrowful age, the few secular festivities assumed greater significance as the celebrants immersed themselves in revelry. They were joyous and widely fêted days in which public parades figured prominently. Among them religious pageantry was frequently represented by priests, monks of various orders, religious statuary on decorated floats, holy banners, and members of religious confraternities dressed in their distinctive robes. Army and militia units—infantry, cavalry, artillery, and support groups—often with drums, bugles, and other musical instruments blaring—paraded too and displayed their distinctive arms, uniforms, and specializations.[29] In contrast to the frequent religious holidays that were generally somber, the Christmas season that stretched to Epiphany (*los Reyes* or Magi) was a cheerful time.

In the midst of these activities, Martín began his economic and social advance. Besides compensation for his Cabildo duties, he received fees for notarial and scrivener services he provided the town's inhabitants. He acquired the privilege on December 12, 1586, upon Gaspar Pérez de Borroto's renunciation of the post. Martín, however, kept it less than four years before surrendering the office to Juan Pérez de Borroto, the son of its former holder.[30] Public scribes were a necessity in a largely illiterate society where reading and writing were unheard of in the lower classes and unknown even among upper-class women. Martín's acquisition of the post put him on the road to economic and social well-being. By the 1580s, money-making ventures in Hava-

29. María Teresa de Rojas, *Índice y extractos del Archivo de Protocolos de la Habana, 1578-1585*, 3 vols. (La Habana: Ucar, García y Cía., 1997), 1: 199, 2: x-xii, 3: viii-x.

30. Real provisión to Martín Calvo de la Puerta, Madrid, December 12, 1786, AGI, IG 527, leg. 1, f. 246v; real provisión to Juan Pérez de Borroto, Madrid, June 6, 1590, ibid., f. 247.

na and its surrounding countryside saw the emergence of a relatively well-to-do group among the various wholesale and retail merchants, food-producing landowners, builders, local manufacturers, and artisans; in addition, these endeavors provided widespread employment for many unskilled workers. Professionals such as physicians, surgeons, lawyers, engineers, financiers, contractors, accountants, and educators rose in number. Inasmuch as many consumer items were produced locally as the population increased, clothes-makers of various kinds—tailors, couturières, milliners, cobblers—and shopkeepers also extended employment. Fishing thrived as did ship-building and repair. Havana businesses also met the needs of the surrounding rural residents, and on holidays the latter thronged into the city for diversion. More than half of Cuba's estimated fifteen to twenty thousand inhabitants in the late sixteenth century lived in the Havana district, and that left the rest of the island scantily populated or totally barren.[31]

As a scribe of the city council, Martín kept the minutes of the weekly meetings of councilmen (*regidores*), read and recorded correspondence to them, wrote and dispatched letters, posted city proclamations, notarized documents, and performed numerous services for city officials. The Havana Cabildo, with which the Calvo de la Puerta family was intimately associated for three centuries, was a complex institution that represented the local elite, and it stood virtually alone as a power-wielding homegrown body. Typical of governments under absolute monarchs, authority flowed down from the crown into a society with slight mobility. In the colonies that were regal properties, royal officials—viceroys, captains-general, audiencia presidents, and governors at various levels—acted for the king. Other than on occasions when a royal official determined a governmental decree was more injurious than beneficial, royal orders prevailed. Local political authority did not exist except for the Cabildo, where city *vecinos* (usually prominent heads of households) held seats and together they exercised control

31. Rojas, *Indice y extractos*, 3: ix; Pérez, *Cuba*, 30-42. See also de la Fuente, *Havana and the Atlantic in the Sixteenth Century*.

over the municipal district.[32]

A venerable institution in Spain, the Cabildo rapidly achieved a similar position in the colonies. Through the sixteenth century, conquistadores founded towns and their municipal governments immediately upon assuming control over a region. As a local governmental body, it represented the important first Spanish settlers, who quickly became landowners and the upper echelons of local society. The councilmen used the institution's power to further their own economic interests and rewarded themselves with prime lands and valuable indigenous labor. In Cuba, with the assistance of the governor in Havana and lesser royal officials in outlying towns, Cabildo representatives regulated virtually all aspects of life in urban centers. The governor's authority on the council was neither absolute nor concerned with mundane problems. Councilmen voted on issues with a majority determining the matter; governors, however, generally possessed the power to veto Cabildo legislation contrary to royal interests. *Regidores* on Cabildos varied in number, and over time, Havana acquired an impressive quantity. Councilmen decided matters such as the construction and maintenance of public buildings; supervised harbor facilities, defenses, and roads within the municipality; and advised the governor on items of interest to the city. Although *regidores* did not receive salaries, specific councilmen performed collateral duties that entitled them to fees. Examples of these duties included inspecting fish and meat markets to guarantee the freshness of their products, cleanliness, and fair weights; fining violators of municipal ordinances; buying livestock for the city's butchers and ensuring an ample meat supply at a fair price; overseeing public safety (law enforcement); and regulating taverns and public inns. As for justice, the city council normally had two *alcaldes ordinarios*, judges who were elected each January 1 by the *regidores* and served only that year. These *alcaldes ordinarios* also voted with the councilmen on municipal measures.[33] Beyond

32. Worcester and Schaeffer, *Growth and Culture of Latin America*, 39-59.

33. See Stephen Andrew Webre, "The Social and Economic Bases of Cabildo Membership in Seventeenth-Century Santiago de Guatemala," PhD diss., Tulane University, 1980. Webre shows that the Guatemala Cabildo changed over time, which also happened in Havana's city government. Irene A. Wright, in "Beginnings of Havana," 501, wrote: "The first *alcaldes* and *regidores* were appointed by [Gov. Diego] Velázquez or his

the Cabildo, governors of the island operated their own civil and criminal tribunals and judged cases involving privileged individuals.[34] Through three centuries, the Calvo de la Puerta family held many of these posts as well as others mentioned below.

Whether the judicial office of *alcalde mayor provincial* (provincial magistrate) was a collateral post attached to a specific *regidor*, as it was in some Cabildos, or if Havana's post was independent is unclear. This official possessed legal authority over crimes and civil disputes arising in the rural district outside the city, and he was expected to visit it frequently to administer speedy justice. Because the *alcalde mayor provincial* usually lacked legal training, government lawyers (*letrados*) assisted him, especially in major cases, in determining verdicts. The *Santa Hermandad*, or mounted rural police force that patrolled the countryside around cities, worked under the direction of the *alcalde mayor provincial* to apprehend fugitive slaves, military deserters, and assorted other lawbreakers.[35]

Other Cabildo posts included the *procurador general* and the *mayordomo de propios*, both of which handled municipal funds.[36] Among

---

representatives. Presumably they were a first and second *alcalde*, and three *regidores*, to constitute the *cabildo* over which the *teniente a guerra* [military commander] presided, as the governor presided over Santiago [de Cuba's] council, without (it developed later) any right to do so. Doubtless there was an *alguacil*; certainly there were *escribanos*. The Cabildo elected the *procurador*, even after the crown had, in 1528, ordered that he be chosen by suffrage yearly. After 1518 the crown appointed *regidores perpetuos*, and the municipal councils of the island, which now elected the *alcaldes*, became the stronghold of a small oligarchy whose members ruled the colony."

34. Wright, *Early History of Cuba*, 325-27; Suchlecki, *Cuba*, 23-25. Despite Havana's Cabildo having more than a two-hundred-year head start on the New Orleans's *ayuntamiento* (city government), they functioned in similar ways, but then officials from Havana started the new Cabildo. The operations of New Orleans's Spanish city government are explained in Gilbert C. Din and John E. Harkins, *The New Orleans Cabildo: Colonial Louisiana's First City Government, 1769-1803* (Baton Rouge: Louisiana State University Press, 1996), 56-100. See also Bayle, *Los cabildos seculares*, and Moore's two volumes *The Cabildo in Peru under the Hapsburgs*, and *The Cabildo in Peru under the Bourbons*.

35. Din and Harkins, *New Orleans Cabildo*, 108-9.

36. It is possible that *regidores* held the offices of *procurador general* and *mayordomo*

the former's responsibilities were collecting revenue (taxes) and debts owed the city, enforcing municipal ordinances, safeguarding the public welfare, and ensuring that city officials discharged their duties honestly. The *mayordomo de propios*, meanwhile, was the city's financial officer who received and managed municipal funds and recorded financial transactions. His obligations included disbursing monies in the execution of city contracts and ensuring their exact fulfillment. Upon leaving office, the holders of the two posts were subject to a *residencia* that investigated their rectitude in the performance of their obligations.[37]

Through their lengthy involvement in the city council, the Calvo de la Puerta family developed an intimate acquaintance with its operations. Their civic participation raised their visibility and prominence in the city and presented them with investment opportunities, usually in contracts, that might otherwise have eluded them. By the 1590s, Martín Calvo de la Puerta had become a notable entrepreneur inasmuch as he shared in the development of sugar. Much earlier sugarcane had been planted near Havana and Matanzas, a neighboring district on the north coast. But little was done with the cane because Cuba lacked an adequate labor force. With Cuba's benign climate, the cane grew wild. In the 1590s, fifteen Havana businessmen, including Calvo de la Puerta, petitioned the crown for funds with which to build sugar mills (*ingenios*) powered by oxen and purchase large Portuguese copper caldrons for boiling cane juice and eradicating impurities. The fifteen petitioners swore that they already owned cane fields and small mills (*trapiches*), with which they produced more than 3,000 arrobas (75,000 pounds) of sugar annually. Their efforts had reduced sugar prices in Havana from what they formerly paid for Santo Domingo imports. Now they exported minor quantities of sugar to Castile. In response, on July 14, 1597, the king agreed to provide 40,000 ducats in loans in amounts dependent on the growers' current sugar production,

de propios in certain Cabildos.

37. Suchlecki, *Cuba*, 23-25; Din and Harkins, *New Orleans Cabildo*, 73-75; Frederick B. Pike, "The Municipality and the System of Checks and Balances in Spanish American Colonial Administration," *Americas* 15 (1958-59): 139-58.

with the most active growers eligible for sums up to 8,000 ducats and smaller producers to only 2 or 3,000. The king further decreed that in time income generated from the tax on sugar would replace the *diezmo* or ten percent duty productive residents contributed to the church's welfare. Calvo de la Puerta's presence among the signers of the petition demonstrated that he had already achieved the status of landowner and sugar producer and engaged in agricultural ventures that probably included cattle and foodstuffs. No doubt in good years farming activities netted him handsome returns. In 1598 Martín sold half his mill called Santiago to Pedro González, a sugar master, perhaps to acquire his knowledge of the mill's operations.[38]

When the loans made in 1602 came due, additional information about the planters' production and holdings emerged. Martín and his wife Beátriz Pérez de Borroto y Alfaro owned their holding; Juan Bautista de Borroto, her relative, had guaranteed their loan of 2,500 ducats. They owned eleven slaves, an undisclosed number of horses and doubtless other animals, and various caldrons. Of the seventeen planters who borrowed money, with loans that ranged from 4,400 down to only 500 ducats, they owned slaves who numbered from two up to fifty-eight. In most respects, Calvo de la Puerta was in the middle ground, with eight planters owning more slaves but only five of them borrowing more money. Together the growers now produced an estimated three hundred thousand pounds of sugar annually.[39]

38. De la Fuente, *Havana and the Atlantic in the Sixteenth Century*, 208. Among the fourteen other petitioners were Hernán Rodríguez, Diego Ochoa de la Vega, Benito Rodríguez, Antonio de la Ribera, Pedro Suárez de Gamboa, Sebastián Fernández Pacheco, Baltazar de Rojas, Melchor Casas, Gínez de Orta, Sebastián de Aragón, Antonio de Matos de Agama, Alonso Jorge, Hernando Rodríguez Tabares, and Hernando Salucio. See also Alejandro de la Fuente, "Sugar and Slavery in Early Colonial Cuba," 115-57, in *Tropical Babylons: Sugar and the Making of the Atlantic World, 1415-1680*, ed. Stuart Schwartz (Chapel Hill: University of North Carolina Press, 2004); Irene A. Wright, ed., "The Commencement of the Cane Sugar Industry in America, 1519-1538 (1563)," *American Historical Review* 21 (July 1916): 755-80. González-Ripoll, in *Cuba*, 38, mentioned Martín Calvo de la Puerta.

39. César García del Pino, *La Habana bajo el reinado de los Austria* (Havana: Ediciones Boloña, 2008), 102-5.

After serving as a scribe and notary and achieving a degree of financial security in urban and rural businesses, the first Martín Calvo de la Puerta moved on to hold the more prestigious office of *regidor*. He was also *procurador general* in 1595, 1597, and 1598, and *alcalde ordinario* in 1608. Quite early, the crown allowed the appointment of permanent councilmen (*regidores perpetuos*) to city governments, but when that happened in the Havana Cabildo is unclear. The sale of a *regidor* seat occurred at least once during the sixteenth century. The practice later became more common, and the Calvo de la Puerta family much later purchased such a seat, which passed down within the family. Overall, the mostly well-to-do members of the city council acted as instruments of the privileged, and, with the acquisition of militia posts, they amassed formidable power within the colonial elite.[40] In the late sixteenth century, while councilmen still belonged to a limited group of individuals who could be regarded roughly as upper middle class—employing modern-day designations based on relative wealth—their status evolved as the colony developed economically and socially and as the fortunes of office holders, who constituted a predominately inclusive group, enlarged. Through the seventeenth century more people, including army officers, served on the Cabildo, and by the early eighteenth century, some office holders reached the pinnacle of political, economic, military, and social success among the Cuban colonial elite.[41]

40. Wright, in "Beginnings of Havana," 501, wrote about the prominent people who served on the Cabildo: "These were intelligent, industrious men. Their activity extended far, for they were masters of the island, from almost the middle of it to its westernmost extremity. They owned, or thought they owned, great cattle ranges over which their half-savage cowmen hunted their wholly wild stock, to kill and cure meat and hides for exportation. They owned, or thought they owned, farms, thereon their red [Indian] encomendados, diminishing in numbers, and their black slaves, prolifically augmenting, grew what crops were in demand, then, for the supply of passing vessels which in increasing numbers frequented Havana bay." Mallén, *Historia de familias cubanas*, 4: 105.

41. On the development of the Havana upper class, see de la Fuente, *Havana and the Atlantic*, 186-222. Many of them had ties to the Havana Cabildo. More people than the Calvo de la Puerta family used Cabildos as stepping stones in their financial and social rise. See, for example, the career of Andrés Almonester y Roxas in late

Few documents aside from marriage and baptismal credentials afford information about the early Calvo de la Puerta family in Cuba. Baptismal records long served as de facto birth certificates but with the birth date often omitted; the church regarded baptism, the day the child became a Christian, as more important, but children were usually baptized shortly after birth. At some time after arriving in Cuba, Martín married Beátriz Pérez de Borroto y Alfaro at the Havana church. She was born in Seville, perhaps shortly before her family emigrated in 1554, and she lived until 1633.[42] Her father, Francisco Pérez de Borroto, after leaving his post as scribe in the Cabildo, became in different years an *alcalde ordinario* and an *alcalde mayor provincial*. He was also a captain in the *Santa Hermandad* at some point.[43] His various positions on or attached to the city council improved his financial standing, and other members of the Pérez de Borroto family seem to have done equally as well. Their rise was probably a wide-spread phenomenon among the ambitious class of Havana's inner circle that was still in its formative stage when Martín arrived. He possibly later held other Cabildo offices as well. Whether he married before returning to Spain in 1583 or after is not known; if it was after his return, he and his wife had a child or two before then. Martín Calvo de la Puerta, the

---

eighteenth-century New Orleans who became one of the richest men in Spanish Louisiana. Din and Harkins, *New Orleans Cabildo*, 5, 29-30, 62, 220-22; Samuel Wilson Jr., "Almonester: Philanthropist and Builder in New Orleans," in *The Spanish in the Mississippi Valley, 1762-1804*, ed. John Francis McDermott (Urbana: University of Illinois Press, 1974), 243-45.

42. Cédula to Sebastián Calvo de la Puerta y O'Farrill, [September or October 1771], [Burgos], signed by Julián Álvarez, a scribe of Burgos, AHN, OM, Exped. 8117. The date for Beátriz Pérez de Borroto's birth in 1578 is incorrect because of the births of her children, especially Bernarda and Hernando. Beátriz was born in Seville prior to her family emigrating in 1554. The births for Bernarda (?) and Hernando (1570-?) allegedly occurred before Martín arrived in Cuba in 1574.

43. On the Pérez de Borroto family in Havana, see de la Fuente, *Havana and the Atlantic*, 188-212 *passim*; Mallén, *Historia de familias cubanas*, 4: 105-6. Possibly children were born to Martín and Beátriz before 1578. More precise information is available about their later children Catalina (1593-1643), Beátriz (1596-?), and Martín (1598-1669).

progenitor of the family in Cuba, died of unknown causes in 1611.[44]

Trying to piece together accurate knowledge about Martín's children presents a formidable challenge because of the contradictory information Cuban genealogists have provided that often raise more questions than they answer. Among Martín's perplexing alleged offspring is Hernando whose birth year of 1570 occurred before Martín's arrival in Cuba. Also, daughters Bernarda and Beátriz were allegedly born in the same year of 1596, but little is known about them or if they were twins or only one child with two given names.[45]

More information exists about Martín's son Sebastián Calvo de la Puerta y Pérez de Borroto, who was born in 1580 and lived until 1651. He was either the first-born or oldest surviving son and did not follow his father into the Cabildo as a scribe. Social status quite likely guided that decision. In imitation of rising colonial affluence, his father groomed him for higher status by providing him with an officer's commission in the Havana Volunteers, a militia unit. In time he became the chief heir to his father's fortune that increasingly moved into landholding, commercial agriculture, and possibly slave labor. During Sebastián's sojourn in the military, he served at St. Augustine, Florida, a military outpost dependent on Havana. In 1604, he accompanied Florida governor Pedro de Ibarra with infantry troops on an inspection tour to the provinces of San Pedro and Guale in present-day coastal Georgia to learn about shipwrecked Spaniards living among the Indi-

44. Ibid. An online posting called "Alcaldes Ordinarios, Corregidores, Gobernadores Políticos y Alcaldes Municipales de La Habana desde 1550 hasta 1919," complains that the Havana Cabildo's *libros de protocolos* from 1578 to 1584 were missing, but they seem to have been misplaced because María Teresa de Rojas, cited above, used them for her work.

45. Mallén, *Historia de familias cubanas*, 4: 106, does not provide a birth date for Hernando Calvo de la Puerta y Pérez de Borroto, but states that Hernando married Isabel Recio y Sotolongo (of Havana) in Madrid on January 22, 1598. He was an *alcalde* of the Havana *Santa Hermandad* in 1624, elected *alcalde ordinario* in 1626, became a councilman (*regidor*) of the Cabildo by royal title and receiver of fines of the Cabildo (a collateral post) in 1630. His brother, Sebastián Calvo de la Puerta y Pérez de Borroto, in old age in the late 1630s married Antonia Recio y Sotolongo (1613-1681), who was possibly Isabel Recio y Sotolongo's sister (see above).

ans, discover the extent of religious instruction, and hear complaints against Spaniards and Native leaders. Although this is the only knowledge of his military service, with all the wars and perils pirates and contrabandists caused, he most likely answered the call to duty on other occasions, too. After his military service ended, he was a municipal magistrate (*alcalde ordinario*) in 1627 and 1642 and managed various rural properties, including the *ingenio*, or sugar mill, his father built on a cane estate with a royal loan.[46] Sebastián and his first wife, Catalina de Arrieta y Gómez de Lara (1586-1633), had three sons: Bartolomé (1608-?), Martín (1614-1669), and Sebastián (1621-1662).[47]

In time, Sebastián's son, Martín Calvo de la Puerta y Arrieta, who belonged to the family's third generation in Cuba, followed similar activities. He held diverse municipal offices and became the captain of a militia cavalry company, which characterized the affluent elite in Havana and in other colonial cities. As an officer, he was instrumental in providing horses, saddles, uniforms, and other paraphernalia for the mostly indigent troopers. His civic responsibility earned him the confidence of governors and higher offices in the city government. Among his known services, he was an *alcalde* (judge), possibly the *alcalde mayor provincial* of the *Santa Hermandad* that patrolled the rural district around Havana; an *alcalde ordinario* of the Cabildo several times; and the *procurador general.* He died in Havana in 1669 at age fifty-five, leaving a substantial fortune of 400,000 pesos *fuertes* (silver pesos that were often hoarded as opposed to pesos *de vellón* or debased pesos that circulated more freely) in a time before wealth began pouring down on the privileged classes. His will assigned the interest earned from 102,000 pesos of his fortune to provide 1,000 peso-dowries for five young women each year as an *obra pía* (a pious deed). The dowries enabled young women of moral rectitude, but who lacked the financial means to contract honorable marriages as he wanted and would contribute toward the formation of a moral populace in the city. Havana's decadence,

46. Mallén, *Historia de familias cubanas*, 4: 105; Manuel Serrano y Sanz, *Documentos históricos de la Florida y la Luisiana, siglos XVI al XVIII* (Madrid: V. Sánchez, 1912).

47. The three sons were Bartolomé (1608-?), Martín (1614-1669), and Sebastián (1621-1662).

at least in the eyes of the upright Martín, must have inspired his decision. The girls could also choose to enter a convent and use the money as dowries to provide for their keep. Between 1659 and 1669, this Martín built a large house in a distinguished neighborhood in central Havana on two ample lots that measured forty-five by forty meters. The house acquired the name *Obrapía* as did its street, and it still stands at 158 Obra Pía. After more than three centuries, the building has become a Havana landmark and a reminder of the generosity and civic responsibility of an early member of the Calvo de la Puerta family.[48]

Nevertheless, Martín's father Sebastián conserved the preponderance of the Calvo de la Puerta fortune, and perhaps he augmented it through successful business ventures. After his wife Catalina died in 1633, Sebastián married again, this time to Antonia Recio y Sotolongo (1613-1681). Both the Recio and Soto or Sotolongo families were financially secure and enjoyed status in the city. Sebastián was then in his fifties and Antonia was more than thirty years his junior. In old age, Sebastián fathered his last child with Antonia, but at this point confusion enters. Sebastián gave this son born in 1639 his same name despite already having an older son called Sebastián. There is no explanation for his baffling decision. But for twenty-three years two sons named Sebastián, the older surnamed Calvo de la Puerta y Arrieta and the younger Calvo de la Puerta y Recio, lived near one another.[49]

The second or younger Sebastián became an octogenarian inasmuch as he lived from 1639 to 1726. Like his father, he had two wives, but his first, Isabel Lucía Calvo de la Puerta y Chacón (1646-67), perhaps a

48. Mallén, *Historia de familias cubanas*, 4: 105-7. Confusion arises about this Martín and his older brother Sebastián who also had a son from his first marriage to Catalina de Arrieta y Gómez de Lara named Martín Calvo de la Puerta y Arrieta, who allegedly lived from 1614 to 1669; he died in the same year his uncle Martín Calvo de la Puerta y Pérez Borroto died. Cuban genealogists have confused them, and it is often impossible to distinguish between them. Francisco Calcagno, *Diccionario biográfico cubano* (Miami: Editorial Cubana, 1996), 148. See also Manuel Fernández Santalices, *Las calles de la Habana intramuros: Arte, historia y tradiciones en las calles y plazas de La Habana vieja* (Miami: Saeta Ediciones, 1989).

49. Calcagno, *Diccionario biográfico cubano*, 148.

first cousin with the same surname as her husband, died childless at age twenty-one. Marriages of the elite to cousins, even first cousins, were not uncommon because paterfamilias sought to concentrate property in the hands of the few, which primogeniture also accomplished. This practice, however, often forced younger siblings, especially sisters, into dependency on the eldest brother. In his youth, the second Sebastián became a militia cavalry captain and later in life held posts in Havana's municipal government. From 1661, he served in the offices of ordinary magistrate (*alcalde ordinario*), in the Santa Hermandad, and as *depositario general.* He became a permanent councilman (*regidor perpetuo*) of the Havana city government and served for years until ailments obliged him to surrender his duties about 1700. Nevertheless, another quarter of a century elapsed before he passed away at age eighty-seven in 1726. Two years after the death of his first wife, Sebastián wed again, this time to Lucía Ana de Gatica y Guilizasti (1654-1716). His fertile new spouse produced six or seven progeny—records are unclear about the last offspring who possibly was a grandchild. Nevertheless, only one of the brood was male, and again he was christened with the family's beloved namesake of Sebastián.[50]

Many members of the fourth generation of the Cuban Calvo de la Puerta family lived into the 1700s with their children. They witnessed the multiple changes taking place on the island and in the Caribbean that gradually advanced economic conditions. Developments in the late seventeenth century prepared the way into a new age that accelerated the pace of life.

Overall, the 1600s were a tumultuous time in the Caribbean, even worse than the previous century. Not only did pirates and corsairs keep raiding Spanish possessions, but enemy nations—France, England, and the Netherlands—became militarily powerful as they profited

50. The daughters were Lucia (1671-1726), Nicolasa (1673-1726), María (1676-1759), Josefa (1678-1765), and Antonia (1689-1721). There is some question about Luciana, who was born in 1707, when her mother was fifty-three years old. Therefore, Luciana was more likely a grandchild. Lucia Ana de Gatica y Guilizasti's maternal name was also spelled Guilisasti. Her father, Nicolás de Guilizasti, was born in Madrid. Calvo de la Puerta genealogy, AHN, OM, exped. 8114.

economically from Spain's decline, erected colonies around the world, and warred on Spanish possessions. They effortlessly swallowed up the vacant smaller Caribbean islands. In 1655 poorly inhabited and defended Jamaica fell victim to a Puritan English onslaught that soon transformed the island into a pirates' nest for assaulting Spanish Caribbean and Central American possessions. Sir Henry Morgan, pirate par excellence, followed up his numerous blood-thirsty raids by becoming a knight and Jamaica's lieutenant governor for a time. Western Hispaniola, meanwhile, confronted incursions by the French from their lair at nearby Tortuga, and Spanish officials evacuated the region in the belief that uninhabited lands discouraged attacks. But that shallow thinking permitted the French to swoop down on the area and claim it. Before the century ended, the new French colony of Saint-Domingue, helped by abundant African slave laborers, had emerged as a thriving agricultural factory, especially in the production of sugar. Spain, which had once asserted dominion over all the Caribbean, in the second half of the seventeenth century was forced to acknowledge its losses. After defeat in the Thirty Years' War (1618-48), Spain gave up the Netherlands in Europe, a Habsburg possession, in the Treaty of Münster, and the Spanish infantry that consisted of the previously invincible *tercios* collapsed into mediocrity. To their chagrin, the Spaniards recognized Dutch possession of the Caribbean colonies of Curaçao, Bonaire, Aruba, and several more located mostly off the northern coast of South America, and the right to trade without molestation. By the Treaty of Madrid in 1670, Spain accepted its loss of Jamaica and English sovereignty over its other island possessions. Finally by the Treaty of Ryswick of 1697, Spain acknowledged the presence of New World French colonies. Although it consumed a century, the three European nations obliged Spain to accept the legitimacy of their territorial holdings. The Spanish-Portuguese Treaty of Tordesillas of 1494 that divided the Western Hemisphere exclusively between the signatories two hundred years earlier had been irreversibly shattered.[51]

51. Knight, *Caribbean*, 53-54; Worcester and Schaeffer, *Growth and Culture of Latin America*, 182-201.

These entrepreneurial rivals, far more quickly than mercantilist Spain, began the large-scale production of Caribbean tropical commodities such as tobacco, sugar, cacao, and dyes that Europe avidly craved. Commercial agriculture initially appeared in small scale tobacco and sugar production. Immigrant European laborers to the Caribbean in the early seventeenth century had first grown tobacco that required skilled labor and was best handled by free workers on small farms. White workers eschewed the backbreaking labor required in the production of sugar, and planters brought in African slaves to perform those tasks. In the early seventeenth century, black slaves in the Spanish Caribbean were still insignificant. But as other European nations acquired more island colonies in the next half century, slave imports rose dramatically as large-scale commercial agriculture took hold. Europe valued sugar, and its insatiable demand turned the British and French Caribbean islands to its production. In time most islands changed to sugarcane produced by African slaves, especially on the smaller islands where lower class white tobacco farmers departed en masse. Spain's seventeenth-century rivals persisted in their attacks or in smuggling as Spanish resistance in the Caribbean deteriorated as some New World colonies plunged into economic hardship. Among factors that contributed to the economic downturn were plummeting Indian populations, slumping colonial silver and gold production, and waning Spanish manufacturing and legal trade. These developments intensified Spain's tribulations under the last two mediocre Habsburg rulers, Felipe IV and Carlos II. The rusty wheels of colonial administration screeched as they revealed antiquated economic, political, and even social systems that were critically in need of repair.[52]

Despite the political and territorial chaos in Spain and its other col-

52. Knight, *Caribbean*, 48-65, 77-81; Céspedes del Castillo, *América Hispánica*, 105-111, 133-35, 139-44, 175-79. Not all colonies suffered the same seventeenth-century economic downturn. The generality began with Woodrow Borah's *New Spain's Century of Depression* (Berkeley and Los Angeles: University of California Press, 1951). An opposing view is Richard Boyer, "Mexico in the Seventeenth Century: Transition of a Colonial Society," *Hispanic American Historical Review* 57 (August 1977): 455-78. Guatemala, on the other hand, experienced growth in the seventeenth century. Webre, "Social and Economic Bases," 11, note 12.

onies, Havana, which had suffered from fewer ships coming to the island in the seventeenth century, at last began taking on symptoms of maturing as the century closed. The neglected island's interior gradually devoted itself more to cattle and hog production that yielded meat for local consumption and for ships of the *flota* or contrabandists. In addition, the value of the animals' hides rose because they had multiple uses in the "leather age." In Cuba the production of food first developed around towns to feed their inhabitants, with the Havana district leading in farms because of its larger population and the *flota* that called there. As a colony dependent on Spain and without direct access to African slave markets, Cuba could not import them freely; by necessity Spain granted other Atlantic nations lucrative monopoly slave contracts called *asientos* to fill their need for laborers. Slave imports, however, never met the colony's demands. Consequently, Caribbean sugar production in Spain's possessions lagged behind those of other nations. In the early seventeenth century, fifty small *ingenios* in Cuba produced 1,250,000 pounds of the commodity. Each plantation operated its own crude cane pressing mill that produced the juice for the manufacture of sugar. As European demand for both tobacco and sugar intensified by the late century, it sparked greater production that could be seen in the prosperity of British Jamaica and French Saint-Domingue. Several thousand Spanish inhabitants and their slaves departed Jamaica in the 1650s when it became an English possession, and they augmented Cuba's modest sugar output around Santiago de Cuba on the southeastern coast.[53] Despite the Caribbean's turmoil, the rise in Cuba's population to about sixty thousand by the early eighteenth century laid the foundation for the future production of sugar, tobacco, cacao, lumber, hides, and more. The eighteenth century held the promise of greater development, and that in turn assured the elite, including the Calvo de la Puerta family, of additional prosperity.

53. Pérez, *Cuba*, 42-46.

2
The Calvos de la Puerta, 1700-1770

Between 1700, when the demise of the genetically impaired and childless King Carlos II ended the Habsburg dynasty in Spain, and 1770, when the discords that preceded the American War for Independence began, the Calvo de la Puerta family continued its rise in prominence among Havana's power elite. With the passage of two generations and at mid-point in the century, Sebastián Nicolás Calvo de la Puerta y O'Farrill was born in Havana on August 11, 1751. In the seven decades prior to this Sebastián reaching adulthood, his grandfather and father exploited the Cuban agricultural market to expand their holdings. Both were well-known planters and members of the Havana oligarchy that the new royal dynasty endeavored to co-opt to its service. Initially, the covetous Bourbon rulers attempted to appropriate the island's developing economy for themselves before they realized that doing so throttled progress and generated hatred since privileged Cuban families zealously defended their economic interests and resented the government's intrusion in their financial dealings. Consequently, the rulers backpedaled and shifted to profiting through the achievements of the planters.[1]

1. The degree to which the Spanish crown exploited its American colonies to augment its treasury has been debated. Because of many European wars in the sixteenth and seventeenth centuries, military expenditures consumed much of the money. This also happened in the eighteenth century, but more of its wealth at that time remained in the colonies to satisfy numerous needs in administration, defense, and development. Many books and articles have appeared on this subject. Among them, see Car-

Placement of the Bourbon Philip of Anjou on the Spanish throne in 1700 as Felipe V, inaugurated a new era in the nation's history, and it affected Cuba in significant ways. As the grandson of the French Sun King Louis XIV who turned France into the powerhouse of Europe, the new monarch immediately sought to restore Spain to international standing to achieve Louis's ambition of creating a potent ally as a counterweight to his many rivals. Transforming Spain's army and navy into formidable weapons, however, required money, and Felipe's French advisers looked to the Spanish American colonies to provide it. To do so, they improved tax collection and curbed contraband traffic. These efforts, however, proceeded slowly, especially in the first half of the eighteenth century when wars erupted with discouraging regularity. Encumbered with numerous obstacles, Spain's administrative, economic, and military makeover lagged behind the development of other European powers. As piratical attacks gradually diminished in the Caribbean in the late seventeenth century, aggressive Atlantic countries employed their national navies and armies to seize revenue producing colonial possessions. Wars were frequent, and peaceful interludes served merely to retool for the next conflict. In the second half of the eighteenth century, Spanish colonial improvements accelerated but not to the extent reformers wished. French advisers, who had accompanied Felipe V to Spain, and later his wife's Italian counselors, pushed their own programs in guiding the king on policy. Other than to collect revenue, European goals, not genuine colonial restructuring, dominated their interests. Not until Felipe V died in 1746 and two sons, Fernando VI (1746-1759) and Carlos III (1759-1788), succeeded him on the throne did Spanish objectives move into motion. Under the latter kings the Enlightenment, a cultural and intellectual revival, grew in Spain among some of the middle and upper classes.[2]

---

los Marichal, *Bankruptcy of Empire: Mexican Silver and the Wars between Spain, Britain and France, 1760-1810* (Cambridge, U.K.: Cambridge University Press, 2007); Regina Grafe and María Alejandra Irigoin, "The Spanish Empire and Its Legacy: Fiscal Re-Distribution and Political Conflict in Colonial and Post-Colonial Spanish America," *Journal of Global History* 1 (September 2005), 1-68.

2. Smith, *Spain*, 245-53; González-Ripoll, *Cuba*, 5; Céspedes del Castillo, *América*

The nation's political directors understood that economic renewal was essential to strengthen its power and that of their American colonies. Geographic obstacles, however, hindered realization of their plans. Spain's mountainous terrain, the elevated plateaus (*mesetas*) of Old and New Castile in the central portions of the nation, and the pervasive shortage of navigable rivers to transport goods did not help. One that was useful, the Guadalquivir, took galleons from the coast to Seville, but silt and debris gradually filled it up. For decades smugglers aboard vessels had unloaded illegal passengers and products, especially bullion, as they journeyed upriver to Seville and taken on unauthorized Indies-bound travelers and goods as they descended. Cádiz finally replaced Seville as the hub of the overseas trade in 1717. Transporting goods by land in Spain, Europe's second most mountainous nation, inflated commodity prices for consumers. Much the same occurred in the mountain-strewn Spanish American colonies; Cuba's streams were likewise negotiable only for short distances. Another obstacle that troubled both Spain and the colonies were economic restrictions. A plethora of medieval taxes imposed stultifying burdens on goods in the colonies: the *almojarifazgo* on imports and exports, the *alcabala* on the sale of goods, the *avería* to cover fleet costs, the *diezmo* (tenth) on commerce that benefited the church, the *quinto* (fifth) that the crown imposed on the production of precious metals, and a veritable host of other taxes on all forms of economic activities. They forced their New World inhabitants, including Cubans, to turn to contraband for cheaper and more available products. Given the difficulties of transporting products to the colonies, Spanish merchants in the Atlantic trade preferred earning large profits from the sale of fewer but costlier items over the gain derived from selling voluminous lower-priced articles.[3]

Economic growth in Spain and its colonies under Felipe V initially fared badly. No sooner was Felipe seated on the Spanish throne than Louis XIV imprudently proclaimed that the Pyrenees had disappeared. His boast led rival European nations to conclude that France and Spain

---

Hispánica, 278-79.

3. Smith, *Spain*, 208-18, 186-89; Pérez, *Cuba*, 53-55.

had merged into a single monarchy under the French king, which tilted the balance of power against them. Consequently, from 1702 to 1713 the War of the Spanish Succession raged to prevent their union, in which Spain experienced losses such as the Low Countries, Minorca, and Gibraltar. At war's end, Great Britain gained the right to supply the Spanish colonies with African slaves and send an annual five hundred-ton trade ship to Portobello, Panama, that faintly masked widespread smuggling. But Spain derived concessions, too, since Felipe remained on the Spanish throne with his French advisors and crushed a secessionist rebellion in Catalonia that brought the semi-autonomous region more tightly into the Spanish-Castilian fold.[4]

Nevertheless, the war racked up tremendous debts that forced the impecunious crown to devise public and private methods to pay for it. One source of revenue came from the secret selling of offices and honors to moneyed individuals. The sales augmented loyalty in the Indies among wealthy subjects from humble backgrounds who in this way boosted their social stature and prominence. Sales of offices occurred in virtually all posts in both Spain and the Indies, and the crown tried as much as possible to conceal these nefarious transactions. Felipe V's family similarly profited from the income, especially the queen whose household operated on clandestine funding.[5]

While contraband trade in Cuba diminished during the War of the Spanish Succession, it quickly rebounded with the return of peace. Perhaps as much as three-quarters of the tobacco produced left the colony furtively while a quarter of the hides from slaughtered cattle found

4. Henry Kamen, *The War of the Spanish Succession, 1700-1715* (Bloomington: Indiana University Press, 1969).

5. Francisco Andújar Castillo, in *Necesidad y venalidad: España e Indias, 1704-1711* (Madrid: Centro de Estudios Políticos y Constitucionales, 2008), discusses the diverse ways the new Bourbon sovereign obtained money from the sales of offices and honors and the impact they had. See also J. H. Parry, *The Sale of Public Office in the Spanish Indies under the Hapsburgs* (Berkeley and Los Angeles: University of California Press, 1953); Regina Grafe and María Alejandra Irigoin, "A Stakeholder Empire: The Political Economy of Spanish Imperial Rule in America," *Working Papers*, no. 111 (November 2008): 32-33.

their way to England. Barrels of salted meat also went to neighboring colonies to feed slave laborers. Overall, nearly half of Cuban products, with an estimated value of 1,400,000 pesos, were smuggled out of the island, primarily through its eastern ports. In return, covert traders provided slaves to tend Cuban livestock and harvest logs for export. Contraband traffic boosted the commerce and populations of tiny port towns noticeably.[6]

With expensive wars to wage, Spain's economic recovery proved thornier than that of its colonies with their greater resources. To counter previous Habsburg maladministration in gathering taxes and the corruption and contraband trade that flourished along side, Bourbon officials tried to refurbish management of the colonies. They introduced new mercantilist methods that monopolized sales to and purchases in the colonies so as to guarantee revenue collection. However, they ignored the multiple causes responsible for the colonies' sluggish development and mercantilism's stifling consequences. Still, the advisers sought to advance colonial trade, reduce illegal imports by sending more legal wares, and encourage Spanish manufacturers and industrialists through a greater colonial production of raw materials. Lording over the Spaniards, the Gallic Bourbons confidently trusted in their ability to transform the stagnant Spanish colonies and control their resources.[7]

Among these possessions, Cuba in the early eighteenth century had changed by moving beyond its earlier situation as a military outpost with only mediocre commercial value. The seventeenth century had witnessed the slow development and diversification of its economy, but it was not tremendous given Cuba's limited population and shortage of both capital and technology. Nevertheless, the island's slight fiscal improvement attracted royal attention. A century and a half of fleets and passengers pouring money into the Havana district had stimulated its financial viability and revenue production. Cuba evolved into the Spanish jewel in the Caribbean Sea, and the island portended

6. Pérez, *Cuba*, 55; Moreno Fraginals, *El Ingenio*, 15.

7. Pérez, *Cuba*, 49-50.

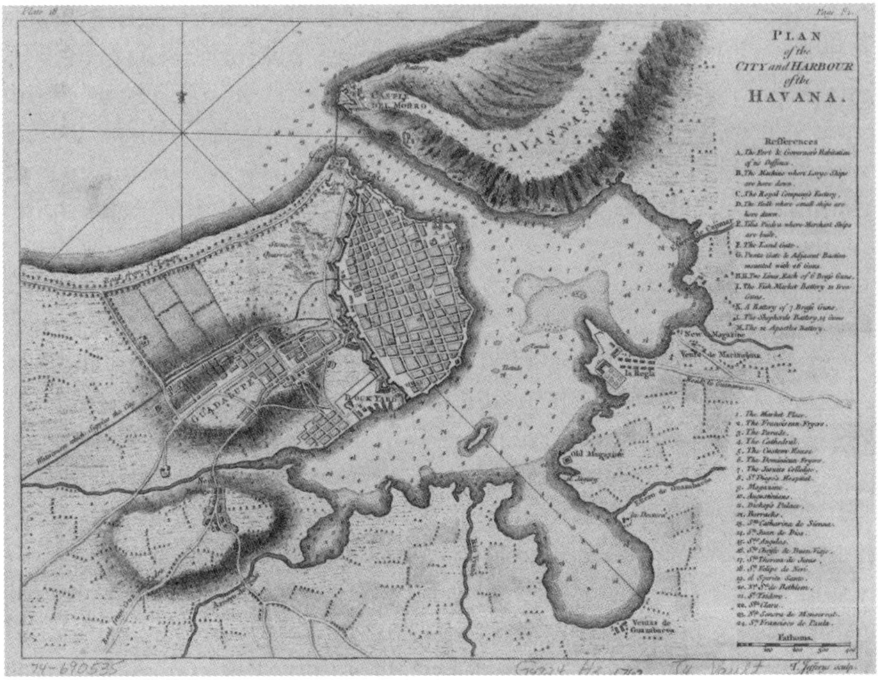

Plan of the city and harbor of Havana
Courtesy of the Library of Congress

further growth. Exports to Europe, especially tobacco, rose steadily. Continental connoisseurs savored the superior quality of its tobacco in cigars, pipes, and snuff. Twenty mills, located mainly in the Havana and nearby Matanzas districts, constituted the colony's tobacco industry and produced the items smoked, chewed, or sniffed abroad. The penurious crown relished the transfer of Cuba's rising profits to Spain and in 1717 established a monopoly to manage tobacco's prices, production, and marketing. Its creation came at a time when other European nations were abandoning their stagnant monopolies. True to form, the Cuban company purchased only a limited quantity of tobacco, not the total amount grown, and it prohibited the sale of the remainder. Largely Spaniards profited from the monopoly as they constituted most buyers in Cuba and all sellers in Spain. In addition, the monopoly limited production to prevent the surplus from entering the contraband market and competing with Spanish sales overseas. Furthermore, Spain wanted to limit Cuban participation exclusively to growing tobacco leaves, which would be shipped to the peninsula for processing and selling. In 1720, the king discouraged the island from sending processed tobacco by boosting its export tax 40 percent over the export duty imposed on leaves.[8]

Still other problems alienated Cuban growers and the public in general. A new governor, Gregorio Guazo Calderón, cracked down on unauthorized production by the *vegueros* (tobacco growers), who were mostly small farmers. His policy, however, affected Cabildo members who also grew tobacco. To crush the opposition, Guazo Calderón clapped some protesting councilmen in jail, one of whom was Sebastián Calvo de la Puerta y Gatica. He probably soon gained his freedom and likely refrained from further spoken criticism.[9]

Tobacco also brought new titles of nobility to eighteenth-century Cuba. Spaniards living on the island and involved in the acquisition of tobacco leaves or in their production for the crown were the first recipients. Only later did Cuban Creoles receive the honors. Laureano de Torres Ayala, the island's Spanish governor, was the first to benefit in 1708 during the War of the Spanish Succession for purchasing large quantities of tobacco leaves for royal factories in Spain; he became the Marqués de Casa Torres. In 1710, Capt. Juan Núñez de Castillo, a Spaniard from Granada, facilitated the Spanish treasury's acquisition of tobacco and founded the settlement of Bejucal; he became the Marqués de San Felipe y Santiago.[10]

By 1740 the constant royal snipping at the Cuban economy had

8. Ibid., 50-51; González-Ripoll, *Cuba*, 41; Moreno Fraginals, *El Ingenio*, 19.

9. González-Ripoll, *Cuba*, 41. A member of a different line of the Calvo de la Puerta family described here and also named Sebastián Calvo de la Puerta, but who was not on the Cabildo, became an agent of a Cádiz merchant and obtained a favorable contract to supply tobacco to Spain from which he profited handsomely. Ibid. His activities as an informant are detailed in J. Rivero Muñoz, *Tabaco, su historia en Cuba*, 2 vols. (La Habana: Comisión Nacional de la Academia de Ciencia de la República de Cuba, 1964/5), 1: 136-74.

10. González-Ripoll, *Cuba*, 40-41, 131.

given the mother country charge of its foreign trade. The king's monopoly, the Royal Havana Company of Commerce, gained exclusive rights over all trade and business transactions between Spain and Cuba and employed the money-making policy of buying cheap and selling dear. Accordingly, the company dropped prices for the purchase of Cuban exports—hides, logs, sugar, coffee, and other commodities—and raised them for Spanish goods sold in Cuba. For example, Cuba's tropical and humid climate prohibited growing wheat, which forced the island to import flour from Spain, where its price of five pesos per barrel skyrocketed to thirty-five in Havana. Meanwhile, tobacco purchased advantageously in Cuba and sold at inflated prices in Europe netted profits that reached up to a thousand percent. With its fabulous earnings, the monopoly company rewarded its Spanish investors generously.[11]

Royal success in squeezing money out of Cuba coincided with a reduction of the island's political power. In 1729 the crown stripped Cabildos of their monopoly to grant land and improved distribution of consumer goods to the island's previously ignored regions to reduce smuggling. The royal government created a coast guard and recovered its costs through the sale of illegal goods found on seized vessels. It further encouraged Spanish privateers to intercept ships of smugglers coming from British Jamaica and French Saint-Domingue, the two major areas involved in the nefarious trade with Cuba. Stopping British smugglers instigated the so-called War of Jenkins' Ear (1739-42) that merged into the War of the Austrian Succession and lasted to 1748. To curb smuggling, in 1746 the Spanish crown issued a royal decree that permitted privateers assisting the coast guard to retain the goods found on apprehended ships; previously, only the king benefited from the seizures. Spanish army officers also replaced civilian administrators throughout the colonies, a measure that tightened the military's grip on colonial life. Militarization in Cuba grew as the crown established fixed infantry battalions in key cities, beginning with Havana. Artillery and cavalry troops supplemented the foot soldiers. Initially, European

11. Pérez, *Cuba*, 51-52.

troops were preferred over colonials, who were considered inferior and potentially disloyal. But as time passed, manpower shortages dictated the enlistment of colonials in militias. Wherever militias were established, they consisted of separate units of local free males—whites, mulattoes, and blacks.[12]

Narrow-sighted imperial efforts, however, brought harmful consequences. Bourbon mercantilist policies limited Cuba's trade solely to Spain, aggressively tried to control Cuban agriculture and ranching, and gave Spaniards financial supremacy over Cubans. These practices deepened Cuban resentment toward Iberian-born Spaniards and their governance of the island. Second-class status in their own homeland and the affected superiority of the alien Spaniards bred enmity among Cubans of all classes.[13]

As the eighteenth century progressed, the island's transformation continued. Racial diversity within the population rose steadily as reflected in censuses started by Carlos III. By 1774, the population reached 171,620, with whites accounting for 56.2 percent, slaves 25.9 percent, and the free people of color 17.9 percent. Only eighteen years later in 1792, the figures increased to a total population of 272,301, with whites at 48.8 percent, slaves 30.8 percent, and free people of color 20.4 percent. While Havana and the adjacent western areas of the island still claimed a disproportionate share of Cuba's inhabitants, older towns in the east such as Bayamó, Santiago de Cuba, and others grew and enjoyed greater trade and development.[14]

As the island experienced these gradual changes, Sebastián Calvo de la Puerta y Recio's family numbered among members of the oligarchy who battled royal economic restrictions. As the family patriarch approached old age (he lived until 1726), bodily afflictions began wearing him down. His lengthy service on Havana's city council grew sporadic as the illnesses progressed. In 1700 he appointed Andrés Rubio Villarreal to fill his post until his son, Sebastián Calvo de la Puerta

12. Kuethe, *Cuba, 1753-1815*, 4-8; Sánchez-Ripoll, *Cuba*, 43.

13. Pérez, *Cuba*, 95.

14. González-Ripoll, *Cuba*, 100-2.

y Gatica (1685-1753), the third consecutive Sebastián to head this branch of the family, had matured sufficiently to assume the posts of councilman and chief magistrate in the municipal government. Rubio Villarreal served for ten years before he relinquished the post to his benefactor's son who reached his majority at age twenty-five. He took over in the last years of the War of the Spanish Succession that had military consequences for the island. British warships often blockaded Havana's harbor and patrolled through the Gulf of Mexico, seizing Spanish vessels. Among the issues Sebastián faced on the municipal council was the suppression of the 1717 uprising of *vegueros* (tobacco farmers) who protested the crown's decision to turn tobacco production into a state monopoly and reduced payments to them. In doing so, he followed orders issued by several governors; perhaps his earlier error in siding with the *vegueros* had taught him the imprudence of defying royal authorities. In 1727, when an enemy force landed outside Havana, Capt. Gen. Dionisio Martínez de la Vega designated two councilmen, Calvo de la Puerta and Ambrosio Zayas Bazán, to gather materials and laborers for the construction of defensive works around the harbor to guard against a seaborne attack on the city. It was only one of this Sebastián's important duties that he carried out throughout his life for the municipal government. Shortly before his death in 1753, he assigned his Cabildo offices to his son and principal heir Pedro José, father of the protagonist of this study.[15]

Pedro José was Sebastian's oldest living son. His father's marriage to María Ambrosia Arango y Loza had been fecund. Between 1713 and 1738, it produced seven or eight children; the number is uncertain because Inés and Luciana had the same years for their births and deaths, and it is likely they were one person. The first born son, Sebastián, died either at birth or shortly after, which left Pedro José (1720-1781), the second son, as the oldest living male heir. Two younger brothers and three sisters—counting Inés Luciana as one person—who reached adulthood followed Pedro José. Among them, only Josefa lived beyond sixty-one years (Pedro José's age when he died), succumbing in 1797 at

15. Calcagno, *Diccionario biográfico cubano*, 148.

age eighty-two. Pedro José earned his father's trust since he proved his ability to carry out duties in agriculture and as a member of the Havana Cabildo. A doctorate in law from the local university no doubt helped him with his chores.[16]

Like his forebears, he advanced the family fortune in succeeding years in both his public and private life. To tie the post of *alguacil mayor* (chief constable) definitively to the family, he bought the office for the then tidy sum of 6,000 pesos *fuertes* (silver pesos). The purchase became the source of a considerable part of the yearly income he and his descendants enjoyed. The Cabildo seat entitled its holder to a fee for purchasing the cattle city butchers slaughtered and sold to the public for consumption. From the mid-eighteenth century as the city grew, the oldest son in the Calvo de la Puerta family controlled the *alguacil mayor* seat on the Cabildo. Annual income from fees the office generated expanded in time to more than three times its purchase price. With the proceeds steadily rising, the heirs clung zealously to the office.[17]

Under Sebastián Calvo de la Puerta y Gatica, the family became closely tied to Ricardo O'Farrill y O'Daly (?-1730), a businessman who arrived in Havana in 1715. As the local manager of the British Company of the South Sea that provided African slaves to Cuba, his ability to dole out workers quickly established his prominence among Havana's well-to-do inhabitants. Born on the West Indian island of Montserrat to Irish immigrants who traced their ancestry back to County Longford in Ireland, his economic endeavors in Cuba earned the respect of the crown. In short order, he emerged as a powerful and influential person in the city's business community. Pleased with life in Havana, around 1720 he left the British company and requested naturalization as a Spanish subject, which he obtained on January 17, 1722. Besides his financial accomplishments, he had equal success in

16. Pedro José's brothers and sisters were Sebastián (1713-?), Josefa (1715-1797), Manuel Nicolás (1717-1767), María Ignacia (1728-1784), Inés and Luciana (both listed as 1730-1751), and Miguel (1738-1777). Mallén, *Historia de familias cubanas,* 4: 336.

17. Although a royal cédula confirmed this on June 27, 1785, the office holder had probably held that right as far back as the town's founding.

the social arena with his November 11, 1720 marriage to María Josefa Arriola y García de Londoño, the daughter of Bartolomé de Arriola y Valdespino, who was the chief accountant in the Royal Accounting Tribunal, a general of the fleet, and the founder of a Havana shipyard. O'Farrill had already garnered a substantial fortune importing Africans from Jamaica, the British slave depot. In addition, he retrieved part of his possessions from that island in 1721, when he returned to Cuba with 260 African slaves of all ages and sexes, household possessions, and materials for construction of a sugar plantation. Besides producing sugar, his business exploits included the importation of slaves and goods.[18]

As early as 1717, O'Farrill became acquainted with Cabildo councilman Sebastián Calvo de la Puerta y Recio, a staunch critic of Havana's royal authorities who dawdled in promoting sugar production on the island. At that time, tobacco and cattle, not sugar, still dominated economic activities in Cuba as they had throughout the seventeenth century. Nevertheless, attracted by the financial success of other Caribbean colonies such as Jamaica, Saint-Domingue, and various smaller island colonies that produced and sold sugar, a coterie of Cuban landowners impatiently sought to boost their sugar output and income. By 1723 O'Farrill, whom the Havana elite had embraced, built two sugar *ingenios* on his lands outside Havana. Calvo de la Puerta y Gatica, meanwhile, also received permission to construct another sugar mill. O'Farrill remained close to the Calvo de la Puerta family during his remaining years of life. Although he died on June 6, 1730, he left a son, Juan José O'Farrill y Arriola (1721-June 17, 1779), who followed in his father's footsteps and became a powerful merchant, and a daughter, Catalina Josefa O'Farrill y Arriola (1723-1796). On December 6, 1746, Catalina married Pedro José Calvo de la Puerta y Arango (1720-

18. Oscar Recio Morales, "When Merit is Not Enough: Money as a 'Parallel Route' for Irish Advancement in Spain," *Irish Migration Studies in Latin America* 5 (July 2007): 121-24; Rafael Fernández Moya, "The Irish Presence in the History and Place Names of Cuba," ibid., 5 (November 2007): 190-91; Ruben C. Arango, *La Sacrocacía: Historia de la aristocracía azucarera cubana* (Miami: Ego Group, Inc., 2006), 106-9; Mallén, *Historia de familias cubanas*, 4: 335; González-Ripoll, *Cuba*, 39.

81), Sebastián's oldest surviving son. Although O'Farrill still had property in Jamaica and had requested permission to transfer it to Cuba, he died before doing so. Nevertheless, royal officials carried out his last wishes. Catalina inherited a portion of her father's property, and in time it joined the holdings of the Calvo de la Puerta y Arango riches.[19]

In numerous ways society functioned primarily to service the elite in eighteenth-century Cuba. The marriage of Pedro José Calvo de la Puerta and Catalina O'Farrill perhaps was arranged by both fathers while their children were young. Havana's close-knit elite most likely attended the wedding as they did all similar marriages.

Pedro José sat on the Havana Cabildo during the momentous Seven Years' War that brought significant changes to Cuba. With his preference for peace over war, King Fernando had not squandered funds on the military. Consequently, Spain's army and navy had deteriorated and were unprepared for hostilities. In addition, Spaniards thought defensively, not offensively, a tactic that emphasized the superiority of fixed positions against enemy attacks. And overall, the Spanish Empire sought to defend lands, not acquire more in the eighteenth century. An exception, however, lay on the west coast of North America where exploration reached up as far as Alaska and claimed lands from California to as far north as Puget Sound. After coming to the throne in 1759, Carlos III saw that France fared poorly in the Seven Years' War, and because it was Spain's sometimes ally in recent conflicts, he wanted to avoid its total rout. In August 1761, he joined France in the Third Family Compact without adequately building up his armed forces. Great Britain, however, anticipated Spain's entry in the hostilities and declared war on January 4, 1762. It then immediately unleashed two invasion armadas against Havana in the Caribbean and Manila in the Philippines, both vital trade centers. The fleet directed against Havana contained more than two hundred warships and troop transports, with a force of 14,000 soldiers and thousands more sailors who outmatched the city's paltry 2,330 regular soldiers and 4,753 poorly disciplined militiamen. Capt. Gen. Juan de Prado y Portocarrero Malleza led the

19. Mallén, *Historia de familias cubanas*, 4: 335; Arango, *La Sacracocia*, 109-10.

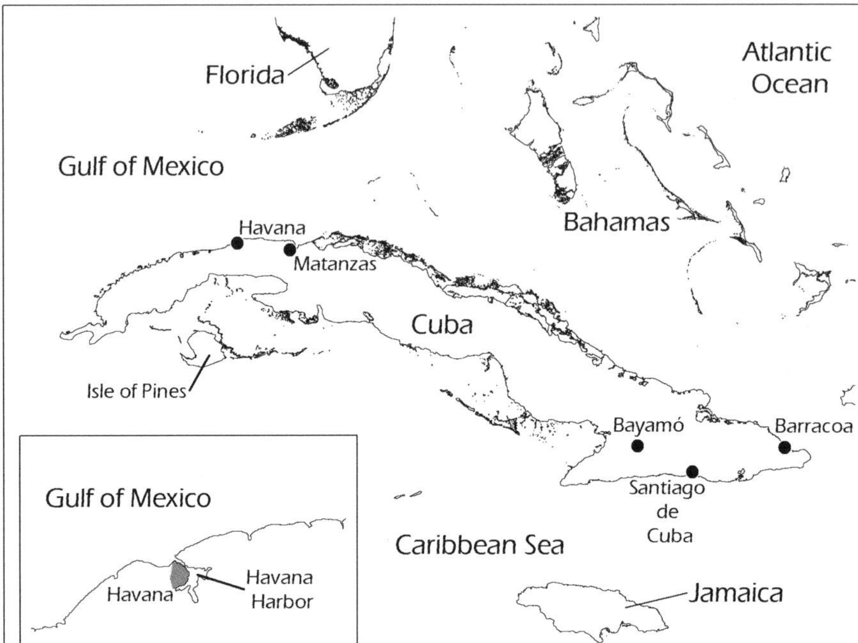

Entrance to the Gulf of Mexico
Map drawn by Alexander Din

defense, with the help of other generals who inadvertently found themselves in Havana. While many of the city's inhabitants rushed to assist in its defense, British troops landed on both sides of Havana in June 1762. Pedro Calvo de la Puerta summoned his slaves from the neighboring sugar plantations of Managua and Buena Vista, and they worked at building up the protective walls that encircled Havana. Soon the British isolated the city and initiated a siege that persisted for two months. Gradually, Havana's defenses deteriorated and reached their nadir when the British captured the heights behind La Cabaña and El Morro fortresses that were across the harbor from the city. By that time, effective Spanish regular troops had fallen to only 631. Many of the more numerous militiamen had ignored the call to arms while those who responded were so badly trained and equipped that they contributed little to the city's defense. Combat, diseases, fatigue, and heat bore down mercilessly on the besieged and diminished their numbers. Determining that further resistance meant only more casualties, General Prado surrendered on August 13, 1762.[20]

For the next eleven months, the British administered Havana. Despite its conquest, many lesser Spanish officials remained at their posts to ease governance of the city. Among them were Cabildo members that included Calvo de la Puerta. As chief magistrate, he had to deal personally with the victors. Verbal clashes ensued when the British insisted that everybody in the city government acknowledge George III as their sovereign. Loyal Cubans, however, unalterably refused, including Calvo de la Puerta. While others later roundly condemned the Cubans who temporarily worked for the British, it was undeserved criticism because the city government provided services to its inhabitants regardless of who had superior authority. Pedro José did not suffer that indignity, however, and instead the public praised him for resisting the British. Through the Treaty of Paris of February 10, 1763, Spain exchanged Florida and territory in Central America for Havana, and in July 1763, the valuable city returned to Spanish rule. France, which lost Canada, also gave up Louisiana, with trans-Appalachia (the territory between the Appalachian Mountains and the Mississippi River) falling to Great Britain except for New Orleans, which Spain received along with the undefined region on the Mississippi's west bank. Unlike other Spanish subjects who solicited compensation for labor given and property destroyed in the war, Pedro José patriotically declined reimbursement for his losses.[21]

Rebuilding defensive measures figured prominently in Spain's actions after the war. The Spanish military had already been preparing an expedition in the Canary Islands to reinforce Havana when word of its capture became known. Santa Cruz de Tenerife was the last port of call for Spanish vessels crossing the Atlantic and, in late 1762 and early the next year, it swarmed with ships and soldiers waiting to depart.

20. Thomas, *Cuba*, 2-11; Kuethe, *Cuba*, 17-20; Calcagno, *Diccionario biográfico cubano*, 148-49.

21. Kuethe, *Cuba*, 17-20, describes the British siege and victory at Havana in 1762. See also Gold, *Borderland Empires*, 13-28.

Only when news of the peace arrived with its assurance of Havana's return to Spanish control did the ships begin to leave. Over the next few years, Spain worked diligently to improve its military installations in the Caribbean, especially in Cuba, Puerto Rico, and the Gulf of Mexico, that were likely targets in another war.[22]

Spanish determination resulted from Great Britain's penetration of the Gulf of Mexico with its acquisition of Florida and the Gulf Coast that stretched to the Mississippi River north of Bayou Manchac, the Amite River, and Lake Pontchartrain. Three types of military units would defend new fortifications: regular Spanish regiments that periodically rotated to the colonies; fixed battalions and regiments that served only in designated locations with both trained Spanish and Creole soldiers; and a disciplined local militia instructed by regular Spanish soldiers. White civilians and free people of color served in separate militia units. To accomplish this enormous task, the Spaniards began with Havana and Cuba and dispatched officers there. At their head were Lt. Gen. Ambrosio de Funes y Villalpando, the Conde de Ricla, and Field Marshal Alejandro O'Reilly. Ricla was charged with rebuilding fortifications and reorganizing the army and militia while O'Reilly was second-in-command and the inspector general of the militia. They left Cádiz on April 27, 1763, and reached Santa Cruz de Tenerife in May. They had orders to recover Havana and push out the British who still occupied it. On June 30, they sighted Havana. Arranging the transfer of possession took several days; it occurred on July 6. The deadline for the English departure was set at September 10.[23]

22. Kuethe, *Cuba*, 25-49; Allan J. Kuethe, "Havana in the Eighteenth Century," 21-22, in *Atlantic Port Cities: Economy, Culture, and Society in the Atlantic World, 1650-1850*, ed. Franklin W. Knight and Peggy K. Liss (Knoxville: University of Tennessee Press, 1991).

23. Bibiano Torres Ramírez, *Alejandro O'Reilly en las Indias* (Sevilla: Escuela de Estudios Hispano-Americanos de Sevilla, 1969), 17-19; Lyle N. McAlister, "The Reorganization of the Army of New Spain, 1763-1766," *Hispanic American Historical Review* 33 (1953), 8-9; Arthur S. Aiton, "Spanish Colonial Reorganization under the Family Compact," *Hispanic American Historical Review* 12 (1932): 269-80; Jaime Delgado, "El Conde de Ricla, Capitán General de Cuba," *Revista de Historia de*

Ricla and O'Reilly immediately began working on the city's defenses that had suffered in the fighting and from English demolition. Ricla renovated the city's bastions, rebuilding the dismantled fortresses of El Morro and La Cabaña and erecting other strongholds to prevent Havana's shameful capture again. It was an expensive task that required abundant local funds. Ricla sought out the wealthiest members in Cuban society and secured planter approval for the needed taxation. In return, the crown facilitated slave imports to expand the production of sugarcane and other crops. While Ricla busily constructed fortifications and obtained funding, O'Reilly supervised the establishment of new military units and reorganized older bodies, especially the Fixed Havana Infantry Regiment that was founded in 1719. Many of its officers had performed poorly in the recent defense of the city, and O'Reilly dismissed or denied them promotion. Newly arriving peninsular officers and soldiers enjoyed preference over their older confreres and Creoles in the unit. The regiment now consisted of four infantry battalions. O'Reilly also created the Spanish Córdoba Infantry Regiment with 1,224 soldier slots for its two battalions, but it initially had numerous vacancies. English deserters who had remained after the evacuation and soldiers from other Spanish units filled some of them. Finally, O'Reilly developed a unit of dragoons (cavalry) composed of 280 men, plus two artillery companies. The dragoon squadron is significant because Sebastián Calvo de la Puerta y O'Farrill, the protagonist of this study, began his military service in it.[24]

Seeking to improve relations with the local population, Ricla rewarded Cubans who had served loyally during the occupation with

---

América 55/56 (January-December 1963): 41-138. Because of his family's noble connections, Ricla became a captain at age seventeen, a brigadier general at twenty-four, and a field marshal at twenty-six. He sharpened his administrative ability through many assignments in Spain. Kuethe, *Cuba*, 25. For sketches of O'Reilly; see David K. Bjork, "Alejandro O'Reilly and the Spanish Occupation of Louisiana, 1769-1770," in *New Spain and the Anglo-American West*, 2 volumes in 1 (New York: Kraus Reprint Co., 1969), 1: 165-82; and David Ker Texada, *Alejandro O'Reilly and the New Orleans Rebels* (Lafayette, La: Center for Louisiana Studies, 1970).

24. Kuethe, *Cuba*, 33-35.

titles of nobility. Only five titles of Castile had been established in Cuba up to this time.[25] To tie the Cuban upper class closer to Spain, between 1764 and 1770 the crown granted seven more titles, five of them to prominent people involved in sugar production, and two to Spaniards in royal service but established in Cuba. The titles to Cubans recognized the growing importance of sugar among the island's leading agricultural crops, and its expansion had only started. According to Pablo Tornero, sixteen Cuban families stood out prominently in agriculture, especially in the production of sugar: the families were the Armentero, Arango, Calvo de la Puerta, Cárdenas, Cruz, Chacón, Garro, Herrera, Montalvo, O'Farrill, Peñalver, Pedroso, Sotolongo, Santa Cruz, Torre, and Zayas. Sixty-nine planters belonged to these families, and they produced much of the island's agricultural crops.[26] Pedro Calvo de la Puerta y Arango figured among the persons Ricla recommended because he had refused to kowtow to the English, and a royal order granted him a title of nobility on April 16, 1766. He became the Conde de Buena Vista; the name came from one of his plantations. In addition, he soon received the rank of colonel and the position of second-in-command in the newly created Havana Militia Regiment. His post had the title of "lieutenant colonel" but it did not determine the holder's rank, only his position as second-in-command in the regiment. A monetary requirement for royal titles stipulated that recipients possess a minimal annual income of 6,000 ducats to ensure that they had a prestigious social standing and a decent standard of living. This fiscal requirement was another reason why wealthy families kept their properties intact through the institution of primogeniture (*mayorazgo*). Moreover, moneyed individuals in Cuba generally purchased their noble titles, and it further required payment of an annual

25. Cuban holders of titles to about 1770 included Juan Francisco Núñez de Castillo, Marqués de San Felipe y Santiago; Manuel José Aparicio del Manzano y Jústiz, Marqués de Jústiz de Santa Ana; Gonzalo Francisco Recio de Oquendo, Marqués de la Real Proclamación; Gonzalo de Herrera y Tapia, Marqués de Villalta; and Francisco José Chacón y Torres, Conde de Casa Bayona.

26. Pablo Tornero, "Hacendados y desarrollo azucarero cubano (1763-1818)," *Revista de Indias* 38 (July-December 1978): 718.

fee to the crown. In 1767 Pedro Calvo de la Puerta had a fortune calculated at 22,034,624 reales (2,754,328 pesos), so that the fee he paid was a negligible consideration.[27] While the first Conde de Buena Vista did not buy his title, he surely paid the yearly fee for holding it.

Elite Cuban families of that time, barring physical impediments, often had multiple children who most often married persons of their own social and economic standing. After several generations, marriage partners were frequently first and second cousins, uncles and nieces, or other combinations of family members. The consanguineous marriages concentrated property more narrowly with each passing generation. A narrow clique of elite families also held offices in the municipal government that became hereditary with time. A similar development occurred in the military where *segundones* (second sons) often found careers. Peninsular Spanish society and its colonial counterparts provided elite males with few career options. Among the favored occupations were those in agriculture, government, church, or army. But contrary to Spain where the older nobility generally shunned business activity outside agriculture, the Cuban elite embraced commerce, especially occupations that were tied to agriculture such as shipping, construction, and slavery. Some well-to-do planter fathers also acquired prominent posts in militia units. Participation in important military offices tied the rich and powerful families to the Spanish crown and gave them unrivaled economic and social clout on the local level. As affluent militia officers, they provided the weapons and uniforms that destitute soldiers from the bottom rungs of the socio-economic ladder could not afford. It was the price the elite paid for leadership positions. Similar to well-heeled civilians, both regular army and militia personnel of all ranks were expected to lend the crown money in wars, usually in affordable amounts.[28] In turn, militia officers received prestigious rewards: the

27. González-Ripoll, *Cuba,* 131, 135-36. A silver ducat was worth approximately the same as a silver peso, with a gold ducat having twice that value. According to one historian, through the colonial era Peru received 411 titles of nobility, Santo Domingo and Cuba each received 234, and Mexico 170.

28. Kuethe, *Cuba*, xiii; Thomas, *Cuba*, 148.

honor of wearing military uniforms on all occasions, which was a vital consideration in a uniform-conscious society, and the military *fuero*, a privilege that moved their law suits from civilian courts to more sympathetic military tribunals.[29]

The Calvo de la Puerta-O'Farrill union seems to have been an excellent and joyous match. In time it produced three sons: Francisco José (1750-96); Sebastián (1751-1820), who was the longest lived of the three sons; and Nicolás (1758-1800). As the eldest, Francisco was expected to follow in his father's footsteps, and he became a planter and inherited the title of Conde de Buena Vista upon his father's demise. He also was a militia colonel and married the daughter of the second Marqués de Jústiz y Santa Ana, who was heiress to her father's title. In the early 1790s, Francisco with other militia officers fought the effort of royal official José Ilincheta to deprive militiamen of the privileges conferred by the military *fuero*. While the crown initially answered favorably, problems remained, and in 1793, Francisco traveled to Spain, where among other things, he petitioned for the *fuero*'s reinstatement.[30]

Pedro Calvo de la Puerta's third son, Nicolás, also became a planter while pursuing scholarly studies. He soon became an ardent advocate for Cuban agriculture. He devoted a decade or more to farming during which time he acquired considerable knowledge about Cuban crops, especially growing sugarcane and manufacturing sugar.[31]

Like many things about Sebastián Calvo de la Puerta y O'Farrill, Pedro's second son, virtually nothing is known about his childhood and education. Furthermore, no known likenesses of him appear to have been made over the course of his life, or if they were, they have not survived. He undoubtedly spent his formative years in and around Havana, with temporary stays in the countryside at one of the family's estates—Buena Vista was probably the largest and most comfortable. On the O'Farrill side of his family, Sebastián had numerous cousins due to his maternal uncle's many children—six girls and five boys.

29. *Enciclopedia Espasa Calpe*, vol. 24, *1505-1506* (Madrid: Espasa Calpe, 1964).

30. Kuethe, *Cuba*, 121, 162-65; Mallén, *Historia de familias cubanas*, 4: 119.

31. Mallén, *Historia de familias cubanas*, 4: 120.

Sebastián probably enjoyed interaction with his O'Farrill male cousins: Ignacio, Juan Manuel, Gonzalo, Rafael, and José Ricardo. Some of them, because of their many male descendants, converted O'Farrill into a familiar Cuban surname. Several of the O'Farrill brothers pursued military careers and achieved high ranks, but none was as successful as Gonzalo. Born on January 22, 1754, he was about two and a half years younger than Sebastián. Gonzalo left Cuba to study at the Benedictine school at Sorèze in southern France, after which he went to Spain to take possession of the officer position his father had purchased for him. Later, as Sebastián journeyed to Spain several times, they sometimes met and rekindled their childhood relationship. With the passage of years and his knowledge of artillery, Gonzalo rose to prominence in the peninsular army.[32]

As an offspring of an elite and affluent family, servants surrounded the world of the youthful Sebastián Calvo de la Puerta and catered to his every need. His privileged position in Cuba's hierarchical society probably seemed natural to him, and he never endured any kind of discrimination, discipline, or other infringement in his life until becoming a cadet; nevertheless, even then he was in the advantageous Havana Company of Nobles. The biggest event in his young life was the British siege of Havana, but where he was is not certain. While his father remained in the city directing his slave laborers in building defenses, perhaps the family, with their many kin, fled to a remote estate to avoid the hardships the siege imposed on the civilian population left behind.[33]

32. Calcagno, *Diccionario biográfico cubano*, 459; González-Ripoll, *Cuba,* 140-42; Arango, *La Sacracocia*, 110-11. Among Gonzalo O'Farrill's brothers Ignacio (1757-1838) became a priest; Juan Manuel (1756-?) became a dragoon captain and lieutenant colonel of the Matanzas militia cavalry; and José Ricardo who often donated money to the military became a militia brigadier general and died at age ninety-three in 1841. Calcagno, *Diccionario biográfico cubano*, 468. See Mallén's lengthy discussion of the O'Farrill clan in eighteenth- and nineteenth-century Cuba in *Historia de familias cubanas*, 3: 334-45.

33. Mallén, *Historia de familias cubanas*, 3: 335, 338; Sebastián's female O'Farrill cousins were María Teresa, María Josefa, María Catalina, María Luisa, Bárbara, and

Some time after the siege ended, Sebastián returned to Havana. On April 1, 1763, several months before he reached age twelve which was the usual minimum age for joining, he enrolled as a cadet in the Havana Company of Nobles. He did so while the city was still occupied but before the war technically ended. Whether Sebastián chose the military as a career or his father did so for him is unknown, but judging from his later behavior as an officer he seemed to have embraced military life, dedicating himself to it until age and circumstance interceded. One can suggest that Sebastián became a cadet as a symbolic protest against the British victory and occupation of Havana. He probably heard his father rant and rave about the indignities the British inflicted upon the city and the Cubans who cooperated with them. About the time he became a cadet, the inhabitants of the city learned that it would soon return to Spanish ownership, but only after that happened did his serious training as a cadet begin.[34]

Like all youthful cadets, Sebastián must have lived at home while he studied the rules and regulations that governed army life at the cadet school.[35] It prepared young men, including boys as young as twelve, to become sublieutenants (second lieutenants), the first officer rank in the army. In the school, they drilled and studied military etiquette, commands, ordinances, tactics, logistics, mathematics, and defenses that perhaps included an exposure to military architecture—the building of forts and defensive works such as moats and stockades among other things. Instruction became more rigorous as the cadets matured. Periodic examinations ensured that students understood their study matter, and those who did not left the program. Through the cadet school, Calvo de la Puerta acquired a secondary education, and private tutors that his parents could well afford probably supplemented instruction in the arts, humanities, and sciences. In the era after

---

Mariana; Recio Morales, "When Merit is Not Enough," 121-24.

34. Sebastián Calvo de la Puerta service sheet, Havana, March 1805, AGM, ES; Recio Morales, "When Merit is Not Enough," 123; Mallén, *Historia de familias cubanas*, 3: 338.

35. Sebastián Calvo de la Puerta service sheet, March 1805, AGM, ES.

the Seven Years' War, with many economic, military, and educational changes taking place, Cuba drew closer to the outside Atlantic world and at a pace that accelerated with each passing year. The educated upper and the upper middle classes felt the impact of new economic and cultural currents far more than the rest of the population.[36]

Though only eleven months long, the British occupation of Havana altered the city and the island forever. As already noted, economic activity had been increasing before the British seized Havana in 1762. Seeking to benefit from Cuban agriculture, they opened the port to free trade, abolished taxes on commerce, and welcomed new merchants from Great Britain and the English Atlantic colonies who offered to sell the Cubans all their needs in return for Mexican silver coins and tropical crops—sugar, tobacco, coffee, cacao, lumber, and more. Planters, above all, needed workers to put new lands into production, and about ten thousand African slaves poured into Cuba during the brief British occupation. With amazing rapidity, the new slaves impacted agriculture as well as other economic areas. Countless foreign ships arrived during the occupation loaded with merchandise for sale at low prices and carried away large quantities of Cuban products. Local merchants quickly learned the advantages of an unfettered trade. In addition to imported products, Cuban commodities found markets abroad that exporters wanted to retain after the occupation ended, and planters fought to enlarge farming and ranching to meet new outside demands and to bolster their fortunes.[37]

At the same time the Cuban economy began feeling the effects of a freer trade, Cadet Sebastián Calvo de la Puerta grew from a boy of twelve to a young man of eighteen in 1769. He became indoctrinated in the trappings of military life, but experiencing it at firsthand

36. Juan Marchena Fernández's *Oficiales y soldados en el ejército de América* (Sevilla: Escuela de Estudios Hispano-Americanos de Sevilla, 1983), is the most detailed work on the Spanish army in the New World; see p. 75 in particular, but additional information is scattered throughout the volume; Pérez, *Cuba*, 49-72; Peggy K. Liss, *Atlantic Empires: The Network of Trade and Revolution, 1713-1826* (Baltimore: Johns Hopkins University Press, 1983).

37. Pérez, *Cuba*, 57-58.

had yet to come. Overall, these years represented a quiet time as Spain strengthened its military hold on Cuba and as its agricultural economy advanced. In October 1768, however, a revolt erupted in New Orleans, Louisiana, and shattered the serenity that had enveloped the Gulf of Mexico after the recent war. The uprising occurred in a colony that the Spaniards had tentatively occupied only two and a half-years before.[38]

Responsibility for the revolt rested on a faction of economically-driven French Creole smugglers and planters who had been the de facto rulers in the "rogue colony" due to France's beneficent neglect. The colony's Creole leaders despised the commercial restrictions that Spain, which officially acquired Louisiana in 1763, intended to impose to make the colony conform to its economic practices in its other New World possessions. Spanish governance of Louisiana had commenced poorly because its policy directors mismanaged relations with its inhabitants. Complaining it lacked troops to claim possession, Spain delayed before it sent a tiny contingent of administrators and a hundred-man company of soldiers composed of many who were ill-disciplined and the refuse from other regiments. They finally arrived in New Orleans in March 1766.[39] Scientist and naval officer Antonio Ulloa, whom the king placed in charge, received a chilly reception from Louisiana's surly local leaders. Guided by their brusque greeting, Ulloa wanted to take control from royal officials, not municipal personages who considered themselves to be in charge. He chose instead to manage the colony's affairs through the acting French governor, Capt. Charles Philippe Aubry. It was an awkward arrangement that produced the false impression that France remained in charge in all aspects, but in finance, defense, commerce, and other vital areas, Aubry was no more than a mouthpiece for Ulloa because he dictated policy. Moreover, had Spain assumed direct control, the French troops who served under Aubry would have demanded repatriation. The Gallic government had assured Spain that their Louisiana soldiers would enlist in the Spanish army, but very few did. Their decision forced Ulloa to appeal to his

38. Moore, *Revolt in Louisiana*, 124-64.

39. Ibid., 42-59.

government for a military force adequate to meet the colony's needs.[40]

While the crown agreed to create a five hundred-man battalion in Louisiana, it sent soldiers slowly from Spain to Havana, where the military unit was to form. Ulloa would take formal charge of the province once the unit reached Louisiana. But as he waited, he determined to post most of his few soldiers throughout the province to proclaim Spanish ownership to the local inhabitants and to the neighboring British who owned the east bank of the Mississippi River from about fifty miles above New Orleans. The disbursement of soldiers along the lengthy Mississippi weakened Spanish strength in New Orleans to the vanishing point. More positively, new posts upriver on the Mississippi flew the Spanish flag and only New Orleans and the pilot's house at the mouth of the Mississippi River still displayed the fleur-de-lis and continued the charade that Frenchmen ran the colony. Spanish silver, when it arrived, paid for the colony's operations. The failure of the viceroy in Mexico City to send sufficient funds to meet Louisiana's expenses, however, forced Ulloa to pay for goods and labor with vouchers that quickly deteriorated in value. His inability to redeem them led to widespread grumbling and opposition. The colony's lack of hard money, moreover, prevented commerce from developing and inspiring confidence in Spanish rule. Matters worsened when in the fall of 1768 Ulloa announced the imminent imposition of Spanish trade restrictions that would drastically infringe on the existing local commercial practices. It induced a clique of already irate merchant-planters who had prospered from the system of neglect to revolt. Spanish impotence in New Orleans and Aubry's failure to use French soldiers against the

40. Ibid., 103-42; Din, "Protecting the 'Barrera,'" 184-88. Shannon Lee Dawdy, in *Building the Devil's Empire: French Colonial New Orleans* (Chicago: University of Chicago Press, 2009), 233-46, refers to Louisiana as a "rogue colony" and assumes that all inhabitants in the colony favored the 1768 insurrection against Spain. This is not true as even farmers from upriver settlements had to be bribed into providing support to the rebel leadership because army officers and their troops refused to participate. More distant settlements throughout the colony were first unaware of, and later, indifferent to the insurrection.

insurrectionists ensured their success.[41]

The rebels easily seized the city on October 18, 1768. To avoid bloodshed, Governor Ulloa declined to resist and quickly ordered the Spanish administrators and soldiers to evacuate the colony. He soon departed for Havana and later to Spain to explain the sordid details of the uprising. Interestingly, the rebel leaders waited until October 29 to issue an explanation of their reasons for the uprising. Many uninvolved inhabitants scattered across the colony remained bewildered by the revolt. The explanation the rebel leaders designed appealed to the colonists' patriotism and desire to return to French rule; justified the takeover as a legitimate process entitled by natural law; and invoked their version of history, laws, and economics to garner support. The explanation, however, foundered.[42]

Contrary to expectations, rebel plans repeatedly misfired for diverse reasons. First, the leaders attempted to return Louisiana to the French king, but since it had been an expensive and unproductive dependency, he declined the offer. Furthermore, the Spanish king had notified him of the uprising first and his intent to recover the colony. The rebels next tried to transform Louisiana into an independent state, but because they lacked money to operate a government or invigorate the economy, and other nations denied them recognition, that plan, too, crumbled. With the colony's frail domestic resources disintegrating, the conspirators desperately appealed to British authorities in Pensacola in West Florida to rescue them from the morass they had created, but the British refused because Spain had already announced its intention to reclaim Louisiana.[43]

From the start, Spanish royal advisors favored the colony's imme-

41. Moore, *Revolt in Louisiana*, 42-142; Rodríguez Casado, *Primeros años*, 99-137.

42. Rodríguez Casado, *Primeros años*, and Moore, *Revolt in Louisiana*, 143-64. James Winston, "Causes and Results of the Revolution of 1768," *Louisiana Historical Quarterly* 15 (April 1932): 181-213, is an early study that relied primarily on secondary sources. See also, Winston DeVille, ed., *The Louisiana Manifesto of 1769* (Ville Platte, La.: Provincial Press, 2004).

43. Moore, *Revolt in Louisiana*, 165-84.

diate retrieval. The revolt set a deplorable example for other Spanish possessions, and Louisiana's loss as a barrier against aggressive intruders from the Atlantic coast boded ill for vulnerable Texas and New Spain. In April 1769, the crown assigned Lt. Gen. Alejandro O'Reilly to regain the colony because of his previous experience in Cuba and the Caribbean. He left Cádiz on May 5, with aides and officers assigned to the Louisiana battalion; he intended to assemble a large force in Cuba, where he personally knew the military leaders. The Cuban units' participation in the colony's recovery would also test their fitness. Capt. Gen. Antonio Bucareli of Cuba put together a force from the troops under his command. They consisted of peninsular regulars from the first battalion of the Lisbon Infantry Regiment, a picket of the Dragoon Regiment of America, and two companies of the Catalan Light Infantry Regiment. Cuban troops consisted of the first battalion of the Fixed Infantry Regiment of Havana, 91 artillerymen, and 294 Havana white and colored militiamen. Altogether they totaled 2,056. O'Reilly arrived in Havana on June 24, and by July 6, a flotilla of 21 ships (3 frigates, 1 packet boat that served as a hospital, 2 brigantines, 3 schooners, 2 sloops, and various others rented for the occasion), 46 cannons, 150,000 pesos, and an abundant cache of supplies were ready to depart. It was an overpowering force directed against a motley crew of rebels who had already lost support in New Orleans. There was little likelihood that the colony's three hundred French soldiers, many of them elderly and sickly, and the untrained militia had the will to defend the humiliated rebel leaders, especially since the French army officers had not supported them. O'Reilly felt that a dominant force would squelch whatever resistance the rebels mustered among the colony's eleven thousand inhabitants, only half of whom were white. Although the expedition was costly, O'Reilly and the crown wanted an indelible impression made on Louisiana's residents—and on other colonies—that royal authority would not tolerate a rebellion. A peaceful takeover was also essential to reconcile the residents to Spanish rule quickly. Reports New Orleans vessels brought to Havana over the last few months indicated mounting dissatisfaction with the insurgent leaders inasmuch as life in the colony had deteriorated under their dismal management.[44]

For Sebastián Calvo de la Puerta y O'Farrill, O'Reilly's expedition to Louisiana presented an extraordinary opportunity. At almost eighteen years of age and after six years at the school for cadets, he volunteered to participate as the next step in his military career. Moreover, he was not going as a cadet, as several classmates were doing, but as a more distinguished member. O'Reilly was probably responsible for appointing Sebastián on July 3, 1769, as the interim captain of the picket of militia dragoons that accompanied him. The general's acquaintance with the Calvo de la Puerta family extended back several years to his first stay in Cuba. At that time he appears to have personally selected Sebastián's father Pedro to fill the slot of second-in-command of Havana's militia regiment. Sebastián's promotion can be seen as a favor to the family, but his selection surely indicated that he possessed ability in leadership, and his sojourns at country estates with horses had undoubtedly given him a proficiency in riding and caring for the steeds, an inherent talent in most males of elite families. But whether the cavalry picket traveled with their mounts is questionable. The appointment occurred only three days before most of the troops boarded their vessels for the voyage to Louisiana. What is interesting as well was that Juan O'Farrill, the forty-eight-year-old lieutenant colonel of the volunteer cavalry regiment of Cuba was Sebastián's uncle. Possibly he, too, helped in the assignment.[45]

It took the fastest ships two weeks to cross the gulf to Balize, the

44. Din, *Francisco Bouligny*, 29-30. Torres Ramírez, in *O'Reilly en las Indias*, 100-101, identified the troops as 679 men from the first battalion of the Lisbon Infantry Regiment, 576 men of the first battalion of the Havana Infantry Regiment, 213 soldiers from Spain sent to join the Fixed Louisiana Infantry Battalion, a 50-man picket of the Dragoons of America, 162 men from 2 light infantry companies of Catalonia, men from the Disciplined Militia of Havana (80 white grenadiers, 80 men from a company of mulattoes, and 80 men from a company of blacks), a picket of 40 men of the Cavalry Militia; 6 noble cadets from the Havana regiment; 8 distinguished volunteers, 60 artillery men, and 31 men from the Louisiana company.

45. Sebastián Calvo de la Puerta service sheet, March 1805, AGM, ES; Kuethe, *Cuba*, 183.

post at the Mississippi's mouth, where the pilot house sat on a small mudflat barely above the water. Vessels of the expedition had not sailed in formation, and some stragglers belatedly reached the mouth a week later, about July 27. The first ships immediately entered the calmer waters of the river but pressed no farther. O'Reilly did not intend to surprise the colony's inhabitants. He first sent a French-speaking messenger, Lt. Francisco Bouligny, to announce O'Reilly's arrival and his wish to assume control peacefully. Bouligny's hundred-mile trip upriver consumed almost four days, and during that time a swifter French pirogue took the news of the Spanish armada's presence. French Governor Aubry immediately declared his intention to transfer the colony; he further informed the city's inhabitants that he would fight anyone who resisted him, which was an unnecessary warning given that the public, if not the heads of the insurrection, were ready to accept Spanish rule. Three former leaders, Pierre Marquis, Nicolas Chauvin de Lafrénière, and Joseph Milhet, went on the boat that took Bouligny's report of conditions in New Orleans downriver since they desperately sought to learn O'Reilly's intentions. He, however, divulged nothing. Over the next two weeks in the hot, humid, and oppressive August weather, the Spanish ships slowly wended their way up river. On arriving at New Orleans, officers first oversaw arrangements for the colony's formal change in possession after the uprising. Aubry assumed responsibility for turning the colony over to Spain. The city displayed no signs of unrest or opposition. Given the colony's isolation and economic hardships of the preceding months, the inhabitants realized the need to move in a new direction. With no support, the insurrection leaders grudgingly acknowledged their failure.[46]

Arrangements for the transfer of authority decreed that it would take place on August 18 on the Place d'Armes (today's Jackson Square in the French Quarter) in New Orleans. After French troops assumed

46. On O'Reilly's voyage to Louisiana, see David Ker Texada, ed., "An Account of Governor Alejandro O'Reilly's Voyage from Havana to New Orleans in July, 1769," *Louisiana History* 10 (1981): 199-207. Texada has a generally accurate account of O'Reilly's activities in Louisiana in his *Alejandro O'Reilly and the New Orleans Rebels*, which is taken from information in his PhD dissertation on O'Reilly in Louisiana.

their positions that day, the more numerous Spanish soldiers disembarked in orderly formations with flags flying and drums beating and took positions around the square that then became the Plaza de Armas. After the governors read their respective royal orders on the colony's change in ownership, the French flag descended and the Spanish banner shot up the pole amid huzzahs from the cheering troops. Capt. Sebastián Calvo de la Puerta was among the two thousand Spanish and Cuban soldiers present that day, with charge of his dismounted dragoons—his first military command. But all was not over yet.[47]

O'Reilly spent the next three days learning the causes for the insurrection. Royal orders prescribed punishing the responsible leaders. Adhering to the testimony of French and Spanish witnesses, O'Reilly arrested a dozen individuals and pardoned the rest of the population. The trials soon began. First, the Spaniards gathered evidence against the indicted persons that consisted of incriminating documents they signed and depositions eyewitnesses provided. In the Spanish legal system, judges, not juries, assessed guilt and imposed sentences. Two lawyers had come on the expedition from Havana for that purpose. O'Reilly issued the sentences that imposed the death penalty on five leaders (Lafrénière, Jean-Baptiste Noyan, Pierre Caresse, Marquis, and Milhet; a sixth condemned man, Joseph Villeré, had died while being apprehended). For lesser crimes, six more received prison terms that ranged from life to three years, but all were freed after a year in response to the French king's petition for clemency. They had been confined in Havana's El Morro fortress and were barred from returning to Louisiana. O'Reilly confiscated the property of the guilty men but returned the dowries of the widows and wives.[48] Calvo de la Puerta likely

47. On Francisco Bouligny in New Orleans, see Bouligny to O'Reilly, New Orleans, July 26, 1769, and [Bouligny] statement, July 20-August 21, 1769, both in Rosemond E. and Emile Kuntz Collection, Howard-Tilton Memorial Library, Tulane University, New Orleans. See also "Relation of how D[on] Alejandro O'Reilly pacified the city of New Orleans," in *Documentos históricos de la Florida y la Luisiana, siglos XVI al XVIII*, ed. Manuel Serrano y Saenz (Madrid: V. Sánchez, 1912), 295-304.

48. Rodríguez Casado, *Primeros años*, 443-82; O'Reilly to Julián de Arriaga, New Orleans, October 27, 1769, SMV, Pt. 1: 105-6; O'Reilly to Arriaga, New Orleans,

witnessed the executions on October 25, inasmuch as he commanded some of the troops.[49]

Perhaps the outstanding event in Sebastián's sojourn in Louisiana happened on September 14, 1769. On that day O'Reilly, as commander of the expedition, appointed him *capitán vivo*, or permanent captain, of his company of dragoons, which the crown subsequently confirmed. The promotion was a reward for his service on the expedition and management of his troops. It also marked the beginning of Sebastián's rise in rank. His membership in the Havana elite no doubt contributed to his rapid promotion. Cadets without advantages who first became sub-lieutenants (the initial officer rank) sometimes struggled twenty years through the bottom two officer ranks to reach captain. In addition, once many officers attained a captaincy (it meant becoming the head officer of a company of soldiers, most often in the infantry), they never rose higher.[50]

Over the next several months, Calvo de la Puerta waited in New Orleans for the colony to settle down to Spanish rule. Nothing is known about him during this time. Meanwhile, O'Reilly inspected the colony and imposed Spanish law on the province; created a Cabildo or city government for the administration of New Orleans; and installed the Fixed Louisiana Infantry Battalion, with a number of French officers who had valuable experience in administering the colony joining the battalion to assist their Spanish counterparts. Spanish officers, however, retained the top posts for several decades. The Spaniards adopted many customs that the French army had developed through a half century in the administration of the colony. O'Reilly sent detachments of soldiers to various forts throughout the colony. He, however, con-

---

December 10, 1769, SMV, Pt. 1: 127-28; O'Reilly to Arriaga, New Orleans, March 1, 1770, SMV, Pt. 1: 160-61; Grimaldi to Unzaga, San Ildefonso, August 25, 1770, SMV, Pt. 1:181-82. Several more people were exiled from Louisiana; see the attachment from O'Reilly to Arriaga, New Orleans, October 17, 1769, SMV, Pt. 1: 103.

49. William O. Scroggs, *The Story of Louisiana* (Indianapolis and New York: Bobbs-Merrill, 1943), 164.

50. Casa-Calvo service sheet, March 1805, AGM, ES.

centrated most troops in New Orleans where they preserved order and rotated periodically with the soldiers at the outposts. Aware that the king loved economy in administration, he tight-fistedly reduced the yearly cost of running the colony to 115,322 pesos, a paltry sum that did not cover many of its needs. While scrimping was a necessity for the cash-strapped monarchy, hard currency stimulated trade and development. Spanish officials quickly learned that most of the subsidy's Mexican silver pesos that paid for the colony's administration quickly vanished from the hands of Louisiana's merchants, farmers, and others to pay for imports. O'Reilly left the colony in the spring of 1770, but for six years he remained its expert for the crown. It was an unwise decision because O'Reilly wanted to please the king with mercantilism and limited costs; moreover, the general was grossly ignorant about the colony's fiscal and economic conditions. Similar to Cuba, where contraband trade long persisted, in the 1770s Louisiana farmers often traded with the Britons who were across the Mississippi River in West Florida, exchanging agricultural products for African slaves, farming implements, and personal necessities. Movement toward a more liberal commercial policy came within a few years, when Francisco Bouligny advised the crown in 1777 that Louisiana needed trade incentives and African laborers to foment its development. In many respects, what he advocated resembled the changes he had witnessed in Cuba during his six years of service there (1763-69). Louisiana's minuscule economy, however, was only a pale replica of Cuba's.[51]

How long Sebastián remained in Louisiana is not known precisely. In December 1769, O'Reilly began returning many of the troops to Cuba other than the Fixed Louisiana Infantry Battalion. The colony had been easily pacified and, aside from angry families that lost members to execution or imprisonment, the other inhabitants welcomed

51. Din, *Francisco Bouligny*, 39-41; "List of Officials Appointed by O'Reilly," February 4, 1770, SMV, Pt. 1: 157-58; "List of Militia Officers Appointed by O'Reilly," February 12, 1770, ibid., 158-59. On the change in Louisiana trade restrictions, see Din, *Francisco Bouligny*, 55-77; Din, *Louisiana in 1776*; and Margaret Fisher Dalrymple, ed., *The Merchant of Manchac: The Letterbooks of John Fitzpatrick, 1768-1790* (Baton Rouge: Louisiana State University Press, 1978).

the Spanish takeover. Although changes in the economy were initially modest, the new regime represented an improvement over the last dismal year since some currency circulated, people returned to work, and a brighter future seemed imminent.[52]

Calvo de la Puerta returned to Cuba in the spring, possibly on the same ship that carried O'Reilly. The young officer's excursion to Louisiana, one of several journeys he made to that colony, had been profitable. He rose from cadet to interim captain of cavalry and returned to Cuba as a full captain. Despite being only a militia officer, the expedition provided his first vivid taste of regular army service, and he developed a yearning for more. Furthermore, at age eighteen he had accepted the military as his chosen profession in life.[53] His participation in the expedition to Louisiana served as the beginning in a maturing process for young Calvo de la Puerta, and he soon continued it with lengthy sojourns in the Iberian nation.

52. O'Reilly to Arriaga, New Orleans, December 10, 1769, SMV, Pt. 1: 126-27.

53. Casa-Calvo service sheet, March 1805, AMS, ES; Laussat to Due Denis Decres, New Orleans, July 18, 1804, in Robertson, ed., *Louisiana*, 2: 43, has biased information. Bradley's sketch of Casa-Calvo in *Interim Appointment*, 484-98, also has errors and claims that French Creoles resented Casa-Calvo for the 1769 executions in New Orleans when he was an inconsequential eighteen-year-old officer, and alleged his "violent character and hatred for the French," a statement taken from Laussat's self-indulgent memoir. See chapter 7 below.

3
Army Service in Peace and War, 1770-1783

Capt. Sebastián Calvo de la Puerta commenced an invigorating new phase in his army career upon returning to Havana from Louisiana. He stayed there only briefly since he soon journeyed to Spain. His military standing was also rising rapidly, and it reflected the influence that membership in an elite family conveyed. In eleven months, his rank meteorically shot up from cadet to brevet cavalry captain (a brevet rank permitted an individual to wear the new insignia but his salary remained unchanged) to permanent militia cavalry captain, and back to brevet captain, but this time in the regular army. He became acquainted with regions beyond the Havana environs that had comprised his world for the first eighteen years of his life, and they sparked his imagination about wider Atlantic horizons. In particular, he learned about New Orleans, a city he revisited several times in succeeding years. He spent a lengthy sojourn in Spain, serving in the peninsular army and calling on Cuban relatives and friends who had also relocated to the mother country. Most significant about his new adventures, he participated in a war on both land and sea in which an energized Spain aided in the defeat of a weaker Great Britain and recovered territories lost in earlier wars. His activities bore witness to an exhilarating age in which he played a role in historic events that contributed to Spain's military successes.

Nevertheless, much of what young Calvo de la Puerta experienced on a personal level during these years remains obscure and unknown. With no extant private letters written by him to family members and friends, or by them to him, only official documents place him at locations and offer meager insights into his activities. In June 1770, he put behind him a full captaincy in the militia to accept an attachment as a brevet captain of dragoons in the Regiment of the King, a Spanish cavalry unit serving temporarily in Havana. Regular army service was more prestigious and financially rewarding than part-time duty in the militia, where planters often bought their high ranking posts and helped pay for the unit's expenses. Calvo de la Puerta's duties in the dragoons are uncertain, but he stayed in the cavalry for several years. His attachment to this branch of the army suggests a devotion to horsemanship. Later in his military career when he was again assigned to Louisiana, he arrived with a brace of thoroughbreds from Havana to pull his ornate Spanish carriage through the unpaved streets of New Orleans, and the beauty of the animals astonished the city's inhabitants. The horses and carriage attested to his status and wealth in society.[1] On many occasions as he grew older, Calvo de la Puerta exhibited the perquisites of privilege that seemed quite natural for a person of his social class.

On June 18, 1770, young Sebastián Calvo de la Puerta entered the regular Spanish army. His father, Pedro Calvo de la Puerta, appears to have purchased the rank of brevet army captain for him. Although no evidence exists that he did this, the selling of army posts was a common practice in the Spanish army.[2] Leaps in rank more often reflected privilege than outstanding service. Sebastián's recent deployment to Louisiana did not include exceptional commissions and tasks that might have entitled him to extraordinary rewards.[3]

Perhaps some of the events that involved him can be explained through his younger cousin Gonzalo O'Farrill's career. No knowledge

1. Casa-Calvo service sheet, March 1805, AGM, ES; Casa-Calvo petition to the King, Madrid, July 25, 1787, AGS, GM, leg. 6880.

2. Din, *Francisco Bouligny*, 83, 86, 116. In Casa-Calvo's service sheets and in the documentation for entering the Order of Santiago, he was sometimes described as belonging to the King's Dragoons and at other times as merely attached to it.

3. Casa-Calvo service sheet, March 1805, AGM, ES.

exists that Cadet O'Farrill journeyed to Louisiana on the O'Reilly expedition, although it was possible he did. In January 1769, he turned fifteen years old, and later that year a group of noble cadet volunteers from Havana accompanied O'Reilly to Louisiana. Possibly they served as messengers and aides to higher ranking officers in New Orleans, but more certain are events that occurred in Havana in 1771. Gonzalo's father Juan José O'Farrill, a wealthy planter and businessman, bought a captaincy for his son in a peninsular regiment. O'Farrill's purchase raises the likelihood that Sebastián's father did the same for his son. In the early 1770s, Juan Gregorio Muniaín, minister of war in Spain, openly sold officer ranks in the army. It was a venerable practice many European nations, including Great Britain, employed to raise money for the army. Selling offices was widespread in nearly every corner of the Spanish and colonial governments, even under the reformer King Carlos III, and Muniaín scandalously practiced venality in the army. Probably early in the 1770s, Sebastián accompanied his peninsular outfit when it rotated back to Spain. Gonzalo also left Cuba in the early 1770s, but his father sent him to France to study in military schools, and he never returned to Cuba. His studies lasted a few years and upon their completion, he traveled south to become an officer in the Spanish army. As for Sebastián, he transferred after several years in the Regiment of the King to a unit that was being assigned to Havana during the American War for Independence.[4]

His service coincided with Carlos III's introduction of change that came from above in the kingdom and empire. In a nation where absolutism reigned supreme, reform trickled down slowly. A triumvirate of entrenched authority composed of the crown, church, and aristocracy dominated the kingdom and held sway over commoners and the unprivileged. In the eighteenth century, a few bold Spanish writers such

4. Recio Morales, "When Merit is Not Enough," 122-23; Casa-Calvo service sheet, March 1805, AGM, ES; Kuethe, *Cuba*, 77; Calcagno, *Diccionario biográfico cubano*, 459. See Miguel Bernal Morán, acting for Sebastián Calvo de la Puerta, petition to the king, (Madrid), June 17, 1788, AHN, OM, leg. 8114. On venality in Spain, see Francisco Andujar Castillo, *El sonido del dinero: Monarquía, ejército y venalidad en la España del siglo XVIII* (Madrid: Marcial Pons, 2004).

as Father Benito Jerónimo Feijóo (1676-1764), of the First Spanish Enlightenment (1737-1760), wrote books critical of the multiple ills in Spanish society and government. Later more writers, influenced by French encyclopedists and *philosophes* (Voltaire, Rousseau, Diderot, and Montesquieu, among others who were in the forefront because France also suffered from absolutism), insisted on greater rights for society's underprivileged middle and lower classes. They questioned the absurdity of blind obedience to authority that exploited their complaisance and the Spanish failure to keep pace economically, educationally, culturally, and even militarily with the leading European nations. By the mid-eighteenth century, the Enlightenment, also known as the Age of Reason, began among small Spanish groups of individuals who skewered tradition-based practices for hindering progress, and advocates for a new society preached the abandonment of antiquated customs. The Baron de Montesquieu's influential *Spirit of Laws* of 1748 alerted the reading public to the irrationality of life in an archaic society.[5] French ideas and books trickled across the Pyrenees into Spain, where readers consisted mainly of minority groups in the well-to-do bourgeois middle classes, some of the clergy, and, oddly, the rich nobility. They comprised the bulk of readers because literacy rates were abysmally low, especially in the lower classes with their few primary schools or opportunities to rise in the entrenched class system that prevailed in Spanish society.[6]

Guided by their growing secularism, Spanish advocates for reform questioned the centuries-old dominance of the Catholic Church in the nation. In particular, they singled-out the powerful and wealthy Jesuit Order and its preeminence in peninsular and colonial society. The Jesuits led in educating the children of the affluent nobility and the influential upper middle classes; many of the latter became mer-

5. Vicente Palacio Atard, *Los españoles de la ilustración* (Madrid: Ediciones Guadarrama, 1964); Bergamini, *Spanish Bourbons*, 75; Gonzáles-Ripoll, *Cuba*, 127-38. On the Enlightenment, see John G. Gagliardo, *Enlightened Despotism* (New York: T. Y. Crowell, 1967), and other works listed below.

6. Palacio Atard, *Los españoles de la ilustración*, 149-61; Richard Herr, *The Eighteenth Century Revolution in Spain* (Princeton, N.J.: Princeton University Press, 1958), 350.

chants, professionals, churchmen, or devoted followers of the order. In addition, the Jesuits did not limit themselves to religion or education and plunged into politics to secure royal favors that augmented their authority and earnings. People of all classes envied the Jesuits for their extensive landholdings, abundant work force, and copious revenue. Jesuit involvement in the Madrid riots of 1764 and 1766 eventually provoked their downfall. Members of the order protested the guile of the Marqués de Esquilache, minister of finance, who followed conservative beliefs and raised the prices of two monopoly foodstuffs, bread and olive oil, that were basic necessities to the poor. His action caused the humble people, who already lived miserably, to protest violently in the streets of Madrid, and their rioting forced the reluctant king to exile Esquilache to his native Italy in 1766. A year later, a government inquiry exposed the Jesuit instigation of the riots. The revelation induced their opponents, as well as the secular (parish) and regular (monastic) clergy, universities, and royalist politicians, all of whom despised Jesuit success, to demand the order's expulsion. In 1767 the king's chief minister (the first secretary of state), the Conde de Aranda, banished the Jesuits from Spain and the colonies. In doing so, he followed the examples of Portugal, France, and the Kingdom of the Two Sicilies.[7] Under Carlos III, Spain moved in a slightly more revisionist and worldly direction, which open-minded members of society's higher echelons, including segments of the literate aristocracy, endorsed. Ironically, many of the uneducated poor viewed the Jesuit ouster as an unwarranted assault on the church and protested. Numerous former students who had been educated by the Jesuit fathers also championed the order.[8]

War, however, repeatedly interrupted measures of reform and development, which is to say efforts at reducing the power of church and aristocracy and promoting trade through the reduction of taxes that hurt not the rich but business and poor consumers. During these times, Spain became involved in conflicts with several nations. They raised the prospect of new fighting in which the army, including Calvo

7. Smith, *Spain,* 248-49.

8. Chapman, *History of Spain*, 286-88.

de la Puerta, would participate. Although the 1770s were not a peaceful interlude between major wars, they appear not to have affected him.

For example, conflict almost erupted over the Falkland Islands (Islas Malvinas to the Spaniards) off the coast of Argentina in 1770-71 because of differing Spanish and English claims to the islands. While a new clash with Great Britain appeared likely, Spain continued arming since French assistance in a future war was uncertain. Protection of Spain and its most valuable colonies required a substantial military force. The crown built up the army's manpower, attracted foreign soldiers with higher pay, and constructed naval warships, especially the larger two gun-decked frigates and the three gun-decked ships-of-the-line, the battleships of the era. Havana's shipyards hummed with activity as they produced many of Spain's fighting vessels. Cuba's abundant forests provided the needed hardwoods.[9]

Another incident involved Spain with nations on the North African coast where it maintained bases to prevent a possible Arab invasion of the Iberian Peninsula, a fear that had persisted since the Reconquest ended in 1492. In 1767 Spain established a treaty of friendship with Morocco. But seven years later, Sultan Sidi-Mohamed-ben-Abdallah had tired of the Spanish presence on Moroccan soil and, persuaded by the dey of Algiers, besieged Melilla. The Spaniards in the city, however, successfully resisted the assault. Rather than attack Morocco where Spanish fortifications were secure, Carlos III's advisers chose to punish the trouble-mongering dey of Algiers, who harbored pirates that assaulted ships of all nations in the Mediterranean and even raided the Spanish coast. The king searched for a general to lead the assault and found Alejandro O'Reilly, who frugally proposed employing the smallest number of soldiers, eighteen thousand to twenty thousand. Informants for the dey leaked news of the coming attack, and spies at Cartagena, on Spain's Levantine (eastern) coast where the expedition slowly formed, kept him alert to the forces he could expect. Armed with this vital intelligence, the Arab leader prepared. O'Reilly's raid on Algiers in the summer of 1775 failed, and he lost several thousand

9. Ibid., 388-90.

soldiers due more to his bungling than to the dey's ability. Widespread Spanish outrage over the disaster and the general's incompetency sent his prestige in the army plummeting.[10] Many officers, who later served in Louisiana and the Caribbean, participated in the attack on Algiers, but not Sebastián, whose cavalry regiment was not called up.

Trouble also arose with Portugal over the undefined borderlands between Spanish possessions and Portuguese Brazil. In 1679, Portuguese soldiers established a settlement at Colonia do Sacramento (today's Uruguay) on the north shore of the Río de la Plata. Its town became a thriving port that smuggled English goods into Buenos Aires across the estuary and served as a base for cattle rustling and Indian slave-hunting in adjacent Spanish Paraguay, home of numerous Guaraní natives and Jesuit missions. In 1750 Spain proposed an exchange of lands in Paraguay for Colonia do Sacramento; however, Paraguayan colonials and Jesuit missionaries affected by the swap prevented its implementation. When the aggressive Marquês de Pombal became minister in Portugal, he encroached on Spanish lands, falsely promised Carlos III that he would refrain from military action, and blatantly denied reports of Portuguese hostility. Pombal expected British assistance should Spain declare war. But in 1775, with Great Britain mired in disagreements with disgruntled North American colonials, aid for Portugal became impossible. When a Portuguese fleet attacked Spanish ships in early 1776 and seized territory, the Spaniards dispatched an armed expedition that captured Sacramento, where they caught twenty-seven British merchantmen brimming with contraband goods. The Portuguese king, José I, died in 1777, and his widow María Victoria, sister of the Spanish king, became regent. She dismissed Pombal, accepted Portugal's loss of Colonia do Sacramento, and ended the century-old dispute.[11]

While these military crises did not involve the Calvo de la Puerta family, Sebastián was active in another way. Before his departure for Spain, his father Pedro sought membership in a religious-military crusading order for himself and his two older sons, Francisco and

10. Smith, *Spain*, 249-50; Chapman, *History of Spain*, 390.

11. Chapman, *History of Spain*, 386, 391-92; Smith, *Spain*, 250.

Sebastián, who all had military affiliations. Entry in a crusading order conferred status on its upper class members. Sebastián's younger brother Nicolás was not included because he was a civilian. Prospective members needed to present a genealogy of their ancestry, which a hired investigator usually compiled. Although the genealogical study was not described as a *limpieza de sangre*, it served the same function as it ensured that no one of an improper (that is non-Christian and non-white) background figured among the petitioner's ancestors through several generations that reached back to the fifteenth century. When the Calvo de la Puerta family inquiry was completed is not known, but it appears that Sebastián took it to Spain.[12]

Perhaps about late 1770 his peninsular regiment rotated home, and Sebastián made his first transatlantic crossing. He sailed in a convoy in which warships guarded troop transports and civilian merchant vessels to ensure their safe arrival. Cádiz in southern Spain was the usual port for Spanish warships, troop transports, and trade vessels that departed for colonial destinations throughout the world. Sebastián landed at the Andalusian port, and aside from his army duties, he had to finish the task his father had begun. He probably did not stay long in Andalusia and moved north by land with the troops. The journey of several weeks perhaps took him northward through or near Seville, Córdoba, and up to Toledo and Madrid, cities on a plateau and higher in elevation. From there, the trek continued and crossed the pass at Somosierra in the Central Mountain system that divides the southern plateau of New Castile from the northern and slightly more elevated plateau of Old Castile. Sebastián finally arrived at his destination of Burgos, a town possessing a medieval appearance with sturdy and ancient stone walls that dated back to about 1000 A.D. Over the next years, Sebastián performed garrison duty and engaged in endless training programs, the task of peacetime soldiers. Earlier, while passing through Madrid or after his arrival in Burgos, he submitted the Calvo de la Puerta ancestral record to the crown. Like many other social climbing and well-to-do

12. By the eighteenth century if not sooner, wealthy individuals with an American Indian ancestor several generations back could purchase membership in an order.

families with titles, members of the Calvo de la Puerta clan sought to "aristocratize" themselves.[13]

Several months passed before the government replied. About September 1771, it contacted Sebastián about appointing him, his older brother Francisco, and their father to a religious-military order. Four such orders existed in Spain: Santiago, Calatrava, Alcántara, and Montesa. They had originated almost simultaneously in the mid-twelfth century, when momentum in the Reconquest swelled and Christian forces reached into Andalusia, the only extensive region remaining in Moorish hands. The orders became a vital component in Christian armies because kings at that time relied on nobles to provide military manpower, especially knights who composed the principal fighting force in medieval armies. Knights, with their protective armor, steel weapons, and large sturdy horses, were expensive but necessary since they facilitated the Christian advance into Muslim lands. The orders changed in the centuries after the Reconquest as the various Christian kingdoms of the peninsula gradually unified until only Castile and Aragon remained. Portugal completed its own ouster of the Moors in the thirteenth century and emerged as a separate nation at that time. The Catholic King Fernando, who terminated the Reconquest in Castile in the late fifteenth century, became the head of all the Castilian religious-military orders and consolidated their military power in the monarchy.[14]

Modern nation-states began their rise in Europe at about the same time, when kings sought dominance over the church, aristocracy, and military. Strong monarchs often absorbed weaker kingdoms through marriage or conquest such as Castile's acquisition of Aragon or England's of Scotland, Wales, and Ireland. Kings gradually came to monopolize the military establishments in their domains, including the crusading orders, by constructing national armies and navies that

13. Much of the information here is supposition based on Calvo de la Puerta's transfer to Spain and the genealogical papers in the Madrid archives. González-Ripoll, *Cuba*, 137-38.

14. Chapman, *History of Spain*, 94, 219-20.

obeyed only the monarch. It was a gradual process that still continued in the eighteenth century. In contrast to early Castilian nobles who joined the orders to acquire loot and power directly from the Moors, later entrants differed in their reasons. By the eighteenth century, the nobility's military power had dissipated except for what their wealth, titles, and membership in exclusive organizations wielded. Consequently, distinguished or worthy nobles and military men sought the luster of membership in the now ersatz crusading orders. Persons who entered these associations became linked more intimately with the crown, but first they needed the king's consent to join. The monarchy held the upper hand and exacted fees for membership. In return honorees received the right to wear the costume of the order, which rarely happened inasmuch as warfare had evolved with the development of modern armies that employed gunpowder, firearms, and cannons as the antiquated knights had been replaced. Nonetheless, inclusion in the orders granted members the right of burial in the habit, which was a treasured honor.[15]

King Carlos III, president of the four religious-military orders, on September 26, 1771, commanded Sebastián, a prospective recipient for the habit of Santiago, to provide the customary genealogical information within thirty days to prove that he possessed the qualities to hold the office of knight. On October 2, the king signed a cédula that granted Sebastián the habit of knight in the order of Santiago, but he needed to sign an important document within two months in the General Accounting Office of the Royal Treasury, where the books that registered the honors (*mercedes*) were kept. The documents left unstated that the government charged for entry in the order. If he failed to pay in the allotted time, the king's cédula lost its value.[16]

By October, the Calvo de la Puerta genealogy that examined Sebastian's paternal and maternal forebears over five generations had been approved. Sebastián requested cédulas for himself and his brother and

15. Ibid., 94-95, 219-20; Smith, *Spain*, 82, 121.

16. Royal cédula to Calvo de la Puerta, San Lorenzo, October 2, 1771, AHN, OM, leg. 8114.

pledged to pay the understood costs—the figures were not given. In Burgos on October 5, 1771, Sebastián signed documents before a notary and witnesses to ensure the legality of the procedure. He also paid an undisclosed sum to Manuel de Larrarte who conducted the genealogical investigation in Spain.[17]

With those tasks completed, another few months passed before the crown acted. On February 1, 1772, the Council of State dispatched the title of knight (*caballero*) in the Order of Santiago to Sebastián Calvo de la Puerta. Later, on May 21, he received a new dispatch that allowed him to wear the habit of the order, but it imposed new requirements. It specified one year of military service in a future war, the first six months in a cavalry unit and the second six months aboard a warship of the royal navy. On completing this obligation, he gained full admittance in the order.[18] For an unknown reason, his brother Francisco was not included. Several years passed before a war broke out in which Sebastián could perform the final requirement.

Despite setbacks, the 1770s progressed reasonably well militarily for Spain as Carlos III strengthened the army and navy, realizing that a new conflict among the imperial powers was inevitable. The king also wanted to recover territorial losses experienced in previous clashes. These wars had occupied the years 1702-13, 1718-20, 1727-29, 1739-48, and 1761-63, when Spain fought alone or with French collaboration. Spain desperately needed a strong military to defend its possessions that were scattered across the world. From the late seventeenth century, Great Britain aspired to become the undisputed master of the seas and owner of the most productive and profitable colonies. Spain's losses in the Seven Years' War shocked its rulers who frantically sought martial improvements to thwart future routs by foreign rivals or dissident colonials. Those aspirations lay at the heart of military expansion

17. Calvo de la Puerta, Burgos, October 5, 1771, AHN, OM, Exped. 8114. Notarizing documents was a well-established Spanish practice. González-Ripoll, *Cuba*, 137.

18. Council of State, February 1, 1772; Juan Francisco de la Torre Lostase to Joaquín de Rozas y Negrete, Madrid, May 21, 1772, both in AHN, OM, leg. 8114. Sebastián had to notify the crown after he completed each phase of his military service, and he would be fined if he failed to do so.

between 1763 and 1779, when Spain entered a new war. While the reforms did not achieve the progress the king had hoped for, the accomplishments represented a shining moment in the century when it appeared that a new era had dawned. Optimism encouraged Sebastián Calvo de la Puerta and the Cuban planters in their endeavors, although the Bourbon reforms (the importation of more slaves, lower taxes, and fewer restrictions in trade) benefited only a limited number of people in the middle and upper classes in Spain, Cuba, and other Spanish colonies.[19]

Furthermore, Spain had reasons for detesting its long-time British rivals. They had seized Spanish territory—Gibraltar, Minorca, and Havana—the last of which they exchanged for Florida, stopped Spanish merchantmen at will on the high seas to search or seize them, smuggled goods into Spanish dominions, obstructed Spanish fishing off the coast of Newfoundland, established unauthorized lumbering camps for dyewoods in Honduras, and occupied islands off its coast. Although Carlos III preferred to avoid war, arrogant British behavior rendered that unlikely. Furthermore, the British government refused to punish the criminal activity of its subjects, especially at sea. Only the Falkland Islands, where Spain had not abandoned its claims, returned to Iberian ownership briefly after Great Britain removed its settlement in 1774. Spanish relations with France also improved when King Louis XV died in 1774, and the pro-Spanish minister Comte de Vergennes came to office. He favored continuation of the Bourbon Family Compact of united cooperation. During the last several years, differences between Great Britain and its inhabitants in their North American Atlantic colonies had escalated as they strenuously objected to continued taxation for defense although their former French rivals in Canada had been defeated.[20]

British efforts to raise money and quarter troops in those colonies generated protests and demonstrations such as the Stamp Act riots, the

19. Chapman, *History of Spain*, 383-85.

20. Ibid., 391. The British seized the Falkland Islands again in 1833, leaving Spain, and later Argentina, with only claims to them.

Boston Tea Party, and the Boston Massacre. Finally, military clashes between British soldiers and colonial militiamen occurred in 1775 at Lexington and Concord, Massachusetts. When the British bolstered their army in North America, the suspicious French and Spanish governments concluded that real British intentions were to seize their possessions. Spanish confidential agents in the North American colonies reported home recent events. By 1776, the dissident colonials had declared their independence, established a government, and raised a continental army to combat the British. The French entered the fray following the rebel victory against British general John Burgoyne at Saratoga since they also wished to humiliate the English for losses in earlier wars. By February 1778, France and the insurgent Continental Congress concluded a treaty of alliance and commerce. The skeptical Spaniards meanwhile dispatched additional agents to gather more facts on the participants and the rebellion.[21] The Conde de Aranda warned the crown that the aggressive expansion of the English colonials would endanger Spain's North American possessions, and if Great Britain defeated the rebels, they would likely band together to attack neighboring Spanish lands. Despite Aranda's misgivings, from June 1776 Spain began aiding American rebels secretly with arms, munitions, clothing, and money shipped from Havana to New Orleans. In 1777 the Conde de Floridablanca came to power as first minister of state in Spain, and he was more amenable to recovering Florida and ousting the English from Honduras. But he and other government officials retained their wariness of the Anglo-American colonials, and it prevented an alliance. Spain first tried to achieve its objectives peacefully by requesting the

21. On Spanish espionage, see Katherine Trimmer Abbey, "Efforts of Spain to Maintain Sources of Information in the British Colonies before 1779," *Mississippi Valley Historical Review* 15 (1928): 56-68; Katherine S. Lawson, "Luciano de Herrera, Spanish Spy in British St. Augustine," *Florida Historical Quarterly* 23 (1945): 170-76; Robert L. Gold, "Governor Bernardo de Galvez and Spanish Espionage in Pensacola, 1777," in *The Spanish in the Mississippi Valley 1762-1804*, ed. John Francis McDermott (Urbana: University of Illinois Press, 1974), 84-99; and especially Light Townsend Cummins, *Spanish Agents in the American Revolutionary War* (Baton Rouge: Louisiana State University Press, 1992), 82-110.

British to return Gibraltar and Minorca in exchange for Spanish mediation in ending the war. Great Britain haughtily refused, and Spain then chose war because British seizures of Spanish vessels and threats to assail their colonies persisted in the spring of 1779. France and Spain, meanwhile, planned an invasion of England that stalled, but the threat kept British warships in home waters and reduced troop shipments to North America. When Spain declared war, Great Britain grudgingly offered concessions in return for Spanish neutrality. Their halfhearted gestures scarcely placated the Spaniards who choose loyalty to France instead.[22]

How soon Sebastián Calvo de la Puerta became involved in the war is unknown. At almost twenty-five years old, he was promoted to permanent captain in the Spanish army on July 23, 1776, a rank he retained throughout the coming war. Two years later, he transferred from the Regiment of the King to the Príncipe (Prince) Infantry Regiment that soon embarked for Havana. His transfer was easily completed because the regiment was under-strength. No doubt he wanted to return home and possibly participate in the coming fray. By October 1778, if not sooner, Calvo de la Puerta was back in Havana. His return was timely because Spain declared war on Great Britain in June 1779.[23]

As soon as the conflict began, Spain immediately besieged Gibraltar, its most important objective in the war. The siege lasted until January 1780, when a British fleet defeated the naval squadron of Juan de Lángara that attempted to blockade the tiny enclave. With the siege thwarted, Spain shifted objectives and prepared an 11,000 troop expedition under Adm. José Solano to reinforce its circum-Caribbean posts, eradicate the British from Central America, and recover Florida. It also planned to capture as much British soil (the Bahamas and Jamai-

22. Chapman, *History of Spain*, 393-97; Chávez, *Spain*, 126-36.

23. Casa-Calvo petition to the king, Madrid, July 15, 1787, AGS, GM, leg. 6880; king's proclamation allowing Calvo de la Puerta to switch military assignments, Aranjuez, June 29, 1778, with copies made in Havana on September 13, 1778, and October 17, 1780; both in ibid. Kuethe, in *Cuba*, 89 and 96, states that the "Regiment of the Prince" arrived in 1777, but other documents place Calvo de la Puerta's arrival in 1778. Whether he reached Cuba with the regiment or alone later is unknown.

ca) as it could to compensate for prior territorial losses. The gigantic fleet of 12 ships-of-the-line and 146 merchant vessels and transports left Spain in April 1780.[24]

Two areas, Cuba and Louisiana, were intimately involved with Spanish objectives and had been slowly shoring up their military strength. Minister of the Indies José de Gálvez appointed his own nephew, Bernardo de Gálvez, as the new governor of Louisiana, where he took command on January 1, 1777. A thirty-year-old army colonel, he had only a battalion of soldiers to protect the sprawling colony against the British in neighboring West Florida. Great Britain had divided an extended Florida into two provinces: East Florida, the peninsula, and West Florida, the panhandle that ran along the Gulf Coast to the Mississippi River. From 1776 to 1778, the British installed troops, many of them German Waldeck mercenaries, throughout West Florida, including on the Mississippi at Manchac, Baton Rouge, and Natchez. Their presence alerted Bernardo de Gálvez to the British intention to assault New Orleans when war came. In 1779, a multitude of discontented Waldeck deserters fled to Spanish territory in small batches, and they confirmed Gálvez's suspicions. Learning of Spain's declaration of war in August before the British did, Gálvez immediately assembled soldiers, militiamen, volunteers, and Indians and attacked and captured the British posts on the Mississippi and most of their 457 soldiers. The victory, however, was only the first of three steps needed to conquer West Florida. In addition, rebel colonials had already seized British forts in Illinois along the Mississippi.[25]

The second step entailed seizing Fort Charlotte at Mobile. The fort was larger than those on the Mississippi and nearer the principal British bastion at Pensacola, but New Orleans's safety hinged on

24. Casa-Calvo service sheet, March 1805, AGM, ES; Beerman, *España,* 67-68; Chávez, *Spain*, 144.

25. Gilbert C. Din, "Lieutenant Raimundo DuBreüil, Commandant of San Gabriel de Manchac, and Bernardo de Galvez's 1779 Campaign on the Mississippi River," *Military History of the West* 29 (Spring 1999): 1-30; Beerman, *España*, 43-62. See also Bettie Jones Conover, "British West Florida's Mississippi Frontier Posts, 1763-1779," *Alabama Review* 29 (1976): 177-207.

eradicating all enemy posts on the Gulf Coast. Gálvez started preparations immediately after returning from Baton Rouge. He sent his second-in-command, Col. Esteban Miró, to solicit two thousand soldiers from Havana. Gálvez did not wait for them and sailed to Mobile by the end of January. His diminutive naval force consisted of one frigate, several galleys, and a handful of armed launches and transports. His 664 Louisiana troops came from the province's fixed infantry battalion, militiamen, carabineers, artillery corps, free black and mulatto militiamen, slaves, and several American volunteers. While the captain general sent him reinforcements after learning of the outbreak of war, they arrived too late for service on the Mississippi, but some of them accompanied him to Mobile Bay. They were 43 soldiers of the Príncipe regiment (Sebastián's unit), 49 from the second battalion of the España regiment, and 50 from the fixed Havana regiment; counting sailors, Gálvez's force exceeded 806 men. Blustery weather, however, prevented him from entering Mobile Bay until early March. Gálvez then gradually moved up to Fort Charlotte on the bay's west side and laid siege with his artillery. After several days of bombardment, the cannons breached the fort's walls, and the British surrendered. Soon troops arrived from Cuba to augment Gálvez's force.[26] Captain Calvo de la Puerta was among them.

Prior to the war's eruption, Sebastián spent many months in Cuba with other members of his Príncipe regiment. It had arrived in Cuba significantly undermanned in late 1778, possessing only 623 troops, the number of men normally found in a single battalion, and soon more soldiers succumbed to tropical afflictions. But once the war began, Calvo de la Puerta used his wealth to help bolster Havana's defenses when an English fleet briefly blockaded the port. He lent gratuitously thirteen of his black slaves to work on improving a port facility, the Fort of the Prince. Furthermore, he contributed 2,000 pesos for the service of paid volunteers. He soon figured among the reinforcements the captain general prepared to send to Mobile, and they sailed on March 7, 1780. Adm. Juan Bautista Bonet, the naval chief in Cuba

26. Chávez, *Spain*, 175-76.

from 1774 to 1781, headed the force of 17 warships, 26 transports, 3,756 sailors, and 2,148 soldiers. Once underway, he sent Gálvez, who was at Mobile, a message that they should coordinate their forces for the conquest of Pensacola. Gabriel de Aristizábal took the letter on his frigate, the *Nuestra Señora de la O*, on which Calvo de la Puerta commanded a picket of soldiers with orders to guard the entrance to Mobile Bay. Bonet's message informed Gálvez that he intended to attack Pensacola and wanted him to travel there overland to surprise the enemy from the rear. Unfazed, Gálvez ignored Bonet since he preferred a naval attack, not an arduous overland trek through the untamed wilderness that would sicken and even kill many of his soldiers.[27]

Once on shore at the entrance to Mobile Bay, Calvo de la Puerta and his unit stood watch to forestall a British naval or land assault to recover Fort Charlotte. Pensacola, however, lacked vessels to transport British troops to Mobile. Instead, a column of over a thousand soldiers led by Gen. John Campbell, Pensacola's military commander, trudged through the backwoods to assist Fort Charlotte, but he turned back on learning that it had fallen. Nevertheless, parties of Campbell's soldiers and Indians attempted to seize *La Aldea* (The Village), a Spanish outpost on Mobile Bay's east bank. The most serious attack occurred on the morning of January 7, 1781, when a two-hundred-man British column tried to overpower the Spanish defenders. A dense fog enveloped the post that morning, making it difficult for Spanish sentinels to recognize the strangers in the mist. Although the Spaniards defeated the attackers, who suffered twenty dead and approximately sixty-five wounded, the clash cost fourteen Spanish lives, twenty-three wounded, and one soldier taken prisoner. Calvo de la Puerta remained at Mobile Bay until Spanish warships secured those waters at the end of summer 1780.[28]

27. Casa-Calvo petition to the king, Madrid, July 25, 1787, AGS, GM, leg. 6880; Beerman, *España*, 97-99. A sketch of Aristizábal's life is summarized in Pezuela, *Diccionario*, 1: 42-43.

28. Calvo de la Puerta service sheet, March 1805, AGS, ES; "Relation of the dead, wounded, and prisoners in the attack of the detachment of The Village on January 7, 1781," AGS, GM, leg. 6912; Beerman, *España*, 115-22; William Beer, ed., "The

Meanwhile, Bonet, without waiting for Gálvez's reply to the message Aristizábal delivered in March, moved his warships, transports, and soldiers to attack Pensacola. He forged an entrance into the bay on March 27. The next morning, Pensacola inhabitants awakened to find a squadron of enemy ships anchored before the town, and it astonished them so much that they hastily destroyed the port cannons and fled to nearby Fort George. For two days, General Campbell fidgeted as he expected a Spanish assault. Possibly Bonet waited for Gálvez's troops to arrive. But on the morning of March 30, the Spanish fleet left the bay without launching an attack; nevertheless, Bonet remained nearby until mid-May, perhaps still expecting Gálvez to appear, before he returned to Havana. Back in the city, fellow officers and royal officials flailed him with accusations of cowardice for not attacking Pensacola.[29]

Gálvez lamented Bonet's squandered opportunity to seize Pensacola, but he remained eager to attack it with the Louisiana vessels under his command. Experienced naval officers, however, cautioned him that his flotilla of seven tiny vessels was insufficient to force his way into the bay because of the British fort near its entrance. Conditions at Pensacola soon worsened for the Spaniards, when eleven British ships reinforced it and a storm came up and destroyed several Spanish vessels outside the bay.[30]

Gálvez's wish for additional troops to recover Pensacola finally received an answer in the expedition of Adm. José Solano that crossed the Atlantic in the late spring of 1780. Solano found the French fleet of Adm. Comte de Guichen in the Caribbean and avoided contact with the English squadron under Adm. George Rodney. At Puerto Rico Solano deposited the soldiers and artillery assigned there and dispatched

---

Surrender of Fort Charlotte, Mobile, 1780," *American Historical Review* 1 (1896): 696-99; Caughey, *Galvez*, 178-86; Starr, *Tories*, 170-74; Beerman, *España*, 94-96; William S. Coker and Hazel P. Coker, *The Siege of Mobile, 1780, in Maps, with Data on Troop Strength, Military Units, Ships, Casualties, and Prisoners of War, Including a Brief History of Fort Charlotte (Conde)* (Pensacola: by the authors, 1982).

29. Beerman, *España*, 97-100.

30. Ibid., 100-3.

other troops to reinforce Caracas and Cartagena de Indias on the north coast of South America. The two allied fleets separated when Guichen left for Cap-Français in Saint-Domingue while Solano proceeded to Havana. He arrived on August 4, two days after Gálvez reached the city to request troops for the conquest of Pensacola. Solano's safe arrival was crucial to Spanish victories throughout the Caribbean and Gulf Coast. From Havana the captain general dispatched soldiers on thirteen transports to Central America with an escort of three ships-of-the-line and two frigates; Spanish forces were trying to remove the British who had infiltrated Honduras using the pretext of obtaining dyewoods. Several thousand soldiers brought by Solano still remained for use against Pensacola. Gálvez learned from a captured enemy report that Pensacola's defenders numbered 1,302 soldiers, 300 sailors, 300 armed blacks, 600 civilian volunteers, and uncounted Indian auxiliaries. The conquest of all West Florida comprised an essential part of the crown's objectives in the conflict, and a Havana council of war quickly agreed to provide the manpower.[31]

Gálvez had left Mobile in May and returned to New Orleans, where he prepared its troops and vessels to strike Pensacola. He sailed to Havana on July 25 to secure the bulk of the soldiers he needed. The king, who showered the Gálvez clan with favors and was impressed by Bernardo's victories, appointed him commander of the Army of Operations in the Gulf and Caribbean. But Gálvez was determined to conquer West Florida himself and chose instead to take charge of the expedition sailing to Pensacola. For this purpose, Solano provided him with 3,700 soldiers and six months of rations. By early October, Gálvez had assembled troops, warships, and transports in Havana for the attack.[32] Calvo de la Puerta, who had returned from Mobile Bay at the end of summer, figured among them.

Gálvez, however, soon erred catastrophically. Against the advice of the more experienced Solano, who suspected inclement weather and

31. In ibid., 97, Beerman declared that Gálvez estimated his white soldiers to number 2,500.

32. Beerman, *España*, 103-6.

wanted to delay sailing, the impatient Gálvez ordered an immediate departure on October 16, 1780. He went on the *Nuestra Señora de la O*, the flagship of Gabriel de Aristizábal, in a squadron of twelve warships, fifty-one transports, and nearly four thousand soldiers. Aristizábal's ship carried Calvo de la Puerta and his picket of ninety Príncipe soldiers. They served as a guard to protect the ship against enemy boarders. But within a half day after leaving Havana, a storm that absorbed energy from the warm gulf waters developed into a formidable hurricane whose winds howled nonstop for several days. It was possibly a remnant of the Great Hurricane of October 1780 that ravaged the eastern Caribbean. The vigorous waves and winds of the gulf tempest shattered Gálvez's squadron and scattered the vessels like fallen leaves. It blew ships to New Orleans, Mobile, the Yucatan Peninsula, and elsewhere throughout the gulf. One battered transport sought refuge in San Bernardo Bay in Texas, where ferocious Indians massacred the Spaniards on board.[33]

The *Nuestra Señora de la O* became separated from the fleet on the first day as the storm heaved it in the direction of Campeche. With two warships and two transports Aristizábal found after the winds subsided, he cruised to a rendezvous point previously designated off Florida's west coast, but not finding other ships there, he continued to the second rendezvous south of Louisiana. He encountered several more vessels on the way, and a bellicose Gálvez summoned the ship captains to discuss an attack on Pensacola with only these forces. The captains all scowled at the idea because of their damaged ships and serious food and water shortages. Their refusal infuriated Gálvez, but he could not dissuade Aristizábal from returning to Havana. As a mere passenger on board, Calvo de la Puerta watched these events unfold, but perhaps he realized that their slender forces rendered Gálvez's proposed venture quixotic.[34]

Thirty miles from Havana, the Spanish ships encountered two English merchant frigates. They were the *George*, with twenty-four can-

33. Ibid., 106-10.

34. Ibid., 110-12.

nons and a crew of seventy, and the *Nancy*, with fourteen cannons and thirty-two sailors. They had left Jamaica on October 29, bound for New York City bearing cargoes of rum. Aristizábal, accompanied by the *Santa Cecilia* and the *San Pío*, approached the enemy vessels and a battle erupted that quickly compelled the enemy frigates to surrender. Calvo de la Puerta's soldiers became the guards of the hundred or so prisoners taken. Upon his return to Havana on November 19, Gálvez found many vessels of his invasion armada there, and it furthered his irritation. Nevertheless, the Spaniards had time to recover from the recent storm because the Great Hurricane of 1780 also ravaged the English fleet under Adm. George Rodney off Barbados; in a calamitous week in mid-October the violent tempest killed more than twenty thousand people in the eastern Caribbean. Gradually, as additional Spanish ships returned to Havana, Gálvez evaluated his losses. The storm sank three transports, probably with all hands lost, and damaged other troop vessels and warships. Many of the latter limped into Havana with the last ship arriving in late January 1781, three months after the storm. The soldiers and sailors aboard these final vessels had a month's respite before they embarked on a new attempt to capture Pensacola. As Spanish preparations continued in February, they learned that Rodney had repaired his battered squadron and seized the Dutch islands of Curaçao and St. Eustatius, along with a purported four hundred Dutch, Spanish, French, and American merchantmen anchored there for elicit trade. The French recovered the islands ten months later. Small islands throughout the Caribbean frequently changed hands in wartime because of their weak defenses.[35]

Calvo de la Puerta did not join the new expedition to attack Pensacola. The frigate *Nuestra Señora de la O* remained in Bonet's fleet to protect Havana and the gulf waters while Gálvez's attack on Pensacola proceeded. By far the subjugation of Pensacola was the most difficult of the three Spanish objectives in West Florida, and it required more troops and vessels. Besides warships of all classes, the expedition held thirty-two troop transports, a hospital frigate, and supply

35. Ibid., 120-25.

vessels. However, it contained only 1,467 troops, far short of the four thousand the crown had specified for Pensacola's conquest, and Gálvez kept prodding Havana to provide more. New Orleans raised eighteen small vessels with more than five hundred soldiers.[36] Gálvez departed for Pensacola on February 28, 1781, and throughout March and April, numerous problems plagued him. They included the shallowness of the water at the entrance to Pensacola Bay and the obstinacy of naval officers who refused to cross the sandbar into the bay; fear of the cannons at Red Cliffs, the fort near the bay's opening; and indecision on how to attack both the town of Pensacola and nearby Fort George. Spanish troops first landed on Santa Rosa Island while naval officers dawdled about entering Pensacola Bay. Disgusted by their refusal, Gálvez gathered his small boats, hoisted a pennant that had "Yo Solo" emblazoned on it, and commanded his Louisiana sailors and troops to enter the bay. Although he hardly entered the bay single-handedly, Gálvez's action shamed all but the officers of the largest warship into entering the bay. The troops on Santa Rosa Island soon moved across Pensacola Bay on barges for the attack on the fort. Gálvez's indecision on how to proceed against it, however, caused him to reposition the troops several times over the next few days. On the mainland, they clashed often with both British soldiers and Indians in the wilderness before a hot cannon ball rolled into an enemy powder magazine at an outpost above Fort George on May 7. Its thunderous explosion inflicted numerous casualties on the British and disoriented the survivors. Spanish grenadiers immediately rushed in and captured the outpost. Its seizure changed the course of battle since it overlooked Fort George and could fire freely upon it. The British quickly realized that prolonging the struggle meant more casualties to no avail and surrendered. The formal capitulation occurred on May 9, 1781.[37] With its capture, the Spaniards controlled all West Florida.

Calvo de la Puerta was not at Pensacola since he was serving on board a ship that made frequent calls at Havana, its home port. His

36. Ibid., 126-31.

37. Ibid., 135.

maritime service continued off and on until the war ended in 1783, making well over a dozen cruises, and they took longer than the six months required for entrance in the Order of Santiago. Despite the Gulf Coast successes and the Franco-American victory in the Battle of Yorktown that followed in October 1781, fighting continued elsewhere. In 1782 the Spaniards still had objectives to achieve, chiefly the capture of Jamaica and the Bahamas. Gálvez, who became commander of all Spanish forces in the Caribbean upon his victory at Pensacola, preferred the more difficult task of conquering Jamaica since it would heap greater luster on his career than seizing the tiny and virtually barren Bahama Islands. Gálvez sailed to Cap-Français in Saint-Domingue to prepare the Franco-Spanish task force that would be used to seize Jamaica, which he hoped to do in the spring of 1782. It never happened, however, because soon after he arrived at the Cap, British warships blockaded the port and terminated Gálvez's string of victories.[38]

Nevertheless, the Bahamas remained. In 1782, Lt. Gen. Juan Manuel de Cagigal, who became the captain general of Cuba at the beginning of the year, undertook the conquest of Nassau, the principal port in the Bahamas. Cagigal left Havana on April 22, with warships, transports, and two thousand regular and militia troops. He easily captured Nassau on May 7, and gained nominal control of the islands. Calvo de la Puerta was then serving on the ship-of-the-line *San Juan Nepomuceno* with a picket of soldiers to defend it against enemy boarding parties. Cagigal's attack was a calculated venture since he used soldiers assigned to defend Havana and other Gulf Coast posts. With Nassau taken, many of Cagigal's warships and soldiers returned to protect the gulf, and Calvo de la Puerta was among them. In two voyages he made during that time, his ship seized two English trading schooners. Danger in the Caribbean, however, rose dramatically when British admiral Rodney defeated the French fleet under Comte de Grasse off Guadalupe Island in July. It presaged new perils since Rodney appeared off Havana in August but found its military bastions too formidable and

38. Ibid.; Don Glickstein, *After Yorktown: The Final Struggle for American Independence* (Yardley, Penn.: Westholme, 2015).

departed. Spanish retention of Nassau, however, was short-lived because British troops ousted the Spaniards before the war ended.[39]

Besides Nassau, 1782 also saw other Spanish victories. In February, the Spaniards with French help recovered the Balearic island of Minorca from the British. The next month, they defeated their rivals on the Honduran island of Roatán, and it began Spanish successes in ousting them from Honduras and Nicaragua.[40]

Between the fighting in the Gulf of Mexico with his expeditions to Mobile, the Gulf Coast, and Nassau, Calvo de la Puerta was often in Havana, where he visited family and friends. More notably, either before Spain entered the conflict or shortly after, he began the courtship of a young and determined beauty from a prominent family. Perhaps the loveliness of María Luisa Peñalver y Navarrete enamored him from the first moment he saw her. When they became acquainted is not known, but it possibly occurred in 1779. By then, and at only fifteen years of age (she was born in Havana on June 29, 1764), she decided to marry Sebastián Calvo de la Puerta. Cuban women often married young, and the thirteen-year age difference with her future husband was far from unusual in that era. Similar to members of prominent and long established Cuban families who were all cousins of various kinds, they shared untold relatives. Because of the war, Sebastián faced the possibility of being sent into the fray on the Gulf Coast. Little is known about what preceded their decision to wed. Despite the social and economic equalities in the two families, her father, Ignacio Peñalver y Cárdenas, vehemently objected to the union and confined his daughter against her will. Perhaps Sebastián's sister-in-law, María Josefa Jús-

39. Kuethe, *Cuba*, 130; Calvo de la Puerta service sheet in AGM, ES; see also Calvo de la Puerta's petition to the King, Madrid, July 25, 1787, in which he summarized his military service, in AGS, GM, leg. 6880. Information on Juan Miguel de Cagigal is in Jacobo de la Pezuela, *Diccionario geográfico, estadístico, histórico, de la isla de Cuba*, 4 vols. (Madrid: Imprenta del Banco Industrial y Mercantil, 1866), 1:226-27. The full account of the Spanish capture and loss of Nassau is told in James A. Lewis, *The Final Campaign of the American Revolution: Rise and Fall of the Spanish Bahamas* (Columbia: University of South Carolina Press), 191.

40. Beerman, *España*, 237-46, 249-60.

tiz, the wife of his older brother Francisco, had acted as a matchmaker with the assistance of her mother, Beátriz Jústiz y Zayas-Bazán, who was the dowager Marquesa de Jústiz y Santa Ana. She possessed an impressive fortune and was a poetess and an ardent advocate of women's rights, such as they were in the eighteenth century. This might have explained her involvement in the matchmaking. The Jústiz family was also distantly related to the Peñalver clan of Havana.[41]

Whatever courting that went on became more complicated when Ignacio Peñalver placed his daughter in the Church of San Francisco to prevent her trysts with Sebastián. Confronted with this dilemma, Calvo de la Puerta took matters into his hands. With the willing participation of his future bride and help from the marquesa and her daughter, he extracted her from the church. The marquesa then ensconced María Luisa in her home, which, because of her title, was inviolate. It began a fierce tussle of wills between Jústiz and Ignacio Peñalver, and the city's inhabitants eagerly took sides. With tongues joyously wagging as they heatedly debated the scandal, Capt. Gen. Diego José Navarro intervened to quell their excited passions. He ordered María Luisa removed from the marquesa's home and put her in the more neutral Convent of Santa Teresa under his protection until the imbroglio could be straightened out.[42] About this time, Sebastián left on his assignment to Mobile.

The brawl between families appears to have stemmed from the British occupation of Havana years earlier. Some sugar producers, among the many who engaged in the export trade, cooperated with the British because they sold their massive stores of coffee, lumber, sugar, and other export commodities that had been stopped by the

41. The Jústiz family's wealth was centered on its large land and forest holdings in the Matanzas region in Cuba. The family sold hardwoods for building warships to the government shipyards in Havana. Alan J. Kuethe, "Havana in the Eighteenth Century," 17, in *Atlantic Port Cities: Economy, Culture, and Society in the Atlantic World, 1650-1850*, eds. Franklin W. Knight and Peggy K. Liss (Knoxville: University of Tennessee Press, 1991), 13-39.

42. Carlos Venegas, "Beátriz Justiz," *Revista de la Arquediócesis de La Habana*, no. 177 (September 2008).

war. After the occupation ended, Pedro Calvo de la Puerta, a foe of the city's occupiers, criticized the opportunists who put business first and benefited from trade with the British, which of course included the sugar producer Ignacio Peñalver. Alejandro O'Reilly also figured in the rivalry because he championed the promotions of individuals who showed their loyalty during the British occupation. Animosity between the two Cuban factions persisted for years and much hinged on which side the king favored. Nevertheless, the Peñalver family, despite temporary disapproval that included many other prominent Cubans, recovered after 1775 when O'Reilly lost royal favor because of his debacle in his attempt to capture Algiers. The Peñalver family regained its place among Havana's elite, and Ignacio Peñalver increased his considerable clout in the city. A long established resident, he became the treasurer general of both the army and navy in the city. He and his brother Gabriel had owned major sugar mills since before the Seven Years' War, and after the conflict ended expanded their holdings rapidly with additional cane fields, mills, cattle, and slaves. María Luisa's deceased mother, María Antonia Navarrete, born in Cartagena de Indias (in today's Colombia), came from a well-known and propertied family, and upon her demise bequeathed part of her personal fortune to María Luisa. Among the prominent members of the Peñalver family in Havana society was José María Peñalver, a priest in the Mercedarian Order and the first director of the Patriotic Society that promoted economic development on the island. María Luisa's paternal uncle and brother of Ignacio, Luis María Peñalver y Cárdenas (August 3, 1749-July 17, 1810), became the first bishop of Louisiana (1795-1801), after which he served as the archbishop of Guatemala between 1802 and 1808, when infirmities forced his retirement to Havana. He famously promoted education, often using his own funds, especially for building the convent of the Ursulines founded in Havana for nuns who had labored in New Orleans and retreated with other Spaniards when Louisiana was surrendered to the United States.[43]

43. González-Ripoll, *Cuba*, 142-43; Calcagno, *Diccionario biográfico cubano*, 487-91. Baudier, in *Catholic Church*, 223-46, provides a lengthy description of Peñalver's

Sebastián Calvo de la Puerta returned to Havana from Mobile Bay at the end of summer 1780. Upon learning of María Luisa's detention, he was determined to rescue her, and marriage appeared to be the way. Plans probably were already moving in that direction. By September or October, he took steps to free her. Following the usual procedure in the army, officers petitioned the crown for permission to marry. It was a royal precaution to ensure that prospective brides of officers belonged to the right social class and their families possessed the means to provide a dowry. Without government permission, the bride was ineligible to receive a pension from the Monte Pío, the military retirement fund, should her husband die in service. In his petition of October 15, 1780, Sebastián assured the crown that his prospective wife possessed the proper qualities. The same day, Gerónimo Girón, a leading military attorney in Havana, pledged to the king that both contracting parties and their families held the correct social credentials; nevertheless, the bride's father obstinately denied his permission. It caused Lt. Gen. Diego José Navarro, the Cuban captain general, to do so in his place. No doubt Calvo de la Puerta and his prospective bride both pleaded for his support, and he provided it. Girón argued that Peñalver's objection to the marriage was irrational, and he further implored the Audiencia de Santo Domingo, the appellate court for Cuban legal issues, to consider the matter sensibly because Peñalver had appealed to it to overturn the captain general's consent. To expedite government consent and as a precaution, Girón simultaneously consulted the king should the audiencia uphold the petition of María Luisa's father.[44]

A few days later, the prospective bride denounced her incarceration as unreasonable and solicited the crown to dispense with its marriage requirements regarding parental permission and dowry. She had the

---

service as bishop of Louisiana.

44. Gerónimo Girón petition to the Crown, New Orleans, October 15, 1780; baptismal record of María Luisa Peñalver y Navarrete, July 9, 1764, by Rector Santiago de Hechavarria; statement by the military attorney of Havana, in the city, February 16, 1781, that summarized events; all in the Sebastián Calvo de la Puerta military file in AGM, EP. The file also includes documents that confirm Girón's statement, such as one made by Juan Saban, Havana, October 16, 1780.

captain general's consent, and her inheritance from her dead mother obviated need of a dowry. To reinforce her petition, she obtained sworn statements from high-placed family friends who attested to her veracity: the captain general of Cuba; the Marquesa Jústiz de Santa Ana; the Conde de Vallellano; the Conde de Lagunillas; the Conde de Casa Montalba; the lieutenant colonel of the Volunteer Cavalry Martín de Aróstegui; and the *síndico procurador general* of Havana, Mateo Rey Gadas. The captain general had the senior army attorney in Havana examine the petition for possible legal flaws on October 12, and quickly dispatched the documents to Spain.[45]

In the peninsula, the crown forwarded the documents to Cádiz. There Alejandro O'Reilly, who still advised the government on Cuban affairs, reviewed Sebastián's petition, acknowledged his personal acquaintance with Maria Luisa's father, and endorsed her request. O'Reilly sent his reply to the crown, and in the spring of 1781 the king's approval crossed the Atlantic to Havana.[46] With royal consent in the captain general's hands, Ignacio Peñalver ended his opposition to his daughter's marriage.

On May 27, 1781, the Calvo de la Puerta-Peñalver nuptials took place in the Havana cathedral, the site of many weddings, baptisms, and funerals of the city's most prominent inhabitants. Since the marriage united two principal families, it was probably celebrated with the participation of many distinguished guests, not to mention throngs of common folk gathered outside the cathedral. Fireworks, music, food, and beverages also enlivened the celebration. Another reason for the festivities was that it occurred less than three weeks after the major Spanish victory at Pensacola that ended the war in West Florida. Calvo de la Puerta was then serving on a ship, and perhaps it had come from the Gulf Coast bringing British prisoners who briefly filled the prison camps outside the city before the inmates were paroled to the British army in the North American colonies.[47]

45. Calvo de la Puerta file in AGM, ES.

46. Alejandro O'Reilly letter, Cádiz, February 9, 1781, in ibid.

47. Miró to Juan Miguel de Cagigal, New Orleans, November 2, 1782, AGI, PC,

Around the time of the celebrations, tragedy struck the Calvo de la Puerta family when its patriarch, Sebastián's father, died in 1781. Nothing is known about the causes of his demise, and perhaps his sons were present when it occurred. A division of parental property soon followed. Usually in such cases, half the property descended on the widow while the children, especially the oldest son, would inherit the rest. But their father had not divided his holdings in the traditional way. Pedro José was an egalitarian and distributed his property among his three sons. The sons, too, would later inherit more when their mother, the dowager Condesa de Buena Vista, died in 1796. At some time in the latter half of the eighteenth century but before 1796, the three Calvo de la Puerta brothers (and possibly including their mother's property, too) owned approximately 12,500 acres of land, most of it devoted to sugarcane, and eight mills to grind the cane. Although this provides indistinct information about their holdings, it is the only description of their real estate after their father's death. No doubt Sebastián's fortune did not develop as rapidly, if at all, as those of his two brothers who actively participated in advancing their properties.[48]

By the day of the wedding, María Luisa was three weeks short of her seventeenth birthday while her fiancé was three months shy of thirty. Their marriage lasted eleven years, during which time Sebastián's army service removed him from Havana for short periods until he departed for Spain on a lengthy absence. When her husband returned from Spain in 1789, she reportedly threw dazzling parties at their Havana residence called "Plaza Nueva." Aside from this sparse knowledge, little information exists on their marriage save for the birth of four children. The first child, María Catalina, was born in 1782 before the war ended. She enjoyed a lengthy life and succumbed in 1857. The second child and principal heir, Pedro José Calvo de la Puerta y Peñalver, was born in 1783 and baptized on August 25. María Antonia, the third offspring, survived childhood, and later as an adult married a Montalvo

---

leg. 1304; Rubén C. Arango, *La Sacarocracía: Historia de la Aristocracía Azucarera Cubana* (Miami: Ego Group, Inc., 2006), 138; Caughey, *Gálvez*, 211-12.

48. Thomas, *Cuba*, 152.

cousin with whom she had about eight offspring. The last of Sebastián's children, Ignacio, was born in 1790, the year after his father's return to Cuba from Spain. Two years following Ignacio's birth, the children's mother and Sebastián's wife, María Luisa, succumbed at age twenty-seven to one of the many infirmities of the era. Details about her death are unknown. Nevertheless, from all appearances the marriage had been felicitous, and it ended far too quickly. Calvo de la Puerta grieved for a considerable period because he never married again.[49] Her death also added responsibility on him as the surviving parent since the children were only ten, nine, eight, and two when she died. Still, army service called their father away, and Sebastián made several journeys away from Havana between 1792 and 1802. Thereafter, Ignacio accompanied his father in all their travels that began in 1803.[50]

Unlike numerous other officers and for whatever reason, Sebastián did not receive a promotion during the war. Nevertheless, his wartime experiences commanding soldiers on land and at sea served him well. He had participated on military expeditions and naval cruises that made him a war veteran. While advancements in rank eluded him, they soon came during the 1780s upon his return to Spain.

49. Arango, *La Sacarocacia*, 138. What little information there is on the Calvo de la Puerta-Peñalver marriage has to be inferred from the documents in his petition to marry and the information provided by Francisco Xavier de Santa Cruz y Mallén. This information was republished in his article, "El Primer Marqués de Casa-Calvo y sus sucesores en el Título," in his collection of biographical and genealogical columns called "Del Pasado" that were printed between 1945 and 1952 in Havana's *Diario de la Marina*. This one on Calvo de la Puerta was published on May 4, 1952. See also the article on the Calvo de la Puerta family in the same collection that has genealogical information on many family members.

50. For more information on the children of Sebastián Calvo de la Puerta, see chapter 8.

4
Spain and Cuba, 1783-1793

While the Spanish participants in the recent war had no doubt avidly prayed for peace, its conclusion produced a dilemma that Sebastián Calvo de la Puerta dolefully welcomed. For the last five years, he had been in and around Havana and his family. Although military obligations forced his occasional absence from the city for several months at a time, he, nevertheless, returned there. But now with hostilities ended, he was required to embark with his Príncipe Infantry Regiment for Spain. Twenty years of service in the militia and regular army had inculcated a dedication to duty, but in addition he had other reasons for returning to Spain. María Luisa, meanwhile, could elect to accompany her husband to Spain or remain in Cuba. She must have pondered the hazards of an Atlantic crossing and unknown conditions in a strange land. Guided by practicality and surrounded by numerous relatives and friends who loathed seeing her leave, she judged Havana a safer choice for her three infant children. Consequently, Sebastián sailed without his family as he probably believed that his absence would be short-lived. Once in Spain, he longed to return to María Luisa and his tiny offspring. Nevertheless, two years passed before he found an opportunity that would eventually allow him to return to Havana in 1789 and retain his military employment and rank, considerations he deemed essential despite his Cuban wealth.

Following a tearful farewell with family members inside the harbor at Havana, Calvo de la Puerta sailed in either late 1783 or early 1784 with the troop transports and warships assigned to convey the Príncipe regiment to Spain. Although only an army captain, a married couple accompanied him as his personal servants. Upon his father's death in

1781, he inherited some properties and monies and could now live more ostentatiously than before. The flotilla of ships sailed to Cádiz, where the arriving military units soon moved on to their home bases. They likely traveled in mule-drawn caravans of wagons that trudged slowly along dusty roads leading to Spain's interior cities. Soldiers filled the wagons while perhaps officers reaped the benefit of journeying on horseback or in a carriage. In the case of Calvo de la Puerta, his regiment appeared to return to its old quarters in Burgos.

Over the course of the several years he spent in Spain during his second stay, Sebastián probably often saw Cuban relatives and friends who were either well established in the mother country or merely visiting. He is not known to have traveled to Cumbres Mayores during this or any of his journeys to Spain. The passage of two hundred years appears to have erased ties to the ancestral homestead and distant relations. During this sojourn in Spain, he spent three years in Madrid and that helped immeasurably in maintaining contacts and staying current with events and his extended family members and acquaintances on the island. Recent arrivals from Cuba also brought news while established residents no doubt shared knowledge obtained through letters. Quite likely his wife, relatives, and friends wrote him often, but unfortunately their epistles, as well as those he penned, have now disappeared. Sebastián's cousin, Gonzalo O'Farrill, was one person he sought out in Madrid. Gonzalo, who was also in the army and slightly younger, nevertheless, served as a model for Sebastián. His multiple talents had enabled him to achieve rapid success as he saw action in several wars. He traveled sometimes to other European nations to study their military systems or serve in a diplomatic post. Spain under King Carlos III tried to a modest degree to modernize the army where privileged individuals, regardless of ability, often attained significant offices to the exclusion of meritorious individuals. In an absolute monarchy bypassing descendants of old titled families was not always practicable.[1]

1. Calcagno, *Diccionario biográfico cubano*, 457-58. On Gonzalo O'Farrill, see Pezuela, *Diccionario,* 4:159-62. Pezuela states that O'Farrill went to France at age nine to be educated. In France he learned French, Latin, and Greek and, because his father bought him a captaincy in the Spanish army, became an officer at age seventeen.

Besides Sebastián, a number of known Cubans from planter families also spent time in Spain in the 1780s. Prominent among them was Francisco Arango y Parreño, who arrived in 1787 to study law and in time he became the most ardent advocate, which is to say lobbyist, for Cuban plantation owners and the development of sugarcane.[2] Gonzalo O'Farrill's nephew, Juan Montalvo O'Farrill, enrolled in the prestigious College of Nobles in Madrid and was later admitted to the Royal Guards as he pursued a military career. Other well-off Cubans in Spain similarly followed military careers, tried to loosen Spanish restrictions on Cuban agriculture, or merely enjoyed the comfort of living near the king. Personal contact at court often yielded more tangible results than petitions submitted from distant colonies. Many Cubans in Madrid shared their unity in values and felt their distinctiveness from both Spaniards and other Spanish Americans.[3] There were exceptions, of course, such as Gonzalo O'Farrill, who assimilated into Spanish society and became a Spaniard in virtually all respects. Differing from his cousin, however, Sebastián clung to his Cuban roots because his loved ones and property were on the island he called home.

Following a year of quiet service in Spain, Calvo de la Puerta emerged from the shadows in 1785. Since the year before, he had worked to straighten out the disposition of the title of nobility his father, Pedro Calvo de la Puerta, had been in the course of obtaining

---

By age twenty-five, he was a brevet lieutenant colonel. He returned to France for a projected invasion of England in 1779, but it never occurred. By 1780 he was at the siege of Gibraltar, and the next year he was assigned to forces that in 1782 recovered Minorca from the British, for which he was made a full lieutenant colonel. In the postwar era, he was assigned to North Africa, and in 1790 became colonel of the Asturias regiment after its head was killed in an earthquake at Oran. In the war, against the French Republic (1793-95), he was first promoted to brigadier and for his actions against the enemy in the Pyrenees to field marshal. Later he became a lieutenant general.

2. Kuethe, *Cuba*, 132-33; Pezuela, *Diccionario*, 1: 32-36. Arango y Parreño visited Spain twice, 1787-94 and 1816-19.

3. María Dolores González-Ripoll Navarro, "Vínculos y redes de poder entre Madrid y la Habana. Francisco Arango y Parreño (1765-1837), ideólogo y mediador," *Revista de Indias* 222 (Mayo-Agosto 2001): 291-307.

when he died. Perhaps Sebastián promised his father during his final illness that he would do it, or possibly Sebastián himself was behind the move to obtain the title. His return to Spain expedited its resolution. The involvement of the Royal Accounting Office suggests that the title of marqués he obtained was purchased as were most titles acquired by wealthy eighteenth-century Cuban planters. By 1790 twenty Cubans basked in the splendor their titles of nobility provided. Either before or after his father died, Sebastián placed in the Royal Treasury in Havana 10,000 silver pesos for the honor. Converting the island's economic and social elite into aristocrats served a royal purpose since it bound them more closely to the crown. Among the documents issued was one involving the royal treasury that acknowledged a receipt of payment—allegedly it was to exempt a nobleman from military service, but that clumsy explanation appears to have been the traditional cover for the money's true purpose. On February 23, 1785, the crown formally bequeathed on Sebastián the title of marqués de Casa-Calvo, which recognized his family rather than him alone. He subsequently called himself by his title, Casa-Calvo, especially in official documents, a prerogative the titled nobility zealously employed. Upon his father's death in 1781, the title of conde de Buena Vista had passed to Sebastián's older brother Francisco.[4]

Even while pursuing his decoration, Casa-Calvo had been searching for a way to return home. His first thought centered on resuming service in his old militia cavalry unit, the Squadron of Havana Dragoons. While still in the Príncipe regiment in 1785, he petitioned the king for reassignment back to the dragoons. To boost the attractiveness of his transfer, he offered to serve without pay until a post of the proper rank, which meant as a captain and head of a company, became available for him. Reasons he espoused for his transfer ranged from his Havana origins, a need to care for his young children, and his diverse

4. AGI, TC, leg. 2. See also the file on Pedro Calvo de la Puerta, Conde de Buena Vista, in AGS, GM, leg. 6855, which has numerous documents on his son, Francisco Calvo de la Puerta, who inherited his title of Conde de Buena Vista. Sherry Johnson, *The Social Transformation of Eighteenth Century Cuba* (Gainesville: University Press of Florida, 2001), 8.

economic holdings that required his personal attention. Lastly, he reminded readers of his petition, and he did so with scant subtlety, that his properties generated considerable income for the Royal Treasury.[5]

The ministry of war, however, first investigated the conditions then present in the dragoon squadron to determine whether a post existed for him to occupy. It required months to gain that knowledge. The squadron's commander in Havana eventually informed the crown of the distressing situation in the unit. In March 1786, the ministry of war announced what it had learned about the unit's manpower. It consisted of four companies with five captains, one captain more than necessary; two of the captains held the rank of brevet lieutenant colonel. The unit's adjutant major, an administrative official, was a lieutenant with the rank of brevet captain; of the five lieutenants in the squadron, one was a brevet captain and one was a captain. More positive, only one of the four sublieutenant posts was held by an officer with a higher rank. Thus the unit that Calvo de la Puerta wished to join already had more than the requisite number of officers, and many held ranks higher than what their posts stipulated. Therefore, royal officials judged Casa-Calvo's inclusion in the squadron as detrimental to all its officers and denied his petition.[6]

Nevertheless, his plan to transfer to Havana was not entirely frustrated. Because of his recent service in an infantry regiment, the crown suggested as an alternative his assignment to the new fixed infantry regiment that the king was creating for Cuba. Minister of War Manuel Lerma and Minister of the Indies José de Gálvez, the Marqués de Sonora, discussed the Casa-Calvo petition, and they noted his readiness to serve without salary. Furthermore, they observed that he was a Cuban planter and, similar with many in the island's oligarchy, his agricultural property benefited the Royal Treasury handsomely.[7] Lerma and Sonora cleverly saw an opportunity to save money with his free services while he enlisted troops for the new regiment. Moreover, perhaps his inclu-

5. Pedro de Lerma to Sonora, El Pardo, March 17, 1786, AGS, GM, leg. 6880.

6. Ibid.

7. Ibid.

sion in the unit would serve to tie his family and other Cuban aristocrats closer to the crown.

Sonora informed Calvo de la Puerta on the impossibility of assigning him to the Havana dragoons. Nevertheless, he could transfer to the new regiment the king had ordered for service in Cuba.[8] His wish to return to the island perhaps belatedly influenced the crown to promote him to brevet lieutenant colonel (the rank of "major" did not exist in the Spanish army). Within days of discussing his petition, the crown advanced him in rank on April 3, 1786. A week later, the king also agreed to appoint Casa-Calvo to the new infantry regiment without a salary until he was officially posted to the unit. That was the reason for denying him pay until then, but it was a specious argument given that the new regiment had numerous vacant posts. His assignment as a recruiter was backdated to April 3.[9] He soon received permission to leave the Príncipe regiment to take up his new duties in Madrid.

Nevertheless, Casa-Calvo kept pestering the government with new petitions because he was without official documentation that specifically designated his new positions. He returned to Madrid about early May before journeying to Aranjuez, which served as the royal capital each spring. The royal family pursued its yearly ritual of changing palaces with the seasons in the year. Aranjuez lay about twenty miles southeast from Madrid, Carlos III's winter residence. Spring arrived earlier at Aranjuez than at Madrid because of its verdant setting on the banks of the Tagus (Tajo) River and its greater distance from the Guadarrama Mountains. On May 29, 1786, Casa-Calvo welcomed his attachment to the new fixed regiment for Cuba, but he simultaneously petitioned for a dispatch that spelled out his attachment to the new unit and his rank. He further requested a royal document that stated the purpose of his commission, which was to form this corps in Madrid and Havana. In return, he would render his best service. He needed the documents, he claimed, to receive a salary from Havana's army ac-

8. (Sonora) to Lerma, El Pardo, March 27, 1786, ibid.

9. Lerma to Sonora, El Pardo, April 3, 1786; Sonora to Lerma, El Pardo, April 5, 1786, both in ibid.

counting office upon completion of his work. For now, he limited his requests to the use of the lieutenant colonel insignia and the uniform of his new unit.[10] He achieved only the first.

Three months later on August 30, Casa-Calvo raised a question about his new rank that exceeded Lerma's knowledge. Therefore, Lerma contacted the inspector general of the infantry, the Conde de O'Reilly, to provide the needed information. O'Reilly approved Casa-Calvo's promotion, and he, in turn, wrote to Col. Pedro Gorostisa, head of the Príncipe regiment. The colonel assured Casa-Calvo of his ascent to lieutenant colonel in the new regiment and that he had been relieved of duty in the Príncipe regiment. But since Casa-Calvo lacked proof of his appointment, he again asked for an official certificate.[11]

Being promoted above the company grade of officers, where he had tarried for seventeen long years, pleased Casa-Calvo enormously. The lengthy stay, however, was typical for purchased ranks, especially for teenaged recipients, since they had much to learn about army life. Nevertheless, it must have seemed an eternity to him, and he had spent approximately eight of those years in Spain, where he demonstrated his equality in ability with his peninsular brethren. Now as a field grade officer and in a new regiment, his promotion opened opportunities for advancement into higher army administrative posts. Perhaps one day, they might lead to the position of general. Although only thirty-five years old in 1786, he could dream about attaining higher posts in the future. First, however, he needed to focus on more immediate ranks, and he was determined to obtain them as quickly as he could. Participating in the formation of a new regiment was a godsend since it could fulfill his cherished wishes, and he soon devoted himself to bringing them to fruition.

He initially requested promotion to full lieutenant colonel in his new employment. He believed he deserved the rank to expedite his duties in recruiting troops. Casa-Calvo petitioned the king again on September 5, 1786, at San Ildefonso. It was the royal summer palace called

10. Casa-Calvo petition to the king, Aranjuez, May 29, 1786, ibid.

11. Casa-Calvo petition to the king, Madrid, August 30, 1786, ibid.

La Granja and in the Guadarrama Mountains, about thirty-five miles northwest of Madrid and near Segovia. Felipe V, Spain's first Bourbon king, had constructed it as a summer refuge away from the heat below in Madrid and Aranjuez. The small palace at San Ildefonso was an airy early eighteenth-century rococo structure set in the midst of grounds adorned with numerous and elaborately decorated water fountains reminiscent of the French palace at Versailles. Felipe V detested the somber mausoleum-like edifice of San Lorenzo de El Escorial, where the crypts of his Habsburg predecessors were kept, and he decreed his burial at San Ildefonso. He became the exception among the kings of Spain.[12]

In his appeal to King Carlos III at San Ildefonso in early September, Casa-Calvo acknowledged that he had served as a captain since 1769. He repeated arguments used in earlier petitions that requested the king's permission to return to Havana without a salary, continue his military career, educate his children, and foment his agricultural estates. Both the king and the Marqués de Sonora permitted him to do these things on April 3, 1786, when they pulled him out of the Príncipe regiment.[13] While the crown considered his promotion valid, he complained that he needed an official document to verify his new rank of full lieutenant colonel. It had an effect. The rank was granted on September 19, 1786. Eight days later, a memorandum among the royal papers stated that Casa-Calvo had been sent an order that he was now attached to the soon-to-be created Fixed Infantry Regiment of Cuba.[14] In a few short months in mid-1786, Casa-Calvo had leapt from

12. Lynch, *Spain under the Habsburgs*, 1: 173; and Henry Kamen, *Philip V of Spain: The King who Reigned Twice* (New Haven: Yale University Press, 2001).

13. Casa-Calvo petition to the king, San Ildefonso, September 5, 1786, AGS, GM, leg. 6880.

14. A document made by an unnamed royal official and sent to the colonel of Casa-Calvo's unit for adjustment, September 27, 1786; royal order to the governor (the captain general) of Havana, San Ildefonso, September 26, 1786, both in ibid. The two promotions are noted in Casa-Calvo's service sheet, end of March 1805, Havana, in AGM, ES. The new regiment was the Fixed Infantry Regiment of Cuba, not the older unit that was the Fixed Infantry Regiment of Havana.

captain to full lieutenant colonel and with a commission to recruit personnel for the new regiment. It was a significant achievement, and his presence in Spain had made it possible. Nevertheless, he was still without a salary or a formal guarantee to a post within the regiment inasmuch as he held only a temporary attachment to it.

In Havana on December 20, 1786, Capt. Gen. José de Ezpeleta informed the Marqués de Sonora that he received a dispatch about Casa-Calvo listing him as a full lieutenant colonel without salary. He noted that Casa-Calvo would receive a position in the infantry regiment of Cuba upon its formation.[15] This was the reassurance he sought, although it is ironic that the Cuban captain general received orders about it before Casa-Calvo in Spain did.

During 1787 and 1788, Casa-Calvo labored in the creation of the new regiment by selecting officers and soldiers in Madrid. In addition, a tidbit of information emerged about his brothers, who had not yet become members of a crusading order. What happened many years before, in 1771-72, when Sebastián sought entry in the order for Francisco is not known. Sebastián had been working on this honor for them in 1787 and learned that he again needed to submit the family genealogical record. However, his personal copy had been misplaced or lost in one of his Atlantic crossings. Therefore, in 1788, he applied for a duplicate to be made from the documents stored in the Spanish archives. His younger brother Nicolás was now an officer in a Havana militia unit, and because of unknown delays he and Francisco entered the crusading Order of Santiago in 1791. At that time both of them presented their lengthy military and civilian achievements to the crown as the reason for being compensated with use of the habit. No doubt, they also paid for the privilege.[16]

While the Marqués de Sonora had entrusted Sebastián with formation of the new regiment for Cuba, recruiting soldiers and officers proceeded slowly. On February 18, 1787, Sonora's first orders on this

15. Ezpeleta to Sonora, no. 270, Havana, December 20, 1786, AGS, GM, leg. 6880.

16. See the documents in AHN, OM, leg. 8114. One document is a cédula from the king, San Lorenzo de El Escorial, October 2, 1771, and it is also in ibid., leg. 8117.

matter instructed the lieutenant colonel to enlist all veteran Spanish troops, particularly corporals and cavalry soldiers who applied because four squadrons had been disbanded in Spain, and many of their career soldiers wanted to continue service in the colonies. Several months later, on July 7, the king ordered Sebastián Calvo de la Puerta to send to Havana three hundred recruits who would form the base of the new regiment under the care of its sergeant-major. Meanwhile, the Cuban captain general was to enroll all Spanish soldiers from the Iberian regiments stationed on the island who had fulfilled their enlistments. Two regiments were returning to Spain, and the crown routinely permitted soldiers who wished to remain in Cuba to transfer to fixed colonial units. In Madrid, Casa-Calvo bore responsibility for the expenses of recruits lodged in private dwellings and apartments. In time the costs grew significantly until they reached 20,000 pesos; nonetheless, he was assured of reimbursement for his expenditures. The crown footed the salaries of some officers and all enlisted men. Whether they engaged in training during their lengthy wait is unknown.[17] The years 1787 and 1788 passed slowly in Casa-Calvo's estimation since he wanted to leave for Havana and his family immediately.

In mid-1788, the ministry of war reviewed the work that Casa-Calvo had accomplished thus far with the new regiment. Two battalions with nine companies each had been formed, but the number of soldiers in them had not yet been designated; soldiers in each battalion usually numbered around six hundred. Cost seemed to be a major factor, and many officers had joined without receiving salaries right away. Since Spain and Cuba could provide only limited recruits, Spanish officials advocated placement of recruiting bands in different lands such as Mexico, the Canary Islands, and Cádiz; seeking foreigners who volunteered to join the Spanish army; raising the cash bonus recruits, who were usually discharged soldiers, received in Cádiz from fifteen to thir-

17. Calvo de la Puerta petition to the king, Madrid, July 25, 1787, AGS, GM, leg. 6880. A memorandum in the same legajo but dated October 3, 1799, made at San Lorenzo, provided reasons why some officers were paid while others were not. It decreed that the royal treasury in Havana should provide the salaries of those who were eligible for payment.

ty pesos for reenlisting for another eight years; and supplying recruits with a daily maintenance allowance of two *reales* (a quarter peso) each until the army assumed charge of them. Discussions ensued about allowing foreigners to comprise one-third of the regiment's soldiers and assigning Casa-Calvo's recruits to other understaffed colonial units in the Spanish army. Not all the soldiers he sent to Cuba thus far entered the new regiment. Recruits arriving in Havana were housed in a military depot and remained there until they received assignments to posts throughout the Spanish American colonies. Three hundred recruits had accompanied Sgt. Maj. Martín Ugarte from Madrid to Havana in 1787. Now, possibly the five hundred additional men Casa-Calvo had enlisted were already in Havana and nearly four hundred more soldiers awaited transportation at Cádiz. Officials expressed a concern about the undermanned third battalion in the Fixed Havana Infantry Regiment, the first army regiment established in the city, and they assigned some of the new recruits to that battalion. The second battalion of the Havana infantry regiment served in Santiago de Cuba while the third battalion saw duty in St. Augustine, Florida. It meant that only the regiment's first battalion served in Havana.[18]

As early as mid-1788 and only two years after leaving his captain's rank behind him, Casa-Calvo announced his wish to be the colonel, which is to say the commander, of the new regiment.[19] The crown, however, was not yet considering an appointment to that position. On September 22, as it appeared Casa-Calvo's departure approached, he enumerated his accomplishments over the last two years. He had formed two battalions for the regiment, each battalion with one grenadier and eight fusilier companies. Since certain officers remained without salaries until they received a posting, Casa-Calvo requested dispatches to enable him to fill the vacant officer slots in the companies and battalions. He also wanted the formation of a headquarters staff

18. Document without names, Aranjuez, June 8, 1788, AGS, GM, leg. 6881. The document from the ministry of war summarizes events and letters associated with the creation of the new regiment. Kuethe, *Cuba*, 129.

19. Kuethe, *Cuba*, 129.

that would handle the customary administrative duties, and he repeated other requests on the establishment of recruiting parties, enlistment bonuses paid soldiers, and the enrollment of foreigners.[20]

During his two years of recruiting and supervising soldiers while they waited in Madrid for assignment to Cuba, Casa-Calvo's confidence in administration grew, and he believed that his familiarity with the officers and soldiers merited another reward. He anticipated in the near future the appointment of the final officers for the regiment and considered himself qualified to become its colonel. In late 1788, he formally petitioned the king for command of the Fixed Infantry Regiment of Cuba. This time, however, he ran into a stone wall. The king deferred the matter, replying that he would attend to Casa-Calvo's petitions if they were meritorious once he reached his destination. Since he would soon sail, the crown instructed him to complete the regiment's formation in Havana. Perhaps his recent promotion to lieutenant colonel had militated against another rapid rise in rank.[21] Nevertheless, it disappointed him enormously. Possibly it stemmed from his relatives and friends in the militia units at home who were now gaining promotions.

Still he held in his favor an important post, duties to perform, and Havana as his next assignment. On January 22, 1789, Casa-Calvo at last inquired about the expenditures he had made in behalf of the recruits in his care. He also asked about his salary since he had not received any kind of remuneration since April 3, 1786. Some recruited

20. Casa-Calvo to Antonio Valdés (minister of the Indies), Aranjuez, September 22, 1788, AGS, GM, leg. 6881.

21. Royal order to Casa-Calvo, (Madrid), December 23, 1788, AGS, GM, leg. 6881; palace memorandum, Madrid, January 13, 1789, AGS, GM, leg. 6842. In 1788 Joaquín Beltrán de Santa Cruz y Cárdenas entered the volunteer infantry as a sub-lieutenant and became a captain two years later. He was the heir to the title of conde de San Juan de Jaruco which he inherited in 1804 along with a fortune in sugar. He was married to María Teresa Montalvo y O'Farrill of the sugar elite. In 1788 he tried to buy the colonelcy of the Fixed Infantry Regiment of Cuba (Casa-Calvo's unit) for 20,000 pesos, a piddling amount of his wealth. He failed because he lacked military merit and the ministry of war loathed selling important posts. Kuethe, *Cuba*, 152-53.

officers, nevertheless, had been paid; there seemed to be no rigid rule for determining which officers received salaries and which did not. Casa-Calvo, for his part, wanted to know what compensation was due him and about the "advanced salary" military personnel traditionally received before they embarked on a journey because they would not be paid for several months, what funds he could expect to receive in Havana, and the reimbursement for the lodgings he had provided his troops.[22] He further grumbled *soto voce* that Sgt. Maj. Martín Ugarte, who had switched from the Spanish Guadalajara Regiment to the new unit on January 27, 1787, and who was a Cuban, had been paid his full salary. Similar to Calvo de la Puerta, he wanted to return home, and in his case, after four or five years in the Guadalajara regiment. His duties as sergeant major involved processing paperwork that dealt with personnel, assignments, equipment, expenditures, and sundry other matters related to the new regiment. About mid-1787, Ugarte left for Havana, where he cared for soldiers arriving from Spain and those recruited locally. The ministry of war sent a royal order on January 23, 1789, to the captain general that discussed Casa-Calvo's expenses, but it did not specify payment.[23]

Casa-Calvo also requested to dress in the uniform of the new unit, but that was impossible since it had not yet been designed. Each regiment in that age wore distinctive uniforms and often of different colors. He complained that he had grown tired of continuing to dress in the garments of the Príncipe regiment, his old unit; he wanted to wear the new uniform, and perhaps become the first person to do so when he officially entered the Fixed Infantry Regiment of Cuba. Undoubtedly, all the recruits in the new regiment still dressed in the uniforms of their previous units, and they must have projected a bewildering assortment of colors whenever they assembled.

In January 1789, the crown at last issued measures to send Casa-Calvo and his remaining troops to Havana. Preparations, nonetheless, proceeded leisurely. In Madrid on February 22, Minister of the

22. Casa-Calvo to Antonio Valdés, Madrid, January 22, 1789, AGS, GM, leg. 6880.

23. War Office memorandum, (Madrid), March 13, 1789, ibid.

Indies Antonio Valdés Fernández de Bazán, who had replaced the deceased Sonora, gave Casa-Calvo permission to leave Spain with two servants and his baggage. The orders instructed Cádiz naval authorities overseeing the sailing of ships and passengers not to interfere with his departure. He probably spent much of April traveling down to the port and reached it before the end of the month.[24]

Thus by the beginning of May 1789, Casa-Calvo anxiously awaited transportation for his journey. Military aides and servants had accompanied him from Madrid. He gave every indication of being an affluent military officer who enjoyed the privileges of riches and rank. He had spent his time in Spain surrounded by retainers, many of them Cubans. Perhaps his most important personal servant was his chamberlain (*ayudante de cámara*), Juan Ramírez, who traveled with his wife Melchora del Castillo and their four children. Possibly they had accompanied him to Spain in 1784. Another servant, Diego de Moya, cared for his employer's sizeable baggage. It included six trunks, two large suitcases, a horse carriage, and thirty boxes filled with household effects; gifts for María Luisa and the children possibly numbered among the contents. Casa-Calvo's military aides consisted of Gren. Capt. Ignacio de la Luz, his wife Melchora, and their male servant, with five trunks of baggage and two beds; and two sublieutenants, Benito Paniagua and Andrés Clar, were each taking one trunk and one bed. In addition, Casa-Calvo's chief military adjutant, Ramón Maudiet y Varela, was expected to join him shortly. Furthermore, he noted that he had acquired a large quantity of linen cloth and other essentials to tailor uniforms for the officers and soldiers of the new regiment. After several inquiries to the government on the regiment's uniform, he offered to design it himself. He chose white as its dominant color. The government authorized him to pick out clothing materials from the army warehouses in Cádiz before he sailed and granted him a large sum of money to cover his expenses. Casa-Calvo, his retainers, and his military aides were all as-

24. Document signed by Valdés, and countersigned in Cádiz, May 5, 1789. AGS, GM, leg. 6842.

signed to the frigate *San Antonio* for their voyage to Havana.[25]

In May, the frigate departed for Cuba, probably accompanied by other vessels. After the customary stop at Santa Cruz de Tenerife in the Canaries that Spanish ships crossing the Atlantic to the colonies made, Casa-Calvo arrived in Havana in July 1789. His wife must have been thrilled to see him. Following an absence of five and a half years, he appeared almost a stranger, especially to his young children. But now he returned as a full lieutenant colonel and attached to an infantry regiment assigned to Havana. His permanence there appeared certain, and the news must have elated his family. His career had received a positive boost, and he seemed destined for higher ranks.[26]

Shortly after arriving in Havana, Casa-Calvo reported on August 13 the number of men who were then in the new regiment. The transport *Santa Florentina* had brought several hundred more recruits, and they were now sufficient to fill the first two battalions with 1,253 men with 254 left over for formation of the third battalion, for an overall total of 1,507 soldiers. Casa-Calvo stated that 142 more soldiers were needed to meet the required number for a regiment. Nevertheless, there was a constant loss and gain with deaths, desertions, imprisonments, enlistments, and the capture or voluntary return of deserters. Moreover, several officers and soldiers were absent because they were recruiting in the Canary Islands and Spain or were gone for other reasons. No officers, however, existed for the formation of the third bat-

25. Kuethe, *Cuba*, 131; Casa-Calvo statement, Cádiz, April 20, 1789, AGI, CC, leg. 5533; royal order to the interim army intendant of Havana, Aranjuez, June 4, 1789, AGS, GM, leg. 6840; royal order to the viceroy of New Spain, Madrid, August 14, 1789, AGS, GM, leg. 6843. The second document above was countersigned on April 30, 1789. It included information that the merchant frigate *San Antonio* was going to Havana with Casa-Calvo's servants, and he had the proper paper work for departure with the needed license. Another document in AGI, CC, leg. 5533, has licenses for the people accompanying Casa-Calvo, but it cautioned him not to help stowaways and other people who attempted to travel without permission. The legajo also contains a license for Casa-Calvo and his people to embark that was given in Cádiz on April 30, 1789, and signed by Manuel González Guiral.

26. Royal order to the Marqués de Casa-Calvo, San Lorenzo, October 31, 1789, AGS, GM, 6843.

talion. Although the soldiers had not completed their training, they helped guard the city and maintain order. Nonetheless, they lacked sufficient arms and uniforms. Some of these last items arrived early in 1790.[27] Two Spanish regiments, the Immemorial and the Hibernia (a unit composed of Irishmen), had completed their tours of duty on the island and left about the time that Casa-Calvo arrived. The crown was anxious that the new regiment be in place with its full complement of soldiers when that happened.[28] The departing regiments had been conspicuously undermanned.

On March 24, 1789, before Casa-Calvo left Spain, the ministry of war decided that his salary would commence as of December 13, 1788, the day the king officially decreed the formation of the Fixed Infantry Regiment of Cuba to be complete. Furthermore, his final expenses in Madrid on behalf of the recruits would be satisfied through the regiment when funds became available. Virtually all agencies in the government functioned on less than adequate budgets.[29] As an aging empire, Spain could no longer generate the assets needed to operate its many possessions adequately nor confront the escalating fiscal challenges rival empires imposed. In addition, Spain still subscribed to the medieval revenue practices of a non-industrialized society that favored a narrow privileged class at the expense of the humble masses who constituted the real taxpayers. As a consequence, the government depended on the colonies to supply the mineral wealth and agricultural commodities it could sell to foreign markets at a profit. It did not

27. Casa-Calvo to Antonio Valdés, Havana, August 13, 1789, with the attachment "Relation of the Force that this Regiment has on this day, with an expression of the surplus for the formation of the Third Battalion," both in AGS, GM, leg. 6880. Casa-Calvo to Valdés, Havana, February 13, 1790, ibid., which also contains letters sent by Valdés to Casa-Calvo. Kuethe, in *Cuba*, 129, discusses army reorganization in Havana in 1787-89.

28. (Valdés?) to the governor of Havana, San Lorenzo, October 16, 1789, AGS, GM, leg. 6880.

29. (Valdés) to the army intendant of Havana, Madrid, March 24, 1789, ibid., and with a letter to Casa-Calvo of the same date. Intendant Domingo Osternani acknowledged the receipt of the order in Havana on May 28, 1789, ibid.

emphasize the manufacture of goods to sell to colonials, and the privileged in Spain shunned commerce and preferred holding land that they regarded as the only true wealth. Moreover, most colonials often did not earn enough money to purchase costly imports, nor did the crown manifest any wish to turn them into consumers.[30]

While Casa-Calvo prepared to leave Spain in early 1789 and during his summer passage, momentous changes began to emerge in the Atlantic world that seriously disturbed international politics everywhere. The new era had actually started with the American Revolution in 1776, but it intensified decisively with the outbreak of the French Revolution on July 14, 1789. Before long the social, political, and economic turmoil began to rattle the fragile cores of other conservative European monarchies and their empires and disrupt the traditional lives of many of their inhabitants. Furthermore, the decades-long crisis involved Sebastián Calvo de la Puerta in different ways since it persisted throughout the remainder of his life, and it had already drawn him into the last war in which he actively participated.[31]

Nevertheless, after Casa-Calvo's return to Cuba in 1789, a peaceful interlude in the Spanish American colonies presented him with an opportunity to take up more tranquil pastimes. He resumed familiar and welcomed obligations as a husband, father, and planter that had ceased upon his departure for Spain because now he was more than an army officer. He probably transitioned to his new life effortlessly, but as a true Bourbon soldier he held civilian obligations subordinate to his

30. María Rosario Sevilla Soler, *Santo Domingo: Tierra de Frontera (1750-1800)* (Sevilla: Escuela de Estudios Hispano-Americanos de Sevilla, 1980), 236. In chapter 6 on the royal treasury, the author discusses the subsidy sent to the colony and the taxes raised within it. Fully 79 percent of Santo Domingo's funds came from outside of Spain in the second half of the eighteenth century.

31. Lester D. Langley, *The Americas in the Age of Revolution, 1750-1850* (New Haven: Yale University Press, 1996); Robert R. Palmer, *The Age of Democratic Revolution: A Political History of Europe and America, 1760-1820*, 2 vols. (Princeton, N.J.: Princeton University Press, 1959-61); Immanuel Wallerstein, *Geopolitics and Geoculture: Essays and the Changing World-System* (Cambridge, U.K.: Cambridge University Press, 1991).

military duties.

Aside from family concerns, Cuba had changed noticeably during his recent absences as each passing decade in the late eighteenth century witnessed its agricultural economy increase appreciably. Production on rural estates typically rose annually as landowners invested steadily in sugarcane, coffee, tobacco, cacao, and other plantation and farm commodities. In doing so, the crops devoured the pristine countryside. At the same time, African slaves arrived in unprecedented numbers to toil in agriculture and numerous other occupations. Moreover, they added to the island's human mix. As Havana's population rose, its residents contributed to transforming the city into a more luxurious cosmopolitan metropolis. No other city on the island approached Havana in size, diversity, and importance. It was the heart of nearly everything of consequence—political, military, economic, social, and religious. In its own world view, Havana functioned as the gateway to the Spanish American colonies and played a significant role in the empire. Nevertheless, the Spanish government controlled the island and determined its economic policies, factors crucial to the wellbeing of a slender group of elite planters and their mercantilist cohorts, who were determined to bolster their wealth and achieve greater political and economic power for themselves.[32]As a professional army officer, Casa-Calvo was not as intimately involved as were other major planters, but because of family connections, he was one of them as were his two brothers who devoted themselves to promoting Cuban agriculture, especially the production of sugarcane that dominated the life of his younger sibling Nicolás.

As a late starter in the expansion of tropical agricultural commodities for export, Cuba initially could not compete with the successful Caribbean islands that had received greater incentives and began their development nearly a century earlier. In this way, they came to dominate the established markets, especially those with the greatest consumption in Europe. The French colony of Saint-Domingue ranked as the most productive, wealthy, and booming agricultural possession in the Caribbean despite it being only one-quarter the size of Cuba. By about

32. Pérez, *Cuba*, 57-62.

1789, in the estimates of a Cuban traveler who gathered information on Saint-Domingue, it had a population of 38,000 to 40,000 whites, 28,000 free people of color (of whom two-thirds were mulattoes and one-third blacks), and 452,000 slaves. The colony had 793 sugar mills, 3,107 coffee farms, 3,150 indigo estates, 799 cotton plantations, and 69 cacao-producing landholdings. These properties annually yielded, among other things: 71,000 tons of sugar; above 30,000 tons of coffee beans, which represented approximately 60 percent of the world's output; more than 415 tons of dyestuffs; and 2,800 tons of cotton. Slaves, many of them recent African imports, outnumbered the colony's white population by more than ten to one, and they performed the arduous labor that produced virtually all these commodities. Saint-Domingue's enslaved workers exceeded those in Cuba by several times.[33]

Despite Cuba's relative backwardness in commercial agriculture, a gradual development had long persisted in the seventeenth and early eighteenth centuries. Many of the popular tropical crops had been grown on the island almost since the Europeans arrived, but a restricted African labor supply and insufficient capital had inhibited growth. Spanish trade policies that included high taxes and few incentives hampered production. Some crafty planters circumvented restrictions through smuggling from isolated ports, especially on the east coast that was near both Saint-Domingue and Jamaica. The British occupation of Havana in 1762 stimulated further expansion, and the Spanish crown, accustomed to Bourbon mercantilism, only gradually adjusted to the rewards of freer trade with the adoption of more favorable policies in the 1760s, 1770s, and particularly the 1780s. Chief among them was the decision in the last decade to open the colonies to the massive importation of African slaves, and the new labor supply enabled agriculture to develop dramatically.[34]

Of course, the insurrection in Saint-Domingue in 1791 and its inability to continue the intense production of commercial crops created

33. María Dolores González-Ripoll, *El rumor de Haití en Cuba: temor, raza y rebeldía, 1789-1844* (Madrid: Consejo Superior de Investigaciones Científicas, 2004), 19, 65.

34. Pérez, *Cuba*, 70.

new marketing opportunities for other regions, especially Cuba. Saint-Domingue's agricultural products had stocked numerous overseas markets for decades, and consumer demand for familiar commodities stimulated Cuban landowners to satisfy them through greater production. Refugee French planters from Saint-Domingue brought capital, skilled slaves, and even machinery to Cuba and infused their knowledge of sugar and coffee production among Cubans. Approximately thirty thousand persons relocated to the island, with many of them initially settling around Santiago de Cuba. Between 1790 and 1800, Cuba nearly doubled its export of sugar, from 15,423 to 28,761 tons. Meanwhile, coffee exports zoomed from 7,101 arrobas (each arroba equals 25.36 pounds in weight) in 1792 to 50,000 arrobas in 1804. Four years later, it had almost tripled to 137,148 arrobas. Exports to the United States soared as it consumed increasing quantities of sugar, molasses, rum, and coffee, with the last commodity soon replacing tea as the more popular non-alcoholic national beverage. The trade converted the United States into Cuba's leading commercial partner. Cubans, meanwhile, imported from the United States textiles, foodstuffs that did not grow in tropical climates, manufactured goods, machinery, and slaves. The decline in Saint-Domingue's production also drove up prices of their former exports and benefited the new growers. Sugar plantations and mills sprang up in diverse locations throughout Cuba; originally, sugar mills relied on rivers to transport the weighty refined commodity to Havana or to other ports from where it was exported abroad. As plantations moved into the interior, roads gradually replaced trails and improved communications.[35]

Payment for this form of internal developments, however, posed a serious question to planters. In 1795, Nicolás Calvo de la Puerta y O'Farrill, Sebastian's brother, penned his tract, "Memoir on the measures that should be adopted so Havana obtains its necessary roads." In it he favored applying church funds to the construction of roads since they would benefit everyone in society. The church and crown, however, delayed consideration of such a bold measure. In the end, the

35. Ibid., 71-4, 77.

sugar planters reduced the *diezmo* or tax they paid to the church on the agricultural crops they produced. Planters avidly sought to maximize their income and minimize the levies they paid.[36]

Sugar was the impetus that sparked the further development of Cuba's export economy and favored the landed elite. Francisco Arango, Pedro Pablo O'Reilly (the second Conde O'Reilly), Nicolás Calvo de la Puerta y O'Farrill, José Agustín Caballero, Antonio del Valle Hernández, and Joaquín Beltrán de Santa Cruz (Conde de Jaruco) numbered among the Cubans who ardently advocated expansion of sugar production. To facilitate its advancement, the privileged class demanded that the government reduce tariffs, import machinery for sugar mills, guarantee a plentiful African labor force, and find more markets for the sale of their sugar.[37]

The introduction of African workers was a salient factor in Cuba's agricultural growth. Since the colony's founding in 1512 until 1763, an estimated sixty thousand slaves had entered it. From 1740 to 1760, the Spanish monopoly company, the Real Companía Mercantil de la Habana, sold 4,986 of those slaves on the island. Spain introduced African slaves slowly, which was caused in part by its poor access to slave markets, and this situation persisted even when agricultural production rose. Finally, however, it changed because new laws allowed the introduction of more than fifty thousand Africans between 1764 and 1790. In 1789, the crown issued decrees that liberalized their entry even more, and their arrival quickly expanded sugar production. Since the days of the first Martín Calvo de la Puerta in the colony, Havana had been the principal center of sugar production and export because of its shipping facilities. In the late 1730s, the island produced 2,000 tons of sugar yearly, and it increased to more than 5,500 tons twenty years later, which saturated its limited markets within the Spanish trading sphere. When the British occupied Havana in 1762, they found a fortune in sugar stored in the warehouses along the harbor that was quickly exported, and sales to foreign markets swiftly stimulated

36. Moreno Fraginals, *El ingenio*, 124.

37. González-Ripoll, *El rumor*, 69; Pérez, *Cuba*, 60-70.

greater production. Spanish militarization of the island that began in 1764 was subsidized in part by planters on condition that the crown allowed them further development of export crops. Taxes on exports and imports were used to defray Cuba's rising military expenses. Sugar production, consequently, expanded as did the hectares (2.47 acres per hectare) in production and the slave laborers who worked the lands. Imported British machinery and new mills improved output over the inefficient traditional sugar mills. By the early 1790s, sugar production reached sixteen thousand tons annually. The value of exports and imports also soared. In 1770 they stood at a nominal two million pesos and grew to sixteen and a half million pesos in the 1790s.[38]

With the growth of exports, Cuba's agricultural economy moved in the direction of monoculture since it focused on export crops and diminished other products, especially comestibles. Soon Cubans found themselves importing food. Spanish merchants controlled imports and exports and profited from manipulating the prices of goods that entered and left the island, all of which hurt Cubans. Furthermore, planters without capital often borrowed money from merchant-bankers, many of them Spaniards since financial institutions or banks were unknown in Cuba, to sustain them from one growing season to the next, and they paid usurious interest rates that reached up to 50 percent per annum for the privilege. Planters deeply resented the avaricious Spaniards who reaped unwarranted rewards from Cuban investments, labor, and profits.[39]

Not all planters fell into financial straits, however, and the elite who prospered often applied their earnings to other purposes. Their civic pride contributed to the beautification of Havana with broad avenues, plazas, churches, and public buildings constructed throughout the city. Cubans also expressed their desire to modernize their capital city in other ways. Although Spain founded its first colonial universities in the sixteenth century, Cuba's University of Havana was estab-

38. Pérez, *Cuba*, 60-63; Hubert H.S. Aimes, *A History of Slavery in Cuba, 1518 to 1868* (New York: Knickerbocker Press, 1907), 23-24; Kuethe, *Cuba*, 54.

39. Pérez, *Cuba*, 62

lished only in 1728. Soon after other institutions opened their doors such as the Colegio de San Francisco de Sales and the seminaries of San Basilio, San Ambrosio, and San Carlos. Education in these institutions often focused attention on the island, and as time progressed they increasingly drew awareness to Cuba's differences with Spain. The first printing press began operations in 1723, and in the course of the eighteenth century a theater, El Principal, appeared to the delight of Havana audiences. Construction of the Cathedral of Havana started in 1748 and continued for many years. The church's designation as a cathedral signified the presence of a bishop or head cleric on the island, the first in Cuba's history. The bishop established a seminary for the training and ordination of priests who were expected to serve the diocese. Planter affluence enabled the island's elite to construct more elaborate urban mansions since they spent lengthy periods of the year in the city besides living on their rural estates, which usually occurred during the busy harvest season.[40]

Thus in significant ways, Cuba in the second half of the eighteenth century experienced never before seen changes. These formative developments were occurring when Casa-Calvo arrived home in July 1789. By October 31 of that year, the crown knew that he had reached Havana with 450 soldiers to finish the creation of the new regiment. While the royal order described the soldiers as belonging to "his command," he knew that his tenure in the formation of the regiment was temporary. Moreover, the crown would soon appoint a commander (a colonel) for the unit. As always, influential supporters could bolster his appeal for appointment to head the regiment, and he quickly gained the favor of interim Capt. Gen. Domingo Cabello y Robles among others. On October 6, 1789, Casa-Calvo began submitting petitions to the crown in an attempt to gain the rank and position he believed he had rightfully earned.[41]

Nevertheless, he was not alone in submitting a petition as several

40. Ibid., 68.

41. To the interim captain general of Cuba (Domingo Cabello), Madrid, February 18, 1790, AGS, GM, leg. 6871.

officers in both Spain and Cuba also applied to head the new regiment. Noteworthy among them was Lt. Col. Felipe Carlos del Cotarro, the lieutenant colonel of the Infantry Regiment of Granada, who had thirty-two years of military service, thirteen spent as sergeant-major of the Cantabrian Infantry Regiment and ten as the lieutenant colonel of the Granada regiment. He had participated in the 1762 war against Portugal and fought in several victorious battles; he was on O'Reilly's failed expedition to Algiers in 1775; and he put in more than five years of garrison duty at Oran on the North African coast. His experience acquired over many years earned him the coveted position of colonel of the Fixed Infantry Regiment of Cuba on February 11, 1790.[42] On that same day, the crown conferred the rank of brevet colonel on both Cotarro and Casa-Calvo, the latter for his service in the regiment's formation and perhaps to placate him because officials in Madrid knew he would be disappointed in not receiving command of the unit.[43] On March 30, 1789, Cotarro, who was in Cádiz, informed the king that he would soon embark on the war frigate *Nuestra Señora del Rosario* with his servant Dimas Lozano. He traveled far more simply than his erstwhile rival had. Cotarro's ship sailed about May, a year after Casa-Calvo had departed for Havana.[44]

Despite not becoming head of the regiment, Casa-Calvo contin-

42. Petition of Felipe Carlos del Cotarro to king, Madrid, February 3, 1790, AGS, GM, leg. 6881.

43. Memorandum without names or place, but probably written in early February 1790, AGS, GM, leg. 6843. Printed patents of promotion to brevet colonel for both Cotarro and Casa-Calvo are in AGS, GM, leg. 6881.

44. Cotarro petition to the king, Madrid, March 30, 1790; statement by Antonio Valdés, Madrid, April 1, 1790; both in AGS, GM, leg. 6881. Francisco Montalvo, commander of the third battalion of the Fixed Regiment of Havana, wanted to be colonel of the Cuban infantry regiment. He had twenty-four years of service, greater wartime experience, and had recruited and outfitted soldiers for service in the Spanish colonies for seven years. He was the sub-inspector of recruits. His and his successor's appointments would not cost the crown additional expense. An inconvenience that the ministry of war suggested, however, was that Casa-Calvo and Montalvo were Cubans, and it possibly would impede them from rendering their best service because of family connections and other ties on the island.

ued as its lieutenant colonel or second-in-command. His lesser experience, seniority, and age had figured prominently in being denied the prestigious office he desired.[45] His failure to achieve the post profoundly disappointed him inasmuch as he had toiled for several years laying the regiment's foundations in manpower and materiel; lent the crown a significant sum of money to do so; spent a year in Cuba finishing its organization; and was personally acquainted with its officers and soldiers. He considered the regiment to be his creation, and he felt abused when the government bypassed him and assigned it to an outsider totally ignorant with the unit and its personnel.[46]

Nevertheless, Casa-Calvo had the consolation of a post in his hometown of Havana. Over the next three years, as the second-ranking officer in his regiment, he commanded the first battalion. The post often constituted a training ground for individuals who eventually assumed charge of a regiment, and although he did not realize it earlier, it was instruction he lacked. Recruiting soldiers and managing a battalion, not to mention a regiment, were different tasks in the unit's operations.

In 1792, as the threat from insurgent French Saint-Domingue developed, Cuba began taking defensive measures. The Fixed Infantry Regiment of Cuba received orders to send a battalion of soldiers to reinforce the understrength battalion from the Fixed Havana Infantry Regiment stationed at Santiago de Cuba. Casa-Calvo took the second battalion to the city nestled near the southeastern corner of the island. Naval transports carried him and his several hundred troops around Cuba to their destination since the island's interior roads ranged from primitive to non-existent. Santiago de Cuba was also the nearest major Cuban port to Santo Domingo, where the battalion would probably be sent. First, however, that colony's governor needed to summon

45. Royal order to the interim captain general of Cuba (Domingo Cabello), Madrid, February 18, 1790, with two other royal orders attached announcing the promotions to the interested parties, all in AGS, GM, leg. 6881.

46. Casa-Calvo's disappointment can be seen through the many petitions he soon submitted.

them if enemy troops invaded Santo Domingo.[47] Refugees from the brutal fighting in the French colony were already streaming into Santo Domingo, and some of them continued on to Cuba, the United States, and Europe. On August 31, 1792, upon the death of Colonel Cotarro, Captain General Las Casas commanded Casa-Calvo to return to Havana to take charge of the first battalion. The summons was only to become the acting head of the regiment because Casa-Calvo as second in command did not rise automatically to the post of colonel of the regiment; instead, the king through the ministry of war usually appointed the top official in army regiments. Casa-Calvo, however, hesitated to return to Havana. On September 15, he indicated his preference to remain in Santiago de Cuba since orders might soon arrive to take the battalion to Santo Domingo to reinforce it as tensions mounted. Furthermore he argued, if he returned to Havana the second battalion would be left leaderless and demoralized in case it sailed to Santo Domingo, by which he implied that he had no subordinate capable of leading the unit. The captain general, he suggested, could oversee the first battalion in Havana. Casa-Calvo wanted to remain with his command until such time as the king assigned a new colonel to head the regiment. Las Casas, however, frowned on Casa-Calvo's absence because he had a similar problem; Cotarro's death had placed the first battalion of the Cuba regiment in the hands of a captain of questionable behavior since he was then under arrest. Nevertheless, Las Casas admired Casa-Calvo's honor, military fervor, zeal, and his earlier willingness to embark with the second battalion for Santiago de Cuba despite the recent tragedy that had shaken his personal life.

The year 1792 was the worst Sebastián had thus far experienced. In the midst of all the developments occurring in Cuba and the international turmoil, his wife came down with a mortal illness. There is no description of it, but it may have been a mosquito-borne disease that caused her demise. How rapidly the infirmity overwhelmed María Lu-

47. The governor of Santo Domingo was sometimes referred to as president because he was the president of the Audiencia de Santo Domingo. Audiencias were the highest courts in the Spanish colonies. Legal matters appealed from the audiencia went to the ministry of justice in Spain for a final resolution.

isa's immune defenses or why she was the only family member stricken by the deadly affliction are unknown. Her death on March 26, 1792, at age twenty-seven, left behind a grieving husband and four inconsolable children. Although married for eleven years, Casa-Calvo had spent more than half those years away from his wife, in Spain and on other military assignments. It was irreplaceable time. Why he insisted on departing with a battalion of soldiers to Santiago de Cuba soon after her death can only be conjectured. No doubt he felt that it was his duty as the second-ranking officer in the regiment to lead a battalion of soldiers as the king had ordered. In addition, he must have yearned to remove his recent misfortune from his mind until the grieving abated; quite possibly it never ended for him. Nevertheless, he left behind his young children. Perhaps the soothing presence of relatives of all ages, headed by Casa-Calvo's own mother Catalina, would help the children recover faster than their father. It was not callousness that drove him from Havana but his helplessness in the face of a calamitous disaster. In placing duty to royal service first, he sought solace for the heartbreaking loss of his beloved María Luisa.[48]

Garrison duty in Santiago de Cuba that was far removed from Havana initially dulled Casa-Calvo's thinking. His first responsibility was to keep his battalion combat ready if and when it sailed to defend Santo Domingo against whatever forces—royalists, republicans, *grand blancs*, free men of color, or slaves who were all battling for their political objectives and control of Saint-Domingue, sometimes singularly and at other times with one or two factions. Residents of Santo Domingo feared that these hostile forces might burst into their peaceful colony. Nevertheless, garrison duty in Santiago de Cuba was repetitious and tedious, and no doubt left the Spanish soldiers wondering when they would sail to the nearby colony and participate in the fighting. While they waited, refugees from Saint-Domingue kept entering Santiago de Cuba with horrifying tales of the brutal fighting, massacres, and devas-

48. Capt. Gen. Luis de Las Casas to Conde del Campo de Alange (Manuel Godoy), no. 487, Havana, October 2, 1792, with Casa-Calvo to Las Casas, Santiago de Cuba, September 15, 1792, both in AGS, GM, leg. 6849.

tation. Then in the spring of 1793, the conflict heated up when Spain, along with the other members of conservative monarchies, sought revenge for the French Republic's executions of King Louis XVI and Queen Marie Antoinette. These kings formed the First Coalition of monarchies determined to overthrow the execrable Republic. Permitting a radical government to execute a king would encourage further mayhem to the established world order of monarchies. News of these astonishing events quickly sped across the Atlantic to Cuba.[49]

That same spring, Casa-Calvo learned from officials in Havana what personally distressed him more than war—the king had chosen Lt. Col. Juan Lleonart to replace the deceased Cotarro as the head of the regiment of Cuba. The appointment of Lleonart, who was an older and more experienced officer, represented another blow to Casa-Calvo's persona, which he took as an affront. Lleonart was the creole son of a Catalonian army officer who served in Cuba. He had become a cadet at age fifteen in 1746 and a sublieutenant around 1754, when he was assigned to Santiago de Cuba. He distinguished himself at the post as a zealous officer by arresting many contrabandists and army deserters. In 1762, probably when the British besieged Havana, he returned to the city to help in its defense. After the war, he served twice at Bayamó, first as lieutenant governor and later as governor. He saw duty again in Santiago de Cuba, where he gradually rose in rank until he commanded the second battalion of the Fixed Infantry Regiment of Havana stationed there. When the position of colonel of the Fixed Infantry Regiment of Cuba fell vacant, the crown selected Lleonart because of his greater experience and lengthier service.[50]

On receiving the devastating news that the government had bypassed him a second time, Casa-Calvo's self-confidence suffered an unforeseen shock. He had expected the king to correct his earlier error

49. Among the many studies on the French Revolution, see Leo Gershoy, *The French Revolution and Napoleon* (New York: Appleton-Century-Crofts, 1964); Crane Brinton, *A Decade of Revolution, 1789-1799* (New York, 1964); and Robert R. Palmer, *The Age of Democratic Revolution: A Political History of Europe and America, 1760-1820*, 2 vols. (Princeton, N.J.: Princeton University Press, 1959-1961).

50. Johnson, *Transformation of Cuba*, 77-79.

and now select him as the regimental colonel. He felt snubbed again because Cuban creoles were beginning to dominate the island's militia establishment. These sons of elite families, who included the offspring of Juan O'Farrill—Casa-Calvo's first cousins—began rising in rank in their units. In fact, the crown seemed to reserve the posts for the highest titled noblemen or the O'Farrills who never sought a noble title despite their wealth.[51] The chief reason for assigning them to these posts was that senior militia officers with their private resources paid for the weapons, uniforms, and other essential equipment used by the common militiamen. Despite Casa-Calvo's service in the regular army and not the militia, he still aspired to equality in rank with them. But it did not happen at this time. His intense disappointment convinced him that he would never command the regiment. He began thinking of going to Spain once more, where he had achieved success earlier, and it again would serve as the path through which he would redress the oversights heaped on him in Cuba.

While in Havana, he resumed writing petitions for his ascent in the regiment. In one of April 15, 1793, Casa-Calvo recounted his thirty years of military duty that included his wartime experiences and prominent role in the formation of the Fixed Infantry Regiment of Cuba. Despite his service, the crown selected seniority and experience elsewhere in assigning command of the regiment. Casa-Calvo dismally concluded that his rejection closed the door to his advancement in the regiment. His depression soon led to a string of petitions, among them one that solicited command of a regiment in Spain. Lleonart

51. Kuethe, *Cuba*, 118-19. Kuethe uses the example of Antonio José de Beitía, the second Marqués del Real Socorro, to note the rise in rank of a privileged person. Beitía began his military service as a fourteen-year-old cadet in 1765. He became a sublieutenant four years later, a captain in 1773 at age twenty-two, and a lieutenant colonel at age twenty-nine. His promotions passed up other officers with more time in grade, and his service sheet noted, "He has no military experience, nor has he noteworthy love for his profession, yet he is young with good qualities and capable of acquiring all essential attributes (for military leadership)." Despite its critical start, the service sheet ends positively and corroborates the preference given to officers who possessed social status over military knowledge which it assumed "might be earned" with experience.

and the sub-inspector general approved his request, and the captain general endorsed it because of the applicant's recognized merit. Soon afterwards, Casa-Calvo sought employment in the Second Spanish Company of American Gentlemen that constituted a unit in the Royal Corps of Guards in Madrid. The corps served as a personal guard to the king, and service in it was an honor. Furthermore, former guardsmen generally prospered in promotions. Despite a plethora of prestigious endorsements favoring his appointment, the king again denied his petition.[52] Casa-Calvo, however, did not learn this for many months, and meanwhile he continued serving in his regiment.

Earlier, in the spring of 1793, Casa-Calvo returned to Havana. Perhaps news had arrived from Europe that Spain and France were near, or possibly already, at war, and that drew him back to the city. France declared hostilities on March 7, 1793, and Spain responded in kind sixteen days later. News of the conflict reached Havana about mid-May. The new war added to the turmoil that was already enveloping the Caribbean because of the catastrophic upheaval then tearing Saint-Domingue apart. All the neighboring Spanish colonies soon felt the brunt of hostilities. Together with Captain General Las Casas, Casa-Calvo helped determine the military equipment and ships needed to transport the second battalion to Santo Domingo. Once these problems were resolved, Casa-Calvo returned to Santiago de Cuba to prepare his battalion for the move.[53]

Although Spain and Great Britain became allies against republican-controlled Saint-Domingue, these alliances were frequently of a

52. Luis de Las Casas to Conde del Campo de Alange, no. 677, July 8, 1793, with Casa-Calvo's petition attached, both in AGS, GM, leg. 6852. Casa-Calvo had submitted his petition in Havana on April 15, 1793, which Domingo Cabello approved on May 4, 1793, both in ibid.

53. The declaration of war was published in Santo Domingo on May 30, 1793, and it was probably published in Havana several days earlier. David Patrick Geggus, "Slavery, War, and Revolution in the Greater Caribbean, 1789-1815," 1-50, in *A Turbulent Time: The French Revolution and the Greater Caribbean*, eds. David Barry Gaspar and David Patrick Geggus (Bloomington and Indianapolis: Indiana University Press, 1997).

temporary nature. On receiving Santo Domingo's call for military assistance, Las Casas responded by sending two battalions, one each from the Havana and Cuba regiments. The soldiers sailed on the frigates *Gloria* and *Ceres* and reached the city of Santo Domingo on July 5, 1793. Because it was wartime service, no one knew what the future held.[54]

Casa-Calvo fully recognized that a successful military career required duty in an active theater of war where he could demonstrate his ability to command as well as his initiative and courage. Coming under enemy fire would add luster to his persona and probably speed promotions and favorable future assignments, especially if he emerged victorious in battle. For now, his greatest aspiration was to be the commanding officer of his regiment. While he had not yet achieved that distinction, he commanded the regiment's second battalion, which he led to war-threatened Santo Domingo. And although the battalion was below—possibly even much below—full strength due to attrition caused by discharges and tropical deaths among its rank and file, he was assigned to a region where combat appeared certain to come.

54. Fernando Carrera Montero, *Las complejas relaciones de España con La Española: El Caribe hispano frente a Santo Domingo y Saint Domingue, 1789-1803* (Santo Domingo: Fundación García Arévalo, 2004), 62n, 128.

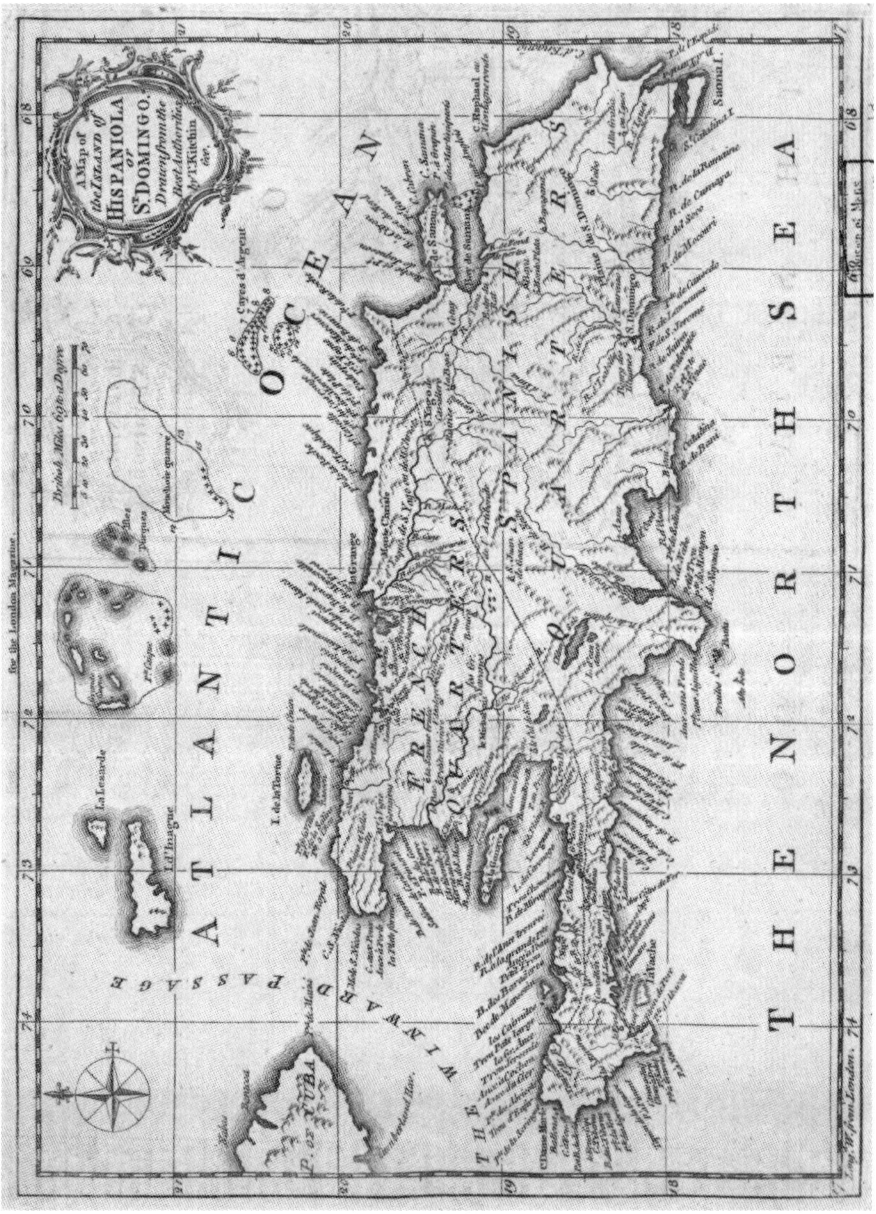

A map of the island of Hispaniola or St. Domingo
Courtesy of the Library of Congress

5
Santo Domingo and Saint-Domingue

Casa-Calvo's return to Cuba in 1789 coincided with the eruption of a new chapter in the political upheaval and warfare that would consume the Atlantic world for several decades. The French Revolution initiated another extensive world-wide conflict. Nevertheless, the new war did not affect Casa-Calvo in the beginning as he spent two relatively quiet years in Havana before the smoldering unrest detonated. It began in France in 1789 and soon repercussions spread to the tinderbox that was French Saint-Domingue (later called Haiti), and the black uprising sent shock waves roiling through the slave colonies of the Caribbean, especially Santo Domingo, with which Saint-Domingue shared the island of Hispaniola. Two years later upon the French revolutionaries' execution of King Louis XVI, conservative European monarchies, including Spain's, banded together in the First Coalition to destroy the French Republic. The war, however, was not confined to Europe, and to protect the lightly populated and militarily deficient colony of Santo Domingo, the Cuban captain general dispatched military reinforcements there. Among them was Casa-Calvo who sailed with his infantry battalion in mid-1793. Hostilities on Hispaniola involved him more intimately than the past war against Great Britain had, and this time he gained prominent commands and promotions.

Despite being Spain's oldest New World dependency, Santo Domingo had sunk into near oblivion. In the two centuries following the exodus of most of its inhabitants to mainland colonies in search of legendary wealth, its population had remained miniscule and the colony undeveloped. Only in the eighteenth century did the neglected possession again display signs of renewal.[1]

Radicalism brought on by the French Revolution's violent upheaval distressed the conservative European monarchies, portended war, and ignited insurrection in Saint-Domingue in 1791. Power groups among the colony's inhabitants quarreled with decrees emanating from France. The French National Assembly helped in no small measure by granting liberties to some of the colony's underprivileged inhabitants. The *grand blancs* (big whites) who were wealthy merchants, planters, and upper class professionals despised the concessions that favored the *petit blancs* (poor to middle class whites) and lesser racial groups, such as the *gens de couleur libre* (free persons of color); *grand blancs* jealously insisted on monopolizing power. Meanwhile, free mulattoes and blacks, many of them wealthy, educated, and slave owners themselves, stridently sought the social and political equality that whites possessed. On the bottom rung of the social ladder were the numerous bondsmen, many recent arrivals from Africa, who yearned for liberation from the brutal slave regime. Angry that rich whites denied them equality, the free people of color initiated the social upheaval. In Cuba, where the authorities anticipated the conflict, military units underwent more training to defend exposed Santo Domingo against the eruption of hostilities in the adjacent French colony. Spain could not send reinforcements since its peninsular army battled French republicans in the Pyrenees and adjoining lands between 1793 and 1795. As the turmoil in Saint-Domingue escalated, agricultural production plummeted due to armed bands of diverse political and social persuasions ravaging plantations and stealing their products and laborers. Faced with unending mayhem, many planter families abandoned the conflicted colony.[2]

1. On Santo Domingo's early history, see Frank Moya Pons, *The Dominican Republic: A National History* (Princeton, N.J.: Markus Wiener Publishers, 1998), 13-89, and Antonio del Monte y Tejada, *Historia de Santo Domingo*, 4 vols. (Santo Domingo: Imprenta de García Hermanos, 1890-92, hereafter abbreviated as HSD).

2. On events in Saint-Domingue (Haiti), see Carolyn E. Fick, *The Making of Haiti: The Saint Domingue Revolution from Below* (Knoxville: University of Tennessee Press, 1990); and C.L.R. James, *The Black Jacobins: Toussaint L'Ouverture and the San* [*sic*]

Although Spanish Santo Domingo at 18,704 square miles in size was nearly twice as large territorially as French Saint-Domingue's 10,620 square miles, it was a neglected and struggling colony by contemporary Caribbean standards and possessed an economy based principally on livestock. The colony's insignificant population developed gradually through the eighteenth century from 18,410 in 1718, to 30,158 in 1739, to 73,319 in 1769, and to somewhere between 80,000 and 125,000 in 1789, with immigrants from the Canary Islands contributing notably to its growth.[3] Unlike the French possession next door, no overt signs of racial tension between free persons and slaves disturbed its tranquility, possibly because of the colony's milder form of slavery, its fewer inhabitants, and the smaller invested capital and economic drive for wealth.

Upon the revolution's outbreak in France, on September 23, the Spanish government instructed fifty-seven-year-old Capt. Gen. Joaquín García Moreno to watch carefully every stranger who entered his colony from neighboring Saint-Domingue.[4] Its society of nearly half a million slaves who outnumbered free people by the ample margin of ten to one began festering after the radical republican National Assembly in France decreed equal political and judicial rights for all free men regardless of color. When the power-hungry *grand blancs* of

---

Domingo Revolution (New York: Vintage Books, 1963).

3. Moya Pons, in *Dominican Republic*, 88, places the colony's population at eighty thousand in 1789. However, in Moya Pons's essay "The Haitian Revolution in Santo Domingo (1789-1809)," in *Yarbuch für Geschichte: Latainamerikas* 28 (1991): 125-62, he puts its inhabitants as 125,000 in 1789. T. Lothrop Stoddard, in *The French Revolution in San Domingo* [sic] (Boston: Houghton Mifflin, 1914), 6, also listed the inhabitants as 125,000 for 1789.

4. Carrera Montero, *Las complejas relaciones*, 24-28. Otto Schoenrich, in *Santo Domingo, A Country with a Future* (New York: Macmillan, 1918), 28-29, states that the colony's population in 1754 was 14,000 whites, 4,000 free mulattoes, and 17,200 blacks. By 1785, inhabitants had risen to 152,640, of whom 30,000 were slaves. Because warfare induced many people to leave, residents declined to about 104,000 by 1810. William Walton, *Present State of the Spanish Colonies* (London: Longman, et al., 1810), 131. With these figures, Walton, on p. 189, estimated that one-third of the colony's population had departed.

Saint-Domingue refused to ratify the Assembly's privileges, the mulatto Vincent Ogé led an uprising with several hundred free men of color in 1790. Colonial troops easily dispersed them, and Ogé fled with supporters to Santo Domingo, where twenty-six were arrested on November 8. García considered them guilty of insurrection. On December 21, the Audiencia, the colony's highest court, decreed that the prisoners be returned to Saint-Domingue but specified that they not be put to death. Aware of the socio-political upheaval in the neighboring colony, Spanish officialdom in Santo Domingo worried that retention of the prisoners might incite disgruntled inhabitants and rouse lower class aspirations. White authorities in Saint-Domingue, however, ignored the Spanish court's resolution and executed Ogé and members of his band with ample cruelty that was designed to suppress unrest. Nevertheless, devoted partisans kept revolutionary sentiments spreading through word-of-mouth and printed literature.[5]

When in 1791 the repressed masses of Saint-Domingue began their uprisings, Gov. Gen. Philibert François Rouxel Blanchelande requested troops from García. He refused, using excuses that ranged from his few soldiers and the rainy season to his wish to avoid entanglement in matters that solely concerned the French colony. By year's end, insurgency had engulfed Saint-Domingue. Because Spanish vessels took weapons to Santo Domingo, stories alleged that the arms found their way to slave bands, and they attributed responsibility to García, accusations he heatedly denied. More realistically, thefts of plantation products enabled slaves to buy guns for sustaining their rebellion, and Santo Domingo's sparse troops were insufficient to prevent sales in secluded regions. The gun-running trade led to efforts to restrain foreign ships loaded with weapons from traveling to Saint-Domingue. Venturesome American vessels, all the same, skillfully maneuvered into out-of-the-way inlets and bays to sell the rebels armaments in return for sugar, cacao, coffee, and more; the ships also spirited refugees to safety in the United States. The arrival of white troops from France to quell the unrest sometimes produced pillaging or worse, such as the November

5. Carrera Montero, *Las complejas relaciones*, 29-34; Schoenrich, *Santo Domingo*, 29.

21 massacre of more than 250 persons in Port-au-Prince by soldiers of the Artois regiment.[6]

As early as May 1791, Spain dispatched the first reinforcements, elements from the Regiment of Cantabria stationed in Puerto Rico, to protect Santo Domingo. Within the colony, García called up the Urban Militia to allow the Santo Domingo Fixed Infantry Battalion to guard roads leading into the province, particularly along the west-central frontier where conflict often flared up near San Gabriel de Las Caobas and on the northern coast at Montecristi. Spanish policy endeavored to protect whites from slave raids; provide food, arms, and munitions to needy persons; and prevent the insurrection from affecting Santo Domingo.[7] At that time the British, who sought additional colonial territory and anticipated the spread of revolutionary unrest, sent troops to the Caribbean, where they placed six thousand regular soldiers and fourteen thousand militiamen in Jamaica alone.[8]

Capt. Gen. Luis de Las Casas of Cuba and Gov. Juan Vaillant of Santiago de Cuba both realized that the slave turmoil in Saint-Domingue threatened the stability of the entire Caribbean. Calming the colony required controlling all its restless groups. From his Cuban vantage post near Hispaniola, Vaillant often received pleas for help from Santo Domingo. Following orders from Madrid, he supported French royalists in their bid to dominate the colony because their views suited Spanish monarchical objectives more closely than those of the *grand blancs*, free mulattoes, or slaves. It led Vaillant to send foodstuffs, especially cattle, to royalist soldiers during 1791 and 1792. However, he stopped shipments by early 1793 as Republican France and monarchical Spain edged toward war. Vaillant also settled French refugees in

6. Carrera Montero, *Las complejas relaciones*, 41n; Mary Treudley, "The United States and Santo Domingo, 1789-1866," in *The Journal of Race Development* 7, no. 1 (July 1916): 112. Like many writers of her time, Treudley used Santo Domingo but meant Saint-Domingue.

7. Carrera Montero, *Las complejas relaciones*, 42.

8. Ibid., 43n.

the Santiago de Cuba region.[9] As French militiamen fought to quash the defiant slaves, the latter retreated into the mountains or to Santo Domingo; some slaves even asked Capt. Gen. Joaquín García to mediate peace for them with French whites. Two black generals, Jean François and Toussaint Louverture, requested only pardons for putting down their arms. Fugitive slaves on the Santo Domingo border worried Spanish officials. Perhaps they did not receive the pardons they sought because in March 1792, Jean François and Jorge Biassou of the "brigands," a term Spaniards used for slave warriors, sought asylum along the frontier and heaped blame on Ogé for starting the uprising. Andrés Heredia, military commandant at Dajabón on the border with Saint-Domingue, believed in neutrality to avoid bloodshed. If blacks violated the peace, whites from Santo Domingo would join the French against them. Blanchelande offered to forgive the rebel slaves if they surrendered their arms and returned to servitude. It happened after a violent era, and many blacks who went back to their plantations soon suffered abuse and even death from irate masters. The disorders perplexed García on what to do, and he used the royal decrees of April 15 and 17 to solicit troops, food, and supplies from Santiago de Cuba in July 1792. The captain general of Cuba, however, refused to send soldiers until the king declared war. García waited until April 20, 1793, after war had erupted, before he asked again.[10]

Spain had moved gradually toward hostilities in both Europe and Hispaniola. In Santo Domingo, García began to modify his attitude toward the French when the commander of Cap-Français, Baron de Cambefort, asked him to round up the rebels hiding inside Spanish territory. García declined to do so because a royal order of June 25, 1792, granted French whites shelter on Spanish soil but far removed from the frontier. Upon the French Republic's proclamation of Sep-

9. Ibid., 44-46.

10. Ibid., 46-50; Fick, *Making of Haiti*, 155-56. Heredia, who came from Puerto Rico, soon died and Col. Gaspar de Casasola replaced him. García to Luis María Quero, Santo Domingo City, July 29, 1793, *HSD*, 3: 71. Jane G. Landers writes extensively on Biassou in her study, *Atlantic Creoles in the Age of Revolutions* (Cambridge, Mass.: Harvard University Press, 2010).

tember 21, 1792, and the execution of Louis XVI on January 21, 1793, whites in Saint-Domingue divided into warring factions as royalists, republicans, and self-serving colonials. Furthermore, free blacks and slaves followed different political factions. As early as August 1792, Spain began to consider fighting France, and it became a certainty after the revolutionaries executed the French king. García intended to enlist the black rebels when war came, and he acted upon learning about the declaration of hostilities.[11]

García proclaimed the war in Santo Domingo on May 30, 1793. The Spanish government advised Dominican officials to enlist the help of black military leaders in the French colony because they identified with monarchical government. French slave owners, in particular, welcomed the war since they considered themselves the chief beneficiaries of the conflict. In addition, in May 1793, Spain and Great Britain united in an offensive-defensive alliance that aimed to destroy Saint-Domingue's republican forces and split the colony between them. The Spaniards in Cuba now diverted their cattle shipments to British soldiers who had seized enclaves on the French colony's southern and western coasts.[12]

Légér Félicité Sonthonax, the most active of the three republican commissioners who arrived in Saint-Domingue in 1792, worked to suppress the colony's insurgency. In August 1793, he tried to persuade rebels and former slaves to forsake the Spaniards, with guarantees of freedom to all who embraced the republican tricolors. In contrast, García advised his subordinates to treat black generals respectfully so as not to alienate them. While the republican commissioners did not initially subvert the fidelity of Spain's black troops or their generals Jean François, Biassou, and Louverture, suspicious Spaniards began to question their loyalty. What helped the French commissioners regain the black warriors was the National Convention's decision on February 4, 1794, to ratify the freedom first granted them in the colony in 1793.

11. Carrera Montero, *Las complejas relaciones*, 53.

12. Bonnaud to the commanders of the Spanish and English forces, Bayajá, October 7, 1793, in *HSD*, 3: 113; Fick, *Making of Haiti*, 160.

The emancipation of slaves began in Saint-Domingue to recover the services of Africans who were fighting for Spain. The strategy worked inasmuch as a number of the military leaders soon deserted the Spaniards.[13]

As already noted, upon learning of the declaration of war, Captain General Las Casas of Cuba prepared an expedition to reinforce Santo Domingo. Col. Matías de Armona, a Spaniard, led it, with Col. Juan Gemir y Lleonart acting as second-in-command. Other officers included Col. Antonio María de la Torre and Capt. Miguel Ortiz de Zarate. Two infantry battalions from Cuba initially entered the colony in early July 1793. Lleonart, as the colonel of the Fixed Infantry Regiment of Cuba, directly commanded the second battalion of the Fixed Infantry Regiment of Havana, and Casa-Calvo acted as his second-in-command with charge of the second battalion of the Cuba regiment. Casa-Calvo spent his first months in and around the city of Santo Domingo, possibly waiting for García to determine the moment to launch a major offensive against Saint-Domingue. Spanish objectives had switched from defending Santo Domingo to conquering the French colony in alliance with Great Britain. While Casa-Calvo waited, he met García, and the two developed a close friendship. García's proclivity for favoring officers who accepted his style of command—unfortunately, he never explained it—helped, and Casa-Calvo dutifully did. Because Cuban soldiers arrived during the summer, rains, floods, and mud deterred an immediate attack. Some time in the late summer, possibly as the precipitation tapered off, black troops allied to Spain initiated action that went beyond border skirmishes to seizing territory inside Saint-Domingue.[14]

13. Carrera Montero, *Las complejas relaciones*, 48-70; Moya Pons, *Dominican Republic*, 95-96.

14. Casa-Calvo kept his military papers and perhaps other letters, all of which have now disappeared. However, del Monte y Tejada, in his book, *HSD*, 3: 159, states that he made copies of the papers relative to Santo Domingo when Casa-Calvo was the commanding general of the Northern Frontier in the war against Saint-Domingue. This was done through the generosity of the general's younger son Ignacio Calvo (de la Puerta). Army officers generally kept the originals of military papers important to

Spain and France in the past had fought over the *Plaine du Nord*, a productive agricultural zone in the northeast corner of Saint-Domingue. Spain eventually lost it in the 1777 Treaty of Aranjuez that laid out the boundary between the two colonies. Slaves inhabiting that region rebelled in large numbers in 1791, and it enabled Spain to enlist the support of various black leaders. Their assistance provided Spanish forces with the possibility of dominating the plain. Black insurgents acquainted with the terrain led assaults into French-held lands while Spanish soldiers followed up and occupied the newly-won areas. The Spaniards sought to minimize casualties caused by virulent tropical diseases such as yellow fever and malaria through the use of black auxiliaries.[15]

While the Spaniards welcomed the black warriors, controlling them presented a dilemma because they lacked discipline and frequently brawled with white soldiers. Reinforcements occasionally arrived from Cuba, Puerto Rico, Mexico, and Venezuela, but they were never enough. Several black generals, who initially swore loyalty to the French crown, joined the Spanish army against the republicans and retained command of their own officers and men. Jean François alone possessed an army of 6,647 men in June 1793. Black auxiliaries boosted Spanish forces in the colony to approximately ten thousand. Nevertheless, treasury officials deplored their incessant demands and the costs they imposed on Spain's meager funds.[16]

Casa-Calvo's movements in the second half of 1793 are sketchy, and the only certain fact was his journey to northwest Santo Domingo. He traveled by ship with a large contingent of soldiers. It was a lively time inasmuch as the Spaniards and their African troops were winning

---

their careers. Casa-Calvo's papers provide a valuable insight into his activities on the island of Hispaniola.

15. While it is well known that yellow fever and malaria ravaged French troops in Saint-Domingue, Spanish soldiers also suffered from these diseases. Moya, *Dominican Republic*, 98, 109. In ibid., 95-96, Moya, however, devotes scant attention to Spanish military participation and their casualties in the war in Hispaniola.

16. Bonnaud to the commanders of the Spanish and English forces, Bayajá, October 7, 1793, in *HSD*, 3: 113; Fick, *Making of Haiti*, 160.

a string of victories inside Saint-Domingue late that summer and fall. With territory falling into Spanish hands, for a brief time it appeared possible they would dominate a significant part of the French colony. Meanwhile, British soldiers from Jamaica already staked out claims on the coastal regions of south and west Saint-Domingue.[17]

Spanish policy aimed to seize as much of Saint-Domingue's northern coast as possible, including the formidable bastion of Cap-Français (in keeping with traditional usage when the Spaniards owned both parts of the island, they continued to call it by its old name of Guárico), the largest city on the north coast. On July 6, the day reinforcements from Cuba arrived, García was overjoyed. He now had the forces he needed to attack Bayajá on the north coast. Nevertheless, he had to wait for several months, no doubt because of the rainy season and time needed to prepare ships, troops, and supplies. He attempted to enlist as many Dominicans as he could for the enterprise. The attack on eastern Saint-Domingue preceded his goal of winning a post on the north coast. In December 1793, after Spanish troops seized lands in the interior of Saint-Domingue, they attacked the city of Bayajá, about twenty-five miles from the Spanish border. Casa-Calvo had sailed with Gabriel de Aristizábal's armada that transported soldiers from Santo Domingo City; they landed at a safe location on the north coast and moved to blockade the city from the rear. With Bayajá isolated, the French defenders capitulated on January 29, 1794. The victors seized 1,031 soldiers, forty cannons of various calibers, and a vast quantity of small arms and munitions.[18] Casa-Calvo was listed as second-in-command of the troops that took the Castle de la Boca, an artillery installation that overlooked the bay. Unfortunately, other details of that victory

17. *HSD*, 3: 139; Joaquín Cabrera to Gomos, November 6, 1793, ibid., 3: 138.

18. Aristizábal to Joaquín del Saso, on board the vessel *San Ramón* in the Bay of Fort Delfín, January 29, 1794, ibid., 4: 180-81; García to Luis Quero, Santo Domingo, July 3, 1793, ibid., 3: 56-57; Sevilla Soler, *Santo Domingo*, 391. See also David Geggus, "The Major Port Towns of Saint Domingue in the Later Eighteenth Century," 87-116 in *Atlantic Port Cities: Economy, Culture, and Society in the Atlantic World, 1650-1850*, eds. Franklin W. Knight and Peggy K. Liss (Knoxville: University of Tennessee Press).

are missing. Nevertheless, the seizure of Bayajá represented a major triumph for Spanish arms. Captain General García learned of the capture on arriving at Dajabón, a town south of Bayajá, and he journeyed north to inspect the impressive gains Spanish troops and their black cohorts had garnered.[19]

Once in the city, García organized the Spanish forces. On February 5, 1794, he ordered an inventory taken of the goods found in Bayajá's warehouses. By his decree, the leading officials assigned a fourth part of the goods for the king, 5 percent more than the traditional "royal fifth" reserved in earlier days. Of the rest, they allotted half to the officers and sailors of the royal fleet, and the other half to the soldiers and officers who occupied the captured forts. That day officials inventoried only a portion of the goods, mostly clothing, and placed their value at 5,452 pesos. They excluded the weapons and other wearing apparel found in the warehouses.[20] In time, Spanish ships brought more war materiel that filled the warehouses, and these supplies soon caught the attention of the many destitute black warriors in the immediate area.

Encouraged by triumphs over the enemy, García contemplated establishing his headquarters in the battle zone to participate in what he believed would be the last military action in that region. It appeared easy to do because Bayajá's capture furnished the Spaniards with a secure harbor on the north coast. From there they momentarily staged assaults along the coastline, aimed at capturing Cap-Français. Victory, at least briefly, seemed at hand.[21]

Following Bayajá's surrender, García described glowingly his successes to the crown and included his protégé Casa-Calvo in a prominent way. García gave him and his battalion interim charge of Bayajá,

19. Sevilla Soler, *Santo Domingo*, 390-91.

20. "Inventory," February 5, 1794, *HSD*, 3: 182-83.

21. Sevilla Soler, *Santo Domingo*, 392. Johnson, in *Social Transformation*, 156, describes Joaquín García as a "broken man" because of territorial losses to the enemy and assumed that he remained in the war zone for many months. It was not until May 1794 that Louverture deserted the Spaniards and began recovering lost French territory. Bayajá, however, stayed in Spanish hands until its surrender to the French in mid-1796.

and the captain general went farther on February 4, 1794, when he appointed him the leading officer of the Spanish Army of Operations on the north coast. Rewards from the Spanish court soon followed. The king approved Casa-Calvo's interim appointment at Bayajá and, in April, named the forty-two-year-old a brigadier general for his role in the Spanish successes. With the promotion, he jumped from brevet colonel, a rank he had held for four years, to brigadier general. The war delayed the travel of his patent of promotion, but once he received it he officially took charge of Spanish forces in the north with his new rank on July 31. However, it was not until eight years later, on July 14, 1802, that he became a true "coronel vivo," or full colonel and head of a regiment. At that time, he received command of the Fixed Infantry Regiment of Havana.[22] Casa-Calvo's participation in the momentous events of 1794 should have delighted him, but that appears untrue.

At the end of 1793 and early in 1794, he persisted in requests for transfer, and he did so even after the Spanish military victories. His petitions went to the Cuban captain general to endorse and forward to the king. Above all, Casa-Calvo wanted command of a regiment in Spain since he resignedly determined that advancement in his Cuban unit appeared unlikely inasmuch as he had been passed over twice. Now a widower, his army career took priority in his life because at that moment his ties to Cuba had weakened considerably. Excluding his lands and income from them, his children remained his only significant connection to the island, and he likely expected his offspring to accompany him to the Iberian Peninsula. Although he had agricultural properties, he was often an absentee owner and mainly sought the income they generated. Unaware of the honors and rewards that were coming his way, he believed a posting in Spain would bolster his career since peninsular army officers generally enjoyed greater opportunities at promotion than their colonial counterparts serving in obscure corners of the empire. The petitions expressed his discontent with his slow progress in ascending the army's ranks. But after submitting his

22. Casa-Calvo service sheet of 1805, AGM, ES.

requests, he could only wait for a favorable royal decision.[23] His cousin Gonzalo O'Farrill, who likely was close to Sebastián, possibly had encouraged him to seek a transfer to Spain, where he could advise and guide his cousin's career.

Among the posts Casa-Calvo solicited in 1794 was that of *alférez* (commander) of the New American Company in the Corps of Royal Guards. In Spain the petition went to the first secretary (minister) of state, the Duque de la Alcudia, Manuel Godoy. He acknowledged on May 31 that he had received Calvo de la Puerta's request for an army position in Spain. At Aranjuez on June 9, Alcudia answered indicating that he would attend to the petition at an appropriate time, by which he postponed a decision.[24] Alcudia's judgment represented another rebuff, but Casa-Calvo also recognized that he was in an active theater of war, and it would be difficult for him to leave without disrupting the military chain of command. Nevertheless, probably like his earlier rejections, the reply deeply disappointed him.

Meanwhile, Captain General García kept pressuring Cuba to send more troops and supplies, but shortages plagued all Spanish islands, and he received only a fraction of what he sought. In the fall of 1793, Las Casas dispatched 450 men of the second battalion of the Regiment of New Spain and fifty artillerymen on two warships, the only vessels large enough to accommodate them. That fall, white French royalists surrendered many of the southern and western coastal forts they still controlled to the more powerful Britons. On the north coast royal-

23. See the letters in AGS, GM, leg. 6851, especially, Luis de Las Casas to the Conde del Campo Alange, Havana, February 17, 1794, Duque de la Alcudia (Godoy) to Campo Alange, Aranjuez, May 31, 1794; and Alcudia to Campo Alange, Aranjuez, June 3, 1794.

24. Several letters in this file that begins with the Duque de la Alcudia to the captain general of Cuba, Aranjuez, June 9, 1794, and includes a letter to Alcudia, Aranjuez, May 31, 1794, all in AGS, GM, leg. 6851. On June 3, 1794, it was decided that Casa-Calvo should continue in his present employment until a more convenient time. Ibid. See also Casa-Calvo's service sheet of March 1805, in AGM, ES. On Godoy, see Jacques Chastenet, *Godoy: Master of Spain, 1792-1808*, trans. J. F. Huntington (London: Batchworth Press, 1953).

ists allied with the Spaniards gave up military positions to them. Aristizábal's naval squadron controlled the northern waters around warzones and blockaded enemy bastions that held out. Spanish command of the coastline was essential for domination of the island's interior lands; otherwise, the enemy could sever communications and block critical supplies and reinforcements from reaching troops in the hinterland. As early as February 1794, when another round of slave uprisings occurred, Spanish authorities became acutely aware of their shortage of soldiers. They felt helpless in trying to control the slaves. Lleonart reported that French republicans were then working diligently to draw them to their side.[25]

Amidst these events in 1794 and to avoid having subversives behind their lines, the Spaniards shipped black prisoners to Havana to sell as slaves. Many white officers in the Cuban battalions purchased large numbers of them for use on their plantations at home. Most likely Sebastián Calvo de la Puerta also acquired some for his rural properties or for those of relatives, and no doubt at bargain prices. The authorities in Havana, however, did not welcome the slaves. When Captain General Las Casas learned that captured "revolutionaries" were on the ships in the harbor, he blanched and refused to let them disembark, a decision the Havana city government quickly endorsed. They feared that the slaves, veterans in insurrection and the military arts, might hatch new plots and induce Cuban bondsmen to rebel. While the fighting persisted in Saint-Domingue, Cuba filled up with unrest and rumors of slave uprisings that kept whites unnerved, particularly the rural inhabitants who lived surrounded by Africans. To smother the incendiary talk, Las Casas shipped the captives back to Bayajá. García, too, objected to their return and immediately dispatched them to Puerto Rico, where they were sold without further objection.[26]

While black soldiers served the Spaniards, keeping order among them was difficult. Sometimes black military leaders became fiercely jealous of their more successful associates. One such case involved

25. Lleonart to Casa-Calvo, San Rafael, February 22, 1794, *HSD*, 4: 186.

26. Carrera Montero, *Las complejas relaciones*, 72-73.

Jorge Biassou who envied the military prowess of Toussaint Louverture. Forces of both generals at different times attacked the other, and it disturbed García who sought to avoid internecine quarrels. He attributed their violent behavior to white advisers, notably two Frenchmen and one Spaniard, whom he arrested and deported to Puerto Rico. But the hostility had deeper roots. The two black generals had been at odds in early 1794, and while García patched up the dispute, peace did not long prevail. The real cause seemed to be that Louverture had secretly decided to abandon the Spaniards and join the French republicans.[27]

Louverture made public his new loyalty on May 4. He trusted the Republic as more likely to preserve the freedom of his troops and all former slaves than the other political factions. With his four thousand-man army, he dealt the effectiveness of Spanish forces a distressing blow since he excelled as a military tactician. Before leaving, he slaughtered the Spanish advisers who were training his soldiers. He despised French royalists, with whom Spain sided, because of their repugnant slave policies. Partisans of the French crown had profited from Saint-Domingue's slave-based agricultural prosperity, and they sought the restoration of their former opulence.[28]

Casa-Calvo, however, was not involved in Louverture's defection. As a senior officer, he served at Bayajá, not in the field battling the enemy. His warm friendship with the older García caused the latter to treat him like a son and call him "Chano" and "Chanito." What endeared the captain general to Casa-Calvo, the origin of the nickname, and whether other friends and relatives also used it are unknown. Casa-Calvo probably received his assignment at Bayajá because of his organizational and logistical abilities, skills he had developed in Spain and Cuba when he put together a regiment. García's appointment of Casa-Calvo

27. Lleonart to Casa-Calvo, San Rafael, March 26 and 30, April 17, 1794, *HSD*, 4: 200-201 and 205-6; Sevilla Soler, *Santo Domingo*, 393. See also chapter 2 of Landers, *Atlantic Creoles*, in which she discusses the shifts in loyalty of the African forces fighting in Saint-Domingue.

28. Sevilla Soler, *Santo Domingo*, 393; Moya Pons, *Dominican Republic*, 96. Much has been written about Louverture; see, for example, Ralph Korngold, *Citizen Toussaint* (New York, Hill and Wang, 1965).

as one of the commanding officers was unexpected because several other officers were senior to him. Besides defending Bayajá and its port facilities and fortifications, Casa-Calvo's duties included obtaining and sending fully equipped troops to interior posts. These logistical tasks were fundamental to the army's success in war, but insufficient shipments in virtually all areas hampered his ability to provide soldiers and supplies in the quantities needed.[29]

At the center of the Spanish offensive into Saint-Domingue was Colonel Lleonart, who held command of the southern and western frontiers of Santo Domingo. In May 1794, he was at the border town of San Rafael de la Angostura, where repeated enemy attacks diminished and exhausted his soldiers, and he desperately needed reinforcements. Troops had left Bayajá proceeding on the road south to Dajabón. Lleonart believed that a battalion or two would be sufficient. Those units coming to help him, however, were distressingly weak in manpower.[30] On May 23, blacks attacked Petite Rivière, where they lost 103 dead while the Spanish troops suffered an officer and 14 soldiers killed and 17 wounded. Despite the victory, troop shortages compelled the Spaniards to withdraw. Louverture also hampered communications by seizing portions of several roads. Lleonart recognized that his capability to fight the French and blacks had deteriorated.[31] Late in the month, he advised that he was leaving the next day to inspect outlying posts. He awaited Jean François's return from San Miguel de la Atalaya, where he had gone to talk with Louverture. Jean François told Lleonart that he would fight Louverture, but only with additional manpower. The first battalion of the Cuba regiment, Lleonart's former command, was in San Miguel under Brevet Sublieutenant Barela because its command-

29. García called Casa-Calvo "Chano and Chanito" in his letters to him, reserved, La Gorra, July 25, 1794, and Santiago, August 22, 1794, *HSD*, 4: 222-23 and 4: 241-42, respectively.

30. Lleonart to Casa-Calvo, San Rafael, May 31, 1794, ibid., 4: 212-13. Juan Lleonart was commander of the South and West zones in the war. Casa-Calvo to García, Bayajá, August 12, 1794, ibid., 4: 237.

31. Lleonart to Casa-Calvo, San Rafael, June 1, 1794, ibid., 4: 213.

er was sick at Hincha, a post that lay further to the west in Saint-Domingue. Shattered remnants of the battalion who were still serving included one sergeant, seven carabineers, and thirty-five soldiers; the rest had died or were recovering from illnesses and wounds at scattered locations.[32] The battalion's integrity had disintegrated, and it existed only on paper.

Recognizing the need to reorganize his defenses, García returned to Bayajá by June 23. Casa-Calvo was then absent on a commission to Montecristi. García assigned Francisco Montalvo, the lieutenant colonel of the Havana regiment, to post a guard around Bayajá against the nearby enemy, and he prepared the city to fight. Montalvo would retain command until Brig. Joaquín del Sasso, a senior officer, returned to Bayajá.[33] On June 16, García had reiterated to Casa-Calvo the need to build hospitals in Montecristi for sick soldiers. First, he had to inspect the town and its hospitals, learn about the local labor supply, and determine the medications useful in healing the infirm. Montecristi needed 450 to 500 beds, for which Casa-Calvo was to enlarge the existing hospitals or build new ones. Lt. Juan Sánchez of the royal treasury accompanied him to assign funds for accomplishing the work.[34]

After ensuring its defenses, García left Bayajá for Montecristi where Casa-Calvo was convalescing from an eye affliction. It appeared to be one of several maladies that troubled him that unpleasant year. García traveled by way of Llano de La Gorra, where he stopped on June 28. He described the settlement as healthy, high in elevation, and mod-

32. Lleonart to Casa-Calvo, San Rafael, June 19, 1794, ibid., 4: 215-16.

33. García to Gaspar de Cassasola, Bayajá, June 23, 1794, ibid., 4: 216. Francisco Montalvo's life was similar to Casa-Calvo's in many respects. He was the son of a prominent Cuban planter, born in Havana in 1754, entered the army as a cadet at age twelve, went to Spain before he was twenty, where he or his father paid 10,000 pesos for his captaincy in the infantry. He served on several expeditions—to Algiers, Colonia de Sacramento, Pensacola in 1781, and Nassau in 1782. He became a lieutenant colonel after the war against Great Britain and returned to Havana, where in time he became the colonel of the Fixed Infantry Regiment of Havana. Penzuela, *Diccionario,* 4: 101.

34. García to Casa-Calvo, Bayajá, June 16, 1794, *HSD*, 4: 214-15.

erate in temperature. Although he was now recovering from his own ailments, his entire body felt frail, particularly his eyes and head. He hoped that the hospitals in Montecristi had been improved. He wanted Casa-Calvo to return to Bayajá for a day or two to collect the latest news. García closed his letter with fatherly advice and suggested that "Chanito" rest his eyes often to prevent his illness from worsening.[35]

Auxiliary troops who aided the Spaniards also created problems. These former slaves fought for the spoils of war since they did not receive salaries. Spanish soldiers were paid in coin, but the army had insufficient specie for whites and none for black troops. They, consequently, lived off the land, taking whatever they found. Initially, they plundered lands recovered from the enemy. One such sacking occurred in April 1794. Troops belonging to the absent Louverture attacked the town of Gonaives, which was allegedly under Spanish control. A shortage of troops, however, had compelled the Spaniards to evacuate it earlier. The black warriors killed about a score of Frenchmen they found outside the town, after which they entered it, massacring everyone they encountered. They pillaged both the town and its nearby plantations. Lleonart and other Spanish officers lamented their inability to control, let alone stop, Louverture's rampaging minions. Nevertheless, black troops became vital when tropical diseases inflicted so many illnesses and deaths among Spanish soldiers that their ability to attack or defend frontier towns virtually collapsed.[36]

As governor of Bayajá, Casa-Calvo became indirectly involved in an atrocity committed by a black ally. Slavery as a labor apparatus employed brutality and inhuman acts to compel Africans to work. Gross abuse by owners and their overseers often led slaves to protest in the only ways they had: they refused to work, ran away, or rose up against their owners. Not all the violence in the war, however, occurred on

35. Juan de Casas to Casa-Calvo, Bayajá, June 28, 1794; and García to Casa-Calvo, Llano de (Plain of) La Gorra, June 30, 1794, both in ibid., 4: 218 and 220, respectively.

36. Lleonard to Casa-Calvo, San Rafael, February 22, 1794; (Casa-Calvo) to (García?), headquarters, March 14, 1794, both in ibid., 4: 186, and 4: 198-99, respectively; Ferrer, "Cuba en la Sombra de Haiti," 191.

the battlefield. Captured rebel slaves sometimes suffered horrendous deaths while former slaves victorious in battle massacred French soldiers and civilians taken prisoner. At Bayajá such a horrific incident took place. French nationals inhabited the city, and they had increased due to the influx from plantations and tiny rural settlements to escape the carnage. Because of their inflated numbers, not all French whites found shelter behind sturdy defenses. Black warriors had a proclivity for killing plantation whites in their sacking rampages, doubtlessly in retribution for the appalling treatment they had received as slaves. By July, Jean François's destitute warriors hungrily eyed Bayajá's bulging warehouses as ripe for plunder. With Spain's military limited to defensive operations, the blacks lost fresh ground to pillage. Eager for spoils, on July 7, 1794, they began sacking the warehouses despite the presence of Spanish troops at a nearby fortress. As the looting proceeded, the blacks encountered some resistance, and the violence escalated until white civilians in the city became targets for the frenzied warriors. The blacks ended up plundering the entire municipality, including Spanish hospitals where they seized medications, beds, sheets, utensils, and anything else of value. They massacred 649 French civilians in one of the largest butcheries of noncombatants in war-torn Saint-Domingue.[37]

Outnumbered Spanish soldiers at the fortress stared at the slaughter in disbelief and did little to stop it since the furious blacks would probably turn on them. African fighters in battle often failed to distinguish between whites of different nationalities. Looters had started by stealing arms, foodstuffs, and clothing in the warehouses and then turned to the property of Spanish officers and soldiers and the treasury offices in search of money. Writers of the Bayajá atrocity who were not eyewitnesses accused the Spanish troops of joining in the plundering, but this would have been dangerous for them and certainly they would not have ransacked their own quarters. When word of the massacre,

37. Mauricio de Zuñiga to Casa-Calvo, San Rafael, August 17, 1794, *HSD*, 4: 240-41. Johnson, in *Social Transformation*, 156, describes the massacre at Bayajá in a confused manner, which is typical of most descriptions of the events on that fateful day.

which was one of many in the brutal colony, became known across the Atlantic, Europeans rebuked the Spaniards, particularly local governor Casa-Calvo, for not protecting the white victims. He, however, was not present when the massacre occurred.[38]

Casa-Calvo had left Bayajá on June 18, to inspect sites and build hospitals for convalescing soldiers in elevated locations free from diseases. He learned of the massacre on July 8 and returned to the city the next day. He took up residence in Fort Dauphin because it housed the acting governor and the Spanish troops. White survivors of the catastrophe had abandoned the city to search for shelter elsewhere. Bayajá remained mostly vacant until July 13, when more Spanish soldiers arrived. The city's two-story treasury building housed French prisoners on the upper floor that Jean François had seized while blacks inhabited the ground floor. The general had not yet dictated the prisoners' fate, but Casa-Calvo liberated them upon his return to the city.[39]

Probably as he was ordered to do, several days after arriving in Bayajá Casa-Calvo returned to Montecristi. While there, he composed a detailed report on how he intended to reorganize Bayajá and its fortifications. He submitted it to García, who was still at La Gorra. When a García official instructed Casa-Calvo to return to Bayajá, he committed his final thoughts to paper.[40] He pointed out that the pestilential city had killed eight hundred soldiers from the time the Spaniards took charge of it five months before. Another six hundred soldiers were then sick, and it shrank the effective troops to a paltry number. He lamented the atrocity that Jean François's soldiers had perpetrated

38. Casa-Calvo to Juan Sánchez, Montecristi, July 30, 1794, *HSD*, 4: 229-30.

39. Lleonart to Casa-Calvo, San Rafael, May 31, 1794; Juan Sánchez to Casa-Calvo, Montecristi, July 28, 1794; Casa-Calvo to Juan Sánchez, Montecristi, July 30, 1794; all in *HSD*, 4: 212-13, 4: 228, and 4: 229-30, respectively. Casa-Calvo was sick in May 1794, and had not yet retired to the mountains. García, who had stayed in the north, developed eye problems and described his mountain retreat of La Gorra as high, healthy, and moderate in temperature. García to Casa-Calvo, La Gorra, June 30, 1794, *HSD*, 4: 220.

40. José Vásquez to Casa-Calvo, La Gorra, July 24, 1794, and García to Casa-Calvo (Chanito), La Gorra, July 25, 1794, both in *HSD*, 4: 222 and 222-23, respectively.

with impunity since the king had ordered preserving the friendship of the indispensable black auxiliaries. Nevertheless, Casa-Calvo vowed to punish them the next time they committed a violent act. More than two thousand armed blacks reportedly roamed through the city, where few whites remained. He felt it necessary to keep Spanish troops in nearby Fort Dauphin, the Castle de la Boca, and the port's naval forces at the Battery of Lanze. In addition, a hospital of four hundred to five hundred beds had to be constructed in the city for ailing personnel. Casa-Calvo assigned hundreds of guards to protect the installations, but it was questionable whether he really had them. Defense of the city fell to Gen. Jean François, who now pledged his complete fidelity to the king, and Casa-Calvo charged the black troops to supply the city, the fortifications, and the naval ships with fresh water, firewood, and foodstuffs at fair prices. Should Jean François and his minions fail in their duties or commit another atrocity, Casa-Calvo guaranteed their extermination. He promised the captain general to remain vigilant and ensure that Jean François and his men behaved properly.[41]

While the massacre was truly a tragedy, the war hindered Casa-Calvo's subordinates in the city from acting more forcefully. The Spaniards had not been able to protect the unfortunate French and, had they tried, the turmoil likely would have turned deadly for them. Still the image of allegedly immobile Spaniards witnessing Africans slaughter whites was a picture that Europeans far removed in time and place could neither accept nor understand. But then they had not grasped the horrendous brutality sadistic whites had long inflicted on defenseless slaves in Saint-Domingue. Nine years was the expected lifespan of field hands, and masters who treated them as property, not humans, habitually preferred to buy "new" workers rather than "coddle" worn-out bondsmen. While the Spanish government investigated the massacre, it neither reached a conclusion on whether it could have been prevented nor held anyone responsible for the events on that dreadful day.[42] It was another terrible consequence attributable to the appalling

41. (Casa-Calvo) to García, Montecristi, July 25, 1794, *HSD*, 4: 423-26.

42. Ada Ferrer, "Cuba en la Sombra de Haiti: Noticias, Sociedad, y Esclavitud," in

institution of slavery and to the brutality of money-hungry captains of agriculture.[43]

Casa-Calvo returned to Bayajá about August 1. While changes had occurred in the city since the massacre, black soldiers still held the warehouses.[44] A week later, Casa-Calvo probably gagged as he informed Jean François that his recent behavior had pleased him. No doubt he judged mollifying the black general necessary to ensure his obedience. Casa-Calvo needed to establish order, tranquility, and defenses in the city. He ejected the black auxiliaries from the city's interior and henceforth prohibited their entry with weapons. Thankfully, white troops were arriving to reinforce him. Casa-Calvo established a black military police force armed solely with sabers to patrol the city. He favored expelling the indolent and leaving only artisans in the city to work on the fortifications and damaged stores of the inhabitants. He planned to collect the guns the black auxiliaries had pillaged, but it is highly questionable whether he succeeded. Nevertheless, he instructed the blacks to exhibit their best behavior, fidelity, love, and respect in carrying out army orders. In return, he pledged to inform the captain general of Jean François's loyal service, and in time the king would reward him and his top subordinates.[45]

García, meanwhile, worried about the numerous French refugees who crowded into Santo Domingo City and, according to him, threat-

---

Dolores González-Ripoll et al., *El Rumor de Haití en Cuba: Temor, Raza y Rebeldía, 1789-1844* (Madrid: Consejo Superior de Investigaciones Científicas, 2004), 193-94.

43. Ibid. Arango was in Spain twice, in 1787-94 and again in 1814-17, ibid., 35. Many owners regarded it more cost effective to buy new slaves than care for "used up" workers. Slave laws, such as the French Code Noir of 1685 granted owners great latitude in the punishment of their slaves.

44. Juan Sánchez to Casa-Calvo, Montecristi, August 3, 1794, *HSD*, 4: 233-34.

45. (Casa-Calvo) to Juan Francisco, August 8, 1794, *HSD*, 4: 234-35. James, in his *Black Jacobins*, 125-26, writes, "Officers of different colors would not accept invitations offered to [only] one [racial] group; as good republicans they refused to bow and scrape before the Spanish Marquis [Casa-Calvo], who raged at the [self-]importance of these blacks."

ened stability and consumed supplies intended for the war effort. Their political sentiments often clashed with Spanish ideology and made them perilous recruits in the colony's small military force. Moreover, if all of them enlisted, they would outnumber Spanish soldiers who kept plummeting in numbers due to illness, mortality, and desertion. The diminutive size of the army, nonetheless, compelled García to accept some Frenchmen.[46]

Colonel Lleonart, commander of the southern and western border regions where fighting first erupted, felt the acute troop shortage. He asked García for additional soldiers, a commodity all military leaders wanted. García instructed Casa-Calvo to send Lleonart only the troops he could spare, and he cautioned him against weakening the garrison at Bayajá.[47]

Spanish troubles, nevertheless, persisted. From San Rafael on August 17, 1794, Lleonart commented that the Bayajá massacre had surprised and saddened him. While he maintained an uneasy modus vivendi with Louverture, the latter's troops sacked and burned houses all around Lleonart, stole animals, and committed countless depredations despite his promises to stop.[48] Bayajá, too, had immediate needs. Many indispensable items had been stolen or destroyed in the city's recent sacking. Hospitals alone required five to six hundred night gowns, the same number of sheets, two hundred or more jars of *ojalata* (a salve), and a thousand wooden spoons.[49]

By September 1794, several months after joining the French republicans, Louverture launched an offensive on the eastern frontier and northeastern corner of Saint-Domingue with great success. He recovered regions Spanish forces had seized until little more than the district of Bayajá remained. Louverture informed the Spaniards that his objective was to recover all occupied territory and push into their col-

46. García to Casa-Calvo, army headquarters at Santiago, July 31, 1794, *HSD*, 4: 232-23.

47. Ibid.

48. Lleonart to Casa-Calvo, San Rafael, August 17, 1794, ibid., 4: 239-40.

49. (Casa-Calvo) to Juan Sánchez, Bayajá, August 18, 1794, ibid., 4: 241.

ony. His intentions and abundant troops led Lleonart and Armona to conclude the futility of fighting in Saint-Domingue, and they retreated back to Santo Domingo. Black forces, however, followed them into Santo Domingo and occupied the towns of San Rafael, San Miguel, Hinchas, Bánica, and Las Caobas in October and November, with little or no combat. It was a calamity not foreseen the year before when the Spaniards confidently invaded Saint-Domingue.[50] Lleonart deplored the new obstacles and his inability to fight back. Furthermore, the Spaniards lost faith in Jean-François's martial proficiency, and food costs soared beyond Lleonart's limited capacity to pay. Despite shortages, he had to stand firm, otherwise the road to Santo Domingo City lay open.[51]

This unexpected turn of events distressed García immensely. Recent losses included two coastal posts, Borgne and Port Margot. After further defeats in November, García relieved Lleonart and others of command. He found Lleonart's operations against the enemy disappointing. The colonel, however, had often complained about his few soldiers, money, and food, all of which inhibited combat. The loss of Fondblanc, a vital coastal artillery post that controlled the water passage to Bayajá, particularly disturbed García. He instructed Casa-Calvo to recover Fondblanc since enemy cannon fire could stop Spanish merchant vessels from entering the bay. Sicknesses and deaths among the crews of Casa-Calvo's warships stationed at Bayajá also weakened his fighting ability. His naval commander Antonio O'Carroll advised the ships to depart for healthier climates; naval officer Francisco Xávier Muñoz had set the example by leaving. Louverture, meanwhile, attempted to convince Jean François to switch sides. About that time, Casa-Calvo's illness abated, and he tried to pursue his duties more vig-

50. Frank Moya Pons, *Manuel de la historia dominicana* (Santo Domingo: Editorial UCMM, 1981), 169; Sevilla Soler, *Santo Domingo*, 394n, who cited a November 20, 1794 García letter to the court on the loss of the ships *San Rafael* and *San Miguel*; Ferrer, "Cuba en la Sombra de Haiti," 192.

51. Lleonart to Casa-Calvo, Bánica, November 6, 1794, *HSD*, 4: 301-302.

orously.[52]

In response to García's inquiries about his troops at the end of November, Casa-Calvo reported on conditions at Bayajá. Military reinforcements had departed the city for Yaquesí on the southern frontier eight days before, leaving him with a garrison of 811men. Beyond these troops, 356 soldiers remained for duty elsewhere. Of them, he sent one hundred to guard the ship-of-the-line *Santa Isabel.* Other troops strengthened the artillery where forty-three gunners had died. Casa-Calvo declared that he had established a police force of 250 mulattoes and a thousand or so blacks inside Bayajá. However, it was impossible for him to send four hundred whites to serve at other locations since it would weaken his land and sea forces considerably. Additionally, with the departure of one of his ships to transport soldiers, only two vessels remained, and their crews were so insignificant, as O'Carroll reported, that they could neither sail nor fire their batteries. The mail sloop *Ventura* that had recently sailed to Havana carried Col. Francisco Montalvo on a commission and escorted a captured American prize and a brigantine that had brought gunpowder. Casa-Calvo argued that he needed all his remaining soldiers to protect Bayajá from nearby enemies.[53]

When García returned to Santo Domingo City near the end of October 1794, he was in a dreadful mood. He revealed his thinking in letters to Casa-Calvo. He granted black auxiliary officers salaries in the hope that they would preserve the loyalty of their troops. His reason for leaving Santiago, he alleged, was its sickly putrefied air and water. The

52. Sevilla Soler, *Santo Domingo*, 392-93; Lleonart to Casa-Calvo, Santiago, November 19, 1794; García to (Casa-Calvo), (Santo Domingo City?), November 19, 1794, O'Carroll to Casa-Calvo, from his ship *Santa Isabel* at Bayajá, November 23, 1794, all in *HSD*, 4: 303, 4: 304, and 4: 304-5, respectively.

53. (Casa-Calvo) to García, Bayajá, November 30, 1794, *HSD*, 4: 305-7. Francisco Montalvo came from a Havana Creole family (his father became the first Conde de Macuriges) and rose steadily in rank from lieutenant colonel of the third battalion of the Havana regiment, to brigadier after the war and head of the same regiment, to sub-inspector of the army in Cuba, to service on the captain general's staff, and in 1813 to viceroy of New Granada. Kuethe, *Cuba*, 126, 152, 161, 170, and 171.

winter season brought frigid winds and sickened troops with colds that frequently developed into pneumonia. He advised Casa-Calvo to leave the disease-plagued Bayajá if illness threatened his life. García's own health problems improved sluggishly because he was burdened with writing dispatches several hours each morning, and rain prevented him from relaxing on afternoon horse rides. It distressed him that disgruntled Dominican families complained that their towns had fallen to the enemy because of the timorous resistance put up by incompetent army officers. He waited for ships to bring him badly needed food, munitions, and money. O'Carroll's wretched decision to leave half the funds assigned to Santo Domingo on board his ships in Puerto Rico devastated the colony's finances. García instructed all commanders to economize drastically since he could not help them. On a personal note, he hoped that Casa-Calvo had received good news from Madrid, from his mother Catalina, and from his children, and he urged him to write if only a paragraph. He added lastly that should Casa-Calvo go to the mountain town of Santiago, García's housekeeper and his physician, Dr. Francisco Espallat, had instructions to treat him as if he were the owner. In a revelatory sentence, García admitted that Casa-Calvo was his favorite among the army officers, and he wished him perfect health and felicity.[54]

Several days later, García had additional news. Knowledge of Casa-Calvo's illness had saddened him deeply. Nevertheless, his spirits had brightened upon learning that he was now mending. Casa-Calvo had acted honorably by remaining in Bayajá despite its unhealthiness, and it made García proud since the king did not expect his highest-ranking officers to risk their lives by living in diseased locations. He was also pleased that Gen. Jean François had rejected the entreaties of French governor Esteban Laveaux to defect, and García would remember the black general's loyalty. Lastly, he trusted Casa-Calvo to manage the

54. García to Casa-Calvo, (Santo Domingo City?), December 1, 1794, *HSD*, 4: 309-11. On García's return to Santo Domingo City, see Sevilla Soler, *Santo Domingo*, 393n.

auxiliaries wisely and the local residents expediently.[55]

The day after Christmas, García notified Casa-Calvo about problems he faced. Answering mail from Spain, Havana, Mexico, and other places exhausted him. At intervals of fifteen to twenty days, headaches and fevers broke out in his body and tormented him fiercely for several days before they abated. The grueling agony left him feeling like he had only a torso and arms but with no legs or head. Swollen feet and abdominal and ankle pains paralyzed his legs. He moved around awkwardly in a "chair with wheels." The five or six hours he spent daily reading and signing documents hindered his convalescence. Aristizábal had written him from Havana in late November that he was returning to Bayajá, but García believed that Montalvo's mysterious commission would delay him longer. García's foremost obstacles consisted of persistent shortages. His two ships, a freight brigantine and the small warship *Volador*, were inadequate to bring in all the supplies he needed or rid the coastline of corsairs and pirates that seized vessels from Bayajá in the north down to Samaná Bay on the east coast. The most notorious pirate was a renegade Catalan, and Casa-Calvo needed to inform O'Carroll about him. He told Casa-Calvo that the government could not delay much longer in naming him governor of Bayajá since he had only an interim appointment. Lastly, García fervently urged his protégé to take care of himself.[56]

Enemy assaults continued near Bayajá in December. On the 23rd they seized the nearby Cerro del Diablo (the Devil's Hill), attacking in three columns that forced the black auxiliaries to flee. They fell back to a place called Valière and to meadows that lay adjacent to Bayajá. Upon

55. García to Casa-Calvo, Santo Domingo, December 5, 1794, *HSD*, 4: 311-12. Capt. José María de la Torre's unauthorized appearance in Bayajá disgusted García. He instructed Casa-Calvo to jail him for a week then return him to his company of soldiers.

56. García to Casa-Calvo, Santo Domingo, December 26, 1794, ibid., 4: 312-13. García included in the letter a paragraph from another letter written to him from Samaná five days before about the Catalan pirate who called himself Josef Riberas but whose real name was Pablo Pullol (Puyol), who had plundered numerous farms. Ibid., 4: 313-14.

learning these events, Lt. Esteban Palomares took to the field to teach the black troops how to stand firm and resist. He left the city with infantry, artillery, and cavalry. Artillery problems delayed Palomares for a day until a gun carriage and gunpowder arrived. Moving forward at 3 p.m., he soon encountered the enemy's vanguard lodged in the hills and on the road below. Fortunately, Jean François's troops came up about that time. Although Palomares intended to fight the following morning, the black troops immediately began firing at the enemy, and it forced him to continue the attack. The black infantry scrambled up the nearest hill and at the summit found signs of a hasty retreat and the dead from previous skirmishes. A scout from Jean François's army reported that at 7 p.m. he saw on the road to Dos Cerros two infantry columns and cavalry hidden in ambush, where they remained for about two hours before departing. Palomares praised the black troops, who displayed punctuality, disposition, and bravery before enemy gunfire. He also lauded the white commanders of the grenadiers, artillery, and cavalry, who all worked tirelessly from the moment they left the city.[57] The resistance at Bayajá proved effective. While the enemy hunkered around the district, they made no headway in seizing it. Casa-Calvo repelled attacks until hostile operations in that sector of the colony ceased.

On November 27, García sent an order instructing Col. Juan Lleonart to come to Santo Domingo immediately to discuss matters that he did not disclose. Left unsaid was Louverture's rout of the Spanish army. García had decided to arrest the officers who allegedly had shown cowardice by fleeing from the enemy. Eight days later, Lleonart, who was in Bánica in west central Santo Domingo and near the fighting, replied that he was leaving as soon as his successor, Col. Joaquín Cabrera,

57. Esteban Palomares to the captain general, Dajabón, December 26, 1794, ibid., 4: 315-17. Not counting about a dozen officers, 571 soldiers of all ranks participated in the sortie. "Statement of the Officers, Troops, and Artillery in the expedition under Capt. Esteban Palomares," Dajabón, December 27, 1794, Palomares to Casa-Calvo, ibid., 4: 317-18. When he learned of the events, Casa-Calvo described them in a shorter letter. (Casa-Calvo) to (García?), Bayajá, December 31, 1794, ibid., 4: 320-21.

took over. Lleonart's illness, however, delayed him slightly.[58]

On reaching Santo Domingo City early in 1795, Lleonart met a livid captain general. A firm believer in his own opinion on how to wage war, no explanation he received satisfied him, and he threw Lleonart into a prison cell. With García behaving irrationally, Lleonart pleaded for mercy from first minister of state Manuel Godoy. He recounted his forty-eight years of faithful service in the army and honorable command of many posts in Cuba. In Santo Domingo, however, he had been assigned to vulnerable locations with insufficient troops, munitions, and food. Appeals for assistance to the captain general had gone unheeded until he suffered defeats, at which point García recalled him to Santo Domingo, where he was imprisoned. He sought impartial justice, honorable treatment, and recognition of his extensive and meritorious service.[59]

Contrary to Lleonart's explanation, García cast blame for the reversals in the war on the officers who retreated. In doing so, he appeared a vivid example of a commander who refused to acknowledge reality. Rather than accept the truth of insufficient troops, munitions, and supplies to fight the enemy successfully, he heaped fault on the officers who failed to perform miracles. And their excuses fell on deaf ears since García recognized only the loss of territory and not the absence of resources. He proceeded with the absurd and incarcerated Brig. Gen. Matías de Armona, Col. José Antonio de la Torre, and Miguel Ortiz de Zarate as well, officers in the battalions sent to protect Santo Domingo. García's behavior was reminiscent of Spanish military leaders who focused on past imperial glories and ignored the current deficiencies in the empire's might. He charged the commanders with dereliction of duty for abandoning occupied lands and refusing to fight, and he eventually dispatched them to Cuba to be court-martialed.[60]

58. García to Lleonart, Santo Domingo, November 27, 1794; Lleonart to García, Banica, December 5, 1794; both in ibid., 4: 312.

59. Johnson, *Social Transformation*, 157-58.

60. Lleonart planned to leave the town of San Rafael, where he was stationed, on June 20, 1794, to go to Havana. *HSD*, 4: 215-16. Captain General García sent Mon-

Upon their arrival in Havana, conditions improved for them. García's hard-nosed decision to prosecute the officers received a slow response. The Cuban councils of war appeared to view the indicted personnel more impartially and judged them hapless pawns in an unwinnable war. Eventually, the drawn-out trials ended favorably for the accused. The Havana judges accepted their explanations of inadequate manpower on Hispaniola and exonerated them. If Lleonart's reputation was briefly tarnished, he and the others rebounded from the imbroglio. As proof of García's misplaced judgment, Lleonart, who was now elderly, served subsequently as the captain general of Central America.[61]

The failed military experience in Saint-Domingue paralleled to some degree the Franco-Spanish war being waged along the Pyrenees. It began well in 1793 with victories that seized lands inside France. Then the successes crumbled as larger numbers of republican soldiers compelled Spain's army to retreat back across the Pyrenees. The French pushed into Bilbao and Vitoria and swarmed down as far as the Ebro River on Catalonia's southern border. Besides military losses, French boots on extensive portions of Spanish soil shook the nation's vitality. The economy veered on collapse and revolutionary strife smoldered throughout the peninsula, rattling society to its core; the calamities pressured the government to move to peace negotiations. Although it held the upper hand, France, too, desired peace inasmuch as manpower and materiel shortages and social unrest at home hindered a more vigorous prosecution of the war. In the midst of this turmoil, Spain eyed

---

talvo to Havana but he was neither one of the accused nor a witness in the trials. After the trials, in February 1810, he was promoted to brigadier general; in 1815 he was raised to field marshal; to lieutenant general, and in 1817 to viceroy of New Granada, where he acted violently against the insurgents. He returned to Cuba in 1818 before going to Spain, where he was named to the Council of State despite his "average intelligence." He died in Spain on October 28, 1821. Pezuela, *Diccionario*, 1: 101.

61. Ferrer, "Cuba en la Sombra de Haiti," 191-92; Johnson, *Social Transformation*, 77-79, 156-57. Johnson's assertion of Las Casas' penchant for removing Creole officers clashes with Kuethe's assertion that Creoles rose in rank in both the army and militia at that time. Moreover, Las Casas retired from army service in Cuba and moved to rural estates he had received from Cubans.

suspiciously British intentions on both sides of the Atlantic. As Spanish negotiations with France progressed, Britons monitored them apprehensively because Spain's abandonment of the conflict would unleash more French troops against them. Great Britain tried vainly to persuade Spain to continue the struggle in Saint-Domingue. The French, meanwhile, tried to wheedle both Louisiana and Santo Domingo from Spain's grasp. Negotiations finally concluded on July 22, 1795, when both nations signed the Treaty of Basel. Article IX returned peninsular lands that France had seized, and Spain surrendered only Santo Domingo to France.[62] The British deplored the treaty since it worsened their military position in Saint-Domingue. Nevertheless, they persisted in the struggle until 1798, when they withdrew, taking many French royalists with them to Jamaica.[63]

Personnel in Santo Domingo first learned of Spanish negotiations with France on the colony's fate about mid-1795. They expected British reprisals if Spain ended the war against France. When English Vice-Admiral Christopher Parker, commander of warships assigned to Jamaica and Saint-Domingue, asked for Spanish help against a French squadron with two thousand soldiers that had left Brest on May 3, Spanish naval commander O'Carroll at Bayajá prevaricated and declared his ships to be few and unseaworthy. But another reason involved the loyalty of Gen. Jean François, whose black troops shielded the Spaniards from French forces. The auxiliaries considered all Frenchmen, regardless of political persuasion, as enemies, and if they could no longer fight for Spain, they would join Great Britain, the other nation still battling France. Aristizábal, meanwhile, worried about a naval attack. On October 14, the captain general of Santo Domingo received a royal communiqué of September 8, announcing the cession of Santo Domingo to France and giving the colonists a year to relocate to Cuba at royal expense with their movable property. Displaced Dominicans would receive royal compensation in Cuba equal to the land they lost. The last

62. Carrera Montero, *Las complejas relaciones*, 97.

63. David Geggus, *Slavery, War and Revolution: The British Occupation of Saint Domingue, 1793-1798* (Oxford: Clarenden Press, 1982).

Spaniards to leave would be the Royal Audiencia and the army, and it suggested that Casa-Calvo should remain with his regiment until the final soldiers departed.[64]

Through the war's second and final year (1794-95), the Spaniards on Hispaniola had fought defensively inasmuch as their military potency had fizzled out. Without more troops from other New World colonies, they now hoped that Spain would send reinforcements, but the mother country could not provide them. Godoy kept an expedition under the naval hero, the Marqués del Socorro, waiting in Cádiz since early 1795 for service in Santo Domingo. French victories in Spain finally awakened Godoy to the futility of the war since it had produced calamities, not triumphs. Seizing Saint-Domingue lay beyond Spain's ability, and Godoy needed to end the struggle and stop hemorrhages of manpower and money. As early as April 1795, the French sought peace and contacted the Spaniards, who initially winced at the thought of accepting defeat. Moreover, Godoy believed that the British invasion of Saint-Domingue presaged their seizure of all Hispaniola and, evincing a defeatist attitude, he preferred black revolutionaries over Britons as owners of the island. Once Socorro received instructions on the likely peace terms, he judged it time to leave Cádiz, but the government reassigned his ships to Santo Domingo's evacuation. Still the squadron delayed departing.[65]

On October 18, 1795, García published the news of Santo Domingo's cession. Rumors about the colony's loss were already circulating, and they filled the inhabitants with dread. The distant government's decision-making proclivities in not consulting the residents of the affected land distressed them tremendously. They worried about falling into the hands of France, a detested enemy, and they publicly condemned Godoy and the king. Local authorities feared that French refugees in the colony might begin demonstrations that would weaken their control. Despite objections, García began the transition to French

64. Carrera Montero, *Las complejas relaciones*, 90-101; Sevilla Soler, *Santo Domingo*, 395.

65. Carrera Montero, *Las complejas relaciones*, 79.

rule, seeking first to neutralize the power of black auxiliaries and the refugee French who could obstruct the transfer. The displaced French, fearful of falling into the hands of the thousands of black troops in the colony, grumbled that the Spanish government had betrayed them. Prospects of renewed hostilities along the frontier, especially in the Bayajá district where black auxiliaries flourished, concerned them. García also instructed Casa-Calvo to evacuate Bayajá upon receiving orders.[66]

As Spain's participation in the war concluded, the anti-French black auxiliaries began exchanging messages with British forces who continued the conflict. Jean François, however, with his officers, their families, and a portion of his troops, entered Bayajá peacefully and laid down their arms. They loathed the French and refused to live under them. On October 20, García granted permission to Jean François and his troops to board vessels bound for Havana. The black general declared his and his people's willingness to live wherever the king assigned them. However, a negligent Madrid had specified only the relocation of Jean François and his highest officers and excluded the rank and file soldiers. The court wanted to leave the latter in place to minimize costs and eliminate risks in transporting to Cuba an army of dubious loyalty.[67]

García then permitted between thirty and fifty of Jean François's officers to settle there. A more contentious Las Casas in Havana, nevertheless, rejected the idea because it would frighten the island's white inhabitants into believing the blacks could incite the Cuban slaves and destroy the colony as they had Saint-Domingue. Havana's faint-hearted municipal government pleaded with Las Casas to keep them out. To its relief, he agreed not to accept black soldiers, and if they arrived he planned to ship them immediately to Florida, the Isle of Pines, or Cádiz. The Spaniards worried that leaving the blacks in Santo Domingo might induce them to join the British. While Las Casas endorsed their evacuation to a safe place, Godoy in Spain denied them entry

66. Moya Pons, *Santo Domingo*, 99-101.

67. García to Casa-Calvo, Santo Domingo, November 9, 1795, AHN, Est., leg. 3407.

anywhere in the empire and left them to find their own sanctuaries in French lands, with people they hated.[68] Casa-Calvo also objected to their settlement in Havana. Writing in December 1795, he compared them to venomous snakes that he had tolerated only because of government orders. It was a telling declaration that reflected a racial bias.[69] Despite the prohibition, Jean François and his family boarded a ship sailing to Havana. When authorities there denied him entry, he continued to Cádiz. He lived out his life near the municipality, dying about 1811. Meanwhile, a fair number of the black soldiers from Saint-Domingue and who had fought for the Spaniards found new homes on coastal Guatemala and Honduras. Removed from the fighting in Hispaniola and slavery, they became the first line of defense to ensure the safety of Spanish Central America should the British launch an invasion in this area.[70]

Although Casa-Calvo learned by fall 1795 that the war had concluded, French representatives did not appear to take possession of Bayajá or Santo Domingo. Chaotic conditions in Saint-Domingue prevented the French Directory that took charge of the government in France in November 1795, from exercising control in the colony. Whites wanted to preserve power over the region and not yield it to a black general. Many months of inactivity in Bayajá caused Casa-Calvo to chomp at the bit and yearn anxiously to return to Cuba or move on to Spain in search of a more promising post. In November 1795, Casa-Calvo wrote home to Cuba on the violence he experienced as governor of Bayajá. He provided lucid depictions of the bloodshed and cruelty. Besides the dreadful catastrophe in Bayajá, he heard about similar events that took place throughout the French colony. It was a

68. Garcia to Las Casas, Santo Domingo, a second letter of November 9, 1795, AHN, Est. leg. 3407; Carrera Montero, *Las complejas relaciones*, 102-9.

69. Ferrer, "Cuba en la Sombra de Haiti," 193-94.

70. Jorge Victoria Ojeda, *Tropas auxiliares del Rey en Centroamérica: historia de negros súbditos de la monarquía española* (San José, Costa Rica: Editorial UCR, 2009); Jorge Victoria Ojeda, *Las tropas auxiliares de Carlos IV: de Saint-Domingue al mundo hispano* (Castellón de la Plana, Spain: Universitat Jaume, 2011).

brutal time, and he had not foreseen that the atrocities he described would alarm the Cubans into believing they would soon experience the wrenching effects of slave insurrections.[71] His depictions of the brutality matched the accounts of refugees and returning soldiers from Saint-Domingue.

Spain ended the war without achieving its goal of expelling the French from Hispaniola. Instead, the fading empire lost the rest of the island. The French, however, still needed to subdue slave unrest in Saint-Domingue, and Great Britain held territory in the colony and continued fighting. The Spanish troops were expected to evacuate the portions of the French colony they held, but a royal order of January 27, 1796, advised Casa-Calvo to stay on guard should Great Britain try to seize territory on Saint-Domingue's north coast. He commanded 1,600 men, which was the size of a regiment, but it was composed of troops from diverse units—Cuba, Havana, Mexico, Venezuela, and elsewhere. Captain General García had instructed him to take his garrison to Santo Domingo City after ceding his command and send sick soldiers to the nearby towns of Montecristi and Dajabón to convalesce. At last on June 14, 1796, Gov. Esteban Laveaux arrived at Bayajá.[72]

Casa-Calvo transferred the Bayajá district with pomp and ceremony on the same day. The troops, dressed in their finest uniforms, paraded with precision before the new owners. No doubt a military band enlivened the ceremonies with spirited music. Giving up occupied enemy territory was not as traumatic as Spain's forthcoming evacuation of the colony of Santo Domingo, a three-hundred-year-old possession. It was Godoy's doing as he appeared to be dismantling the Spanish Empire. Only two months later in 1795, he gave up more territory, this time in the Mississippi Valley when he capitulated to exaggerated American claims that their territory extended down to the present-day Louisi-

71. Ada Ferrer, "Noticias de Haiti en Cuba, 1791-1804," *Revista de Indias*, no. 229 (2003): 675-94.

72. Casa-Calvo service sheet of March 31, 1805, AGM, ES; Sevilla Soler, *Santo Domingo*, 404. Sevilla Soler states that Santhonax took over at Bayajá after the Spaniards departed.

ana-Mississippi boundary on the east bank of the Mississippi River. The surrender of much of West Florida did not extinguish American ambitions, however, as they aspired to seize all of Spain's northern Gulf Coast possessions.[73]

Two hours after surrendering Bayajá, the Spanish troops embarked on Aristizábal's ships. Although scheduled to sail early the next morning, the absence of favorable breezes detained them for several more days. During this time, mail arrived overland from Santo Domingo, including official correspondence from the captain general. It included news that Socorro was sailing to Santo Domingo. Aristizábal then consulted naval commander O'Carroll, who agreed that proceeding to Havana was the best recourse because they had food for only a month and the ships were deteriorating. It was impossible to repair them in Santo Domingo City or at its nearby anchorage at Ocoa. With the colony's transfer soon to take place, the authorities at Bayajá agreed to transport the troops to Havana.[74] García had already informed Casa-Calvo that he soon expected the arrival of Citizen Philippe Roume, agent of the French Directory, who was to take possession of the city and colony.[75] García's letter seemed to endorse that sailing to Havana

73. A century ago, Isaac J. Cox, in "The American Intervention in West Florida," *American Historical Review* 17 (January 1912): 290-311, disproved the validity of the American claims to West Florida. He followed up his article with his book, *The West Florida Controversy, 1798-1813: A Study in American Diplomacy* ([Baltimore], 1918). The Spanish side of events is explained in Gilbert C. Din's unpublished paper, "Seven Troubled Years: American Claims and Aggression on Spanish West Florida, 1803-1810."

74. Casa-Calvo to the Príncipe de la Paz, Havana, June 28, 1796, AGI, Estado, leg. 5A Aristizábal to Casa-Calvo, no. 8, on board the *San Eugenio* at Bayajá, June 16, 1796.

75. Casa-Calvo to Aristizábal, on the *San Eugenio* at Bayajá, June 16, 1796; Aristizábal to Casa-Calvo, no. 8, on board the *San Eugenio* at Bayajá, June 16, 1796, *HSD*, 4: 347. On June 10, García wrote Casa-Calvo that the brigantine *Resolución* of the Royal Navy arrived at Santo Domingo City the day before. It brought official mail on the transfer. After reading the contents, García immediately informed Citizen Roume that he should take possession of Santo Domingo City and the rest of the colony immediately. García to Casa-Calvo, June 10, 1796, Santo Domingo City,

was the proper decision. As Socorro from Cádiz had also advised Casa-Calvo that he was leaving for Santo Domingo to evacuate people and property from the colony, Aristizábal concluded that his rightful destination was Havana, especially since the hurricane season was at hand. With Casa-Calvo deprived of transportation to Santo Domingo, he took his men to Cuba despite its violation of García's earlier order.[76]

Although hundreds of miles away, favorable easterly breezes finally aided the passage and the ships arrived in several days. No doubt Casa-Calvo rejoiced at being back with his children; his absence from Cuba had lasted three years and again he missed out on important events in their young lives. The three older children were now teenagers, and they had endured long stretches without his presence. His younger son, Ignacio who was born in 1790, was only six when his father returned from Santo Domingo as nearly a stranger. He had written occasional letters to his children from Santo Domingo, probably sending messages on birthdays or at Christmas and Easter, and the letters helped assuage his absence. Nonetheless, letters were a poor substitute for his presence.

In retrospect, the Cuban army's journey to neighboring Santo Domingo had been a failure. Nevertheless, on a personal level, it helped Casa-Calvo immeasurably because the victories around Bayajá netted him the rank of brigadier general. Furthermore, he had held command positions in a war zone for nearly three years, and his presence assisted in the retention of the Bayajá district until the conflict ended. He gained valuable experience in wartime logistics and in the command of troops. All these factors were vital ingredients in furthering his military career.

Only after returning to Havana did Casa-Calvo explain to García

---

AGI, Estado, leg. 5A. On board the ship-of-the-line *Príncipe de Asturias* in Cádiz Bay, on May 3, 1796, the Marqués del Socorro wrote to Captain General García. His principal news was that his squadron was sailing soon to Santo Domingo. Its purpose was to transport the persons and property who had decided to relocate to Cuba.

76. Joaquín García to Casa-Calvo, Santo Domingo City, July 18, 1796; Nicolás de Toledo to Casa-Calvo, on board the *Princesa de Asturias*, May 3, 1796; both in AGS, GM, leg. 7161.

on June 28, 1796, the change in ownership at Bayajá. He had not written earlier because of the rush to depart, and now he enclosed inventories of the artillery and other military equipment that the French had demanded. In order to leave with the expedition, Casa-Calvo surrendered them but under protest.[77]

Perhaps after receiving Casa-Calvo's June 28 letter, García explained to Miguel de Azanza in Spain's ministry of war what had happened. He wrote that Casa-Calvo had disregarded García's explicit instructions to go to Santo Domingo City and Godoy's order of January 27, 1796, to maximize Spanish forces because the British were nearby and represented a threat. García felt that he could no longer rely on support from the disillusioned Dominicans, who had become hostile to Spain from the moment they learned of the colony's cession to France. They felt the mother country had sold them out to recover conquered regions in the peninsula. Looking at the positive side, however, the transfer of troops to Cuba was cost-saving but only if the British did not attack. At the same time, García did not have the funds to pay troop salaries, nor could he provide much in the way of materiel support for them. Finally, the arrival of both Socorro to evacuate Spanish inhabitants and the French representatives to claim the colony were proceeding slowly. Spanish ships had already decided to winter in Havana over 1796 to 1797, and he did not expect their return to Santo Domingo in the near future.[78]

Five months later, the king directed a royal order to García on the matter. He disapproved the reasons Casa-Calvo had given for returning to Cuba. But it went no farther and, given the positive reasons for sailing to Havana, the king did not suggest punitive action against

77. Casa-Calvo to García, with attachments, Havana, June 28, 1796, AGI, Estado, leg. 5A, no. 67. Laveaux, Chief General in Santo Domingo, to Casa-Calvo, commander of the troops of His Catholic Majesty. Esteban Laveaux to Casa-Calvo, in Port of Liberty, 27 of Praireal, year 4 of the French Republic, acknowledged that he kept two cannons of 25 caliber, two of 8 caliber, and seven campaign pieces as they constituted part of the city's defenses in spite of Casa-Calvo's protest.

78. García to Miguel de Azanza, Santo Domingo, July 18, 1796, AGS, GM, leg. 7161; Moya Pons, *Santo Domingo*, 100-102.

him.[79] Perhaps the crown recognized that with troops and funds short everywhere, pursuing a time- and money-consuming investigation that would yield negative results was a losing proposition. Therefore, the reprimand was soon forgotten, and for the next three years Casa-Calvo stayed in Havana before he received his next assignment. During this time, he served as a brigadier general and the acting commander of the Fixed Infantry Regiment of Cuba.

79. Royal order to the captain general of Cuba, San Lorenzo, December 8, 1796, ibid.

6
Cuba and Louisiana, 1796-1801

Upon returning from his three-year tour of duty in Hispaniola, Casa-Calvo remained in Cuba for a similar length of time with his children and other family members. Although he served as commandant of the Fixed Infantry Regiment of Cuba while its colonel Lleonart faced a court martial, when it ended Casa-Calvo resumed his post as the number two officer in the regiment and head of its second battalion. Among his military duties, he tried to reform the battalion and the regiment as he worked to add and train whatever recruits he could obtain to replace the losses suffered in Hispaniola. More important, he ended his petitions for a post in Spain as Havana became more accommodating; perhaps his children who had endured his lengthy absences persuaded him to stay. Furthermore, he possessed the rank of brigadier general in addition to a title of nobility; enjoyed status as a prominent planter; and was well established in the highest echelons of the island's society. As he adjusted to Cuba again, he resumed direction of his estates and often joined with other landowners to advocate for agricultural and commercial reforms. Finally, he spent the last years of this period as the interim governor of Louisiana, where he exercised more power than in any previous post.[1]

1. Kuethe, *Cuba*, 152. Brief expositions of Casa-Calvo's work in Louisiana are discussed in Gilbert C. Din, "Marqués de Casa-Calvo," in *A Dictionary of Louisiana Biography*, general editor Glenn R. Conrad, 2 vols. ([Lafayette, La.]: Louisiana Historical Association in cooperation with the Center for Louisiana Studies of the University of Southwestern Louisiana, 1988), 1: 158-59; and "Francisco Bouligny; Marqués de

As well as his life progressed professionally and materially, on his return to Cuba he learned that two senior members of his immediate family lay dying. His mother, Catalina O'Farrill y Arriola de Calvo de la Puerta, had been ailing from an undisclosed malady. Realizing that the affliction would claim her, on June 10 and at age seventy-two, she summoned a notary to make out her last will and testament. After doing so, her hardy constitution clung to life for several more weeks, and the time enabled Casa-Calvo to complete his journey from Bayajá. He spent approximately two weeks with her in Havana, and they undoubtedly exchanged final confidences. It must have given him a measure of solace to be present when she died on July 9, because army duty had kept him away for the last three years of her life. Probably more than anyone while she was able, she cared for his children during his absences and now related to him whatever relevant news about them he did not know. With her demise, their responsibility again devolved on him. He possibly inherited some possessions that had once belonged to her father, Ricardo O'Farrill, the progenitor of the O'Farrill clan in Cuba, and to her husband (Sebastián's father) Pedro Calvo de la Puerta.[2]

Casa-Calvo's older brother Francisco, the Conde de Buena Vista, also died that summer. His status as the first-born son had made him the wealthiest member of the family and enabled him as colonel of the Havana militia regiment, a post that conferred abundant prestige, to provide much of the unit's military equipment and uniforms. In 1793 he traveled to Spain to lobby for more privileges for the Cuban plantocracy that was trying to replace Saint-Domingue, where the African insurrection had destroyed commercial agriculture, as the chief sugar producer in the Caribbean. He journeyed despite the government's tendency to limit visits by favor-seekers and prevent reduction of the colonial population. Francisco used his illness of hydrocele, the

Casa-Calvo; Manuel Juan de Salcedo; Pierre Clement, Baron de Laussat; Colonial Governors, 1799-1803," in *The Louisiana Governors: From Iberville to Edwards*, ed. Joseph G. Dawson III (Louisiana State University Press: Baton Rouge, 1990): 74-79.

2. Calcagno, *Historia de Familias Cubanas*, 335-36; information provided by Jorge Auñon.

seepage of a watery fluid into body cavities, for going. It was the same affliction that killed his uncle Juan O'Farrill, and it seemed to be an O'Farrill genetic affliction. In an age before anesthesia and antibiotics, Francisco survived an operation in Havana that drained the fluid but did not cure him. His uncle was not as fortunate and succumbed to the procedure. Possibly Europe held a solution to his ailment, and Francisco went there. He arrived in Spain several months after his younger brother Sebastián sailed to Santo Domingo, and he returned to Havana in 1796, slightly before Sebastián did. In Spain Francisco and several more Cubans successfully petitioned the crown to reinstate the *fuero* for the militia, among other things.[3]

Francisco also used his presence in Spain to gain advancements in military rank since he had been denied promotion to brigadier general in his petitions from Havana. Now in Madrid he flaunted his New World riches by paying substantial sums to the money-hungry wartime treasury to secure promotions to brigadier general in 1794, the same year Sebastián earned that rank in the field, and then, presumably for a larger sum, to field marshal in 1795. The new ranks must have delighted Francisco, but he had no time to exercise whatever authority they wielded. His disease worsened in Spain, and with the pangs of death bearing down on him, he returned home to Havana. He succumbed on July 29, 1796, in the city of his birth not long after his return.[4]

His title of nobility and his property descended upon his only child, María Francisca Calvo de la Puerta y Aparicio del Manzano (November 8, 1778-1846). Several months before her father's departure for Spain and at the age of fourteen, on November 11, 1792, she married Pedro Pablo O'Reilly de Las Casas (1769-1832), son of the first Conde de O'Reilly, Alejandro O'Reilly, and nephew of Luis de Las Casas, then the Cuban captain general (1790-1796). The marriage il-

3. Pezuela, *Diccionario,* 4: 191; On the "Fuero Militar," see Lyle McAlister, *The "Fuero Militar" in New Spain, 1766-1800* (Gainesville: University of Florida Press, 1957).

4. Conde de Vallellano (Fernando Suárez de Tangil y de Angulo), *Nobiliario Cubano: Las grandes familias isleñas* (Madrid: F. Beltrán, [1929]), 252. See also the file on the Conde de Buena Vista in AGS, GM, leg. 6855, that deals with Francisco Calvo de la Puerta's requests for military promotion.

lustrated the standing of both families in the highest circles of Havana society. Shortly after the wedding, O'Reilly's father died in Spain, and Pedro inherited his title.[5] In 1796 María Francisca became the condesa de Buena Vista as she gained her father's title on his death. Several titles in wealthy families were not uncommon. Earlier in the 1760s, Alejandro O'Reilly had acquired estates in Cuba that his son now inherited. With his lands and title, the faction of the Havana elite that had continued to support his father, even after his humiliating failure in the invasion of Algiers in 1775, welcomed Pedro O'Reilly into their fold. In addition, Pedro was attached as a colonel and a liaison at the headquarters of the Cuban military.[6]

Finding two immediate family members on the verge of death on arriving in Havana distressed Casa-Calvo deeply. Instead of the anticipated joyous homecoming, their pending demise had already shrouded the family in grief. On the eve of becoming the family patriarch, Sebastián tried to assuage his mother's and his brother's final days by carrying out their last wishes. He surely felt a great helplessness since their illnesses lay beyond remedy and the understanding of eighteenth-century medicine. While his mother had reached an advanced age for that era, his brother Francisco, only a year older than Sebastián, expired at forty-six. Fortunately, the new head of this branch of the Calvo de la Puerta family exhibited no signs of hydrocele, and he outlived Francisco by more than twenty years.

As a planter Sebastián demonstrated an avid interest in agriculture between 1796 and 1799, especially as he searched for more efficient ways to augment sugar production on his lands. It can be seen in his subscription to the Havana newspaper, the *Papel Periódico* (founded in 1791 as a weekly and converted to a daily two years later) that carried

5. Pezuela, *Diccionario*, 4: 191. Kuethe, *Cuba*, 164-65; information provided by Jorge Auñon. María Francisca's son, Manuel Francisco O'Reilly y Calvo de la Puerta received his mother's title of condesa de Buena Vista upon her death in 1846.

6. Sánchez-Ripoll, *Cuba*, 140, and note. Pedro O'Reilly held posts in the Havana Cabildo as a *regidor* and *alguacil mayor*, which María Francisca inherited from her father, the Conde de Buena Vista. She was Sebastián Calvo de la Puerta y O'Farrill's niece.

articles on agricultural science, techniques, and machinery. The journal also published articles written by his brother Nicolás on these subjects. Both brothers belonged to the *Sociedad Económica de Amigos del País* (Economic Society for Friends of the Country), and Nicolás became one of its early directors. It strove to disseminate knowledge on agriculture and sugarcane, stockraising, industry, mining, and commerce, and its subscribers included the powerful landowners. Nicolás's studies on growing sugarcane and its conversion into sugar made him a respected authority. No doubt Casa-Calvo frequently sought his advice.[7]

Although Nicolás received a doctorate of theology from the Royal and Pontifical University of Havana on January 27, 1781, in reality the subject matter was more related to agriculture and chemistry than religion. He started his acquisition of knowledge and experiments on lands inherited from his father. Some of the techniques he promoted had originated in French Saint-Domingue. His mill at his estate of La Holanda, near Güines, figured prominently in his experiments and creation of methods to extract juice from the cane stalks more efficiently. He advocated the formation of the Patriotic Society that propagated new ideas throughout the island. Soon Nicolás acquired a professorship at his university as the spread of colonial universities and numerous other institutions of learning in the eighteenth century reflected a growing maturity in Spain's overseas possessions. Nicolás's studies quickly earned him distinction as a scholar. He ardently advocated furthering sugar production on the island, and he was second only to the noted writer Francisco Arango y Parreño in doing so. Nicolás was one of the most important investors, along with Luis de Las Casas and Arango y Parreño, in a society dedicated to the production of sugar. In April 1799, Nicolás borrowed 300,000 pesos from Juan Santa María, who with a partner, possessed investment capital to lend to sugar planters who were expanding their operations. As they bought up properties from the *vegueros* in districts around Havana, the remaining smaller tobacco growers appealed to the crown for protection from the rapacious sugar barons. There was a reason for concern. Sugar, the planters

7. Pérez, *Cuba*, 65-66.

argued, was a weightier and bulkier crop and more difficult to transport than tobacco leaves. The crown, however, rejected their arguments on March 15, 1798, and the decision severely disturbed Nicolás. With other planters, he believed that those lands belonged in the hands of sugar growers, and he wrote a tract on November 6, 1798, condemning the protection given to tobacco farmers and urging the crown to provide the *vegueros* with lands farther removed from the coast. Egotism probably led him to conclude later that *veguero* domains should be seized without compensation. Sugar growers were then investing heavily in their agricultural endeavors. But when the crown specified that sugar growers erect chapels and put a chaplain on their payroll for the religious instruction of African slaves who were arriving in growing numbers, Nicolás publicly denounced the measure. He despised charging plantation owners 400 pesos for each priest's annual salary, which was in addition to the fees he received for burials, marriages, wakes, baptisms, and perhaps for confessions. Nicolás married a first cousin, Bárbara O'Farrill y Herrera, with whom he had seven children. After Nicolás's early death in 1800, she wedded Sebastián Peñalver y Borroto, no doubt a Calvo de la Puerta relative through more than one connection.[8]

Nicolás differed from his older brothers in another respect. He agreed with other wealthy Cubans who refused to acquire a title, which perhaps was a subtle protest against the crown. His O'Farrill cousins were among them since none capitulated to the allure of a title of nobility. In the 1790s, Nicolás condemned the Spanish crown for refusing to provide the sugar oligarchy with all the slaves, lands, machinery, and tax avoidance they wanted. Sebastián undoubtedly shared many of Nicolás's economic convictions, but as an army officer in royal service

8. Pérez, *Cuba*, 205-7; Gonzalez-Ripoll, *Cuba*, 141, 154; Calcagno, *Diccionario biográfico cubano*, 148-49; Thomas, *Cuba*, 79 and note. Nicolás Calvo de la Puerta married the daughter of his uncle José Ricardo O'Farrill. Alexander von Humboldt, *Personal Narrative of Travels to the Equinoctial Regions of America*, translated and edited by Thomasina Ross (New York: B. Bloom, 1971). See J. W. Pierson's article, "Francisco de Arango y Parreño," *Hispanic American Historical Review* 16, no. 4 (November 1936): 451-78.

he knew it was better to stifle his private opinions.[9]

Despite the planters' complaints, the crown promoted agricultural improvements in several ways. It allowed the importation of more African slaves. After it founded the Royal Economic Society for Friends of the Country in 1792, it followed up with the establishment of the Consulate of Agriculture and Commerce in 1795 to further the circulation of knowledge in these important areas. Francisco Arango y Parreño, who headed it, had earlier lobbied the government on behalf of planters while studying law in Madrid. As Cuba widened its horizons in trade, its planters sought to modernize their antiquated methods to catch up with the agriculturally advanced colonies. Inasmuch as neither Cuba nor Spain manufactured the implements needed to grind cane faster or the newest boilers that extracted sugar from the juice more efficiently, they had to be imported. Later, steam-powered engines replaced the plodding animals that moved the machinery that ground the cane stalks. The production of sugar and its other marketable products soon generated even larger fortunes for the planters, including the Calvo de la Puerta clan. Sebastián probably spent time on his estates and looked in on the operations of managers. Nicolás almost certainly guided him on ways to improve mechanical techniques. Much had to be done, and Casa-Calvo's presence on his estates helped in furthering those tasks.[10]

Nevertheless, he was first a soldier, and Spain was soon in another war. Great Britain declared hostilities a few months after Casa-Calvo returned to Cuba in 1796, and the island quickly felt its effect when enemy warships cruised off the coast or seized its ships. Perhaps more serious, the conflict impeded Spain from trading with its colonies. Aware that they would traffic illicitly if denied lawful commerce, Spain

9. Moreno Fraginals, *El Ingenio*, 128.

10. Roland T. Ely, "Cuba Emerges from Isolation: Economic and Social Changes Between 1760 and 1839," 160-63, in *Background to Revolution: The Development of Modern Cuba*, ed. Robert Freeman Smith (New York: Alfred A. Knopf, 1966), 159-67; Jaime Suchlicki, *Cuba, from Columbus to Castro* (Washington: Pergamon-Brassey's, 1986), 44-46; John Edwin Fagg, *Cuba, Haiti, and the Dominican Republic* (Englewood Cliffs, N.J.: Prentiss Hall, 1965), 26.

opened its overseas possessions to commerce with neutral nations that also sought to sell the colonies food and machinery. Trade, consequently, quickly surged upwards.[11] As demand for Cuban exports widened, the island's planters eagerly increased the production of sugar, coffee, hides, cacao, rum and tafia (undistilled rum), and other commodities, and they welcomed new buyers and markets. They also sought more African slaves to perform the backbreaking labor demanded by agricultural tasks, especially sugarcane.[12]

While work on his estates kept Casa-Calvo occupied, he, nevertheless, was a high-ranking officer and administrator. As such, the captain general chose him to employ his talents when the governorship of Louisiana fell vacant. His effort at building up the Fixed Infantry Regiment of Cuba had not been very successful since Spain stopped sending troops. In addition, part of the regiment stayed in Santo Domingo until 1799. The second battalion that was stationed in Havana had only 273 men of an authorized 626 in 1796, and the number slipped to 203 two years later. When the unit was reorganized in early 1799, it counted 467 men. It was at that time that Casa-Calvo was selected to return to Louisiana, a colony he had not visited for several decades. His role there now differed significantly from his duties as an inexperienced teen-aged captain in 1769 and 1770. Since then, he had acquired extensive military knowledge during two lengthy sojourns in Spain, where he became intimately acquainted with the peninsular army, formed a regiment, and dealt not only with soldiers and officers but with the ministry of war. In addition, he gained proficiency in field operations in Cuba and in his relations with superior officers, particularly the captain general. In war-torn Santo Domingo, he led troops in battle, first a battalion in the capture and fighting around Bayajá and later a regiment in defense of the city; furthermore, he built hospitals

11. Fagg, *Cuba, Haiti, and the Dominican Republic*, 26.

12. Sugar mills increased from 245 in 1792 to 305 in 1800 while boxes filled with sugar rose from 30,487 in 1769 (there is no figure for 1792) to 230,000 in 1802 (80,500,000 lbs). Each box weighed about sixteen arrobas (184 kilos or 350 lbs). Pablo Tornero, "Hacendados y desarrollo azucarero cubano (1763-1818)," *Revista de Indias* 38, nos. 153-54 (July-December 1978): 715 and note.

for infirm soldiers. Casa-Calvo's intelligence and fluency in the French language acquired either in Saint-Domingue or earlier helped significantly. Lastly, he had emerged from the imbroglio in Santo Domingo relatively unblemished, except for the minor criticism on his decision to sail to Havana instead of the city of Santo Domingo. His new assignment made him the interim military governor, the top official in Louisiana and West Florida while he waited for the royally-appointed governor to arrive.[13]

The origins of Casa-Calvo's new assignment came on July 18, 1799, when a malignant illness, probably yellow fever, struck down Louisiana's governor, Brig. Manuel Gayoso de Lemos.[14] With his demise, the head of the Fixed Louisiana Infantry Regiment, Col. Francisco Bouligny, assumed the military governorship, a post he desperately wanted. But he suffered from unrelenting maladies that often prevented him from leaving his bed. On September 3, 1799, Cuban Capt. Gen. Salvador de Muro y Salazar (1799-1812), better known by his title of Marqués de Someruelos and in charge of Cuba, Louisiana, and the Floridas, concluded that Louisiana needed a fit governor. Since military men filled political posts in the eighteenth-century Spanish colonies, he chose Casa-Calvo, who received orders to depart as quickly as possible. On the death of a royally appointed governor, his duties were divided between two interim governors. Authority in civil matters that were mostly legal descended in July on Nicolás María Vidal, the government attorney in Louisiana, while Casa-Calvo acquired "military" authority, but it extended beyond army matters to include po-

13. Kuethe, *Cuba*, 141, 152; military service sheets of the Cuban army, June 30, 1803, AGI, PC, leg. 1771A. In Louisiana, Casa-Calvo communicated with Francophone post commandants in French. Although his scribes were undoubtedly versed in the French language, he gave every indication that he knew it too. Examples of his letters in French are in AGI, PC, leg. 69.

14. Jack D. L. Holmes, *Gayoso: The Life of a Spanish Governor in the Mississippi Valley, 1789-1799* (Baton Rouge: Louisiana State University Press for the Louisiana Historical Association, 1965), 266-67. Holmes incorrectly asserts that Nicolás María Vidal acquired political power on Gayoso's death; he did not, he acquired civil authority. Casa-Calvo's position as military governor included political power.

litical and diplomatic duties. He was by far the senior official in the dual arrangement, and the public generally accepted him as the real governor.[15]

In naming Casa-Calvo the military governor of Louisiana, Someruelos requested a greater salary for him since he was not making enough in his post as second-in-command of the Havana regiment (140 pesos monthly) to cover his new expenses. He favored an increase to 236 pesos monthly. On the other hand, if the king decided to pay him only his salary as a brigadier general then he was entitled to 218 pesos. Someruelos considered Casa-Calvo worthy of the larger increase because he was leaving his family and business interests behind and doing so without hesitation. In Madrid on March 15, 1800, the government agreed to the increase in pay.[16]

With only a few days to arrange his affairs, Casa-Calvo assigned caretakers, undoubtedly relatives, to take charge of his children. His business interests and estates needed a different solution inasmuch as they involved slaves, commercial crops, comestibles for home consumption, livestock (cattle, oxen, horses, donkeys, mules, and pigs), poultry of many kinds, and everything else used or consumed in the countryside. One can speculate that during his three years in Havana, his lands had increased in productivity. The most difficult part of his departure was leaving his sons behind, especially Ignacio who was only nine years old. Pedro, on the other hand, was now seventeen, and perhaps assisted with his younger siblings. On September 11, 1799, Casa-Calvo boarded a ship in Havana's inner harbor and began the voyage across the Gulf of Mexico to New Orleans.[17] As a high ranking army

15. Gilbert C. Din, *Francisco Bouligny: A Bourbon Soldier in Spanish Louisiana* (Baton Rouge: Louisiana State University Press, 1993); Domingo Rosain, *Necropolis de La Habana* (Havana: Imprenta El Trabajo, 1875), 181-82. Someruelos lived from 1754 to December 14, 1813.

16. Royal order to the captain general of Cuba, Aranjuez, March 15, 1800, and attachments, AGS, GM, leg. 6926. See also in ibid., Someruelos to Juan Manuel Alvarez, no. 27, Havana, September 14, 1799; and Casa-Calvo to Someruelos, Havana, September 6, 1799.

17. Casa-Calvo to Someruelos, New Orleans, September 20, 1799, AGI, PC, leg. 1550.

officer, a personal bodyguard of several soldiers from his regiment plus a servant or two accompanied him to Louisiana.

The crossing on the royal brigantine *Saeta* took roughly seven days as winds blew in favorable directions. On arriving in New Orleans in mid-September 1799, after a three-decade absence, Casa-Calvo found the city almost unrecognizable.[18] From a tiny settlement of about three thousand whites and blacks thrust between a riverbank and a swamp in 1769, it had sprouted to nearly fifteen thousand people living in the city and its adjacent areas. It represented a significant growth for that age as it was the province's only municipality. The colony, in turn, had increased from about eleven to twelve thousand inhabitants to approximately fifty thousand. All this occurred as commerce changed from a trifle, much of it eked out from smuggling, to nearly two hundred legal ships per year engaged in its foreign trade, and many of them cluttered the city's river wharves and banks when the new governor arrived. Besides the Louisiana river boats, foreign vessels came from ports in the United States (New York, Philadelphia, Charleston, Baltimore, and Boston were the most common), Cuba, Spain, Jamaica, France, and Mexico. Many more commercial activities operated in the city than in 1770, since it serviced all regions of Louisiana and West Florida. The city's inhabitants and transients communicated in a multitude of languages, not merely in French as they had several decades before. Development of the port's cosmopolitan character was well underway.[19]

New Orleans bore similarities to Havana, at least until the coming of numerous Americans in the late 1790s. Society revolved around class status, political or military position, and the economic fortunes of the wealthiest planters and merchants who were ensconced at the top of a commercial or bourgeois social pyramid. They were followed by holders of professional offices: physicians, attorneys, engineers, clergy, and other university trained persons of which there were few in all cat-

18. Ibid.

19. Someruelos to Álvarez, no. 39, Havana, October 20, 1799, AGS, GM, leg. 6926; Clark, *New Orleans*, 228, 251. Although Clark's figure for ships is for 1801, it probably approximated the number for 1799.

egories. Below them were the more numerous artisans or commoners knowledgeable in a multitude of manual skills that made up the nebulous lower middle class. The unskilled poor constituted the bottom rung of whites in New Orleans, many of whom lived in miserable and squalid conditions and usually performed back-breaking manual labor. Often little distinguished them from free blacks who were gradually increasing numerically and occasionally through tireless work rising above lower class whites in economic circumstance. African slaves, of course, made up the lowest social group, but they, too, differed in position, more so in the city than in the countryside. If their owners were wealthy, select blacks sometimes trained as servants (barbers, cobblers, tailors, cooks, carpenters, coachmen, etc.), skills useful should they gain their freedom. They often had opportunities to work for pay and used their accumulated earnings to buy their freedom or that of kin and even start businesses. As the Spanish period progressed from the 1760s to the 1790s, a substantial class of free people of color emerged. Among them were mulattoes and quadroons, fathered by white men and sometimes freed by them. The major difference between New Orleans and Havana was the French language that Louisiana descendants of the first inhabitants and their slaves continued to speak. Spanish, however, was used by soldiers, sailors, government officials, and even settlers like the Canary Islanders. Many French New Orleanians acquired a functional knowledge of Spanish similar to the Spaniards who learned French. Spanish was the idiom of the government and official documents were written in it, although proclamations posted in New Orleans were usually printed in both languages. At older civilian settlements, commandants were often French, and they communicated with the governor in this idiom. For French Creoles who were army officers, however, learning Spanish was obligatory inasmuch as the army employed it exclusively as nearly all soldiers were Spaniards.[20]

20. Kimberly S. Hanger, *Bounded Lives, Bounded Places: Free Black Society in Colonial New Orleans, 1769-1803* (Durham, N.C.: Duke University Press, 1997); Hans W. Baade, "The Law of Slavery in Spanish *Luisiana, 1769-1803*, in *Louisiana's Legal Heritage*, Edwin F. Haas, 43-86 (Pensacola: Perdido Bay Press, 1983). On the use of the Spanish language in New Orleans, see Din and Harkins, *New Orleans Cabildo*,

As it kept changing, Louisiana was in many respects a province, society, and economy in rapid transition. By the late 1790s, Americans were accelerating in numbers as settlers, merchants, and sailors, who among others entered the colony by ship from the Atlantic coast and by barge and flatboat from the upper reaches of the Ohio and Tennessee Rivers, especially during spring floods when travel downriver was faster and shorter. In the late 1790s, hundreds, if not more, of Americans arrived each spring on boats packed with agricultural products, and not all the personnel on board returned home.[21]

Changes in political ownership in the Mississippi basin had altered boundaries in the last decades of the eighteenth century. After losing the Seven Years' War (also known as the French and Indian War) in 1763, French dominion over both banks of the Mississippi River as well as over Canada terminated. France ceded the river's west bank and the small area around New Orleans (the Isle of Orleans) on the east bank to Spain. Great Britain won Canada and trans-Appalachia (the region from those mountains westward to the Mississippi) and down the east bank as far as Bayou Manchac; at war's end Spain swapped Florida to recover conquered Havana. Twenty years later, with the defeat of the British in the War for American Independence, Americans gained the Mississippi's east bank down to West Florida that Iberian arms had seized in the conflict; Great Britain also yielded East Florida to Spain. The Treaty of Paris at war's end acknowledged these territorial transfers. Spain acquiesced to another change in territorial limits on the east bank in its 1795 Treaty of San Lorenzo, when Manuel Godoy, Spain's principal minister, ceded territory to the United States down to the 31st parallel, and colonial officials implemented the transfer in 1798. The last two territorial exchanges brought the Americans nearer

9-10. See also Samantha Perez, *The Isleños of Louisiana: On the Water's Edge* (Charleston, S.C.: The History Press, 2011).

21. Whitaker, *Mississippi Question*, 97; John G. Clark, *New Orleans, 1718-1812: An Economic History* (Baton Rouge: Louisiana State University Press, 1970), 237-49 and 251-74. In *The Accidental City: Improvising New Orleans* (Cambridge, Mass.: Harvard University Press, 2012), 314-51, Lawrence N. Powell discusses the influx of Americans into New Orleans in the 1790s and the changes they introduced.

to where the bulk of Louisiana's population resided. Americans also gained passage on the river where Spain owned both banks and the right of deposit in New Orleans that permitted American goods to pass untaxed across Spanish soil. The ominous presence of Americans in the lower reaches of the Mississippi delta created a worrisome dilemma for Spain, and Casa-Calvo felt their hovering presence when he arrived in New Orleans.[22]

His first tasks in September 1799 consisted of learning how to handle the issues that confronted the colonies in his charge. Military scribes, who dealt with the voluminous paper work that Spanish bureaucracy required to maintain communications with all regions of the provinces, issue orders, and document events, helped him greatly. The records were stored in the governor's archives and informed him of the orders Madrid had sent and the measures taken by predecessors. He also became acquainted with the people he had to deal with, both Spaniards and foreigners. Casa-Calvo quickly discovered that problems abounded, some originating in and around New Orleans while others came from military and civilian posts scattered across Louisiana and West Florida. Resolving them required knowing past experiences and exercising his best judgment. Because the captain general in Havana could overrule him, he reported often on critical events and requested approval for the decisions he made. Ships, however, sailed irregularly to Havana, which meant that weeks or even months might elapse, especially in wartime, before he received instructions.[23]

The most unrelenting issue Casa-Calvo faced was the United States, which had already cast a shroud on Spanish lands in the lower Mississippi Valley. At times rumors starting far up the rivers portended a forceful seizure of Louisiana. Spain had tried to forestall growth of the western American settlements by closing the Mississippi River to

22. DeConde, *This Affair of Louisiana*, 91-105; Jon Kukla, *Wilderness So Immense*, 187-94; and Frederick Jackson Turner, "The Policy of France toward the Mississippi Valley in the Period of Washington and Adams," *American Historical Review* 10 (January 1905): 266-67.

23. Din and Harkins, *New Orleans Cabildo*, 228.

its citizens in 1784, but the settlements grew nonetheless, and that increased the risk of invasion. Despite Spain's expenditure of substantial sums of money to augment Louisiana's Catholic inhabitants, primarily with Acadians, Canary Islanders, and French Canadians, it achieved only modest results. Spain then turned to encouraging Protestant Americans if they settled at their own expense. But they, too, entered in limited numbers as governors in the 1790s preferred Europeans, whom they judged more loyal and trustworthy despite the difficulty in attracting them.[24]

Casa-Calvo's predecessor, Gayoso, had tried to restrain Americans from entering Louisiana. He grew displeased with them when the last newcomers to arrive between 1795 and 1797, in the Natchez district where he was then the local governor, exhibited anti-Spanish proclivities after the territory technically became American and Spain delayed yielding it until 1798. He ordered post commandants to withhold land grants to unmarried and penniless males until they demonstrated their loyalty and industriousness through several years of toil. He further required children of settlers to be raised as Roman Catholics and limited religious tolerance to their parents only. Casa-Calvo adopted these policies since he agreed with Gayoso; possibly Louisiana's bishop also influenced him.[25] Following in Gayoso's footsteps, Casa-Calvo instructed post commandants to drive out vagrants who entered the province without written permission, and he advised against creating new settlements on the Mississippi's Spanish bank. While these policies probably slowed the entry of Americans, they did not halt the influx.[26]

In 1800 an exasperated Casa-Calvo commented about American desires to expand westward. To a superior official in Spain, he complained about "their unwarranted ambitions that they constantly try

24. See Gilbert C. Din, *Populating the Barrera: Spain's Immigration Efforts in Colonial Louisiana* (Lafayette, La.: University of Louisiana at Lafayette Press, 2014).

25. Gayoso to the Prince of the Peace (Godoy), New Orleans, November 22, 1798, AHN, Est., leg. 3900.

26. Gilbert C. Din, "Spain's Immigration Policy in Louisiana and the American Penetration, 1792-1803," *Southwestern Historical Quarterly* 76 (January 1973): 255-76.

to impress upon their youth from their most tender years."[27] Trying to wean them from their entrenched ambitions seemed impossible. Casa-Calvo understood well the formidable presence the Americans constituted and the difficulty of dealing with them.

In a proposal of the same year, Philippe Enrique Nering, who was a would-be land impresario and a bogus nobleman who called himself the Baron de Bastrop, generously offered to introduce five hundred families and pay all their travel expenses, rations, and settlement costs. Most likely he possessed few of the funds he needed to do these things. Bastrop had earlier solicited land from Governor Francisco Luis Héctor, barón de Carondelet to raise cotton with newly introduced African slaves. Inasmuch as Gayoso, who received the proposal, died, Casa-Calvo "inherited" and approved it.[28] He preferred slaves over Americans in Louisiana. A fly in the ointment appeared when Bastrop tried to capitalize on his grant by selling part of it to Col. Abraham Morhouse of Kentucky. An alert Intendant Ramón López y Angulo, however, suspected that Bastrop wanted to leave the colony, and he stopped the sale. Going farther, López y Angulo halted sales of all land grants, to which Casa-Calvo protested that this strategy harmed immigration.[29]

Government officials in Spain, meanwhile, questioned the usefulness of giving land to Americans entering Louisiana and West Florida. Following the rejection of Bastrop's petition, Secretary of the Treasury

27. Casa-Calvo to Mariano Luis de Urquijo, New Orleans, October 8, 1800, AHN , Est. leg. 3888, and cited in Sylvia L. Hilton, "Movilidad y expansión en la construcción política de los Estados Unidos: 'estos errantes colonos' en las fronteras españolas del Misisipí (1776-1803)," *Revista Complutense de Historia de América* 28 (2002): 63-96.

28. Gayoso to Morales, New Orleans, October 5, 1797, AGI, PC, leg. 44; Francisco de Saavedra to the Prince of the Peace, Aranjuez, February 23, 1798; Bastrop to the Marqués de Casa-Calvo, New Orleans, June 18, 1800; Casa-Calvo to López y Angulo, New Orleans, July 10, 1800; all in AHN, Est., leg. 3901.

29. Casa-Calvo to Luis de Urquijo, New Orleans, August 8, 1800, AHN, Est., leg. 3901; López y Angulo, nos. 94 and 95, both reserved, New Orleans, August 12 and September 25, 1800, respectively, both in AHN, Est., leg. 3888. The crown rejected Bastrop's commission in 1802. Soler to Pedro Cevallo, Madrid, July 13, 1802, AHN, Est., leg. 3901.

Cayetano Soler stopped land grants to Americans inasmuch as the United States gave explicit signs of wanting to annex those provinces.[30]

After eight months in the colony, Casa-Calvo informed Captain General Someruelos on observations he had made on several vital topics. The concessions granted to the United States in the 1795 Treaty of San Lorenzo and the proximity of Americans (they were approximately forty miles above Baton Rouge and settled intermittingly upriver for many hundreds of miles) compromised Louisiana's safety. He emphasized two points: land grants to settlers and defense. He complained that a royal order had transferred his authority to grant land and determine where to build settlements to the intendancy. The transfers destroyed his ability to encourage immigration. Furthermore, not satisfied with the law, the intendant had established new regulations that hurt settlements Casa-Calvo considered necessary. He believed in placing new immigrants in West Florida and expanding their settlements north toward the American border (the Mississippi Territory). Expecting scurrilous accusations that alleged he sought personal gain, he vigorously insisted that he only wanted to benefit the province.[31]

Casa-Calvo's second point dwelt on Louisiana's defenses. He believed the colony's military leadership had grown ineffectual. The illnesses of Bouligny, colonel of the regiment, worsened each day. The next in command, Lt. Col. Carlos Howard, although he possessed a keen mind and had experience, was elderly. Casa-Calvo suggested that the province would benefit if Bouligny retired and the king rewarded Howard with an appointment to another post, possibly St. Augustine, Florida. He urged the selection of able and patriotic officers to replace them. Expanding on this matter, he added that the colony needed more Spaniards because outsiders often seemed unaware that Spain owned the province. For this purpose, he advised permitting Spanish officers from other army units to swap posts with the French Creole officers

30. Soler to Pedro Cevallo, Madrid, July 13, 1802; statement by Cayetano Soler, Palace, July 20, 1802; both in AHN, Est., leg. 3901.

31. Casa-Calvo to Someruelos, New Orleans, May 21, 1800, AHN, Est., leg. 3901. Morales's land regulations are in Gayarré, *History of Louisiana*, 3: 632-40.

in the Louisiana regiment. Although Casa-Calvo knew that the transfer of Creole officers to foreign posts contradicted the purpose behind Louisiana's "fixed", i.e., stationary regiment and staffed with local personnel, he believed it necessary. He further questioned the worth of the colony's numerous infantry, artillery, and cavalry militia organizations, and a special unit that admitted only distinguished (well-born and moneyed) individuals given that they never met, trained, or knew their duties. Officers were unacquainted with their personnel and soldiers with their superiors. Even though scattered settlements throughout the province usually had militia forces, great distances separated them and limited their defensive and supportive capabilities.[32]

Finally, he considered the large sums of money the king spent annually on Louisiana. The expenditures, he alleged, did not enhance the love of the province's unenthusiastic vassals for their monarch. Unless their devotion increased, he predicted that they would separate from Spain's sovereignty. He dismissed the willingness of New Orleans's Creole and American inhabitants to defend the city against a potential foe, and he lamented that the city's Spaniards alone could not protect it. He ended his observations by declaring, "[I]t is painful to consider that an important royal possession is inhabited by persons who are not truly devoted to the Spanish monarchy. And as my patriotism cannot tolerate this ingratitude, I must manifest it to you."[33]

In this instance, a xenophobic Casa-Calvo seemed to focus his attention on the disgruntled few while ignoring the vast majority of Louisiana's inhabitants who were dedicated to the monarchy. This became apparent several years later when they learned that the colony was to be transferred to the United States. At that time, many residents demonstrated their addiction to the only system of governance they had known. Casa-Calvo's letter further illustrates that he was not accustomed to life in a Spanish possession inhabited by people of different ethnic origins. Perhaps, too, he had acquired an anti-French bias from his wartime experience in Saint-Domingue and from the social

32. Casa-Calvo to Someruelos, New Orleans, May 21, 1800, AHN, Est. leg. 3901.

33. Ibid.

revolution that had destroyed the French Bourbon monarchy. Within a few years, he would again demonstrate his devotion to monarchy even though it was not a genuinely Spanish government.

If he did not know it before arriving, Casa-Calvo quickly learned that he had a relative of sorts in New Orleans. Luis de Peñalver y Cárdenas, the bishop of Louisiana, probably was among the welcoming entourage that greeted him in September 1799. He had known him in Havana since he was the paternal uncle of Casa-Calvo's deceased wife. Peñalver was only a year or two older than the governor. He had arrived in Louisiana on July 17, 1795, as the colony's first Catholic bishop, and he remained throughout Casa-Calvo's tenure as interim governor. As a Cuban, his proclivities resonated with those of Casa-Calvo. Peñalver found religious observance by the colony's Catholics halfhearted, and he tried to stimulate their devotion through more public celebrations. One important to the Spaniards was Corpus Christi that was celebrated in June sixty days after Easter Sunday. It became a huge public event. Following Mass on the designated day, a procession would wend through the streets of New Orleans with the religious, including the bishop, participating. A Protestant American writer described the 1797 Corpus Christi pageantry in which the priests marched in front of the bishop dressed in their assorted costumes and carried crosses and candles. The writer, with his ingrained sectarian partiality, described a portion of the procession: "After [the clergy] came the bishop, walking in solemn state under a canopy supported by half a dozen priests, and scattering his fruitless blessings around on a gaping multitude. Close to the bishop followed the Baron de Carondelet, the governor of the province, together with his suite, and at the close of these a party of horse and foot to preserve order, and to keep off the rabble which followed behind."[34] No doubt Casa-Calvo participated in similar processions in June of 1800 and 1801.

The bishop renewed his friendship with his former nephew-in-law after a four-year hiatus. They saw each other on both private and public occasions. It is known that the bishop sometimes met with Casa-Calvo

34. Baily, *Journal of a Tour*, 174.

in Pointe Coupee to seek assistance in dealing with religious issues at the outlying posts. One such meeting involved the *charivari*, which was a spontaneous French custom of razzing newlyweds on their wedding night with pots, pans, horns, and other noise makers. It happened when the marriage partners included a widow, widower, or an older groom with a young bride. Unfamiliar with the raucous custom, the bishop deemed the commotion a violation of the marriage ceremony's sanctity; with the recent exception of Protestant settlers, all marriages in Spanish Louisiana and West Florida were Catholic. At the bishop's urging, Civil Governor Nicolás María Vidal ordered the instigators of the mayhem to come to the city for judgment. Casa-Calvo also instructed the post commandant to determine which militiamen had been involved and to stop those "pagan abuses." Otherwise, he hinted, criminal action would be taken.[35] Apparently, the mischief makers had exceeded customary limits and word of the turmoil reached New Orleans. On another occasion, Casa-Calvo stopped the marriage of a girl who was possibly younger than twelve but had the mother's consent to wed a much older man. He ordered a two-year delay to the nuptials; locals accepted fourteen as the marriageable age for girls. If the mother, Madame Vallière, objected, the commandant was to send her to New Orleans, where her son, army Capt. Antonio Vallière, awaited her. Casa-Calvo warned the Pointe Coupee commandant that by no means was he to permit such an irregular and scandalous marriage.[36]

35. Casa-Calvo to Guillermo Duparc, New Orleans, (date illegible but it is 1800), AGI, PC, leg. 69. In Vidal's letter to Casa-Calvo, (New Orleans), October 8, (1800?), in ibid., Vidal said he had informed the Pointe Coupee commandant not to permit the charivari for any reason in the future and to arrest violators. He further asked Casa-Calvo to support his measure. A description of the charivari can be found in Winston DeVille, "Charivari at Pointe Coupée in 1800," *Louisiana Genealogical Register* 40, no. 4 (December 1993): 356-58.

36. Casa-Calvo to Carlos de Vilemont, New Orleans, March 18 and May 9, 1800, both in AGI, PC, leg. 69. Throughout Roger Baudier's study, *The Catholic Church in Louisiana* (1939; repr. New Orleans: Louisiana Library Association, 1972), he does not provide a minimum age for minors to marry and states that they needed only the consent of their parents. However, the Catholic Church decreed marriage ages as fourteen for girls and sixteen for boys. John Burke, *Catholic Marriage*, 67.

Peñalver, who had tired of Louisiana, learned in 1801 that his religious superiors had appointed him archbishop of Central America, with his seat in Guatemala City. Religious laxity among Louisiana's Catholics and the growing presence of foreign Protestants and freemasons upset him considerably. In his many years of religious service, he had never confronted such a blasphemous situation. Cuba did not share a contiguous border with a Protestant nation, and aside from merchants, few of the Protestants who arrived on the island chose to settle down. Peñalver finally departed from Louisiana in November, several months after Casa-Calvo's governorship ended.[37]

The governor quickly learned that dealing with subordinates could be arduous, especially when they sought to advance their private agendas. One such example was the egotistical Lt. Col. Vicente Folch y Juan, governor of the Pensacola district, who regarded himself skilled in all areas of political and military government. He was the nephew of the erstwhile governor of Louisiana Esteban Miró (1782-1791), during whose governorship and after, subordinate officials treated Folch deferentially. His abrasive personality, however, generated enemies, and he habitually disparaged governors since he regarded his knowledge superior to theirs. On Gayoso's death, he proclaimed himself governor of West Florida and free from the Louisiana governor's authority, but Captain General Someruelos immediately quashed his faulty judgment.[38]

While Folch was in far-away Pensacola, acting civil governor Vidal presented a more troubling figure in New Orleans. As both a judge and a lawyer, civil legal matters in the colony fell under his purview. Nevertheless, he unashamedly exploited his government positions to

37. Gayarré, *History of Louisiana*, 3: 407; Baudier, *Catholic Church in Louisiana*, 223-46; Garnie William McGinty, *A History of Louisiana* (New York: Exposition Press, 1951), 95; Actas del Cabildo, vol. 4, (3), pp. 140-41, New Orleans, November 6, 1801.

38. David Hart White, *Vicente Folch, Governor in West Florida, 1787-1811* (Washington, D.C.: American Academic Press, 1981). See also by White, "The Indian Policy of Vicente Folch, Governor of Spanish Mobile, 1787-1792," *Alabama Review* 28 (July 1975): 145-55; and Din, *Bouligny*, 214-16.

strengthen his power and extort the public. No other executive in the colony exhibited a similar degree of venality. Although forced at times to interact with him, Casa-Calvo maintained a respectful distance from the disreputable Vidal.[39]

Casa-Calvo and Vidal clashed over the New Orleans theater that the latter tried to destroy. It had been built in 1792 and had financial problems virtually from the day it opened. It was located in a small building on St. Peter Street between Royal and Bourbon streets. It measured only 31 feet wide and 128 feet deep, had a dozen boxes, an amphitheater, a gallery for white spectators, and a balcony for free people of color. Because of high costs, or a public that was priced out of attending, financial straits shut it down several times. Nevertheless, among its known achievements, the theater held the city's first opera on July 17, 1796, put on by a touring musical company. Three years later, on September 3, 1799, shortly before Casa-Calvo arrived in the city, the theater put on a play called *Renaud d'Ast*.[40] These productions signified a growth in the city's cultural sophistication.

More important, the theater's financial problems involved city officials and the Cabildo.[41] The Cabildo rented one theater box using city revenue to pay for it, which perhaps was a misappropriation of money. The box was divided into two sections, the larger side to seat the council and the smaller section for the governor and his family. In 1797, when the councilmen added six more members, the twelve (or fourteen with the two ordinary judges who were also councilmen) could no longer fit in their side of the partition. For two years, they struggled with the seating arrangement. On July 27, 1799, when Governor Gayoso de

39. No adequate biography on Vidal has yet been written. See for now "Account of the Merits and Services of Dr. D. Nicolás María Vidal," Madrid, November 8, 1804, Biblioteca Nacional (Madrid), Sección de Manuscritos, CDL, Vol. 19,509, ff. 270-75; and Jack D. L. Holmes, "*Dramatis Personae* in Spanish Louisiana," *Louisiana Studies* 6 (1967): 152-55.

40. Grace King, *Creole Families of New Orleans* (1921; repr. Baton Rouge: Claitors, 1971), 377; René J. Le Gardeur, Jr., *The First New Orleans Theatre, 1792-1803* (New Orleans: Leeward Books, 1963).

41. LeGardeur, *First New Orleans Theatre*, 16-18.

Lemos died, his duties as civil and military governor were divided with Vidal becoming the acting civil governor who handled legal affairs. He declared that the military governor (Col. Francisco Bouligny was then serving in that post) was not entitled to half the box, and Vidal ordered the theater manager to remove the partition. This happened shortly before Casa-Calvo's coming, and when he arrived, he refused to bow down to Vidal's impudent behavior. Nevertheless, Vidal closed the theater on February 8, 1800, for an unknown reason, and it remained shut until a royally appointed governor, Salcedo, arrived in mid-July 1801, and Vidal lost his authority.[42]

Juan Ventura Morales, the acting intendant, was another rancorous official Casa-Calvo had to work with. An economic bottleneck appeared soon after Casa-Calvo's arrival when Louisiana officials received the king's revocation of his decree that permitted the Spanish colonies to trade with neutral nations in wartime. It was an unfortunate decision since commerce had boosted the fortunes of Louisiana merchants, agriculturalists, businessmen, contractors, and others, who all employed hosts of artisans and laborers. The economic boom further expanded New Orleans in size, a phenomenon still underway when Casa-Calvo appeared. Consequently, virtually everybody of importance, from Morales to Cabildo councilmen, planters, and the corps of merchants voiced their opposition to the royal order. Within several days of his arrival, Morales solicited Casa-Calvo's opinion, which he submitted on September 25.[43]

The interim governor advised that suspending trade with neutral

42. Ibid.,18; Casa-Calvo to Someruelos, New Orleans, December 27, 1799, AGI, PC, leg. 1550; and Salcedo to Someruelos, New Orleans, March 2, 1802, and its enclosure, "The Cabildo and the Theater Box in the Casa de Comedias," Salcedo, New Orleans, February 24, 1802, both in AGI, PC, leg. 1553. Vidal was venal and tried to humiliate officials he did not like.

43. Juan Ventura Morales to Miguel Cayetano Soler, no. 354, New Orleans, November 30, 1799, and attachments, AHN, Est., leg. 3892*bis*, exped. 1. These documents are named "File on the enlargement of rules for the trade of Louisiana through neutrals." See also Actas del Cabildo, New Orleans, September 27, 1799, vol. 4, (3), pp. 79-80; October 4, 1799, vol. 4, (3), p. 89; October 8, 1799, vol. 4, (3), pp. 89-97.

nations, as the royal order decreed, would seriously impact Louisiana's exports. To forestall that prospect, he suggested that the local Cabildo, commercial corps, and government representatives (governor, intendant, and treasury officials) collectively appeal through the intendancy to persuade the king to reverse his decision. Until that time, the decree should not be enforced. He recounted that when the same announcement arrived in Havana, the captain general permitted trade to continue while he petitioned the king. Casa-Calvo further urged that William Panton of Panton, Leslie, and Company be allowed to carry on his trade with the southeastern Natives, especially now that they were restless. The adventurer William Augustus Bowles, who had escaped from Spanish imprisonment the year before, was returning to the Florida Gulf Coast where he was certain to instigate greater mayhem than he had between 1787 and 1792, all in an attempt to install himself as director general of the Creek Confederation. The various organizations in the city followed Casa-Calvo's advice and submitted representations that Acting Intendant Morales bundled into a petition and forwarded to the crown.[44] Trade proceeded uninterrupted during Casa-Calvo's interim governorship in Louisiana.

Bowles represented a nagging quandary for Casa-Calvo, who tried to maintain control over an inadequately defended colony. Not until October 22, 1799, did he enlighten the captain general about the impending crisis in West Florida. He described the defenses in his two provinces as wretched. He lacked a ship capable of navigating the shallow waters along the Gulf Coast or stopping corsairs and contraband. Mississippi River gunboats were his only functional government vessels for operating in shoals, and he had few soldiers and sailors to intercept Bowles's return to West Florida, a region inhabited overwhelmingly by Indians. Nevertheless, he offered the Pensacola commandant a river

44. The "File on the enlargement of rules" cited above and which is in AHN, Est., leg. 3892*bis*, contains all the documents, including Casa-Calvo's letter of October 10, 1799, in support of the decision to keep trade with neutral nations operating. On Panton, see William S. Coker and Thomas D. Watson, *Indian Traders of the Southeastern Spanish Borderlands: Panton, Leslie and Company and John Forbes and Company, 1783-1847* (Pensacola: University of West Florida Press, 1986).

galley and twenty soldiers to augment the Gulf Coast's scant protection.[45]

To overcome Louisiana's naval inferiority and the Bowles menace, Casa-Calvo requested the captain general to build a powerful corvette with twenty-four cannons to shield West Florida's exposed coastal waters, a suggestion Someruelos dismissed most likely due to meager funds. A week later word arrived that Bowles had reached the Apalachicola River, fifty miles west of Fort San Marcos de Apalache. A storm, however, wrecked the British brigantine that carried him on a barrier island and destroyed nearly all his arms and gunpowder. Undaunted, he ascended the Apalachicola to the Lower Creek towns. Buoyed by Bowles's return, many Seminoles and Lower Creeks became aggressive because they detested Panton's inflated prices on the goods sold them. Employees at the merchant's store on the Wakulla River immediately sought protection at Fort San Marcos four miles downstream. They feared that Bowles would sack the store as he had in 1792. With the fort hundreds of miles from New Orleans, news about Bowles trickled in slowly. Casa-Calvo vowed to seize Bowles, but he faced formidable obstacles.[46]

It took him a month to assemble five weather-beaten galleys and gunboats and several smaller troop and supply vessels. He recruited fifty black and mulatto militiamen and sixty-six white soldiers and assigned thirty of the latter and one officer to reinforce Fort San Marcos. Casa-Calvo considered the expedition sufficient to capture Bowles or foil his intentions, after which it was to return because Louisiana needed the soldiers. His judgment, however, showed his ignorance about Indians and Spanish power in that part of West Florida. The expedition finally left in early 1800 for the Apalachicola River, where it

45. [Casa-Calvo] to Someruelos, no. 1, New Orleans, October 22, 1799, AGI, PC, leg. 154B. On the Mississippi River gunboats, see Abraham P. Nasatir, ed., *Spanish War Vessels on the Mississippi, 1792-1796* (New Haven: Yale University Press, 1968).

46. Gilbert C. Din's "William Augustus Bowles on the Gulf Coast, 1787-1803: Unraveling a Labyrinthine Conundrum," *Florida Historical Quarterly* 89 (Summer 2010): 1-26, offers new insights into Bowles and the propaganda machine he employed.

narrowly missed catching Bowles. After dropping off the soldiers assigned to Fort San Marcos, the vessels returned to the Apalachicola and remained to intercept Nassau craft carrying goods and arms to Bowles's cohorts. The Spanish gunboats seized one schooner loaded with arms, and it prompted more Indians to bolt to Bowles's side since he railed relentlessly on how Panton fleeced them in their purchase of hunting and domestic goods.[47]

In April Bowles gathered several hundred livid warriors, surrounded Fort San Marcos, and severed its communications. Without knowing the formalities of combat, the Indians embarrassed Bowles by firing on the fort before his declaration of war arrived. During the five-week siege, foodstuffs at the fort ran short, potable water quickly vanished, few artillery pieces functioned properly, and the cannoneers rapidly exhausted fuses for their weapons. In addition, guarding the barricades day and night fatigued the garrison's sixty-odd soldiers, and the fort's decayed stone walls and dilapidated wood stockade could not resist a determined attack.[48] Perhaps the most crucial error was galley commander Manuel García's failure to maintain communication with the fort. Had he given the post a gunboat or galley as Casa-Calvo had instructed him, the commandant could have informed the expedition of Bowles's attack. The turning point in the siege came when Bowles caught a Panton brigantine going up the San Marcos de Apalache (today's St. Mark's) River that provided him with food, supplies, and two 4-pound cannons. The artillery pieces shattered the exhausted officers' last hope of retaining the fort. Anticipating a barrage followed by an overpowering assault that would inflict numerous casualties, the officers chose to surrender, provided Bowles released the fort's defenders and civilians. He agreed because capture of the post constituted the

47. Din, *War on the Gulf Coast*, 95-112.

48. Gilbert C. Din, "In Defense of Capt. Tomás Portell: An Episode in the History of Spanish West Florida," *Revista Española de Estudios Norteamericanos* 12, nos. 21-22 (2001): 143-58. Arthur P. Whitaker's description of the capture of Fort San Marcos in *The Mississippi Question, 1795-1803: A Study in Trade, Politics, and Diplomacy* (repr. Gloucester, Mass.: Peter Smith, 1962), 162-63, 166-72, badly misinterprets events.

first step in the creation of Muskogee, the Indian nation he planned to rule. He often boasted that he dominated the Seminoles and Creeks, but the cheaper goods that merchants from Nassau in the Bahamas introduced explains the cooperation Indians provided him. Bowles's sway extended only to the Seminoles and a few Lower Creek towns when they agreed with him, which they did not always do, while the more numerous Upper Creeks detested the opportunist and saw through his charade. Nevertheless, they did nothing to apprehend him to avoid intra-tribal conflict and waited for Lower Creek and Seminole opinion to turn against him. The Upper Creeks relied on the persuasive powers of Native "speakers" who harangued Bowles's supporters and on the Spaniards to intercept Nassau vessels bringing in trade goods. Spain's weakness in West Florida, which replicated conditions in Santo Domingo, allowed a small number of British vessels to quietly introduce a smattering of wares for the Indians. [49]

With Bowles's capture of Fort San Marcos, Casa-Calvo needed to recover it without delay. He quickly prepared an expedition of vessels, soldiers, and supplies to oust the interloper and to garrison the fort. He did not know that Folch had decided without orders to regain it himself and demonstrate his martial talents. He realized that Bowles's victory was a stroke of luck that could be remedied with bold measures. Using the vessels and soldiers at Pensacola, Folch struck before Bowles gathered white adventurers to reinforce his warriors. A month after Portell surrendered, Folch sailed into the San Marcos River with his galleys and, after Bowles declined to surrender, began lobbing shells. The fort responded with desultory cannon shots, but when two galley shells exploded on the fort's walls, the Indians fled to the safety of the forests, followed shortly by Bowles's few white followers. Nearly all the defenders escaped with Bowles leading the way. After the fort's recovery, Folch spent three weeks installing troops and officers, ordered reconstruction of its defenses, and wisely assigned two armed vessels to

49. Gilbert C. Din, "Mississippi River Gunboats on the Gulf Coast: The Spanish Naval Fight against William Augustus Bowles, 1799-1803," *Louisiana History* 47 (Summer 2006): 277-308.

remain on the San Marcos River for additional protection.[50]

Only after his return to Pensacola in mid-July did Folch report his departure and victory to the governor. He trusted that Casa-Calvo would approve his fait accompli. But irritated by Folch's failure to follow orders, the governor complained to the captain general about Folch's innate tendency to act on his own, ignore superiors, and report after the fact. Folch also instituted criminal proceedings against the officers who surrendered the fort, a step Casa-Calvo probably would have avoided given the valid reasons that compelled their submission. But after receiving Folch's warped explanation that skirted the true reasons for the capitulation, he acquiesced. He found dealing with the quarrelsome Folch exasperating, and the captain general had already accepted his explanation. Knowing that he had violated orders, Folch informed the captain general first with his self-serving account of events. Someruelos overlooked his breach of protocol because he judged the fort's recovery crucial. At this time in 1800, Casa-Calvo had his testiest relations with Folch. Bowles roamed free through the Gulf Coast's forests trying to instigate disorder for another three years before his Indian support withered. The Upper Creeks finally convinced the war-weary and goods-deprived Seminoles to surrender him, and they did so for a Spanish reward. Casa-Calvo, who was again in New Orleans in June 1803, probably saw Bowles before his shipment to Havana to stand trial for his depredations.[51]

An unusual event occurred during Casa-Calvo's stay as governor. Americans, who were increasing in number as merchants, sailors on commercial vessels, settlers, and assorted other professions in New Orleans, expressed an interest in commemorating the life of former president George Washington on learning of his death. Two leaders of the city's American community, Evan Jones and William Hullings, requested Governor Casa-Calvo's permission for the event. He consented, and on February 5, 1800, they held a ceremony that included a procession from one of their homes, where undoubtedly several of

50. Din, *War on the Gulf Coast*, 126-42.

51. Ibid.,143-213.

them spoke on the president's accomplishments. Upon its conclusion, the participants walked to the levee for the final activity. An American warship on the river ended the commemoration with a salute from its cannons. Afterwards, the crowd quietly dispersed.[52]

Native American relations constituted an important part of Casa-Calvo's duties as governor. In November 1799, the governor of the Mississippi Territory, Winthrop Sargent, wrote to the acting American consul in New Orleans, Evan Jones, that he heard Casa-Calvo had called a conference with the Choctaw Indians who lived on American soil as an infringement of authority. Sargent acknowledged that he had no written evidence and that the oral report might be inaccurate. Nonetheless, he regarded that the information required investigation, and informed Jones to consult the Spanish governor.[53] By December 31, Jones's reply to Sargent had reached him. Casa-Calvo had no knowledge of such a conference nor had the Spanish government proposed one. Despite the Spanish official's denial, Sargent inserted in his letter to Secretary of State Timothy Pickering a decoded message that the Choctaws had dispersed. According to the mysterious informant, several chiefs, when they were in Spanish territory, had received certificates signed by Casa-Calvo and his secretary Andrés López Armesto. Jones further informed Sargent about the Spanish expedition of gunboats that Casa-Calvo prepared late in 1799 to reinforce Spanish posts in the eastern reaches of West Florida against the adventurer Bowles.[54] Despite Sargent's allegations, there is no proof that Casa-Calvo gave certificates or medals or tried to subvert Indians living on American soil.

52. The information on the ceremony is in Casa-Calvo to Vidal, New Orleans, February 4, 1800, in which he replied to Vidal's letter of February 3, 1800; both letters are in AGI, PC, leg. 71A. Vidal claimed that the right of approval belonged to him, but Casa-Calvo disagreed and cited the Royal Ordinances to show that jurisdiction was his.

53. Dunbar Rowland, compiler and editor, *The Mississippi Territorial Archives, 1798-1803: Executive Journals of Governor Winthrop Sargent and Governor William Charles Cole Claiborne* (Nashville: Brandon Printing Company, 1905), 187-88.

54. Ibid., 188-200.

A more serious Native American problem existed far up the Mississippi River, where Casa-Calvo commanded Upper Louisiana, or the west bank of the Mississippi, through a lieutenant governor stationed at St. Louis. Hides, furs, and agricultural products, particularly wheat that was ground into flour, made up its economy. Aside from the omnipresent threat of foreign invasion from British Canada or the United States, the Osage Indians constituted the most formidable dilemma in that distant quarter. The large Osage tribe's bellicosity had produced nettlesome relations with the French in the first half of the eighteenth century, and it continued with the Spaniards. Many Osage males were committed to combat and often warred on neighboring tribes for honors. Not only did they kill other Indians but also whites, especially when they were alone in the wilderness. Many Osage braves clung to the "mourning-warrior ceremony" that believed a deceased tribal member required the scalp of an enemy or a non-Osage for admission into the afterlife. Other tribes, however, despised the Osages for their wanton killing, and it included the French and Spaniards who tried to forge peaceful relations among all Natives.[55]

News of Osage murders came down to New Orleans repeatedly, but a shortage of soldiers in the colony prevented the adoption of forceful measures against them. Trade embargoes on the tribe to compel obedience failed because money-hungry merchants surreptitiously trafficked with it. Osage ability to gather more hides and furs than other Indians because of their numerous hunters disinclined traders from halting commerce with them. Osages exchanged their hunting proceeds for guns, powder, flints, pots, cloth, knives, and other manufactured items that quickly turned into necessities. The French and Spaniards never attempted to destroy the tribe but strove to find an accommodation that promoted peaceful relations. By the end of the eighteenth century, pacifist elements in the tribe had wearied of the warrior mentality and

55. Carl J. Ekbert, *French Roots in the Illinois Country: The Mississippi Frontier in Colonial Times* (Urbana: University of Illinois Press, 1998); Carl H. Chapman, "The Indomitable Osage in the Spanish Illinois (Upper Louisiana), 1763-1804," in *The Spanish in the Mississippi Valley, 1762-1804*, ed. John Francis McDermott (Urbana: University of Illinois Press, 1974), 294-95.

made several peace agreements. Nevertheless, these measures failed because a handful of chiefs and young warriors stubbornly clung to their traditional practices and commitment to warfare, especially along the Arkansas River.[56]

Casa-Calvo, who during his term as interim governor never ventured far from New Orleans, could not help settlers living in exposed areas. Lacking manpower, he only commiserated with Indians and whites who suffered from Osage depredations. For example, on March 6, 1800, he expressed his regret over their recent murders in the Natchitoches district, and he could not advise Commandant Felix Trudeau on how to handle them.[57] That changed when the lieutenant governor of Upper Louisiana, Carlos Dehault Delassus, informed him that Osages had killed at least two persons and stolen many horses. In June 1800, Casa-Calvo advised the prominent Osage chief Cheveux Blancs to destroy the responsible warrior band, and he instructed post commandants to treat them as enemies. He even applauded other Indians who fought them, particularly the Kickapoos who in one raid on an Osage village took forty-five scalps, many of women and children. As Casa-Calvo commented on Spanish policy vis-à-vis the Indians: "As long as the Osages do not change their perfidious behavior, they will be targeted by other Indians and in the end destroyed.... [W]e should not mix in Indian affairs except to talk to them of peace and encourage its implementation."[58]

56. The extensive literature on the Osages includes Gilbert C. Din and A. P. Nasatir, *The Imperial Osages: Spanish-Indian Diplomacy in the Mississippi Valley* (Norman: University of Oklahoma Press, 1983); Willard H. Rollings, *The Osages: An Ethnohistorical Study of Hegemony on the Prairie-Plains* (Columbia: University of Missouri Press, 1992); Carl H. Chapman, *Origin of the Osage Tribe* (New York: Garland, 1974), and Chapman's "The Indomitable Osages in Spanish Illinois (Upper Louisiana), 1763-1804," in *The Spanish in the Mississippi Valley, 1762-1804*, ed. John Francis McDermott, 272-84 (Urbana: University of Illinois Press, 1974); James Owen Dorsey, *An Account of the War Customs of the Osages* (Philadelphia: n. p., 1884).

57. Casa-Calvo to Trudeau, New Orleans, March 6, 1800, AGI, PC, leg. 71A; Din and Nasatir, *Imperial Osages*, 307.

58. Casa-Calvo to Carlos Dehault De Luzières Delassus, New Orleans, June 9, 1800,

That same summer the possibility of an invasion of Upper Louisiana from Canada loomed on the horizon. The war with Great Britain that began in late 1796 continued. To gather intelligence, Casa-Calvo dispatched scouts to discover if an enemy force was headed toward St. Louis. At the same time, Lieutenant Governor Delassus investigated the arms available at the neighboring posts. Their reports, however, were disheartening because they had few arms and little gunpowder.[59] When a war scare broke out in Upper Louisiana in 1800 with the British in Canada, Casa-Calvo ordered officials in St. Louis to be as prepared as possible since he could offer little help.[60] Fortunately, the invasion story proved false, but new tales kept surfacing to the end of Casa-Calvo's governorship.

The Indian skin and fur trade out of St. Louis constituted the most important task Casa-Calvo managed from New Orleans. To minimize conflict between traders and their exploitation of the Natives, both France and Spain regulated the commerce through monopolies given to traders to commerce with only specific tribes for their skins and furs. Similar to earlier governors, merchants and companies petitioned Casa-Calvo for trade monopolies with the tribes.[61]

By 1801, as Casa-Calvo's time in Louisiana grew short, the government in Spain under Godoy had taken steps to dispose of the colony through the several treaties of San Ildefonso of October 1, 1800. They called for the retrocession of Louisiana that Spain had received in 1763

---

cited in Din and Nasatir, *Imperial Osages*, 312.

59. Ibid., 313. See also Nasatir, ed., *Before Lewis and Clark*, 2: 614n.

60. Casa-Calvo to Someruelos, no. 12 reserved, New Orleans, May 20, 1800, AGI, PC, leg. 1573.

61. See Nasatir, "Anglo-Spanish Rivalry on the Upper Missouri River," *Mississippi Valley Historical Review* 16 (December 1929-March 1930), no. 3: 359-82; no. 4: 420-39; Nasatir, ed., *Before Lewis and Clark*, 2: 608-11. See also Jacques Clamorgan to the governor and intendant of Louisiana, New Orleans, January 29, 1800, AGI, PC, leg. 1573. When Casa-Calvo heard about the war scare with the British in Canada in 1800, he ordered St. Louis to be as prepared as possible. Casa-Calvo to Someruelos, no. 12 reserved, New Orleans, May 20, 1800, AGI, PC, leg. 1573.

to France in exchange for a kingdom in Italy for a royal relative.[62] The retrocession, however, took three years to complete, and Spain never received the Italian kingdom.

Casa-Calvo's administration faced another major problem when Philip Nolan intruded into Spanish territory. He had already achieved a reputation for rounding up wild horses on the plains of Texas, which was a part of the Spanish Interior Provinces. People like Nolan represented an escalating dilemma for Spain as western American settlements grew and their inhabitants entered Spanish soil searching for easy money. This time a captured confident insinuated that Nolan intended to rob the caravan carrying the payroll to the Texas military posts along the Louisiana border, but it was questionable if this was his real objective. On October 28, 1800, Nolan initiated his newest foray into Spanish lands. Before long, commandants at Ouachita, Rapides (present-day Alexandria), Natchitoches, and elsewhere in Louisiana reported his passage as he traveled with thirty armed men from Natchez that was now in the American Mississippi Territory. Other countrymen followed Nolan in later days. On being notified of the intrusion, Casa-Calvo warned post commandants along the Red River to stop Nolan's raiders.[63]

The commandant of Nacogdoches in eastern Texas, Miguel Francisco Muzquíz who had the largest military force, took action. He left his post on March 4, 1801, searching for the bandits. He found them

62. DeConde, *This Affair of Louisiana*, 95; E. Wilson Lyon, *Louisiana in French Diplomacy*, 79-98, 108-9. The treaty that ceded Louisiana to France did not call for the cession of West Florida that Spain had gained in 1783 from Great Britain. Spain never joined the two colonies as the United States under Thomas Jefferson and James Madison contended.

63. Casa-Calvo to Mariano Luis de Urquijo, New Orleans, November 18, 1800, AHN, Est., leg. 3901, exped. 2; Casa-Calvo to Trudeau, New Orleans, November 18, 1800; Casa-Calvo to Duralde, New Orleans, December 23, 1800; both in AGI, PC, leg. 69. Studies on Nolan include Maurine Wilson and Jack Jackson, *Philip Nolan and Texas: Expeditions to the Unknown Land, 1791-1801* (Waco: Texian Press, 1987); John Edward Weems, *Men Without Countries* (Boston: Houghton Mifflin, 1969); and Noel Loomis, "Philip Nolan's Entry into Texas in 1800," in *The Spanish in the Mississippi Valley, 1762-1804* (Urbana: University of Illinois Press, 1974): 120-32.

near the Brazos River, where they had built a strong stockade. Muzquíz ordered Nolan to surrender, but he refused and began shooting. A Spanish ball to the head quickly silenced him, whereupon his men scattered, but most were soon captured. Muzquíz returned to Nacogdoches with the prisoners and horses he found at the encampment. On April 7, he wrote to José Vidal at Concordia, asking him to convey the news to the Louisiana governor. Vidal obliged and sent Casa-Calvo a letter on April 22.[64] Although the governor was not directly involved in liquidating the Nolan menace, he, nevertheless, advised posts commandants in Louisiana on the adventurer's intrusion, and he instructed the commander at Nacogdoches to do everything in his power to seize Nolan. Muzquíz further proved that the intruder had not been the formidable peril he was believed to be. Thus the recovery of Fort San Marcos in 1800 and the elimination of Nolan in 1801 ended positively for Spanish arms, and they represented two constructive military actions that occurred during Casa-Calvo's tenure as interim governor.

Another incident of concern took place in December 1799, when Casa-Calvo assumed personal command of a military excursion. The military commander at Balize, the island or mudflat at the principal mouth of the Mississippi River that housed the pilots who guided vessels across the sandbar into and out of the river, sent a report to New Orleans that a powerful English frigate was nearby in the gulf. Casa-Calvo called up the armed vessels he had in New Orleans, which were only a gunboat armed with mortars and a galiot that was smaller than the galleys. With a party of soldiers on board, he descended the river to station the vessels in the most useful places. It was at this time that the war galleys he was sending to the eastern Gulf Coast to seize Bowles also went down to the Mississippi's mouth. Those vessels exited the river through the east pass that was away from Balize and not as exposed to foreign marauders; Casa-Calvo, meanwhile, guarded the main

64. José Vidal to Casa-Calvo, no. 112, April 22, 1801, with enclosure Miguel Francsico Márques to Vidal, Nacogdoches, April 7, 1801; Trudeau to Casa-Calvo, Natchitoches, April 28, 1801; all in AGI, PC, leg. 72. Several prisoners, Robert Ashley, Michael Noors, John House, and Black Joe, fled from detention in Nacogdoches and went to Natchez.

channel. During the several days that he patrolled the river's mouths, a five-ship convoy arrived safely from Havana. Perhaps its size forced the enemy frigate to slink away, and it caused no trouble. Corsairs generally preyed on smaller and unarmed ships since most of them sought to avoid casualties. With the convoy's arrival, Casa-Calvo returned to New Orleans. While he was away, Colonel Bouligny, whose illness had momentarily abated, governed in his stead.[65]

Casa-Calvo and Bouligny were long aware of each other. Fifteen years separated the two in age, with Bouligny the older man. He was from a merchant family in Alicante, Spain, but he chose a military career; spent six critical years, from 1763 to 1769, in Havana; and traveled with the young Calvo de la Puerta, possibly in the same ship, to New Orleans in 1769 in O'Reilly's expedition to recover Louisiana after the French Creole revolt. In New Orleans, Bouligny provided important services as a messenger and later as a translator at the trials of the rebel leaders. At that time, Calvo de la Puerta was no more than an immature militia captain. Upon O'Reilly's departure, Bouligny remained in the colony as a part of the Louisiana Fixed Infantry Battalion and captain of one of its companies. By 1791 Bouligny had risen to colonel and head of the Louisiana infantry regiment while Casa-Calvo because of combat duties in Santo Domingo in the 1790s had ascended the ranks to brigadier general although he had not yet achieved the formal position of colonel of a regiment.[66] While in New Orleans, Casa-Calvo had numerous talks with Bouligny before the latter's illnesses finally claimed him on November 25, 1800.[67]

Casa-Calvo soon reported to the captain general Bouligny's death to an apoplectic stroke. He did this to advise that a replacement for colonel of the regiment was needed, and he recommended three individuals on the basis of seniority. It was the usual method in selecting replacements. His nominees were Lt. Col. Carlos Howard, the regiment's

65. Casa-Calvo to Someruelos, New Orleans, December 26, 1799, AGI, PC, leg. 1550.

66. Din, *Francisco Bouligny*, 222.

67. Ibid., 223.

lieutenant colonel; Lt. Col. Maximiliano de St. Maxent, a Louisiana native who was the commandant of the third battalion in Pensacola; and the Frenchman and refugee from France Lt. Col. Carlos Dehault Delassus, who served as lieutenant governor in St. Louis. Casa-Calvo also reminded Someruelos of his earlier dispatch of May 21, in which he discussed the need to conserve the province and advised naming Spaniards to the high posts in the regiment. Casa-Calvo expressed suspicions about his three nominees since the names Howard, Delassus, and St. Maxent were not characteristically Spanish. Despite his fifteen months in the province, he apparently had not yet accepted its multinational character. He added that the regiment's colonelcy should have an individual who was knowledgeable in accounting because Bouligny's repeated illnesses had muddled the unit's finances. Of the three men, Casa-Calvo favored Howard, who should be promoted to colonel. As the Irishman had applied for the governorship of East Florida earlier that year, Casa-Calvo regarded him fit for that post when the time came. Lastly, he recommended Delassus for the position of lieutenant colonel of the regiment.[68]

The three-battalion regiment over which Bouligny presided had reached its apogee in manpower in the early 1790s. From that time, it gradually lost strength so that on Casa-Calvo's arrival in the fall of 1799, death, rotation home, and discharge had whittled the 1,600-man regiment down to 851, and that created shortages everywhere because few new recruits entered to bolster its ranks. When Casa-Calvo complained about the loss in troop strength, Captain General Someruelos instructed him not to discharge anyone, neither the able-bodied nor the lame since the latter could still function as hospital orderlies and as honor and barracks guards; their service would free able soldiers to perform critical duties. In addition, Louisiana's non-Spanish population disturbed Casa-Calvo; while civilian males between fifteen and fifty in years theoretically served in the militia, few men enlisted in the regiment. Its army officers, however, were a mixture of Spaniards

68. Casa-Calvo to Someruelos, no. 155, New Orleans, November 30, 1800, and his attachment of the same date, AGI, PC, leg. 1552.

and French Creoles whose army and planter fathers wanted military careers for them. In some respects, the situation bore a similarity to the regiments in Havana. As time progressed, French Creoles increasingly replaced Spanish officers who retired or died. In Louisiana Casa-Calvo deemed the change as demoralizing, and he advised Someruelos several times to supply the regiment with more Spanish-born officers.[69] Although Creoles were also achieving the highest militia and regular army posts in Havana, there he sided with Cuban officers whom he considered equal to Spaniards.

Among other issues Casa-Calvo dealt with was resuming the importation of African slaves. Governor Carondelet, at the request of the frightened Cabildo councilmen, had stopped their entry in 1796 after the Pointe Coupee slave conspiracy. Newly imported African slaves from several plantations in the district plotted in 1795 to rise up against their oppressive masters. Upon discovery of their plans, a legal investigation began and gathered evidence through confessions and witnesses. Judge Manuel Serrano decreed death sentences for twenty-eight slaves and prison sentences for twenty more. The conspiracy's unearthing alarmed Louisiana's infant plantocracy about the rapid increase in African slaves in the early 1790s. Newly imported Africans were more inclined to resist bondage, run away, and cause assorted mayhem than Creole slaves who had grudgingly adjusted to the abominable institution and had more to lose by defying masters. Following the punishment of the conspirators, the planters who dominated the New Orleans Cabildo urged Governor Carondelet to halt importing slaves, and he soon banned their entry.[70]

69. Casa-Calvo to Someruelos, New Orleans, October 12 and 22, 1799, AGI, PC, legs. 1551 and 1550, respectively; "General Statement of the [Army] Corps," enclosed in the second letter; [Someruelos] to Casa-Calvo, [Havana], November 7, 1799, AGI, PC, leg. 154B; Casa-Calvo to Someruelos, New Orleans, May 21, 1800, AHN, Est., leg. 3901, exped. 1.

70. Gilbert C. Din, *Spaniards, Planters, and Slaves: The Spanish Regulation of Slavery in Louisiana, 1763-1803* (College Station: Texas A&M University Press, 1999), 154-76. See by the same author, "Carondelet, the Cabildo, and Slaves: Louisiana in 1795," *Louisiana History* 38 (Winter 1997): 5-28.

For the next three years, except for individual slave owners relocating to Louisiana with their bondsmen, slave imports stopped. By 1799, the earlier slave unrest had receded, and planters again sought to advance the new labor-intensive agriculture crops of cotton and sugarcane. Casa-Calvo's background as a planter and amenability to slave imports in Cuba influenced him, and he sided with the councilmen who wanted workers. On August 1, 1800, however, the city government voted six to five against the introduction of slaves. Stunned, Casa-Calvo reprimanded them for thinking that they alone could decide this vital matter. In the end, it was Intendant López y Angulo who resumed African imports on November 29, 1800. He also called for tighter controls on slaves. However, he soon left the colony, and Morales, who again took the office, opposed the entry of more slaves and stopped their importation. In Spain, the king's council examined the New Orleans petition for slaves and informed the Cuban captain general that French slavers had received permission recently to introduce five thousand blacks in Louisiana, and it was not prepared to do more for the present. Nevertheless, inasmuch as Governor Carondelet had halted the introduction of slaves on his own authority, the king's permission to resume it was not needed.[71]

Before this decision reached Louisiana and in an effort to convince the captain general to permit the entry of slaves, Casa-Calvo confided that masters now treated their bondsmen better. He did so because earlier governors had reported that French treatment of slaves had been abhorrent. But it was debatable if owners had indeed improved their behavior. Abusive slave management can be seen in the example of Madame LeBlond who beat, chained, starved, and dressed them in rags; her outrageous conduct seemed psychotic, and she was not alone in abusing slaves. If the governor had indeed investigated life on plantations, his examination reached only as far as the wealthy planters of the New Orleans district and not to their slaves. As a Cuban sugar baron and as a governor, Casa-Calvo firmly believed in the institution since,

71. Gayarré, *History of Louisiana*, 3: 407.

except for his stays in Spain, it had always been present in his life.[72]

Slave treatment was a problem discussed several times during Casa-Calvo's tenure in Louisiana. Civil Governor Vidal strongly disagreed that master behavior had improved as Casa-Calvo and others contended, and he blamed planters for their wretched conduct. His denunciation shocked slave owners because they were not accustomed to blunt criticism; Vidal rejected their requests for new slave regulations, and insinuated that owners would probably follow the example of the inhabitants of the French islands and impose a harsher management of slaves. Overall, Spaniards who were acquainted with Louisiana favored a gentler treatment while many planters opted for the reinstitution of the stringent laws of the French Code Noir of 1724 against all blacks, free and slave.[73]

Shortly before Casa-Calvo's governorship ended, he unexpectedly clashed with the Cabildo. It began on April 24, 1801, when two councilmen walked to his house to request his presence at a Cabildo function to celebrate the arrival of the new governor, Col. Manuel Juan Salcedo. The captain general had sent word that Salcedo was in Havana and would soon embark for New Orleans. Much to the councilmen's chagrin, Casa-Calvo informed them that he, too, planned a reception, and should the Cabildo decide to have one, he invited the councilmen to have it at Government House, a large building in central New Orleans that held the colonial government's offices. The councilmen, however, had planned to host the reception at their own *casa capitular* or office structure that had been rebuilt in 1799 after the devastating fire of 1788.[74] The governor's unexpected announcement

72. Casa-Calvo to Someruelos, no. 37, New Orleans, May 26, 1800, AGI, PC, leg. 1551; Din, *Spaniards, Planters, and Slaves*, 137. Documents on Madame LeBlond are scattered in AGI, PC, but see, for example, those in legajo 106A between Casa-Calvo and the commandant of Baton Rouge Carlos de Grand-Pré written in the spring of 1800.

73. Vidal to the Cabildo, New Orleans, October 21, 1800, in Morazán, "Letters," I: 195-203; Ingersoll, "Old New Orleans," 614.

74. Din and Harkins, *New Orleans Cabildo*, 5. Mail arrived in New Orleans in April 1801 indicating that the new governor would be arriving soon. Even Gen.

created a quandary and sent the two men rushing to report it to the city government. After further discussion, the two officials returned to the governor's residence to explain their customary procedure. Councilors usually sent selected members to greet the incoming governor several miles downriver from New Orleans, accompanied him to the city, and immediately celebrated his arrival. If, however, the governor insisted on holding his own welcome on that day, the Cabildo would cancel its reception. Nevertheless, it pledged to inform the king about the incident so that he could determine how the Cabildo should celebrate the future arrival of governors. Their grumpy answer astonished Casa-Calvo since they considered the gubernatorial welcome a serious matter. He informed the councilmen that when Salcedo arrived, he would do what was necessary according to his position as the departing governor. The councilmen were free to do what they believed was their duty—celebrate his arrival, provide furniture for his household, and employ their generosity in whatever way they wished. Furthermore, they were at liberty to inform the king, and Casa-Calvo would also furnish his own explanation.[75]

The governor's clash with the councilmen occurred more than two months before Salcedo arrived. In the interim, Casa-Calvo learned how previous governors had been received, and upon further consideration he yielded to the customs of the municipal council. During this time, he received several letters from Salcedo in Havana, and perhaps they persuaded him to be more flexible. Nevertheless, he waited until July 15, before he informed the councilmen to hold an extraordinary meeting at their facilities for the new political and military governor. That

---

James Wilkinson posed the question directly to Casa-Calvo. On April 19, 1801, Casa-Calvo replied that he would keep Wilkinson advised on Manuel Juan Salcedo's forthcoming arrival. Casa-Calvo to Wilkinson, New Orleans, April 19, 1801, Collections in the Center for American History, University of Texas, Austin. Information provided by Jorge Auñon.

75. G(abriel) Fonvergne and Domingo Bouligny to Casa-Calvo, New Orleans, April 27, 1801; (Casa-Calvo) to the regidores, New Orleans, April 29, 1801, both in AGI, PC, leg. 72; Actas del Cabildo, New Orleans, April 24, 1801, vol. 4, (4), pp. 86-87; Actas del Cabildo, New Orleans, May 8, 1801, vol. 4, (4), p. 89.

was the day Salcedo reached the city. Reports five days earlier from Balize and Fort Plaquemines, posts respectively at and near the mouth of the Mississippi River, announced his presence and that a powerful summer storm detained him. Casa-Calvo's tenure in Louisiana would have been shorter had misfortune not plagued Salcedo as he crossed the Atlantic and shipwrecked in a tempest. After stumbling across several Caribbean islands, he reached Cuba, where his wife sickened and died, and he was left to care for two adolescent sons, one a sublieutenant and the other a cadet. Salcedo finally took the oath of office on July 15, 1801, a year and a half after the king appointed him. On that day, Casa-Calvo surrendered authority to Salcedo who became the last Spanish governor of Louisiana. [76]

With no reason to remain in the province, Casa-Calvo originally intended to use the vessel that brought Salcedo to return to Havana. But obtaining funds for the money-straitened colony quickly forced him to hold discussions with Salcedo and treasury officials. As Louisiana produced paltry revenue to defray its operating expenses, the silver mines and mint in Mexico provided a subsidy for Louisiana since it became a Spanish possession and for other Caribbean colonies, even sugar-rich Cuba. As war costs were then soaring because of numerous expenditures, the funds arrived haphazardly or not at all, and when they did come they never covered all expenses. As early as mid-1800, acting intendant Juan Ventura Morales began dispatching ships to Veracruz to request the viceroy to remit Louisiana's subsidy. Morales used private vessels loaded with goods that were meant to enter Mexico without paying the customary duties. He allegedly resorted to this subterfuge because he lacked the money to hire ships. Eventually, he dispatched so many that Casa-Calvo questioned Morales's activities and authority. The intendant further claimed that he had the power

76. Actas del Cabildo, New Orleans, July 15, 1801, vol. 4, (4), pp.108-113; two letters of Pedro Favrot to Casa-Calvo, nos. 169 and 170, Plaquemines, both dated July 10, 1801, both in AGI, PC, leg. 72. See also Salcedo to (Casa-Calvo), Havana, May 30, 1801, in ibid. No biography or adequate sketch of the less than able Salcedo has been written. Whitaker, in *Mississippi Question*, 160, 192-93, 197-98, traces some facets of Salcedo's administration.

to issue paper money because of the calamitous shortage of funds.[77] In November 1800, he notified the governor that unless the subsidy arrived soon, he intended to issue paper certificates on January 1, 1801, which he did. In mid-May, the new intendant, López y Angulo, also approached Casa-Calvo on the urgency to obtain money. He wanted Casa-Calvo, who was leaving Louisiana, to deliver in person a message to the viceroy since his own letters had not produced funds. With the approval of Louisiana's treasury office, Casa-Calvo accepted the task. He would travel with a Captain Fletcher, a wealthy planter and owner of estates and slaves in Louisiana who had long aspired to trade with Veracruz. Fletcher planned to load his schooner *Josephine* with seventy barrels of pitch and thirty barrels of tar to cover his costs. Casa-Calvo instructed him, however, to reduce his cargo to forty barrels of pitch and twenty of tar, possibly to boost speed and outrace privateers that preyed on shipping in the Gulf of Mexico. Salcedo had brought official correspondence from Havana with orders to forward it to Veracruz. On July 24, he gave Casa-Calvo permission to depart with the mail.[78]

Casa-Calvo's ship left New Orleans in August, exiting the Mississippi by the west pass. The schooner, however, did not reach Veracruz and landed outside Tampico in the province of Nuevo Santander. Fletcher's contraband did not escape detection as customs officials found goods not listed on the ship's manifest. While Casa-Calvo was ashore at nearby Aguayo, he learned that two Louisiana officers, army Capt. Celestino St. Maxent and militia Capt. Tomás Power, were nearby. St. Maxent had been sent to Mexico City to beseech the viceroy to dispatch funds to money-strapped Louisiana, but he failed. Power, meanwhile, was involved in recruiting soldiers for duty in Louisiana and had been looking for a ship sailing to Havana. St. Maxent was

77. Casa-Calvo to Mariano Luis de Urquijo, no. 42, New Orleans, November 22, 1800, AHN, Est., leg. 3901, exped. 2, and attached enclosures.

78. López y Angulo to Casa-Calvo, two letters, both reserved, New Orleans, May 15 and 28, 1801, both in AGI, PC, leg. 72. In (Casa-Calvo) to Salcedo, New Orleans, July 28, 1801, AGI, PC, 77B, Casa-Calvo acknowledged his receipt of letters for officials in Mexico, including two for the viceroy asking for money and one for the superintendant of the mint.

at Pánuco when he heard that Casa-Calvo was close by, and he traveled there to see him. No doubt he learned that Mexico, too, suffered in the war-induced financial exigency. Nevertheless, on September 8, Casa-Calvo sent five bundles of dispatches via the royal mail service to the viceroy. Hoping for success, Casa-Calvo intended to proceed to Mexico City on September 15, journeying more comfortably by coach. If delayed by unknown causes, the dispatches would still inform viceregal authorities of the importance of his mission to obtain desperately needed funds for Louisiana.[79]

Casa-Calvo left for Mexico City after his talks with St. Maxent and Power, and he used both men to take letters back to Salcedo in which he explained the results of his journey thus far.[80] When after several months information about him next surfaced he was in Veracruz, and it can only be assumed that he saw the viceroy in Mexico City. Veracruz was the viceroyalty's chief gulf port, and he must have been anxious to return home to Havana. By September 1801, he had been away from his children for two years. Casa-Calvo yearned to resume his roles as father to his children and as the full-time commander of his regiment. During his absence, he kept in touch with the acting head of the unit. Even from Mexico he sent letters that dealt with personnel problems and replacements in the regiment. A permanent appointment to commandant of his regiment had not been made and, consequently, matters of importance were routinely routed to him despite the slowness in decision-making. Although it was an awkward situation, a shortage

79. Casa-Calvo to Juan de Diós Fernández, Aguayo, September 8, 1801; and two letters of Casa-Calvo to Salcedo, Aguayo, September 14, 1801; and Felix Berenguer de Marquina to Casa-Calvo, Mexico City, July 15, 1801; all in AGI, PC, leg. 72. Apparently, Casa-Calvo's mailings created a problem, and Fernández wrote to him in September 1802, asking for a reimbursement of sixty-three pesos. Casa-Calvo replied from Havana in November, explaining that the mail was government business and the Department of Mails or the viceroy should bear the expense. Fernández to Casa-Calvo, Aguayo, September 2, 1802; and (Casa-Calvo) to Fernández, Havana, November 13, 1802; both in ibid.

80. Casa-Calvo to Salcedo, Aguayo, two letters dated September 14, 1801, both in AGI, PC, leg. 72.

of personnel prevented naming a replacement. After several months in Mexico, his task seems to have been completed when the viceroy agreed to send funds. Not long after that, Casa-Calvo found a ship sailing to Havana, and he departed. By March 1802, he was once again at home.

That same spring, the viceroy dispatched a million pesos to Cuba, which included money for Louisiana. However, only 20,000 silver pesos reached New Orleans in June, and it was assigned to the intendant. Salcedo wrote to treasury officials in Havana in April for the money owed to Louisiana, but the Havana treasury argued that many of its own expenses had not been covered.[81] Although the funds were few, Casa-Calvo had achieved a modicum of success in his journey to Mexico, and the viceroy followed up the initial shipment with others.

Aside from his trip to Mexico, an assessment can be made about Casa-Calvo's success during his twenty-two month governorship of Louisiana and West Florida. He had been assigned there temporarily and he was not to implement new policies or transform them in any meaningful way. Moreover, money, as already noted, was in short supply to support changes had he wished to institute them. He did not know that in Spain Godoy, who was running the government for Carlos IV, had retroceded Louisiana to France in October 1800 as a way of reducing expenditures. Therefore, Casa-Calvo's governorship and that of his successor, Salcedo, occurred during an unstable era. The governors' principal objective, which was unknown to Casa-Calvo and he learned it only during Salcedo's administration, was to keep control over Louisiana until the transfer to France took place.

81. Juan de Araoz to Salcedo, Havana, June 1, 1802, and (Salcedo) to Araoz, New Orleans, June 25, 1802, both in AGI, PC, leg. 77B.

7
A Return to Cuba and Louisiana, 1802-1806

In 1801 the warring European powers that pitted Great Britain on one side against France and Spain on the other began negotiations to halt the conflict, and after protracted talks they finally produced the Peace of Amiens (1802-03) that temporarily stopped hostilities. Slightly before, Casa-Calvo left his post as acting governor of Louisiana, journeying first to Mexico and finally back to Havana in early 1802. Aside from making his travel safer, the quiet interlude greatly facilitated trade and allowed Cubans to sell their products in ever larger quantities than during the war years when neutral shipping bore responsibility for transporting the island's rising exports.

Upon returning home after an absence of nearly two and a half years, Casa-Calvo again resumed life in the city and on his estates. Undoubtedly, his children rejoiced at having their father, who had been absent so long, among them. Furthermore, Capt. Gen. Salvador de Muro y Salazar, Marqués de Someruelos, pleasantly surprised him soon after his return by appointing him commanding officer of the Fixed Infantry Regiment of Havana; whether the appointment had royal approval or Someruelos named him on his own authority is unknown. He replaced Col. Francisco Montalvo, son of the first Conde de Macuriges, who received a post on the governor general's staff.[1] Casa-Calvo's new position was an honor inasmuch as the regiment was the oldest and most prestigious military unit in Cuba, and it gave

1. Kuethe, *Cuba*, 152.

his military career another boost. He had finally realized his wish to become the legitimate colonel of a regiment, a posting that he had wanted for more than a dozen years. His lengthy service as the acting colonel of the Fixed Infantry Regiment of Cuba, the unit that he had formed, prepared him to serve effectively. Attaining its leadership also satisfied his aspirations, at least for the present. His successful stint as the interim governor of Louisiana helped him, too, since the experience made him Cuba's most knowledgeable official in military, diplomatic, and administrative matters. He was fifty years old and, while he had suffered annoying setbacks, his army experiences and his social background continued to propel him forward. Furthermore, he was precisely where he wanted to be since he had abandoned thoughts of moving to Spain to advance his military ambitions.

However, his return to Cuba recalled to mind the loss of his scholarly younger brother Nicolás. He had sickened and died on December 16, 1800, while Sebastián was absent in Louisiana. The nature of his illness and how long he had been ailing are unknown. His demise must have mystified Casa-Calvo as well because only a few years before his older brother Francisco, wealthy in money and property, had expired. Nicolás, in contrast, had become a respected scientist and mathematician. Among his scholarly accomplishments, he learned Latin, Greek, Italian, English, and French. He kept a botanical collection, painted, and dabbled in astronomy with his own telescope and celestial spheres. Mechanical contraptions fascinated him, and he tried to learn as much as he could to apply his learning toward improving the machinery that produced sugar. His publications and rise to scientific prominence in promoting sugarcane garnered attention in Cuba and abroad. It is not known whether Alexander von Humboldt, the renowned natural scientist, met Nicolás prior to his death when he visited Cuba in December 1800. Humboldt became acquainted with Francisco Arango y Parreño, a friend of Nicolás who accompanied Humboldt in his inspection of the developments that were then taking place in Cuba and turning the island into the Caribbean's foremost sugar producer. It has been said that Humboldt employed Nicolás's statistics on Cuba's agricultural output and exports in his study on the

Spanish American colonies that he published several years later.[2]

The loss of his younger brother temporarily dimmed Casa-Calvo's cheerfulness. With Nicolás's passing, Sebastián became the sole surviving member of his first nuclear family, which of course did not include his children. He now centered his attention entirely on them, and he rejoiced in their development as on his return to Havana his older offspring had turned twenty-one, twenty, and nineteen. Young blond-haired Ignacio trailed behind as he was only twelve in 1802. Throughout this year and into early 1803, Casa-Calvo relaxed in Cuba, enjoying his children and the yields from his estates. While he was in Louisiana, he had become a grandfather. His older daughter Catarina had married Francisco Chacón y O'Farrill, a wealthy cousin from a titled family. His parents were the Condes (counts) de Casa Bayona. Catarina's child received the formidable name of José María Luis de Jesús Chacón y Herrera de Calvo de la Puerta.[3]

While resting at home after his travels, Casa-Calvo no doubt yearned for a conclusion to the disruptive Napoleonic wars in Europe that had extended across the ocean and into the Caribbean. His participation in the struggle in Santo Domingo had taught him that peace was infinitely preferable to hostilities on either side of the Atlantic

2. Calcagno, *Diccionario biográfico cubano*, 149; Arango, *La Sacarocracia*, 168-69; "Elogio del señor Nicolás Calvo y O'Farrill," in *Escritos varios*, ed. José Agustín Caballero (Havana: Editoriales de la Universidad de La Habana, 1954), 179-96; José Manuel Serrano Álvarez and Allan J. Kuethe, "La Familia O'Farrill y La Élite Habanera," in *Élites Urbanas en Hispanoamérica*, coordinated by Luis Navarro García (Sevilla: Universidad de Sevilla, Secretariado de Publicaciones, 2005), 205. Because Humboldt had met Gonzalo O'Farrill, who at the time was the Spanish minister in Berlin, Humboldt used him to have money sent for his expenses in Cuba. Alexander von Humboldt, *Personal Narrative of Travels to the Equinoctial Regions of the New Continent During the Years 1799-1804*, trans. by Helen Maria Williams (London: Longman, Hurst, Rees, Orme, 1829), 289.

3. Baptismal certificate of José Maria Luis de Jesús Chacón de Calvo de la Puerta, Havana, August 30, 1801, Book 19 of Baptisms of White Persons, folio 40, number 149, in the Sagrario of the Cathedral of Havana, copy made in Havana, June 28, 1900, and provided by Jorge Auñón. Casa-Calvo's son Ignacio was baptized on June 1, 1790, and he was probably born shortly before. Vallellano, *Nobiliario cubano*, 251.

world. He could not imagine that violent upheaval improved life or furthered economic productivity. As a royal army officer, he represented the status quo politically and socially, although that did not apply to the economic modernization that had gradually been picking up momentum in Cuba during the past century. Investments by upper class entrepreneurs in the production of sugar and other commercial crops in recent decades had increased their fortunes still more and provided employment for numerous free people of all colors. Slaves, however, who involuntarily supplied the arduous toil needed to generate the fortunes, inhabited the abused and scantily rewarded bottom rungs of society. Nevertheless, a surprising number of slaves, more urban than rural, had become free by the various means available to them—self-purchase, emancipation, and reward for good service—which among other reasons were designed to instill obedience among those still in servitude. Casa-Calvo, a servant of the crown and entrenched in the Cuban privileged class, thought only about preserving life as he knew it, and he detested any kind of political, economic, or social catastrophe that would devastate the affluent in Cuba. The last thing Casa-Calvo wanted was a lower-class insurgency that loosened racial mayhem on the white-dominated Cuban social order, a sentiment shared by slaveholders throughout the Atlantic world.[4]

While life on the island was pleasurable for the well-to-do, the French Republic had moved on to a Directorate, which Napoleon Bonaparte soon dominated. During the brief time it governed France, the Directorate tried to return Saint-Domingue to slavery since in the past the colony had served as a royal cash cow. Louisiana also figured prominently in Bonaparte's overseas plans as he wanted it to supply foodstuffs for sugar-producing Saint-Domingue; even prior to 1791 the French possession had imported huge quantities of comestibles from Cuba, Santo Domingo, Jamaica, other neighboring islands, and the United States. Bonaparte's ambition to create an overseas empire,

4. Although the Cuban sugar planters knew about the terrible events in Saint-Domingue, they continued to push the growth of sugarcane on the island, helped by many refugees from the war-torn colony. These issues are discussed in González-Ripoll et al.'s *El rumor de Haiti en Cuba: Temor, raza y rebeldía.*

however, quickly foundered. Yellow fever and malaria broke out among his victorious soldiers in Saint-Domingue who crushed the slave insurrections, and soon they began to die in horrendous numbers. Their deaths enabled the black generals to win back the colony. On realizing that he could neither establish profitable dependencies overseas nor dominate the British navy while he fought wars in Europe, Bonaparte abandoned Saint-Domingue and sold Louisiana to the United States to gain funds to pay his soldiers, a decision that intimately affected Casa-Calvo. Soon the Corsican adventurer resumed hostilities in Europe as he preferred success over stalemate.[5]

These events took place in the Caribbean between 1799 and 1803. In addition, problems in leadership troubled Louisiana. Letters coming from New Orleans justified Captain General Someruelos's negative opinion about Governor Salcedo. He had met the appointee when the latter passed through Havana in 1801, and Someruelos could not fathom what had inspired Manuel Godoy to assign a foolish and undistinguished man who did not appear to understand his duties as governor of Louisiana. The royal order of July 24, 1802, that announced the retrocession of the colony to France, baffled Salcedo because he soon inquired whether it included West Florida; he wanted its governorship if it remained Spanish. Not only that, but he wrote to Vicente Folch, the commandant in Pensacola, to tell him what he was seeking and asked about suitable housing in the town. Folch, of course, immediately notified Someruelos about Salcedo. After an interval, an irritated Someruelos instructed Salcedo to abide by the treaty's literal meaning that specified only the return of territory received from France in 1763.[6]

5. DeConde, *This Affair of Louisiana*, 193-225; Jon Kukla, *A Wilderness so Immense: The Louisiana Purchase and the Destiny of America* (New York: Anchor Books, 2004). Saint-Domingue's exports had been providing income to the French government, and with the decline of revenue Bonaparte needed to obtain funds wherever he could.

6. Manuel Salcedo to the Marqués de Someruelos, New Orleans, October 22, 1802; Someruelos to the governor of Louisiana, Havana, November 10, 1802 and February 23, 1803; all in MPA, SD, vol. 8, ff. 29-38, 39-43, and 43-44. Spanish dealings with France between 1795-1800 on returning Louisiana are examined in Arthur P. Whita-

Reading Salcedo's official correspondence reveals that he spent much of his time attempting to further the army careers of his two sons who had accompanied him to Louisiana. His older offspring, named Manuel María, welcomed his father's authority as governor. Once in New Orleans, he gathered a group of seedy officials and quickly manipulated the governor's power toward satisfying their personal ends. In addition, the son had become entangled in a mysterious relationship with Marie Elisabeth d'Estréhan. Nicolás María Vidal, the government attorney who received her complaint, informed the governor that its seriousness merited his son's arrest, to which Salcedo suggested holding him at the city's Fort San Carlos. Perhaps what upset Marie Elisabeth was Manuel's breach of a marriage promise. With the governor exerting authority, the incarcerated suitor was almost immediately released to house arrest because of an alleged illness, and home confinement lasted roughly two weeks. In the midst of this disorder, in June 1803 Manuel María received royal permission to marry María Guadalupe Prieto y Laronde, which he later did. To rehabilitate his son's tarnished image, Salcedo appointed him head of the military squad that escorted the prisoner William Augustus Bowles to Havana in that same June, and the governor went farther and heaped undeserved praise on his son for the adventurer's capture when in actuality he had not been involved. Nevertheless, the strategy worked, and the misinformed peninsular government promoted both sons. For whatever reason, the crown also elevated Salcedo to brigadier general about the same time and freed him from the *residencia* or investigation into his conduct while governor.[7]

---

ker, "The Retrocession of Louisiana in Spanish Policy," *American Historical Review* 39 (April 1934): 454-70. Salcedo solicited the office of governor of West Florida in his letter to the Prince of the Peace (Manuel Godoy), New Orleans, December 13, 1803, in James Alexander Robertson, ed., *Louisiana under the Rule of Spain, France, and the United States, 1785-1807*, 2 vols. (Cleveland: Arthur H. Clark, 1911), 2: 145-49.

7. (Salcedo) to Vidal, New Orleans, May 24, and June 2 and 6, 1803; Vidal to Salcedo, New Orleans, May 24 and June 2 and 6, 1803; all in AGI, PC, leg. 78; (Salcedo) to Someruelos, New Orleans, four letters all dated June 4, 1803, all in AGI, PC, leg. 155B. The promotions of Salcedo's sons are also noted in Someruelos to Casa-Calvo, Havana, April 26, 1804, AGI, PC, leg. 156A; (Casa-Calvo) to Someruelos, New

This sorry episode was only part of the corruption and non-enforcement of royal laws that plagued New Orleans, and conditions had worsened under Salcedo's doddering leadership. Inasmuch as he needed assistance in governance, Someruelos preferred that it come from a knowledgeable and upright government servant. Furthermore, doing that was less complicated than removing a royally-appointed governor since the deposed official might instigate a royal inquiry. Besides, by the spring of 1803, the inept Salcedo had only several months left to serve if arrangements for the province's transfer to France could be quickly finalized.[8]

Someruelos chose as Salcedo's adviser the most informed official on Louisiana he knew, Casa-Calvo, recently the colony's acting governor. About mid-March, he was ready to return to New Orleans, which he had left less than two years before. A major difference from his earlier journeys, however, was that his younger son Ignacio now accompanied him. Casa-Calvo did not wish to deprive him of his

---

Orleans, June 4, 1803, AGI, PC, leg. 155B. Even Claiborne mentioned that Salcedo's older son possessed a degenerate character and had a ruinous influence over his father. Claiborne to James Madison, New Orleans, January 2, 1804, in *Official Letter Books of W. C. C. Claiborne, 1801-1816*, edited by Dunbar Rowlands, 6 vols. (Jackson, Miss.: Mississippi Department of Archives and History, 1917), 1: 326-29. Stanley Clisby Arthur and George Campbell Huchet de Kernion, in *Old Families of Louisiana* (repr. Baton Rouge: Claitor's Publishing Division, 1971), 414-16, in their section on the d'Estréhan family do not mention Marie d'Estréhan.

8. (Salcedo) to Manuel María Salcedo, New Orleans, June 13, 1803, AGI, PC, leg. 76. See also Pitot, *Observations*, 21, who calls Salcedo an old man, infantile, poor, almost paralyzed, angered by family reverses and who sought to profit from his position. Historians have long known that Governor Salcedo epitomized the worst features of Spanish officialdom and that he could not compare with Louisiana's earlier governors. On the complaint of Marie Elisabeth d'Estréhan against Salcedo's older son, Nicolás Vidal investigated and found the officer deeply involved, with enough evidence to arrest him or send him to Havana to be placed at the captain general's disposition. But Vidal left it to the father to determine if this should be done. Vidal to Salcedo, New Orleans, May 24, 1803, AGI, PC, leg. 78. After two weeks, Vidal suspended the arrest of the younger Manuel Salcedo under his word of honor until the captain general answered. (Salcedo) to Vidal, New Orleans, June 6, 1803, ibid. A week later the son left for Havana with a guard of soldiers and Bowles in tow. Laussat comments on Bowles are in his work, *Memoirs of My Time*, 36-39.

tutelage as he had done with Pedro, who now exhibited symptoms of a spoiled upbringing. Casa-Calvo's decision to keep Ignacio close to him must have delighted both of them, and from this point forward for the remaining seventeen years of his father's life, with the exception of brief interludes, Ignacio was his father's constant companion. Moreover, he had entered the army as a cadet in March 1802, just short of age twelve, and although he did not attend a cadet school, his father supervised his military instruction.[9] Someruelos informed Casa-Calvo that his new duties consisted of ensuring that the transfer of Louisiana proceeded smoothly. Left unsaid was that Salcedo should avoid advice from intrusive quarters. To prevent this, Casa-Calvo received authority that equaled Salcedo's in the reassignment of Louisiana. In fact, sub rosa Casa-Calvo's power was probably greater since all matters of substance on the transfer cleared his hands before the documents became public.[10]

Casa-Calvo reached Louisiana in April as the province was learning of its return to France. Someruelos had sent this information to Salcedo on September 25, 1802, after receiving a royal order dated the previous July 31, from Spain's chief minister. The Louisiana governor appears not to have acknowledged the letter until January 12, 1803.[11] By the following summer, rumors circulated that Bonaparte had sold Louisiana to the United States. Before that happened, New Orleans's French population awaited the arrival of Bonaparte's officials, and in-

9. Enlistment certificate of Ignacio Calvo de la Puerta, in the Company of Justo Muñoz of the Battalion of the Infantry Regiment of Havana, Havana, March 26, 1803. AMS, ES.

10. (Casa-Calvo) to José Martínez, (New Orleans), March 2, 1804, and Martínez to Casa-Calvo, New Orleans, March 3, 1804, both in AGI, PC, leg. 73. The second document contains a royal order of October 3, 1803, from the Secretary of War on the king's wish to send Salcedo into retirement in the Canary Islands. It was approved in Spain on March 1, 1803. Casa-Calvo would assume direction of Salcedo's military and political commands. Also, Martínez as a sergeant major of the Royal Engineers would act in concert with Casa-Calvo in the matter of boundaries, according to a royal order of September 16, 1803. Ibid.

11. (Salcedo) to Osorno, New Orleans, January 12, 1803, AGI, PC, leg. 78.

deed, Prefect Pierre Clément Laussat, who was designated as the civil governor and authorized to receive Louisiana from Spain, appeared on March 26. But the anticipated expedition of several thousand French soldiers under Gen. Claude Perrin Victor, who was to be the captain-general or military governor and was charged with taking physical possession of the colony, never sailed as Bonaparte had abandoned his plans for a New World empire. If the colony's Francophone inhabitants had rejoiced upon learning the first news, they soon lamented the Corsican's heartless decision to alienate them. Unlike most citizens of the new United States, the French inhabitants of Louisiana yearned to retain political ties to the motherland. Through 1803, each passing month became gloomier for the colony's population. Spain had already exhibited its waning potency by governing the colony inadequately with fewer resources and personnel and by imposing a mediocrity as the last royal governor. In doing so, the-less-than-brilliant Carlos IV and his second-rate minister Manuel Godoy had reduced Louisiana's government to shambles, never mind Spain's diminishing strength. Although the colony only occasionally received the monarchy's full attention, newcomers to Louisiana did not realize that its decline was mostly a recent phenomenon due to the seemingly endless European wars.[12]

Years after the events of 1803-04, the French prefect recounted in a memoir the colony's transfer as he saw or preferred to remember it. He recalled that on May 12, Governor Salcedo honored both him and the Marqués de Casa-Calvo with a banquet, and the following Sunday, Laussat returned the compliment with another dinner.[13] This ended the official feasts until October 14, when Casa-Calvo gave one to commemorate the saint's day of the Prince of Asturias, the king's son and heir Fernando. When Laussat learned that a French general,

12. Kukla, *Wilderness So Immense*, 228-29; Claiborne to Wilkinson, Washington, Mississippi Territory, November 16, 1802, 1: 225-26; Eberhard L. Faber, "The Passion of the Prefect: Pierre Clément De Laussat, 1803 New Orleans, and the Bonapartist Louisiana That Never Was," *Louisiana History* 54 (Summer 2013): 261.

13. Pierre Clement de Laussat, *Memoirs of my Life*, 44.

the surly Charles André Burthe who had accompanied him across the Atlantic, had also been invited, he bluntly announced his departure to the startled host, declaring that he could no longer abide Burthe. Laussat soon went farther and tried to have the hapless general arrested, but the Spanish authorities refused to consent to such a bizarre request.[14]

Laussat had arrived in Louisiana as an arch Bonapartist and an arrogant advocate of his political, racial, and cultural superiority over the colony's and the New World's inhabitants. Upon reaching the mouth of the Mississippi on March 20, 1803, he wrote Salcedo in an attempt to take immediate control of Louisiana. That did not happen although the colony's Creole population initially kowtowed to his self-importance, and to his mind it confirmed his ability to lord over the masses. Casa-Calvo, on the other hand, came from a different cultural and economic background and refused to stoop before the pretentious middle-class bureaucrat. Moreover, he had learned from his lengthy stays in Spain that the notion of European superiority over New World Creoles, an attitude that also permeated Spanish society, was no more than Old World ethnocentrism, and he refused to be intimidated.[15]

Only a week after his arrival, Laussat published in the New Orleans newspaper, *Le Moniteur de Louisiane*, a proclamation in which he all but announced that he was taking over since it was time to correct the crass error the French king committed four decades before. Laussat wanted to be in charge when the French soldiers arrived and deploy them as he saw fit. Moreover, he sent fraudulent reports that he was making progress in preparations for the arrival of the troops, which

14. Ibid., 42-46; Jon Kukla, ed., *A Guide to the Papers of Pierre Clement Laussat* (New Orleans: Historic New Orleans Collection, 1993), 5.

15. Laussat arrived in New Orleans on March 26, 1803. Grace King and John R. Ficklen, *A History of Louisiana* (rev. ed; New York-New Orleans: University Publishing Company, [1893]), 150. On Laussat's pretentiousness, see Faber, "Laussat," 261-91; Ronald D. Smith, "Napoleon and Louisiana: Failure of the Proposed Expedition to Occupy and Defend Louisiana, 1801-1803," *Louisiana History* 12 (Winter 1971): 32-34.

he could not do as he lacked both authority and money. In time he learned that the expedition was not coming, the Spaniards were not yielding power, and he remained powerless to enforce his diktats. He further insulted the Spaniards by condemning the executions of the 1768 rebellion leaders. His repugnant behavior alienated the people with real authority, and his self-importance soon evaporated. Upon New Orleans receiving word that France had sold Louisiana to the United States, his status in the colony plummeted from being the future civil governor or prefect of Louisiana to surrendering it, thus placing him in an identical position with Casa-Calvo and Salcedo.[16]

Laussat's irrational behavior convinced Casa-Calvo that his decision to improve the image Spain projected during Louisiana's last months as a royal possession was right. On returning to New Orleans, he wanted to be perceived differently from his 1799-1801 stay, when he was the interim governor. This time impressing the inhabitants was important and, for this purpose, a personal entourage of about twelve soldiers and several servants accompanied him. He flaunted his wealth by bringing his ornate Spanish carriage from Havana and at least a pair of spirited thoroughbreds to pull it through the streets of New Orleans. Colorful dress uniforms that he delighted in filled his wardrobe, and he relished the occasions that required formal wear. He intended to leave an indelible impression on as many people as he could, especially the Americans who were now entering the province in rising numbers.[17]

In May, important documents emerged from the governor's office that bore Salcedo's and Casa-Calvo's signatures on the colony's transfer. But routine provincial matters stayed solely under Salcedo's control. Much as Laussat wanted, he had not supplanted Salcedo in any

16. Faber, "Laussat," 269-74; Smith, "Napoleon and Louisiana," 21-40. While Smith claims that the Spanish government delayed in ceding Louisiana, the French did not send personnel to take control of the province. Only a handful of officials accompanied Laussat, far fewer than those Ulloa brought in 1766. The Spaniards did not cause the delay in the retrocession.

17. Henry E. Chambers, *Mississippi Valley Beginnings: An Outline of the Early History of the Earlier West* (NewYork: Knickerbocker Press, 1922), 207-8.

regard; moreover, officials at military posts scattered throughout the colony were Spaniards and loyal French Creoles who would not obey the orders of a strange and conceited outsider. Nonetheless, Salcedo's reaction to the reduction of his authority in the province by Casa-Calvo's appointment must have displeased him, and Someruelos wanted as little attention drawn to his decision as possible.[18] Only letters in which he registered his dissatisfaction with Salcedo and Casa-Calvo's signature on documents that originally required only the governor's name attested to the new situation. Their first important joint proclamation was issued on May 18, 1803, and announced the forthcoming retrocession of Louisiana. While waiting for the transfer, Casa-Calvo received additional duties: He was to oversee the Spanish evacuation and determine the boundary line between Spanish Texas and soon-to-be American Louisiana. For the latter purpose, he received the title of commissioner of boundaries.[19]

In advance of Louisiana's retrocession, the Spanish government appointed Col. Vicente Folch y Juan, commandant at Pensacola and Casa-Calvo's old nemesis, the first Spanish governor of solely West Florida on September 16, 1803. Inasmuch as time, distance, and terrain hampered communications between Pensacola and the Florida Parishes, which was the western-most part of West Florida (the Pearl River to the Mississippi), the commandant at Baton Rouge, Carlos de Grand-Pré, served as deputy governor to early 1809, and Carlos Dehault Delassus followed until 1810. Their presence sped up the resolution of purely local matters.[20]

18. Many documents in AGI, PC, legajos 70B and 78, illuminate Casa-Calvo's new status in Louisiana and Salcedo's reduction in authority.

19. Proclamation of Manuel Salcedo and the Marqués de Casa-Calvo, New Orleans, May 18, 1803, AGI, PC, leg. 70B; Arthur Preston Whitaker, *The Mississippi Question, 1795-1803: A Study in Trade, Politics, and Diplomacy* (1934; repr. Gloucester, Mass., 1962), 184. See also Carlos Howard to Salcedo and Casa-Calvo, no. 257, New Orleans, May 23, 1803, AGI, PC, leg. 78.

20. Carlos de Grand-Pré to Casa-Calvo, [Baton Rouge, February 1804] and February 9, 1804, both in AGI, PC, leg. 73; David Hart White, *Vicente Folch, Governor in Spanish Florida, 1787-1811* (Washington, D.C.: American Academic Press, 1981),

Shortly before the retrocession, the two Spanish commissioners notified key officials in the city of the event and instructed them to wrap up their unfinished tasks as quickly as possible. Casa-Calvo took more of a role in this activity than Salcedo, whose authority was near its end. These messages had Casa-Calvo's name in first place and stated simply that tomorrow the province would be turned over to the French Republic. In one he advised Thomas Hassett, the colony's prelate following the bishop's departure, to meet with the city's clerics at 11:30 a.m. to finish arranging their part in the transfer.[21]

Celebrations accompanied the territorial change that was carried out with all the pageantry a remote colonial town could muster. New Orleans's inhabitants organized festivities, banquets, dances, and musical and theatrical presentations. It was *laisser le bon temps roulé* if only for a fleeting moment. The colony's retrocession to France occurred at midday on November 30, 1803, at the building that housed the municipal government. Salcedo presided at the gathering, and it represented his final notable duty. At the ceremony, Casa-Calvo announced that the colony's inhabitants who wished to remain in Louisiana were released from their oath of fidelity to the Spanish king. The town's inhabitants rejoiced upon the change in ownership despite their knowledge that Bonaparte had already alienated the colony.[22] For nearly three weeks the few French officials who had come to Louisiana and the Creole population tried to ignore the pending transfer. American delays in putting together an armed force in Natchez for the takeover created the interregnum, and it gave the peevish Laussat time to abolish the city government or Cabildo and Spanish law, reinstate the harsh French slave *Code Noir*, and attempt to eradicate other reminders that Louisiana had once been Spanish. But without soldiers to serve as a police force, the prefect faced a dilemma until Casa-Calvo tried to solve it by helping him form a body of militia. However, in-

77, 104.

21. Casa-Calvo and Salcedo to Thomas Hassett, New Orleans, November 29, 1803, AGI, PC, leg. 78; King and Ficklen, *History of Louisiana*, 152.

22. Chambers, *Mississippi Valley Beginnings*, 208.

stalling new laws presented more problems since it took time for the public to accept them, and Laussat's thoughtless manipulations ended up muddling Louisiana's legal procedures for several years. While the pompous official in his book depicted Salcedo as an impotent manikin, he denounced Casa-Calvo, a more formidable adversary, as "violent" and "filled with hatred for the French," no doubt since he had resisted the Frenchman's arrogance more effectively than Salcedo.[23] Laussat's characterization of Casa-Calvo, however, was highly questionable and his narrative of events in New Orleans reeked with a rabid Hispanophobia.

Laussat's conceit early on convinced Casa-Calvo not to take him seriously. To demonstrate that he was the better man on December 8, he held a large banquet and dance for the French official and for the city's distinguished people at the municipal dancehall that accommodated both whites and free blacks on separate days of the week. According to the prefect, 150 French, American, and Spanish ladies were in attendance, not counting the more numerous men. Casa-Calvo presided over the festivities with his usual finesse and began the dancing with the widow Madame Almonester. As was often the custom in New Orleans, the revelry persisted until 8 a.m. the next morning. At that time, Laussat as the guest of honor left with his entourage, and Casa-Calvo brought the soiree to a merciful close. Not to be outdone, Laussat returned the honor with another all-nighter on December 16.[24] Despite the celebrations, the two men barely dis-

23. Kukla, *Wilderness So Immense*, 319-20; Laussat to Louis André Pichon, [New Orleans], December 12, 1803, in Kukla, ed., *Guide*, 101. See also Mark F. Fernandez, *From Chaos to Continuity: The Evolution of Louisiana's Judicial System, 1712-1862* (Baton Rouge: Louisiana State University Press, 2001). A century after the Spanish era ended, historian Alcée Fortier tried to tell Louisiana inhabitants that Spain's four-decade long rule had no significant impact on the French colony. This interpretation lasted until the twentieth century when historians began visiting Spanish archives and microfilm copies of the documents became available in Louisiana. Their works provide a vastly different narrative of events than Fortier's biased judgment.

24. Laussat, *Memoirs of My Life*, 85. King and Ficklen, in *History of Louisiana*, 154, describe the elegance of the dinner parties given by Casa-Calvo and Laussat in their rivalry. See also Georges Oudard, *Four Cents an Acre: The Story of Louisiana under the*

guised their contempt for each other.

With the transfer of Louisiana accomplished, Salcedo recognized that his authority had ended. On December 9, in a letter to Commandant Joaquín de Osorno at Mobile, the former governor declared unabashedly that he had ceded Louisiana in the exact terms prescribed by the crown to Prefect Laussat. Furthermore, he also claimed to have instructions to remain in New Orleans with Casa-Calvo until completion of the province's physical transfer to the United States. Salcedo barely mentioned Casa-Calvo in his letter as if his presence did not matter. Since West Florida remained in Spanish hands, Salcedo confided that he had advised superior authorities to keep Osorno as commandant at Mobile.[25] While he wrote in a restrained manner, Salcedo's letter projected subtle indications that the reduction of his authority had pained him, and in recommending Osorno he attempted to demonstrate that he still possessed a modicum of power.

Following the transfer of the province to the United States on December 20, a ceremony in which only Americans cheered, the balls continued in early 1804. The new city officials who were now mostly French Creoles gave one on January 3, in honor of Madame Laussat. This time the festivities concluded at about 6 a.m. Nothing extraordinary happened at it, unlike the public ball of January 8, which many of the dignitaries still in the city attended. Laussat claimed that at the dance American rowdiness had produced a great commotion when the newcomers demanded more of their own kind of quadrilles, and the new governor had attempted futilely to quell the unrest. Meanwhile, Casa-Calvo with his natural savoir faire offered several alarmed ladies his protection and served them gumbo all the while he somehow continued playing cards. Laussat spun the story to depict Casa-Calvo in a disagreeable light. He also vaguely described the enmity between Casa-Calvo and the governor of West Florida, Col. Vicente Folch,

---

French (New York: Brewer and Warren, 1930), 259. According to Chambers, in *Mississippi Valley Beginnings*, 207, Laussat tried to engage Casa-Calvo in a duel. However, neither Laussat nor Casa-Calvo mentioned a duel in their writings.

25. (Salcedo) to Osorno, New Orleans, December 9, 1803, AGI, PC, leg. 78.

who was in New Orleans with his two sons. Laussat alleged that Folch "was highly successful" without specifying how while the Cuban "both detested and flattered [Folch]."[26] In reality the difficulties between Casa-Calvo and Folch had occurred in 1799-1800, when the former was governor of Louisiana and West Florida. Folch, who was then commandant at Pensacola, had repeatedly shown his insubordination, and on one occasion daringly proclaimed himself governor of West Florida.[27] In Laussat's description of the January 8 ball, he tried again to denigrate Casa-Calvo.

As the highest ranking Spanish official left in Louisiana, Casa-Calvo supervised Spain's withdrawal and transfer of men and equipment to Pensacola. It fell to him to find the ships, food, and supplies to sustain the troops until they reached their destination. His work took months to accomplish as many posts up the Mississippi evacuated slowly because the commanders waited for American authorities to replace them; the transfer at St. Louis occurred only in March 1804. On February 26, Casa-Calvo dined with the inexperienced twenty-eight-year-old American governor, William C. C. Claiborne. He had arrived in New Orleans more than two months before with Gen. James Wilkinson, the American military commander, to receive the province from France. To put him at ease, Casa-Calvo reported news that he had recently received from Spain that his government desired peace in Europe and America. Claiborne, however, felt vulnerable because he spoke neither French nor Spanish and his entrenched ethnocentrism caused his imagination to run wild in a land inhabited by people of other cultures. His qualms, if not paranoia, led him to complain frequently of his few troops and what he labeled the unhurried Spanish evacuation. He neither appreciated the amount of work it required nor recalled his own sluggish descent to New Orleans. He informed

26. Laussat, *Memoirs of My Life*, 93, with the quotations on p. 96. Claiborne claimed that on the raising of the American flag occurred "amidst the re-iterated acclamation of thousands." But even Hatfield described Claiborne's comment as a "pardonable exaggeration." Joseph T. Hatfield, *William Claiborne: Jeffersonian Centurion in the American Southwest* (Lafayette: University of Southwestern Louisiana, 1976), 112.

27. Din, *War on the Gulf Coast*, 141-42.

James Madison, the American secretary of state, that Casa-Calvo was now the sole commissioner since Salcedo was leaving in retirement to the Canary Islands, which he and his sons did in May.[28]

Probably acting for the Americans, Laussat encouraged the Spaniards to evacuate their troops from Louisiana without delay. Laussat then left New Orleans in April incognito to avoid possible detention by English privateers at the mouth of the Mississippi and sailed to the Caribbean to assume a new post in the government of Martinique.[29]

Spain's soldiers in Louisiana disturbed Claiborne who often complained since he learned virtually nothing about them. Earlier, in May 1803, Salcedo reported the number of soldiers he had. At that time the regiment was short nine hundred men, without counting nearly two hundred more who awaited discharge as they had served their time while others were unfit for service. They stayed in uniform be-

28. Claiborne to Madison, New Orleans, February 26, 1804, in his *Official Letter Books*, 1: 387-88; see also Josef Martínez to Casa-Calvo, New Orleans, March 3, 1804, AGI, PC, leg. 73; (Casa-Calvo) to Someruelos, (New Orleans), May 29, 1804, ibid., leg. 156B. On May 25, 1801, President Jefferson appointed an ardent follower, William C. C. Claiborne, as the governor of the Mississippi Territory at the age of twenty-six. *Official Letter Books*, 1: 2-5. Casa-Calvo wrote a report to Pedro Cevallos detailing what he believed were the western boundaries of Louisiana. For the lower portion, he wrote, "All agree, generally, in assuring that the *San Francisco de Sabinas River* is the true boundary...." A. P. Nasatir attributes the letter to Salcedo but the author is really Casa-Calvo, the boundary commissioner. [Casa-Calvo] to Cevallos, New Orleans, [April 17, 1804], in A. P. Nasatir, ed., *Before Lewis and Clark: Documents Illustrating the History of the Missouri, 1785-1804*, 2 vols. (St. Louis: St. Louis Historical Documents Foundation, 1952), 1: 745-50, with the quotation on p. 746. Nasatir made this error again in a letter of August 1804, when Salcedo was clearly no longer in Louisiana. American historians have not appreciated the work required to oversee the Spanish evacuation from Louisiana and Casa-Calvo's reasons for delaying his examination of the Texas-Louisiana frontier. See, for example, Philip C. Brooks, "Spain's Farewell to Louisiana, 1803-1821," *Mississippi Valley Historical Review* 27 (June 1940): 30.

29. Laussat, *Memoirs of My Life*, 149-50; Laussat to Casa-Calvo, New Orleans, April 9, 1804; Gayarré, *History of Louisiana*, 4: 7.

cause of the critical shortage of manpower, which also caused him to summon to arms sixty free colored militiamen who were always eager to demonstrate their loyalty. By 1804, the scarcity of soldiers had become acute. Troops who transferred to Pensacola numbered fewer than five hundred.[30] They were anything but a fearsome military body since many suffered from ailments and disabilities, were elderly, and stayed in service because replacements did not come. Moreover, shortages in working guns, supplies, and especially money reduced their usefulness still more.[31] Americans, however, insisted that they constituted a potent force, and a shaky Claiborne kept reminding Laussat while he stayed in New Orleans of the unacceptable Spanish presence. Claiborne, a civilian with limited military experience, repeatedly projected signs of being easily rattled.

When Claiborne again implored Laussat to inquire about the Spanish evacuation, Casa-Calvo replied on March 5, that several factors had delayed their departure. Salient among them was the lack of transportation. Besides troops, Spain needed to ship artillery, munitions, and military equipment of all kinds. For this purpose, the frigate *Nuestra Señora de las Nieves* would soon remove much of this paraphernalia and some of the dragoons who were still in the city. Nevertheless, it still took several trips. Other personnel remained behind because they were on special assignments, and some had obtained permission to settle their business affairs in the city before departing.[32]

Among the numerous matters that Casa-Calvo supervised were the army officers who would remain in Louisiana's fixed regiment after they moved to Pensacola. Many were Louisiana residents and wished to remain in their native province. Soon after the transfer, a large number began resigning their commissions, which harmed the feeble regiment still more. Later in West Florida, the unit continued

30. (Salcedo) to Juan Caso y Luengo, New Orleans, May 4, 1803, AGI, PC, leg. 78.

31. Gilbert C. Din, "'For Defense of Country and the Glory of Arms': Army Officers in Spanish Louisiana, 1766-1803," *Louisiana History* 43 (Winter 2002): 5-40.

32. Casa-Calvo to Laussat, New Orleans, March 5, 1804, in *Memoirs of my Life*, Laussat, 139.

to shrivel as resignations persisted and adequate funding and replacements failed to come. Before long the regiment collapsed into a rickety shadow of its former self.[33]

Money shortages also affected continuing Spanish officials and army officers in New Orleans who received their salaries irregularly. Over time, they accumulated debts to New Orleans shopkeepers. The regiment's transfer to Pensacola in 1804 alarmed the merchant community, and they sought out Claiborne for help. He, in turn, consulted Casa-Calvo, who expressed his willingness to resolve the dilemma. He suggested that in conformance with Spanish law the debtor officers would have a third to half of their monthly salaries assigned to the merchants until they liquidated their arrears. Claiborne accepted Casa-Calvo's suggestion.[34]

Another chore unexpectedly arose after the Americans took charge in Louisiana. The Catholic Church in the province had been under the Spanish government that held the *patronato real*, or royal patronage, that gave the king and his subordinates power over it. But as the United States was a secular nation, it did not take charge. Instead, Casa-Calvo assumed responsibility for the wages of the churchmen, which he paid in 1804 and 1805. In the latter year, however, he inadvertently became embroiled in the rivalry between the leading Catholic religious in New Orleans, Father Patrick Walsh and Father Antonio de Sedella, otherwise known as Père Antoine. In that year, Walsh attempted to assert greater authority in New Orleans and told Casa-Calvo that the United States had not given him the power of papal legate, nor did he have authority over church property. A gathering of the church parishioners entrusted its holdings to Jean Castillon, who in turn dele-

33. Ibid. Among the many documents on this topic, see Carlos Howard to Salcedo and Casa-Calvo, New Orleans, May 23, 1803, ibid., and its attachment, "Relation that the Officers of the Fixed Infantry Regiment of Louisiana present today in this City." It indicated which officers then preferred to resign from the regiment. See also Howard to Salcedo and Casa-Calvo, no. 14, New Orleans, July 11, 1803, ibid., which told that only one officer of the regiment's third battalion stationed in West Florida wished to leave Spanish service.

34. (Collell?) to Casa-Calvo, no. 32, New Orleans, March 17, 1804, AGI, PC, leg. 73.

gated them to Sedella, whom they chose as their priest; such elections, however, were against Catholic custom. Church funds, moreover, had been entrusted to the city government that in 1805 no longer wished to handle them. As the parishioners had elected an assembly called the Marguilliers, or trustees of the Cathedral, the money went to them to administer. Castillon then introduced a discordant note when he said that the French-Vatican Concordat governed the church in Louisiana. This, however, clashed with the Marguilliers and Père Antoine who had named Casa-Calvo as their grand counselor. Conditions became murkier when the Marguilliers claimed to hold the right of patronage under Spanish law and custom. Part of the turmoil was relieved when Father Walsh, who contended that he was the legitimate Vatican appointee, died of yellow fever in 1806. By that time, Casa-Calvo was no longer involved as he had left the province.[35] Before long, the bishop of Baltimore assumed oversight of Catholic affairs in Louisiana, which ended the disorder.

In the immediate post-transfer era, Casa-Calvo also became indirectly involved with Gen. James Wilkinson, who was a notorious schemer and knew no loyalty except to his pocketbook. He sought money everywhere, even in treasonous dealings, as he sought to satisfy his wife's lavish spending habits. As early as 1787, the Spanish crown had employed him as their secret agent Number Thirteen to foil American attempts to encroach on Spanish territory as their inhabitants relentlessly moved into Kentucky and Tennessee and toward the Mississippi River. At that time, he sought the defection of Kentucky from the American republic and creation of a sovereign nation. Although Wilkinson received payments from the Spanish government for several years, he did little to stem the American push westward, especially after Kentucky and Tennessee became states in the union.

35. Baudier, *Catholic Church in Louisiana*, 255-58. See also Charles Edwards O'Neill, "'A Quarter Marked by Sundry Peculiarities': New Orleans, Lay Trustees, and Père Antoine," 421-55, in *The Louisiana Purchase and Its Aftermath, 1800-1830*, ed. Dolores Egger Labbe, vol. 3 of *The Louisiana Purchase Bicentennial Series in Louisiana History* (Lafayette, La.: Center for Louisiana Studies, University of Southwestern Louisiana, 1998).

Despite having opponents occasionally claim that he was a traitor, he skillfully deflected the charges and continued with his American army career mostly unblemished. Because of his experiences in the west, he became the military chief assigned to Louisiana on its takeover and later governor in the upper part (St. Louis) of the colony.[36]

But as Wilkinson's need for money remained constant, soon after the transfer he sought out Vicente Folch (the nephew of Gov. Esteban Miró who first employed him as an agent) with promises of aiding the Spaniards to halt the American territorial juggernaut that demanded territory. He wrote out a document called "Reflections" that laid out his thoughts on the alternatives Spain could employ. For his involvement, he wanted his former pension of $2,000 per year resumed and ten years of back pay satisfied. When Folch announced that he lacked funds, Wilkinson quickly cut his demand by half. Folch then said that other officials had to be informed to secure the funds, including the former intendant Morales and Casa-Calvo; the latter was receiving money to pay for his surveying expedition going to the Sabine River. Wilkinson then scurrilously denigrated Casa-Calvo's personality, allegations that some historians have bought wholeheartedly despite the charges coming from the master of deception and an inveterate liar. He charged that Andrés López Armesto, Casa-Calvo's secretary, dominated his boss who was a dilettante and not dedicated to government service (Wilkinson showed his total ignorance about Casa-Calvo's many decades of army labor in various capacities). He further described López Armesto as the soul of indiscretion who would tattle everything to Morales. He, in turn, worked hand in glove with Daniel Clark Jr., a businessman, to sell him lands illegally in West Florida. Furthermore, Clark communicated directly with President Jefferson.

36. Wilkinson has generated a number of studies; see in particular, James Ripley Jacobs, *Tarnished Warrior: Major-General James Wilkinson* (New York: Macmillan, 1938); Juan Navarro Latorre y Francisco Solano Costa, *¿Conspiración española?1787-1789: Contribución al estudio de las primeras relaciones históricas entre España y los Estados Unidos de Norteamérica* (Zaragoza, España: Editoriales Librería General, 1949); and Andro Linklater, *An Artist in Treason: The Extraordinary Double Life of General James Wilkinson* (New York: Walker Publishing Company, 2009).

When Casa-Calvo offered López Armesto's services to translate Wilkinson's Reflections to Spanish, Wilkinson adamantly refused, and Folch did it instead. In his clandestine endeavors, Wilkinson toiled to turn his associates against each other as he created a maze of deceit in which no one trusted the other.[37]

Folch, who was more involved than Casa-Calvo, wanted Spanish retention of the west bank of the Mississippi for the protection of Mexico and the Floridas to shield Cuba. While he rejected paying off the United States' national debt for Louisiana, a suggestion someone had made, he was amenable to returning what the United States had paid France. Casa-Calvo, meanwhile gave Wilkinson $12,000 from funds he had. Wilkinson then invested that sum in sugar to ship to the United States, which resulted in rumors about where he had obtained the money. The general initially explained it as payment for an earlier purchase of tobacco, but soon switched it for his alleged services in securing Indian treaties. However, Spanish account books showed no payment for tobacco, as Clark learned from Morales. This was the extent of Casa-Calvo's involvement with Wilkinson. He later included the 12,000 pesos paid to Wilkinson as expenditures made to Morales and Pensacola as he prepared his expedition to the Sabine.[38]

The year 1804 marked the start of a struggle over the western part of West Florida that later became known as the Florida Parishes, and it persisted well into 1810. As he prepared to supervise the evacua-

37. Cox, "Wilkinson and His Later Intrigues," 794-99. Wilkinson's "Reflections" are published in *Louisiana under the Rule of Spain, France, and the United States, 1785-1807*, James A. Robertson, 2 vols. (Cleveland: Arthur H. Clark), 325-47, and it can be found AGI, PC, leg. 2355. In his *Official Letter Book* (New Orleans, May 24, 1804, 2: 166), Claiborne wrote to Madison, "There exists a great hatred between the Marquis of Casa Calvo and the late [*sic*] Intendant Morales and at this time their exertions are mutual to ruin each other....My private opinion is that the Marquis is infinitely the most deserving character and I therefore wish and hope he may triumph over his rival."

38. Casa-Calvo to Andrés López Armesto, Madrid, February 23, 1808, with the attached document, "Notice of the investment of One Hundred Thousand Pesos received in New Orleans that came from Veracruz," Casa-Calvo, January 22, 1807; both documents in AGI, PC, leg. 70B.

tion from Louisiana, Casa-Calvo learned to his bewilderment about the aggressive intrigues of the Thomas Jefferson administration in the United States that seemed to foreshadow attacks on Spanish territory. Jefferson had already been working to secure use of the rivers that flowed southward from the Mississippi Territory into the Gulf of Mexico. Because the rivers crossed West Florida where Spain owned both banks, Jefferson wanted to claim the colony from Spain that it had won through conquest, and its ownership was ratified by the Treaty of Paris of 1783. In 1802, when he learned that France had acquired Louisiana, he thought the Gallic kingdom might help him achieve his objectives, and Jefferson assigned two diplomats, Robert R. Livingston and James Monroe, to buy West Florida and New Orleans. Spain, however, was unwilling to part with West Florida. Given that Bonaparte's overseas ambitions collapsed about the same time, Napoleon then decided to part with Louisiana, which France was soon to receive from Spain. François Barbé-Barbois, the French foreign minister, received the task to engage the Americans in negotiations, and he caught them off guard by unexpectedly offering to sell them Louisiana and New Orleans. Buying the sprawling Louisiana colony, however, was not the purpose of their commission; nevertheless, they could not resist the offer since they felt they needed some kind of diplomatic success to salvage their failure over West Florida. While recognizing that the colony had been left outside the purchase since it was not territory Spain had received from France in 1763, the Franco-American treaty defined the boundaries loosely and left the Americans with wiggle room to make claims, not that West Florida in any way constituted a genuine part of Louisiana. Despite their acquisition of land that doubled the size of the United States, public reaction in the eastern states, particularly New England, was initially hostile as they regarded the unknown wilderness as a worthless desert. Some Americans even considered exchanging the western bank of the Mississippi for Spanish West Florida, a swap that appealed to many Louisianans.[39]

39. E. Wilson Lyon, *The Man Who Sold Louisiana: The Career of François Barré-Mar-*

By January 1804, American representatives in New Orleans started making exaggerated claims on lands they alleged comprised the Louisiana Purchase, and they revealed the exponential growth of Jefferson's territorial ambitions. Monroe and Livingston had both been working on how to include West Florida in the Louisiana Purchase, and they made several suggestions that alleged the sale included the province. In time Jefferson's new version of the Purchase's territorial limits took in not only West Florida but Texas as well. Laussat reported that American authorities had inquired unofficially about Louisiana's boundaries, declaring that West Florida and Texas were integral parts of the colony. He, however, rejected their insinuations.[40] The American claims came despite the proclamations issued at the time of Louisiana's transfers from Spain to France on November 30, and to the United States on December 20, 1803, that did not hint at the inclusion of West Florida or Texas. Moreover, Jefferson himself had written to Salcedo on July 4, 1803, announcing the United States purchase of Louisiana and New Orleans from France, and he mentioned neither one of the two provinces. But soon after, his scheme

bois (Norman: University of Oklahoma Press, 1974), 118-22; François Barbé-Marbois, *The History of Louisiana,* ed. E. Wilson Lyon (Baton Rouge: Louisiana State University Press, 1977); Kukla, *Wilderness so Immense*, 259-83, 289-90; Cox, *The West Florida Controversy*, 66-67; DeConde, *This Affair of Louisiana*, 161-75. See also Jared W. Bradley, "W.C.C. Claiborne and Spain: Foreign Affairs under Jefferson and Madison, 1801-1811, Parts I and II," *Louisiana History* 12 (1971): 297-314, and 13 (1972): 5-26. Gayarré, in *History of Louisiana*, 4: 18, errs in believing that the area known as the Florida Parishes was part of the Louisiana Purchase and that the inhabitants favored annexation to the United States. This was an interpretation that long persisted.

40. Laussat, *Memoirs of My Life*, 91. On the dispute over Louisiana's western boundary, see Philip Coolidge Brooks, *Diplomacy and the Borderlands: The Adams-Onis Treaty of 1819* (Berkeley: University of California Press, 1939); and Luis de Onis, *Negociaciones entre España y los Estados Unidos de América*; 3rd ed. (Madrid, 1969). Jefferson's claim that Texas extended to the Rio Grande will not be discussed here, but on this matter see Isaac Joslin Cox, *The Louisiana-Texas Frontier*, 2 vols. (Austin, Tex.: University of Texas Press, 1906). Casa-Calvo's first warning to Spain on American exploring expeditions was his reserved letter to Pedro Cevallos, New Orleans, March 20, 1804, in Nasatir, ed., *Before Lewis and Clark*, 2: 727-78.

to gain more territory led to his ex post facto declaration that the Purchase meant Louisiana's size prior to 1763, when France owned both sides of the Mississippi River. The Spaniards regarded the assertion as patently absurd. Jefferson based his sketchy contentions on seventeenth-century French claims to Texas, which he now said the United States acquired through the Purchase. France, however, had years before discarded its pretensions to lands it never settled. Pushed by his expansionist agenda, nevertheless, Jefferson dismissed Spain's early eighteenth-century occupation of Texas, conquest of West Florida from Great Britain between 1779 and 1781, and obligation to retrocede only what France had ceded it in 1763. Jefferson foraged on tenuous ground as he rejected earlier political accords and accepted history, and going farther, he deep-sixed President Washington's recognition of West Florida as Spanish territory in Pinckney's Treaty of 1795, as apparently Jefferson's own interpretation of what constituted the Louisiana Purchase took precedence. He was interested only in the acquisition of territory, not in the legitimacy of his arguments since he possessed the military clout to grab all the Mississippi Valley. But his political critics at home and possible hostile foes abroad restrained his embellishments, and the claims alone sufficed for now.[41]

41. Casa-Calvo to Pedro Cevallos, New Orleans, January 13, 1804; Cevallos to Casa-Calvo, Aranjuez, April 2, 1804; both in MPA, SD, vol. 8, ff. 236-37 and 237-41, respectively; (Jefferson to Salcedo), "Cession of Louisiana," Washington City, July 4, 1803; and Salcedo and Casa-Calvo to Someruelos, New Orleans, August 8, 1803, both included in Someruelos to Cevallos, Havana, August 27, 1803, AGI, Estado, leg. 2. Historians familiar with Spanish documentation do not accept Jefferson's inclusion of West Florida as part of Louisiana. See, for example, William S. Coker and Susan R. Parker, "The Second Spanish Period in the Two Floridas," in *The New History of Florida*, ed. Michael Gannon (Gainesville, Fla., 1996), 154; and Whitaker, *Mississippi Question*, 308, n. 20. Claiborne showed his subordination to Jefferson by immediately calling West Florida a part of Louisiana despite public opinion in New Orleans that said it was not. Claiborne to James Madison, New Orleans, January 24, 1804, in *Official Letter Books*, 1: 344-49. Hatfield's *William Claiborne*, 238, is a sympathetic study of Claiborne and describes him and James Wilkinson, the American commissioners assigned to receive Louisiana, as not insisting on West Florida's inclusion to avoid "some Embarrassment." Indeed! Louisianans said that it was not a part of the territory. Barbé-Marbois, *History of Louisiana*, 240. See also David E.

As early as January 19, 1804, Casa-Calvo, who was uninformed of Louisiana's western dimensions, asked Laussat for a verification of its boundaries. Unlike his superiors in France, however, Laussat took scant interest in doing so. He merely recited that he would adhere to the vague description found in the 1800 Spanish-French agreement. Since that accord defined boundaries imprecisely, it did not resolve Casa-Calvo's dilemma.[42] After further consultation, he decided to place the dividing line between Texas and Louisiana at the Sabine River and Spain's post of Los Adaes located not far from Natchitoches.[43] As Laussat's information did not help, Casa-Calvo called upon Spain to provide further instructions. On March 26, Laussat informed Wilkinson and Claiborne that the Spaniards rejected American contentions. Casa-Calvo categorically described Spain's hold on West Florida and the lands beyond the Sabine as non-negotiable, and he asked Laussat to consult his government on this matter, which he did by writing to Denis Decrès, minister of the navy and the colonies in Paris.[44] Decrès, however, did not provide helpful information.

On March 27, 1804, the United States commissioners Claiborne and Wilkinson placed in Laussat's hands a protest in which they called West Florida American, an assertion Jeffersonians repeatedly made

---

Narrett, "Geopolitics and Intrigue: James Wilkinson, The Spanish Borderlands, and Mexican Independence," *William and Mary Quarterly*, 3rd ser., 69 (January 2012), 101-46. Narrett follows a pro-Jefferson interpretation and writes, "To acknowledge this historical reality [Jefferson's acceptance of freebooters operating in West Florida] is neither necessarily to praise nor condemn Jefferson but rather to see him as a statesman who employed a variety of means to induce Spain to make large territorial concessions. His tactics were not above the intrigues and power politics of the Old World, however much he believed himself to be acting on a higher moral level." Ibid., 118-19.

42. Laussat, *Memoirs of My Life*, 76.

43. Salcedo and Casa-Calvo to Laussat, New Orleans, January 19, 1804, in Laussat, *Memoirs of My Life*, 125.

44. Laussat to Salcedo and Casa-Calvo, New Orleans, January 20, 1804, in Lassaut, *Memoirs of My Life*, 126; Salcedo and Casa-Calvo to Laussat, 20 January 20, 1804, ibid., 126; Claiborne and Wilkinson to Laussat, New Orleans, March 26, 1804, ibid., 144; Casa-Calvo to Laussat, New Orleans, March 31, 1804, ibid., 145.

until its occupation. Following instructions from Washington City, they insisted that Louisiana's size was what it had been on October 1, 1800 (the day Spain agreed to the treaty of San Ildefonso that would retrocede Louisiana to France and which Americans now claimed included West Florida), and when France had possessed it prior to 1763 (Louisiana then consisted of both sides of the Mississippi). These boundaries, they insisted, passed on to successor nations, a contention the inventive Americans put forth to benefit their point of view as they hoped that Spain would capitulate to their demands as Godoy had done in 1795. Unimpressed, Laussat merely passed the note on to Casa-Calvo. In an effort to gain French support, Claiborne and Wilkinson used Laussat to deliver the message, but Spanish policy refused to accommodate their pretensions. Despite its multifold weaknesses, the Iberian nation displayed no inclination to surrender the province to bogus arguments.[45]

Nevertheless, a group of disgruntled American supporters in Louisiana, the Mississippi Territory, and even a few in West Florida were prepared to go farther in the acquisition of more lands. After receiving news of American unrest in West Florida in May 1804, Casa-Calvo delineated their intentions clearly in reporting their plans to seize the Florida Parishes, the roughly hundred-mile portion of West Florida that extended from the Mississippi River to the Pearl River. He wrote, "They wait no other moment to realize the intervention than the appeal for help from the inhabitants of that district [West Florida], for which the Americans would offer them protection, and as much aid as might be needed to ensure [the success of] the uprising."[46]

45. Laussat, *Memoirs of My Life*, 98-99. See also Jared W. Bradley, "W. C. C. Claiborne and Spain: Foreign Affairs under Jefferson and Madison, 1801-1811," in *The Louisiana Purchase and Its Aftermath, 1800-1830*, ed. by Dolores Egger Labbe, 110-37, vol. 3 of *The Louisiana Purchase Bicentennial Series in Louisiana History* (Lafayette, La.: Center for Louisiana Studies at the University of Southwestern Louisiana, 1998). While some United States historians have argued that Jefferson had valid claims to West Florida, in reality it is no more than bluster.

46. Whitaker, *Mississippi Question,*, 155-56, 181-82. Robertson's translation of Ca-

Jeffersonians wanted to use the Americans of that region to achieve their aims. Settlers had been moving into the Florida Parishes since 1787, when Spain opened up West Florida with offers of free land despite most of the newcomers being American Protestants. By 1804, after the colony's reduction in size by Pinckney's Treaty of 1795, its inhabitants could be found in scattered agricultural settlements along the Mississippi and on the interior Amite, Tangipahoa, Tchefuncte, and Pearl rivers that flowed south through the Florida Parishes. After 1795 the largest communities were on the Mississippi at Bayou Sara and Bayou Tonica in the Feliciana District, which lay below the Mississippi Territory, and at Manchac and Baton Rouge further south. Baton Rouge was the district's principal settlement. The inhabitants raised cattle, indigo, corn, sugarcane, and cotton; and produced pitch, tar, and wood products, especially boxes and barrels, from the region's piney forests. Well-to-do landowners—and most West Floridian were not—brought in slaves for the arduous labor needed to clear and level land, log, and plant and harvest crops.[47]

Meanwhile, Jefferson threatened that peace with Spain was impossible until the United States acquired West Florida. While some historians have attributed Jefferson's concerns to national security, they should have known that the tiny strip of the Gulf Coast in question lacked economic and defensive viability. Alone it was a worthless possession to European nations, and it was unlikely that they would fight to seize it, especially since they had no bases nearby to support their aggression. Honor, however, compelled the Spanish court to retain it; at the same time, the government did not invest scarce resources to guarantee its preservation. Jefferson's declaration, meanwhile, appeared to indicate that he wanted his territorial demands met in what-

sa-Calvo to Cevallos, New Orleans, May 18, 1804, in his *Louisiana*, 2: 187, is extremely awkward, and I have revised the quotation without changing the meaning.

47. Carlos de Grand-Pré to Casa-Calvo, Baton Rouge, May 10, 1800, AGI, PC, leg. 106A; Antonio Acosta Rodríguez, *La población de Luisiana española, 1763-1803* (Madrid: Ministerio de Asuntos Exteriores, 1979), 465-66. Since the 1770s, West Florida had been exporting wooden boxes for use in the Cuban export of sugar. Boxes were used before sacks made of fabric.

ever way necessary. France, whose support the American president sought, steadfastly refused to provide it, and Louis-Marie Turreau, the French minister to Washington, advised Secretary of State James Madison that neither Spain nor France recognized American claims to West Florida.[48]

Casa-Calvo remained in Louisiana for slightly more than two years after its transfer to the United States. Outside newspapers and government dispatches informed him of the diplomatic wrangling that went on by the United States to acquire West Florida, and he learned at first hand the devious manipulations of American citizens in the Mississippi Territory and even in New Orleans to seize it. Internal disturbances by a small group of the Florida Parishes' dissidents created the appearance that many of them were involved in the disorders. Perhaps five thousand or more individuals, both whites and slaves, inhabited the Parishes at that time.[49]

Simultaneously, the corrupt Intendant Juan Ventura Morales of New Orleans operated a profitable racket that sold off lands in the parishes to non-residents. In this way, the city's well-known and affluent merchant Daniel Clark Jr. acquired thousands of acres for speculation as he sought to enrich his pockets from their subsequent sales.[50]

48. Cox, "American Intervention," 296. The British attempt to conquer New Orleans in the War of 1812 was a foolhardy venture since even had they won the battle and the city they surely would have lost the city had the war continued.

49. Carlos de Grand-Pré to Casa-Calvo, Baton Rouge, AGI, PC, leg. 106A; Acosta Rodríguez, *La población,* 465-66.

50. Andrew McMichael, "Maintaining Loyalty in the West Florida Borderlands: Land as Cause and Effect in the West Florida Revolution of 1810," in *Coastal Encounters: The Transformation of the Gulf South in the Eighteenth Century*, ed. Richmond F. Brown (Lincoln: University of Nebraska Press, 2007), 210-30, discusses Spanish land policy and land holding. On Daniel Clark, see Andrew McMichael, "William Dunbar, William Claiborne, and Daniel Clark: Intersections of Loyalty and National Identity on the Florida Frontier," in *Nexus of Empire: Negotiating Loyalty and Identity in the Revolutionary Borderlands, 1760s-1820s*, eds. Gene Allen Smith and Sylvia L. Hilton (Gainesville: University Press of Florida, 2010), 285-89. Even Claiborne acknowledged the bad relations then present between Casa-Calvo and Morales. See his letter to James Madison, New Orleans, May 24, 1805, in his *Official Letter Books*, 2: 166.

Acting as if the United States had a valid claim to West Florida because of the Purchase, Claiborne tried to stop Morales from alienating land. He argued that West Florida was disputed territory and land transfers should await a resolution of its ownership. Spain, however, had regarded West Florida as its legitimate possession for more than twenty years before Claiborne's arrival and insisted that the Louisiana Purchase had not invalidated its title. Claiborne finally stopped Morales from selling land in New Orleans by ejecting him from the city in 1806. Not dismayed, however, the enterprising intendant relocated to Pensacola where he soon resumed his sales from a new land office.[51]

Maintaining order was Spain's greatest problem in the Florida Parishes. Opportunists, outlaws, army deserters, and adventurers, almost all Americans from the neighboring Mississippi Territory, took advantage of Spain's handful of soldiers to raid, steal slaves and livestock, and commit other crimes. Lawlessness was an inherent characteristic of the American frontier, and it was pervasive in the trans-Appalachian West before it occurred in the Plains or the Far West. To quell the disorders coming from Mississippi, Spanish officials used Anglo-American settlers in West Florida in local militias and as *alcaldes* (magistrates) to preserve the peace in the countryside while the Spaniards employed their soldiers primarily to garrison the fort in Baton Rouge. In the spring of 1804, the Kemper brothers, Reuben, Nathaniel, and Samuel, began their violence in the parishes. It started with their complicated business dealings with a John Smith, a landowner who evicted them from his property, and they resisted expulsion by rising up against Smith and the Spanish authorities. The Kempers

51. McMichael, *Atlantic Loyalties*, 64-67; Claiborne to Casa-Calvo, New Orleans, August 3 and 9, 1805, *Official Letter Books*, 3: 146 and 161; Claiborne to Madison, New Orleans, June 26, 1806, ibid., 3: 346-47. United States claims to West Florida incited some West Floridians who supported annexation. Although he was committed to seizing West Florida, Claiborne denied responsibility to provoking unrest there. Claiborne to Madison, New Orleans, June 27, 1804, ibid., 2: 227-29. Casa-Calvo persisted in believing that land on the Mississippi River's west bank would eventually be returned to Spain. Claiborne to Madison, New Orleans, July 25, 1804, and January 21, 1806, both in ibid., 2: 266-67 and 3: 246-47 respectively.

soon joined a small group of dissidents who favored American annexation, and they purposely provoked unrest as a way to elicit American intervention. Reuben Kemper spent most of his time in New Orleans and had ties to Claiborne who was disinclined to curb the criminal deeds of the two Kemper brothers in the Feliciana district. The outraged inhabitants of the Florida Parishes, however, used the militia to quell the Kemper rampages.[52] Although Gen. James Wilkinson once detained Nathaniel and Samuel Kemper in the Mississippi Territory, he soon released them despite Spanish objections. In doing so, he exemplified the American refusal to prosecute or extradite persons wanted for crimes in West Florida.

Kemper disorders grew serious in May 1804. To combat them, Spanish soldiers, who were evacuating upriver posts and the Galveztown fort on the Amite River, reinforced the Baton Rouge garrison.[53] Nevertheless in July, Grand-Pré reported that brigands in the Feliciana district had burned the home of militia captain Vicente Pintado. Grand-Pré quickly dispatched a boatload of soldiers to restore order. Elsewhere the inhabitants remained quiet. Grand-Pré offered the arrested amnesty on condition they left Spanish territory and never returned.[54] Such measures, however, merely provided the

52. Andrew McMichael, "The Kemper 'Rebellion': Filibustering and Resident Anglo American Loyalty in Spanish West Florida," *Louisiana History* 43 (Spring 2002): 136-38; McMichael, "Dunbar, Claiborne, and Clark," 285; Nugent, *Habits of Empire*, 104. Early nineteenth-century interpretations of the Kempers hailed them as heroes in the American acquisition of the Florida Parishes. See Stanley Clisby Arthur, *The Story of the West Florida Rebellion* (St. Francisville, La.: St. Francisville Democrat, 1935). An example of American lawlessness is in Claiborne to Madison, New Orleans, March 15, 1804, in *Official Letter Books*, 2: 41-42. In contrast, Claiborne noted in a letter to Madison, "The Louisianans have as Little Mischief in their dispositions and as much native goodness as any people." New Orleans, July 7, 1804, ibid., 2: 239-40.

53. Grand-Pré to Casa-Calvo, Baton Rouge, April 21, and May 9 and 13, 1804; (Casa-Calvo) to Grand-Pré, New Orleans, May 22, 1804; all in AGI, PC, leg. 73. Many Canary Islanders at Galveztown were then migrating to Baton Rouge, where they created Spanish Town.

54. Grand-Pré to Casa-Calvo, Baton Rouge, July 6 and 19, 1804, AGI, PC, leg. 73.

Kempers with new opportunities for more mayhem.

The Kempers constituted a grave menace inasmuch as they moved about with armed men threatening the inhabitants. They operated in several bands of twenty or so men who displayed a flag with seven white and blue stripes and two stars at the front. On August 3, Samuel and Nathaniel murdered a constable and savagely mistreated another. In New Orleans Reuben Kemper unleashed threats against *Alcalde* Alexander Sterling in the parishes. Four days later, the outlaws momentarily seized Pintado, *Alcalde* John O'Connor, and other persons; attempted to capture Grand-Pré at his home; and attacked the fort to no avail. Several reports from Feliciana told of "insurrections" there and in Bayou Tonica [*sic*], but they were all minor flare ups unworthy of the word insurrection since the inhabitants quickly extinguished them. Casa-Calvo requested that Claiborne order commanders in the Mississippi Territory and Pointe Coupee to deny the rebels sanctuary and to arrest Reuben who was printing "incendiary publications" in New Orleans.[55] Claiborne, however, denied that he coddled dissidents, had a talk with Reuben, and advised commanders near Spanish territory to prevent American involvement. Disorders in Spanish territory, nevertheless, persisted into September. By that time, Claiborne declared to Casa-Calvo, "I do not feel that my Authority permits me to direct or allow the seizure of [insurgents] within the Limits of the United States." In doing so, Claiborne consented to their activity. The governor of the Mississippi Territory acted in a similar manner.[56]

Casa-Calvo dispatched eight soldiers of his personal guard to Baton Rouge as he had no other troops to send.

55. Casa-Calvo to Claiborne, New Orleans, August 11, 1804, *Official Letter Books*, 2: 307-9; Grand-Pré to Casa Calvo, Baton Rouge, August 4, 1804, MPA, SD, vol. 2, ff. 397-401; McMichael, *Atlantic Loyalties*, 77-78.

56. Claiborne to Casa-Calvo, New Orleans, August 28 and September 13, 1804, *Letter Books*, 2: 309-10 and 330-31; William C. Davis, *The Rogue Republic: How Would-Be Patriots Waged the Shortest Revolution in American History* (New York: Houghton Mifflin Harcourt, 2011), 49. Claiborne, however, cautioned Mississippi territorial governor Cato West and the commandant at Pointe Coupee Julien Poidras to prevent persons residing near the Spanish boundary from intervening in the "dispute."

In August, Grand-Pré reported that a militia company that tried to capture the rebels resulted in many of them escaping to Pinckneyville, a village no more than a mile inside the Mississippi Territory. If Claiborne could not arrest them, Casa-Calvo requested their removal from the border to prevent further incursions and dissemination of incendiary writings designed to stir up discord. His request disturbed Claiborne, who admitted to Madison "that [as Casa-Calvo was] becoming troublesome I shall probably in a Short time refuse to hold any correspondence with him, until he shall have been acknowledged by the President of the United States as a Public agent on the part of Spain."[57]

Raids into the Spanish province continued from bases in Pinckneyville and Pointe Coupee across the Mississippi River, and they worried Grand-Pré. Since it took many days for reinforcements to reach him from Pensacola, Grand-Pré sought help from Casa-Calvo who had only his small military escort and limited funds. Nevertheless, in August he sent a galiot and Sublieutenant Bernardo Molina with a handful of grenadiers and 1,500 pesos. Later that month, Folch in Pensacola dispatched a force of 150 grenadiers and fusiliers to quiet the unrest. By the time they arrived several weeks later, tranquility reigned once again.[58]

Claiborne to West, New Orleans, August 29 and 30, 1804, ibid., 2: 311-12 and 313, respectively. Claiborne to Madison, New Orleans, September 8, 1804, ibid., 2: 327. Nevertheless, American intervention in West Florida persisted.

57. Casa-Calvo to Claiborne, New Orleans, September 13, 1804; Claiborne to Madison, New Orleans, September 23, 1804; both in *Official Letter Books*, 2: 331-32 and 340, respectively. Grand-Pré explained the insurgents' failure in his letter to Folch, no. 65, Baton Rouge, August 28, 1804, MPA, SD, vol. 7, ff. 704-23. Davis, in *Rogue Republic*, 50, mentions an unsigned letter that circulated widely in eastern American newspapers and stated that up to a dozen Spanish regiments were coming to reinforce Pensacola and stop disorders in their territory. While several persons attributed the letter to Casa-Calvo who denied it, others pointed at a Spanish officer in Baton Rouge who was grossly ignorant in military matters.

58. Casa-Calvo to Folch, New Orleans, August 11, 1804, MPA, SD, vol. 2, ff. 396-98; Casa-Calvo to Grand-Pré, New Orleans, August 13, 1804, AGI, PC, leg. 70B; McMichael, *Atlantic Loyalties*, 91-94. Gayarré, in *History of Louisiana*, 4: 19, gives

Another incident involved the detention of an American, D. B. Morgan, in West Florida. He had been a surveyor for the Spaniards for some time. At Baton Rouge for unknown reasons he was arrested by Capt. Manuel García, who had been the second officer in command of the Spanish gunboats on the Mississippi River. Morgan and his property were put aboard García's galley that was sailing to Pensacola. He, however, escaped when the boat stopped at American Bayou St. John, and he fled to nearby New Orleans. There he first asked Governor Folch, who happened to be in the city, for his property on the galley. Not obtaining redress, Morgan then applied to an American court for the return of his goods from García, who was also in the city. A magistrate ordered García's arrest, but he resisted, stating that he had been following orders and declined to post bail. He asked for a delay until Governor Folch arrived, to which the sheriff agreed. As he was ill, Folch sent his son with instructions that García not submit to bail and resist any force used to remove him from the house he was in. When Folch's son reached García, the situation had become agitated, but as Claiborne, Casa-Calvo, and Folch were nearby, perhaps they could resolve the problem peacefully. The sheriff then consulted a judge who declared that the arrest warrant took precedence. On returning to García's house, he took four constables with him as a crowd of about two hundred had gathered there. Many, however, were sympathetic to García and drew their swords, and that stopped the sheriff. Eventually, García surrendered to a detachment of American soldiers. Casa-Calvo, nevertheless, took umbrage at Claiborne's actions to redress an incident—the seizure of Morgan's property—that occurred on Spanish soil. Claiborne, on the other hand, objected to the tone of Casa-Calvo's letter, exalted the American judiciary's ability to determine the legality of García's arrest, and deplored Casa-Calvo's alleged use of provocative language. All of Casa-Calvo's protests, Claiborne boldly remonstrated, would not impede him from exercising his duty. A lengthy correspondence ensued between Casa-Calvo and Claiborne

---

the impression that Casa-Calvo had an armed vessel and sufficient soldiers to stifle the unrest. His military escort consisted of twelve grenadiers.

on whether García, who was passing through American soil, had immunity from American prosecution for events that occurred in Spanish territory. It apparently was settled satisfactorily out of court.[59]

A similar situation began almost immediately. This time it involved Spanish authorities in West Florida issuing judgments for tax evasion against individuals who had fled upriver to American territory. The American courts refused to honor Spanish judicial rulings. Despite that, Claiborne declared that the courts were open to Spanish officials to file their grievances. Perhaps with Claiborne's intervention the issue was resolved.[60]

Troubles, however, persisted. On December 11, 1804, Claiborne described another "insurrection" at Baton Rouge involving perhaps thirty persons who were mostly local residents. It quickly dissipated, and Folch granted most of the arrested amnesty after he expelled the leading troublemakers from the Florida Parishes. Nevertheless, American assertions to ownership of West Florida persisted. Claiborne regarded the American claim as a "little misunderstanding," but as a true Jeffersonian, he expected Louisiana's eastern (Florida) and western (Texas) boundaries to be achieved. Moreover, he gave no credence to the rumor of Spain's possible recovery of Louisiana in exchange for West Florida, which Casa-Calvo stubbornly clung to. In doing so, he confounded the West Floridians who were satisfied with Spanish rule but wondered whether they were to be sacrificed for the return of Louisiana. Casa-Calvo, however, seemed to advocate retention of both

59. Gayarré, *History of Louisiana*, 4: 29-32; Davis, *Rogue Republic*, 58. Davis cites a Claiborne letter from his *Official Letter Books*, 3: 17-19 of November 18, 1804, and states that after November 1804, Claiborne no longer communicated with Casa-Calvo. But this seems questionable. Jared William Bradley describes a riot outside Casa-Calvo's house in late 1804 because of an incident involving his guards which led to their removal. Soon afterwards, the house was robbed of $700. Bradley, ed., *Biographical Sketches*, 18. Claiborne told Madison that a "drunken" Spanish guard at Casa-Calvo's house had attacked a passing American sailor. Then a crowd intervened and severely beat the guard. Claiborne to Madison, New Orleans, February 4, 1804, *Official Letter Books*, 1: 358-60. In writing to superiors, Claiborne tried to please them and, in my opinion, took liberties in describing events.

60. Gayarré, *History of Louisiana*, 4: 32-33.

West Florida and Louisiana, which represented a formidable challenge and one that Spanish politicians were disinclined to consider.[61]

Unrest in the Florida Parishes continued through 1805, with the Kempers operating freely from American territory into Spanish lands. Requests for their arrest had no effect. Many residents in the Parishes identified the activities of Samuel and Nathaniel Kemper as designed to instigate dissention toward Spain. Inasmuch as the exasperated inhabitants knew who the real troublemakers were, in late August they planned a raid on Pinckneyville to apprehend the two Kempers. Late one night in early September disguised men rode into the settlement, entered a house, and seized them. The raiders rode back to Spanish territory where they collided with a mounted militia patrol. The raiders immediately decamped, leaving the prisoners behind. The patrol officer quickly realized who the bound men were and took them to the Mississippi River to send them to Baton Rouge by boat. Once under way, the boat commander inexplicably veered to the American bank, where Nathaniel identified himself to a settler and shouted that he was being taken to Baton Rouge as a prisoner. Without delay, a rider dashed off to the Pointe Coupee fort to alert the commander. As soon as the Spanish boat passed the fort, a gunboat with numerous soldiers apprehended it. Once on shore, the Kempers quickly gained their freedom, but their guards spent two weeks in prison before a judge under Spanish pressure released them. This incident illustrated the frustration of the West Florida inhabitants who objected to the protection afforded the Kempers and regretted that American authorities did nothing to quell the lawbreakers.[62]

61. Claiborne to Madison, N.O., December 11, 1804, in *Official Letter Books*, 3: 25-26. The Spanish government instructed its minister in Washington "to withdraw the objection to the [Louisiana] Purchase, which he did early in 1804." Philip C. Brooks, "Spain's Farewell to Louisiana, 1803-1821," *Mississippi Valley Historical Review* 27 (June 1940): 31. Casa-Calvo appeared not to know about this decision.

62. Grand-Pré to Folch, Baton Rouge, December 21, 1805, MPA, SD, vol. 8, ff. 575-76, and the accompanying documentation of letters and depositions in ibid., ff. 576-629. Davis, in *Rogue Republic*, 70-76, provides a version different from the traditional pro-Kemper viewpoint. However, he states that the three Kemper brothers

West Florida constituted a problem for the Spaniards and Casa-Calvo while he remained in New Orleans. The threat from the United States grew stronger over these two years as more of their citizens came down the Mississippi and their ships arrived from the Atlantic coast. Casa-Calvo did not have the resources to help the embattled Spaniards. His protests produced only avoidance from American officials who had the authority to act. Instead, he had to focus on his mission and leave the problem in the Florida Parishes to Folch inasmuch as he was the colony's governor.[63]

Meanwhile in Havana, not everybody in Cuba knew why Casa-Calvo had gone to Louisiana other than to assist in the territorial transfer. That became evident when in January 1804, the Conde de Mopox, the army inspector general, inquired about why he had not returned after the retrocession. The captain general informed Mopox that Casa-Calvo would be delayed without specifying a time. Despite his absence Casa-Calvo was still expected to act as head of his regiment in many matters, such as promotions to fill vacant slots; securing more soldiers through recruiting teams placed in the Canary Islands, Cadiz, and Mexico; and obtaining a steady supply of money, arms, and equipment for the unit. Fulfilling his many tasks required a steady flow of letters between Louisiana and Havana.[64] The delays caused by Casa-Calvo's absence forced Mopox to insist that the regiment's lieutenant colonel should temporarily assume certain functions, especially naming replacements to the unit. Before long that chore vanished from Casa-Calvo's duties.[65]

In May 1804, Casa-Calvo's Havana regiment lost its lieutenant colonel, José de Saavedra, who was promoted to colonel of the regiment of Cuba, Casa-Calvo's old unit. In turn, José Sastre took over as

---

were seized there.

63. On Folch, see White, *Vicente Folch*.

64. Conde de Mopox to José de Saavedra, Havana, January 18, 1804, AGI, PC, leg. 73. This legajo contains many of Casa-Calvo's letters to officials in Havana, Texas, and Mexico.

65. Conde de Mopox to José de Saavedra, Havana, January 18, 1804, ibid.

the lieutenant colonel of the Havana regiment, and he became the official with whom Casa-Calvo communicated. Not until August 17 did the absent commander hear about the changes and approved them. It was Sastre who first mentioned that Casa-Calvo sought promotion to *mariscal de campo* (field marshal, the rank above brigadier general in the Spanish army) for his recent work in Louisiana.[66] He must have petitioned for the new rank soon after the transfer.

Casa-Calvo's final duty was to determine the Texas-Louisiana boundary, but delays halted his expedition. When he left Havana, the task had not been assigned to him, and, consequently, he arrived in Louisiana unprepared for the work. Once he received the appointment, he needed competent surveyors, proper surveying equipment, and money to hire and pay employees. In early 1804, Casa-Calvo began searching for the necessary instruments among the government's effects in Louisiana, later bought them wherever he could, or had them sent to him. In addition, the viceroy in Mexico parted with funds very slowly. When money had not come by late 1804, Casa-Calvo dispatched Lt. Benigno García Calderón to Cuba to obtain it. He reached Havana in January 1805, and Someruelos, whose finances were short, sent him to Mexico to make a personal appeal to the viceroy. In addition, García Calderón had taken to Cuba a large quantity of promissory notes, perhaps amounting to a million pesos, used to cover expenses incurred in the transfer of the colony as Casa-Calvo had not received money to pay them. The debts also illuminated his extravagant spending. Many of them were entertainment expenses as he had spent lavishly trying to impress the dignitaries present for the transfers of territory. After several months in Mexico, García Calderón returned to Louisiana with specie, but it was an insufficient amount to liquidate the debts or to fund the expedition adequately.[67] Casa-Calvo

66. José Sastre to Casa-Calvo, Havana, two letters of June 5, 1804, both in ibid.

67. Someruelos to Casa-Calvo, Havana, January 22 and 29 and February 7, 1805, all in AGI, PC, leg. 156A. It was later stated than 100,000 pesos had been assigned to the surveying expedition, but more than half of it was spent outside Louisiana. Casa-Calvo to Armesto, Madrid, February 23, 1808, and enclosure, AGI, PC, leg. 70B.

further informed Madrid that he had raised 70,878 pesos in vouchers from the sale of objects belonging to the royal treasury. Perhaps expecting trouble from Claiborne, Casa-Calvo notified superiors that possibly his surveying expedition would be obstructed and, if it happened, he believed he should go to Madrid to explain the unsettled conditions on the frontier.[68]

What makes Casa-Calvo's surveying trip notable was that it coincided with the American exploratory expeditions of Meriwether Lewis and William Clark, Zebulon Montgomery Pike, and several more. While Casa-Calvo's did not explore new territory, it set the boundary that Spain claimed with proof in subsequent negotiations with the United States. Far-fetched Jeffersonian arguments had failed to procure a vastly expanded western boundary.[69] Casa-Calvo also tried to stop the Lewis and Clark expedition because he believed that it would infringe on Spanish soil, but without military forces he was powerless to do so.

As early as the end of March 1804, Casa-Calvo informed Pedro Cevallos, the foreign minister in Spain, of the personnel he had picked for his expedition to the Sabine. His immediate subordinate was the engineer José Martínez. For surveyors, he chose Nicolás de Finiels, Stephen Minor, and Thomas Power, all of whom had served the Spaniards on many commissions. Other personnel accompanying Casa-Calvo included his son Ignacio and the accountant Ramón Viguri, both members of his Havana regiment; and the scribes Antonio Fornamira and Luis Fernando de Velasco. In addition, he

68. Indices of Casa-Calvo to [Pedro Cevallos], nos. 57 and 58, New Orleans, both dated April 27, 1805, AGI, Est., leg.17, exped. 24.

69. Isaac Joslin Cox, *Early Explorations of Louisiana* (Cincinnati, Ohio: University of Cincinnati Press, 1906); Zebulon M. Pike, *The Southwestern Expedition of Zebulon M. Pike*, ed. Milo Milton Quaife (Chicago: R. R. Connelley and Sons Company, 1925); Trey Berry, Jeanne Clements, and William Dunbar, *The Forgotten Expedition, 1804-1805: The Louisiana Journals of Dunbar and Hunter* (Baton Rouge: Louisiana State University Press, 2006). Casa-Calvo also relayed information to Pedro Cevallos in Spain that he received about the American expeditions. See indices of his letters dated in New Orleans, July 18 and 19, 1805, in AGI, Est., leg. 17, expeds. 15 and 16.

praised the addition of Andrés López Armesto who had served him well in many public and private ways. Still other officials included the surgeon Joaquín Alamedo, Chaplain Sebastián Gilly, and Lts. Benigno García Calderón and Antonio Molina. Casa-Calvo announced that all he sought in return for his service in which he risked both his life and fortune was the king's gratitude. He hinted but provided no explanation that his absences from Cuba had resulted in losses to his properties. Lastly, Casa-Calvo declared that as he had served as a brigadier general for ten years, he would welcome a new promotion. Like career officers who enhanced their accomplishments, Casa-Calvo wanted to include his efforts in designating the Louisiana-Texas boundary if the king approved his service in Louisiana.[70]

His assignment took Casa-Calvo to the eastern fringes of Texas, where its inhabitants had dreaded learning that the United States was their new neighbor. Earlier, knowledge of Louisiana's retrocession to France had created a dilemma in Texas and even in northern Mexico. The eastern Commandancy General of the Interior Provinces had its administrative center in Chihuahua City. Spaniards recalled that early in the eighteenth century French Louisiana had been a constant concern for them in northern Mexico, and their proximity pushed Spanish colonization into Texas (New Orleans and San Antonio were both founded in 1718). The preoccupation ended when Spain acquired Louisiana. But in 1803 the same but now far more critical problem surfaced again. In June of that year, Nemesio Salcedo, commandant-general of the Interior Provinces (New Mexico, Texas, Coahuila, and Nueva Vizcaya or today's Chihuahua) and who was not related to Gov. Manuel Salcedo of Louisiana, wanted information in order to protect the Spanish lands he commanded. During the time when he believed that France would again occupy Louisiana, he wanted knowledge on the French military in the colony—commanders, forts, troops, boundaries, and other related data. Less than three weeks later, Nemesio Salcedo was shocked to learn that Prefect Laussat had

70. Casa-Calvo to Pedro Cevallos, New Orleans, March 30, 1804, in Robertson, ed., *Louisiana*, 2: 173-77.

requested Texas to supply 120 horses for a cavalry corps he expected from France. Salcedo pointed out that Spain had historically prohibited trade between the two provinces and exceptions to the rule required royal approval. But as the two nations were currently allies, he ordered Natchitoches to supply the horses and to expect payment upon their delivery.[71] No doubt the order was rescinded when Salcedo learned that France had sold the province. The more territorially aggressive United States then became Spain's rival. Acting as commissioner of boundaries, Casa-Calvo communicated often with Nemesio Salcedo in Chihuahua City and his subordinates in Texas on vital matters such as Philip Nolan, Laussat, the United States, and placement of the boundary.[72]

Nemesio Salcedo attempted to strengthen his forces since he faced an antagonistic rival next-door. He believed that danger from the Americans was greatest from Natchitoches and along the Nacogdoches trail to San Antonio and from the many paths along the Red, Arkansas, and Missouri rivers that led to Santa Fe, a settlement two hundred years old. Spanish opinion labeled the so-called American "scientific" expeditions as pretexts for locating routes to facilitate their military intrusion upon the eruption of war; Pike's foray into Spanish territory was a prime example. To counteract them, Nemesio Salcedo opened Texas as an asylum for runaway slaves, military deserters, and other fugitives who possibly could help defend the province. Border officials received orders to examine carefully suspicious people coming to settle, and in 1805 Salcedo designated places where they could establish themselves such as San Antonio, settlements on the Trinity River, and military posts. In September of the same year, he transferred his government from Coahuila to San Antonio because the Texas governor was mor-

71. Nemesio Salcedo to the governor of Louisiana, Chihuahua City, June 21 and July 10, 1803, both in AGI, PC, leg. 78. On the founding of New Orleans and San Antonio, see Powell, *The Accidental City*, 43-51, and David J. Weber, *The Spanish Frontier in North America* (New Haven: Yale University Press, 1992), 161-65.

72. Many Casa-Calvo letters to officials in Texas and northern Mexico and theirs to him are in AGI, PC, leg. 73, and in other legajos.

tally ill. He desperately needed reinforcements inasmuch as half of his three hundred soldiers had gone to Nueva Vizcaya and Coahuila in Mexico.[73]

In the summer and fall of 1805, the Spaniards devoted time to examining their defensive options. Antonio Cordero, who arrived as the new governor in Texas late in the year, declared that he needed 1,500 men to protect his colony. As 1806 began, his forces increased to four hundred, and three months later they stood at seven hundred, but the men lacked military training and an adequate food supply. By the end of June 1806, his troops had swelled to a thousand under the command of Lt. Col. Simón de Herrera of Nuevo León. While Cordero cited his forces realistically, Wilkinson reported roguishly that Aaron Burr was raising ten thousand troops in Kentucky and Tennessee for use against Spanish territory. The falsehood worried the Spaniards. These menacing events served as a background for Casa-Calvo's activities during his time along the Texas border.[74]

Nemesio Salcedo had sent a report on the boundary on September 26, 1803, in response to a royal order of the previous April 17. Casa-Calvo probably had a copy when he dictated an unsigned draft of his investigation of the boundary on August 1804. Although A. P. Nasatir attributes the letter to Manuel Salcedo, it was the work of Casa-Calvo, the boundary commissioner, because this Salcedo had left Louisiana the previous May.[75] In the past, Spain had not defined the dividing line between Texas and Louisiana precisely inasmuch as both provinces were Spanish. However, information the Spaniards gathered from the inhabitants living along the border agreed that in the lower reaches the dividing line was the San Francisco de Sabinas (Sabine) River.

73. Isaac Joslin Cox, "The Louisiana-Texas Frontier during the Burr Conspiracy," *Mississippi Valley Historical Review* 10 (December 1923): 275-78. Cox reported that the Spaniards received important news of American military movements from Felix Trudeau, who had been the Spanish commandant at Natchitoches.

74. Ibid., 279-84; Gayarré, *History of Louisiana*, 4: 14-15.

75. (Casa-Calvo) to Pedro Cevallos, (New Orleans), August 20, 1804, in Nasatir, ed., *Before Lewis and Clark*, 2: 745-50, with the original in AGI, PC, leg. 2368.

Casa-Calvo, however, went farther in his report and discussed earlier French traders on the west bank of the Mississippi and exploration up the Missouri River. His historical inquiry recounted that Spanish explorers from Santa Fe had traveled to St. Louis and Natchitoches, which he asserted bestowed Spain with rights in those areas. He advised using the governor of New Mexico to gain the friendship of the Upper Missouri Indians. Going farther, he said that he would try to extend the border from the Sabine eastward to the Calcasieu or Mermentau rivers and would steadfastly resist ceding anything west of the Sabine. Money at that time was a major problem because Casa-Calvo had only 12,000 pesos, and it was insufficient to begin his journey.[76]

In October 1805, after considerable waiting for finances, personnel, supplies, and vessels, Casa-Calvo was ready to map the Louisiana-Texas border.[77] He was then recovering from fevers that had struck him in September. He explained that he intended to travel first to the Mexican Gulf by way of Bayou Lafourche. He requested a passport from Claiborne so as not to rile him by traveling through American territory without permission. He further invited the American governor to appoint an officer to journey with the expedition and observe their work. Claiborne soon issued the requested documents and assigned an officer to accompany Casa-Calvo. Approximately sixty-three persons, who constituted thirteen officers, five servants, and the crews of several boats, made up the expedition.[78]

On October 19, the party left New Orleans proceeding upriver in several boats to Bayou Lafourche, roughly to where Donaldsonville stands today, and down the bayou on which both Canary Islanders

76. Ibid. See also Noel M. Loomis and Abraham P. Nasatir, *Pedro Vial and the Roads to Santa Fe* (Norman: University of Oklahoma Press, 1967); and Henry Folmer, *Franco-Spanish Rivalry in North America, 1524-1763* (Glendale, Calif.: Arthur H. Clark Company, 1953), 277-320.

77. Marcos Aragón to Casa-Calvo, New Orleans, October 9, 1805, AGI, PC, leg. 73.

78. Jack D. L. Holmes, "The Marqués de Casa-Calvo, Nicolás de Finiels, and the 1805 Spanish Expedition through East Texas and Louisiana," *Southwestern Historical Quarterly* 69 (January 1966): 326-27, 329.

and Acadians lived. From the Lafourche, the expedition used various routes but mainly the Atchafalaya River to descend to the gulf. Once there it proceeded westward and stopped at the mouth of the Mermentau River; the explorers, however, found the tiny stream inadequate for navigation. Acadians had already settled along its lower banks. Only seven leagues to the west lay the Calcasieu River, which was a bigger waterway and more suitable for vessels. He explored the lower river before moving on to the Sabine, which was another eleven leagues to the west.[79]

At the Sabine's mouth, he encountered a welter of descending streams, some of them rapids and others jammed with logs. The area was then uninhabited. In early December, Power and his guides used four small canoes to reconnoiter about ten leagues of the river before moving on to the Angelina and Neches rivers that lay farther to the west. At San Bernardo (Matagorda) Bay, the expedition split into two parts; the naval component continued examining the bay and coast under Benigno García Calderón while Casa-Calvo, Power, de Finiels, and the surveying party went ashore and proceeded on land. Casa-Calvo had earlier written to the San Antonio commander, Antonio Cordero, requesting pack mules and horses to carry them and their equipment on their land journey. He found a Spanish post at Atascosito, not far from the Trinity River, where his party lounged about until the animals and supplies arrived.[80]

After the surveyors completed their work on the Sabine, they and the soldiers from San Antonio journeyed to Nacogdoches, where Casa-Calvo's party relaxed for about three weeks. At that time they obtained more mules and wagons for the return journey to New Orleans. While waiting, Casa-Calvo inspected the documentation at the San Miguel de los Adaes mission and presidio. Records revealed that the mission had been founded in 1716 and that its jurisdiction extended east as far as Arroyo Hondo, which lay two and a half leagues from

79. Holmes, "Casa-Calvo-de Finiels Expedition," 330-33.

80. Ibid., 333.

Natchitoches.[81]

Shortly before, on December 15, 1805, Casa-Calvo had written again to Cevallos in Spain requesting permission to go to court to discuss the results of his expedition. French engineer de Finiels, who had been in Spanish service for a number of years, drew up a comprehensive map of the areas the expedition covered. Casa-Calvo reported that it definitively proved the Sabine River was the boundary line and felt that he should present it at court immediately to strengthen Spain's position against Jefferson's outrageous claims. By this time, Casa-Calvo had already formulated a plan to retain as much territory in this area as possible. It consisted of the introduction of Irish settlers. Unfortunately, Spain did not have the money to pay for the massive program he proposed. Moreover, inasmuch as the British occupied Ireland and Spain was at war with Great Britain, no one in the Spanish foreign office considered such a project feasible.[82]

At Nacogdoches on January 3, 1806, Casa-Calvo requested sixteen saddle horses, with riding equipment for eleven of them. He also intended to rent mules in Natchitoches for wagons he was sending down to New Orleans with his equipment and men. Since Natchitoches was close to Los Adaes, he quickly traveled there. At Natchitoches, he rented a boat for the journey down the Red River to New Orleans. The overland trek apparently had exhausted him, and he wanted an easier and faster trip back. During his travels in Texas, Casa-Calvo communicated with many Spanish officials, including the bishop of Nuevo León. Because vast distances separated them, he was unable to meet the bishop or as many other officials as he would have liked.[83]

81. Ibid., 334-35.

82. Ibid., 338. The letter Holmes cites in which Casa-Calvo requested permission to go to court is Casa-Calvo to Cevallos, n. p., December 15, 1805, in AGI, PC, leg. 179B. Holmes, however, believes that the letter was written in 1806. But it is my opinion that Casa-Calvo wrote the letter in Louisiana in late 1805, possibly in Natchitoches. On Spanish immigration policy and why officials in Madrid refused to consider Casa-Calvo's project, see Din, *Populating the Barrera,* 105-31.

83. Casa-Calvo to Sebastián Rodríguez, camp ten leagues from Nechas, December 8, 1805, and Nacogdoches, January 3, 1806, both in AGI, PC, leg. 73.

While Casa-Calvo's surveyors completed their work, Claiborne, who had long relished ridding himself of the Spaniards, displayed unmitigated antagonism toward their continued presence in Louisiana. Soon after Casa-Calvo's expedition had departed, Claiborne or his henchmen let fly a pack of stories that had little factual basis behind them. In one, Casa-Calvo allegedly left New Orleans with $32,000 with which he intended to take command of several thousand Spanish troops on the Texas border. A different version stated that the money was to be used to buy Indian friendship and employ them in the coming war against the Americans. An older rumor that Claiborne recounted was that Casa-Calvo spread discontent in the province and alleged that it would soon return to Spanish control. Casa-Calvo had indeed talked about the exchange of West Florida for Louisiana, and eastern Americans had also considered that possibility in 1804; Spain, however, beset with many problems and little money took no steps toward its recovery. Tension arose on the border about the same time, when an American military force of 150 men ordered an eighteen-man Spanish patrol from Nacogdoches back to the west side of the Sabine River. To reinforce this, an American officer from Natchitoches appeared at Nacogdoches and warned the Spaniards not to tread on American soil.[84]

Still another tale has been repeated by several recent historians who suggested that Casa-Calvo was involved in a slave conspiracy while he was in Louisiana. The story originated with the "confession" the free black Stephen made in January 1806 to Governor Claiborne. His tale, however, lacks credibility, which these historians should have recognized. African resentment following Claiborne's removal of colored officers from the black and mulatto militias in New Orleans initiated

84. Holmes, "Casa-Calvo-de Finiels Expedition," 335; Gayarré, *History of Louisiana*, 4: 150-54; Hatfield, *Claiborne*, 171-72. When Claiborne consulted Casa-Calvo in 1804 about Spanish efforts to incite Indians against the United States, he responded that he would look into the matter. I, however, found no documents that he was involved. Hatfield also alleges (in ibid., 180) that "Casa-Calvo and some of his associates . . . covertly encourag[ed] slaves to runaway." There is no proof that they did, but rumor mills operated freely.

the story. The account Stephen spun had Africans, both slave and free, conspiring to rise up against American forces in Louisiana, and they expected a Casa-Calvo led invasion force from Florida to help them. Serious problems, however, plagued this tall yarn since it was pure fantasy. First, Spain lacked both soldiers and ships in Florida for an invasion of Louisiana; second, the government would have to order such an invasion, which it had not done; and third, had Casa-Calvo wanted a fight he would have relied on whites, not blacks. His experience in Saint-Domingue had taught him to deplore racial upheaval. Stephen's so-called confession was designed by blacks to frighten Claiborne and perhaps restore the colored officers to their lost militia posts. But a key fact that Stephen mangled badly was Casa-Calvo's whereabouts. In January 1806, he was on the Texas-Louisiana frontier finishing up his reconnoitering task, which was well known to Claiborne, and not in Florida forming an invasion flotilla. Furthermore, his surveying expedition had few arms and soldiers, certainly not enough to support an African uprising that Louisiana's whites would shun, not join. As an experienced soldier, Casa-Calvo knew he could not expect help from Cuba or Spain in such an enterprise or find it in Louisiana. Finally, except for participation in the War for American Independence when Spain had numerous allies, it had painstakingly refrained from hostilities in the Mississippi Valley since its arrival in 1766.[85] The govern-

85. Kukla, in *Wilderness so Immense*, 325, merely mentions Stephen; but Hanger, in *Bounded Lives*, 166, and Bell, in *Revolution, Romanticism, and the Afro-Creole Protest Tradition*, 35-36, gave the conspiracy some creditability. It deserves none. The source for their allegations is "Statement of Stephen, a Free Negro, to Governor Claiborne," New Orleans, January 23, 1806, in Carter, ed., *Territorial Papers*, 9: 475-76. Joseph F. Stoltz III, in "'The Preservation of Good Order': William C. C. Claiborne and the Militia of Louisiana Provisional Government, 1803-1805," *Louisiana History* 54 (Fall 2013): 424-47, mentions Claiborne's dealings with the free colored militia of Louisiana. However, Stoltz is overly favorable to Claiborne and states that American rumors about a Spanish instigated slave uprising were done to counter Spanish denunciation of American aid to West Florida insurgents. Stoltz's source for the suggestion is the easily rattled Claiborne who saw enemies on all sides of him. Claiborne to James Madison, New Orleans, September 20, 1804, *Official Letter Books*, 2: 337-38. See also Gayarré, *History of Louisiana*, 4: 131-35, which is based on Claiborne letters.

ment knew its multiple weaknesses, and its three-decade-long effort to build up Louisiana's population had achieved scant success in the gigantic colony.[86]

Later in 1806, Claiborne traveled to Natchitoches to gain the friendship of the nearby Indians as he planned to use them against the Spaniards if an occasion arose. Americans had believed for several months that warfare on the frontier was possible, and it had stirred up passions. Further complicating problems, a disagreement arose on the Arroyo Hondo that lay several miles east of the Sabine River and possibly could lead to war, which Spain did not want. By September 1806, more than 1,200 Americans assembled at Natchitoches ready to advance into Texas and perhaps Mexico. The Spanish commander Herrera had already withdrawn across the Sabine. As Wilkinson also sought to avoid a clash, he called for negotiations, and he and Herrera drew up the Neutral Ground Agreement that declared the region from the Sabine to the Arroyo Hondo a neutral zone and off limits to the armed forces of both sides. The accord quieted the turmoil to a degree on the Texas-Louisiana frontier and preserved the peace until a formal agreement was made in 1819. Spain, however, lost the "neutral ground" in the final treaty since it was on the east side of the Sabine River.[87]

The presence of numerous rumors about Spanish actions and the duplicitous maneuverings by the Kempers in West Florida and Aaron Burr in the Mississippi Valley turned New Orleans into a hotbed of unrest. Societies for the invasion of Mexico thrived in the city. Amidst

86. Spanish efforts to build up the Louisiana and West Florida populations are examined in Din, *Populating the Barrera.*

87. Cox, "Louisiana-Texas Frontier," 279-84; Brooks, "Spain's Farewell to Louisiana," 31, 32-6. Gayarré, *History of Louisiana,* 4: 123-30. The Wilkinson and Herrera agreement to preserve the peace in 1806, undercut the machinations of Aaron Burr who sought to provoke disorder. John Thornton Posey, "Rascality Revisited: In Defense of General James Wilkinson," *Filson Club History Quarterly* 74 (Fall 2000): 338. Posey is very favorable to Wilkinson. On the Adams-Onis treaty of 1819, see Brooks, *Diplomacy and the Borderlands,* and Onis, *Negociaciones entre España y los Estados Unidos de América.*

all the fables unloosed on the public, Claiborne did not fare well. From the start of his governorship, he grumbled about the presence of the Spaniards, and Casa-Calvo in particular, in New Orleans. He wanted them gone but doubted his own ability to oust them. He waited until Casa-Calvo left the city before he requested Jefferson to issue such an order, and the president complied. Claiborne received the expulsion order about early January 1806, and he then sent Capt. George F. Ross to Natchitoches to deliver it to Casa-Calvo. The nervous Claiborne also instructed the Natchitoches commander to prevent Casa-Calvo from returning to New Orleans. However, while Ross journeyed to that post by road, Casa-Calvo had started his return on January 22, on the Red River, and their paths did not cross. No doubt his reappearance in New Orleans startled the American governor.[88]

By the evening of February 4, Casa-Calvo had reached the Crescent City after a journey that consumed 111 days and covered 500 leagues (approximately 1,350 miles). On his second day back, he unexpectedly received a copy of Jefferson's order to expel him. Claiborne gave him a week to depart, which caused Casa-Calvo to protest for more time to put his affairs in order, but Claiborne refused. Then in the midst of treating Casa-Calvo shoddily, the clueless governor asked him to grant William Dunbar and Thomas Freeman passports for the exploration of the Red River to its source, which was in Spanish territory. Casa-Calvo indignantly replied no. On February 12, the commissioner received a passport from Claiborne and three days later, he left the city by boat for Pensacola with his son and several aides and servants. Only two soldiers embarked with him. The travelers left from Bayou St. John, a small port for boats on Lake Pontchartrain that was behind the city and used by persons engaged in activities on the lakes that extended halfway to Pensacola. His abrupt departure forced him to leave behind baggage, carriage, horses, and probably more. What happened to the rest of his Cuban soldiers is unknown; perhaps they later escorted his property on a ship that sailed to Pensacola.[89]

88. Holmes, "Casa-Calvo-de Finiels Expedition," 335-36.

89. Ibid., 337.

Casa-Calvo's voyage to Pensacola unexpectedly took weeks. About February 19 and near Bay St. Louis, a storm hit his overloaded boat, and the sailors headed for shore seeking shelter in shallow waters. As the storm continued for hours, they finally made land at Pass Christian. He and his party spent several weeks there until everyone recovered from injuries and repaired their boat. Only then did they continue their journey to Pensacola. The delay angered Casa-Calvo but he could do nothing about it. At last on March 24, at 8 p.m. in the evening, he reached his destination. He described his experience on the Gulf Coast as the worst of the twenty or so voyages he had made, even worse than the gulf hurricane he had weathered in 1780. Vicente Folch commanded Pensacola as governor of West Florida, and undoubtedly Casa-Calvo remembered his unpleasant relations with him in 1799-1800. Dealings with him, however, had improved several years before when Casa-Calvo returned as a commissioner to oversee the surrender of Louisiana and determine the Texas boundary. They met several times in New Orleans, mostly to discuss problems that American officials were giving the West Florida inhabitants. While he could commiserate with Folch and his problems, resolving them was unlikely as the colony's retention appeared doubtful. Casa-Calvo remained in Pensacola more than two months, and perhaps mindful of his recent sailing experience, he waited for a decent vessel in which to cross the gulf to Havana. Nevertheless, he enjoyed the springtime weather in Pensacola. And once he fulfilled certain obligations in Havana, he was determined to go to Spain. On March 26, he wrote an explanation of recent events in his journey.[90]

Among other things, Casa-Calvo mentioned ten boxes of documents for the archives that he had received from Antonio López Armesto. They dealt with a wide variety of subjects such as royal orders, correspondence from government ministers, and reports from post commanders in Louisiana and West Florida. Among them were maps, legal papers, and even documents in English. Casa-Calvo was taking them to Havana. Perhaps this assortment of records remained

90. (Casa-Calvo to Someruelos), Pensacola, May 26, 1806, AGI, PC, leg. 70B.

separate from the Louisiana-West Florida documentation and stayed in Havana after the main collection was moved to Spain.[91]

Casa-Calvo left Pensacola about June 4, took sixteen days to cross the gulf to Havana, and arrived there on June 20. Eleven days later, just before his departure for Europe, he wrote to Folch about his journey and plans. He commented that he needed to travel immediately to Madrid. Apparently, he had consulted Captain General Someruelos who agreed with his plans. He was sailing that afternoon by going first to Boston since it was wartime. From there he planned to take any ship sailing to a port in Spain, Portugal, or France. With God's help, he wrote, he could be at court by mid-September. He sent his regards to Folch, his wife and children, and to Maximiliano St. Maxent who was the commander of the troops in Pensacola. As Casa-Calvo had left some mules and a horse in Pensacola, he informed Folch that if he did not buy them, to sell them to anyone else. He also sent a gift to Folch's wife on the mail boat that was returning to Pensacola, perhaps for putting him up while in that settlement.[92] Aside from fulfilling these chores, however, most of his brief stay in Cuba was spent with his children and grandchild.

In looking back at his experiences in Louisiana, Casa-Calvo had visited the colony and the Gulf Coast four times over the last thirty-seven years in different capacities. His recent visits that began in 1799 had made him the most knowledgeable Spanish official on the newly alienated province, which he still considered vital to the Spanish Empire. Above all, he wanted to enlighten royal personnel of its importance and persuade them to undertake the formidable task of recovering it. He had spent the last three years in the colony and had told various people that Spain would retrieve it. Top government officials in Spain, however, had many issues that extended across the empire to consider. In doing so, their broader perspective gave Louisiana lesser weight among the multiplicity of dilemmas they dealt with. By the time he reached Madrid, those other concerns had grown even

91. Ibid.; Casa-Calvo to Folch, Pensacola, May 29, 1806, ibid.

92. Casa-Calvo to Folch, Havana, July 1, 1806, ibid.

more acute, and his plans for Louisiana disintegrated.

Casa-Calvo's narrow thoughts on Louisiana clashed with harsh reality since he either was unaware of the empire's financial straits or did not comprehend the political and economic relationship between the colonies and mother country. As his views tended to focus primarily on Cuba, he probably had not given serious consideration to the causes behind the popular uprisings that had shaken the Spanish colonies of Paraguay, Peru, Bolivia (or Upper Peru), New Granada, and even Mexico in recent decades. Perhaps the reason lay in that his own colony enjoyed a vastly different relationship to Spain with its upper class resolve to maintain stability and its intimate dependency on the monarchy. Possibly for this reason Cuba stood virtually alone among the Spanish American colonies as the "ever faithful" possession.[93] That privileged status most likely influenced Casa-Calvo who seemed amenable to Bourbon reforms—or change from above—in development, but he and others of his class deplored anything that undermined the established order in government, economy, and society. In that respect, Casa-Calvo remained a representative of the late eighteenth century with his attitudes and opinions unchanged. In traveling across the Atlantic Ocean in the early nineteenth century, however, he would unexpectedly encounter a similar conundrum in Spain and Europe where the social order had already suffered cracks and upheavals brought on by the French Revolution. French *philosophes* had long ridiculed their stagnant society, and as social conditions continued to worsen, they finally produced an awareness in the lives of the middle and even the down-trodden classes whose aspirations were inexorably coming into play. Although these forces had expressed themselves in the past, they now exerted a greater impact in some European nations inasmuch as trade and manufacturing had enlarged the urban-based laboring and middle classes that no longer demon-

93. Charles E. Chapman, *Colonial Hispanic America: A History* (New York: Macmillan, 1933), 215-21; Franklin W. Knight, in "Origins of Wealth and the Sugar Revolution in Cuba, 1750-1850," *Hispanic American Historical Review* 57 (1977): 231-32, attributes "ever faithful" to Cuba's loyalty that furthered the upper class's accumulation of property and wealth.

strated a willingness to accept the inferior status that absolute monarchy, aristocracy, and theology had dictated upon them for countless generations. As the Atlantic world grew progressively more malleable against the persistent winds of change, Casa-Calvo as a soldier felt the need to defend the empire, and this reason compelled his journey. But in doing so, he inadvertently traveled to another region where vigorous social and economic aspirations were also stirring up turmoil. These forces, and the resistance to them, exerted a powerful impression in shaping Casa-Calvo's thoughts in his final years.[94]

94. Holmes, "Casa-Calvo-de Finiels Expedition," 335-38.

8
Journey's End, 1806-1820

In the summer of 1806, Casa-Calvo began a journey that would eventually take him and his son Ignacio to Spain. As he left Havana at nearly fifty-five years of age, he likely did not realize that he would never see Cuba or his three older children again. Instead, he dwelled on instructing the government about the boundary he had recently surveyed, conditions in Texas, and his plan on how to recover Louisiana, which perhaps was uppermost in his thoughts. Thinking positively, he reflected on whether his recent work would earn him a promotion, perhaps as a capstone to his lengthy career. Since it was wartime and few Spanish ships were sailing, he boarded a neutral merchant vessel to reach the United States from where he planned to cross the Atlantic to anywhere in Europe. Unfortunately, he left no information about his time-consuming journey or when he reached Spain.

His return was the first since 1789, when he completed recruiting troops for the Fixed Infantry Regiment of Cuba. Over those seventeen years, Spain's relations with France had deteriorated due to the revolution and their war of 1793-95. French governments that followed the radical Republic—the Directory, the Consulate of Bonaparte, and the empire Napoleon created in 1804—moderated its excesses. Spain, under Carlos IV, meanwhile, had crept on slowly as an absolute monarchy which Manuel Godoy as chief minister directed with an unsteady hand. Although a political novice, the nymphomaniac queen María Luisa thrust her brash intimate on the government to the detriment of virtually every Spaniard. In contrast, the "enlightened despotism" of Carlos III had operated under the cautious guidance of the more liberal Conde de Floridablanca and the more conservative Conde de Aranda alternating as chief minister. But now the political voices had dissolved into raucous noises that championed a variety of dissenting groups: aristocrats, bourgeoisie, clergy, and even the lower classes. Naturally, they disagreed on policies about the social order, economy, and government. France, despite its drastic reformist tendencies as opposed to Spain's chronic traditionalism, continued to influence the peninsula with ideas that at times were accepted and at other times emphatically rejected.

The Spain that Casa-Calvo returned to remained overwhelmingly rural and underdeveloped. In a population of about ten million, a sparse forty towns had inhabitants that exceeded ten thousand. Largest among them was Madrid with fewer than two hundred thousand residents composed mainly of the upper and lower classes with few industrial laborers or members of the middle class. Most educated people belonged to the nobility, clergy, and middle sectors of society who all made up a small percentage of the population. Illiteracy continued unabated given that schools and books for the lower classes remained few. Newspapers circulated poorly and had negligible influence over the masses. Priests, on the other hand, enjoyed tremendous sway over the peasantry who slavishly followed their bidding and scorned as un-Spanish anything new or different. Animal husbandry predominated in a land with little industry or commerce and even limited agriculture. Sheep owners still exercised unwarranted control in politics and economics, and their flocks continued to trample fields and crops as they alternated seasonally between pastures. The centuries-old *Mesta* or Honorable Council of Sheep Men enjoyed long-established authority over new economic groups and refused to accommodate their needs. Despite that, Spain often produced insufficient wheat or other grains to feed its population and had to import them at a yearly cost of 147 million pesetas, or three-quarters of the annual bullion that arrived from the Indies with the remainder of colonial imports paying for European manufactured goods. Religious groups, nobility, and communes owned most of the agricultural lands, which they held in entailed estates that tenant peasants and day-workers labored on, eking out a miserable living. The eighteenth-century Enlightenment had bypassed all but the cultured and literate few, and even many of these people did not support it.[1]

While society in Spain had changed little, Casa-Calvo found that recent events had sent the nation tumbling down another rabbit hole. Spain ended the Peace of Amiens in 1804, when it declared war on Great Britain after it demanded Spain stop arming and seized four of its ships-of-the-line laden with New World bullion. Their loss inflicted a devastating blow since the government was bankrupt and the countryside faced widespread famine and disease. British actions drove Spain back to its former ally France that despite its reformist agenda appeared a better partner. Napoleon was then battling the British fleet and the armies of the conservative monarchies. In an action after the Spanish alliance began, Britain's Horatio Lord Nelson engaged a fleet of combined enemy warships off Cape Trafalgar on October 21, 1805, and decisively defeated them although it cost the famed admiral his life. The victory allowed Great Britain to dominate the seas and thwart a French invasion of England. As a by-product, Spain's colonies also enjoy unrestricted trade for several years, which pleased them enormously.[2]

By 1807 turmoil swept over the Spanish court as different political groups vied for power. A new faction appeared led by Fernando, son of Carlos IV and heir to the throne. He surrounded himself with nobles, many of them *grandes*, who despised the opportunist Godoy and sneered at his lowly *hidalgo* rank. They conspired to overthrow the ineffective king and seize power. Fernando and his clique favored Britain as they sought to end Spain's shameful subjection by France. Seeing the royal family finagle for kingdoms in Italy led the ambitious Godoy to aspire to a realm of his own, and he plotted with Bonaparte. But the

1. A. Ramos Oliveira, *Politics, Economics, and Men of Modern Spain, 1808-1946*, trans. Teener Hall (London: Victor Gollancz, Ltd., 1946), 19-25.

2. Smith, *Spain*, 161-62; Chapman, *Colonial Hispanic America*, 215. Allan J. Kuethe, in "Havana in the Eighteenth Century," in *Atlantic Port Cities: Economy, Culture, and Society in the Atlantic World, 1650-1850*, eds. Franklin W. Knight and Peggy K. Liss (Knoxville: University of Tennessee Press, 1991), 28, states, "By 1808 the royal treasury had reached a state of de facto bankruptcy."

fickle and contradictory Godoy soon began considering a connection with the Russians until Napoleon trounced them and the Austrians in battle at Austerlitz in December 1805, and it forced Godoy to again grovel at the Corsican's feet. The next year, the emperor achieved another victory at Jena-Auerstedt on October 14, 1806, that gave him control over Prussia and soon ended the Holy Roman Empire. To weaken Spain, he insisted that Godoy send twenty thousand troops, about all the nation had, to Germany in 1807, and their removal left the kingdom vulnerable to French intrusion. Godoy's intrigues against the royal family were so blatant that nearly everybody at court and throughout the kingdom despised him.[3]

Amidst all the scheming, Casa-Calvo arrived in Madrid around the end of 1806 following what appeared to have been a protracted journey. He eagerly looked forward to renewing old friendships. Fortunately, he had connections at court, especially with officials in the ministry of foreign affairs who were eager to learn more about his recent examination of the Louisiana-Texas boundary since Spain wanted a secure border with the United States. They were less interested, however, in Casa-Calvo's pet project of recovering Louisiana because they deemed it a needless and impractical imbroglio.

His cousin Gonzalo O'Farrill, whose talents and presence in the mother country had facilitated his rapid rise in the army, was then not in the peninsula where his career had blossomed. After his arrival in Spain from France in the late 1770s, he became an army officer, studied artillery, and became so proficient that in time he rose to head the military college at El Puerto de Santa María across the bay from Cádiz and afterwards the Royal Academy of Artillery in Segovia. In the 1793-95 war with France, he won victories in the Pyrenees and promotions to field marshal and later to lieutenant general. He also became the inspector general of the infantry in 1798 and spent time as the minister plenipotentiary at the Prussian court in Berlin. His travels took him

3. Carlos Corona, *Revolución y reacción en el reinado de Carlos IV* (Madrid: Ediciones Rialp, 1957), 328-52; Smith, *Spain*, 262-63; Payne, *History of Spain and Portugal*, 2: 419-21.

through Germany, Switzerland, Italy, Holland, and England to acquire political and military knowledge. According to the Englishwoman Lady Holland (Elizabeth Vassall Fox Holland), O'Farrill's many abilities had earned the admiration of the younger army officers. He gladly would have welcomed Casa-Calvo and filled him with insights about contemporary Spain, but duty had taken him to Tuscany, Italy, in 1806 to command a Spanish division.[4]

Nevertheless, Louisiana affairs initially occupied Casa-Calvo. In January 1807, perhaps soon after arriving in Madrid, he submitted his report to the ministry of foreign affairs. He also presented a financial statement made by Andrés López Armesto on the costs of the boundary survey. But the ministry delayed acting on the matter until the next year, and Casa-Calvo spent the time waiting for answers. At last one came in February 1808 on expenses for the survey. Casa-Calvo wrote to López Armesto at that time telling him that Pedro Cevallos had received the clarification on how the 100,000 pesos allocated to the survey had been used. Among the expenditures, Havana had provided supplies, equipment, and naval services that cost approximately 23,000 pesos; Juan Ventura Morales as acting intendant had consumed 8,000 pesos; and the posts of Pensacola and Baton Rouge claimed more than 26,000 pesos for men and services. These and other expenditures had amounted to slightly more than 87,000 pesos. The salaries of the men who went on the expedition and their supplies had cost 29,000 pesos. Therefore, the amount spent on the expedition had exceeded the 100,000 pesos assigned.[5] Perhaps the viceroy in Mexico City made up

4. A sketch of O'Farrill is in Charles Frederick Partington, *British Cyclopedia of Biography: Containing the Lives of Distinguished Men of All Ages and Count* (London: W. Orr, 1837), 686-87; Elizabeth Vassall Fox Holland, *The Spanish Journal of Elizabeth Lady Holland (1791-1811)*, ed. Earl of Ilchester (New York: Longmans, 1910), 278. The Ilchester edition, however, omits Holland's discussion of Madrid under José I. See also *Memoria de D. Miguel Jose de Azanza y D. Gonzalo O-Farrill, sobre los hechos que justifican su conducta política, desde marzo de 1808 hasta abril 1814* (Paris: P.N. Rougenow, 1815), 289-91, in which O'Farrill provides a modest sketch of his accomplishments. Azanza and O'Farrill both sought pardons from Fernando VII.

5. Casa-Calvo to Andrés López Armesto, Madrid, February 23, 1808, with attached

the deficit.

Among Casa-Calvo's other known activities in Madrid in 1807 and 1808, he participated in the festivities that fellow colonials enjoyed. Several Cubans had been in Spain for years, including some of his relatives. They took part in court intrigues vicariously through their attendance at *tertulias*, social and literary gatherings held in the late afternoons or evenings. Towards the end of the eighteenth century and into the next, tertulias served to spread court gossip and discuss a multitude of contemporary events, including Cuban affairs. The more successful gatherings frequently had a raconteur who entertainingly commented on happenings at court and in *madrileño* society, which made people in the upper social realms relish them. Tertulias sometimes served as useful functions for individuals without court influence or connections. The most prominent tertulias in the early years of the nineteenth century were those of the Duquesa de Alba and the Duquesa de Benavente, both of which attracted many prominent court figures. But there were others.[6]

One was that of Cubans who had spent years in Madrid. Noticeable among them was the planter Joaquín Beltrán de Santa Cruz y Cárdenas, Conde de Jaruco, who had gone to Spain in 1790 with his wife María Teresa Montalvo y O'Farrill. She was the daughter of the Conde de Casa Montalvo and granddaughter of Juan O'Farrill (Casa-Calvo's uncle). María Teresa remained at court after her husband returned to Havana in 1797. With Godoy's assistance and Mexican silver pesos, Beltrán de Santa Cruz secured the additional title of Conde de Santa Cruz de Mopox, the rank of army brigadier general, an appointment

---

document, "Notice of the investment of One Hundred Thousand pesos received in New Orleans that came from Veracruz," Casa-Calvo, Madrid, January 22, 1807, both in AGI, PC, leg. 70B. Undisclosed payments to Wilkinson seem to have been included in the accounts for Morales and Pensacola.

6. On *tertulias*, see the *Diccionario de Autoridades* (Madrid: Editorial Gredos, 1979). Many Spanish writers have commented on Madrid's tertulias of this era. José Luis Prieto Benavent, "Mercedes de Santa Cruz y Montalvo, Condesa de Merlin: 'une femme du monde,'" *Revista Hispano Cubana* 13 (Madrid: May-September, 2002): 85-86.

as the inspector general of the army in Cuba, and the privilege of importing one hundred thousand barrels of flour at Havana. His wife, the Condesa, purportedly stayed on to manage the Madrid-end of their business interests. She turned into a fixture as a hostess to government officials under Carlos IV and later José I during the French intervention in Spain. She promoted reformist ideas congenial to enlightened individuals and was devoted to art and literature, too. Among persons who graced her salon were government officials such as Miguel de Azanza, and cultural icons like the poet and playwright Leandro Fernández de Moratín and the artist Francisco Goya. No doubt Gonzalo O'Farrill attended her tertulias when he was in Madrid, as did Casa-Calvo. In time and as a widow, the Condesa María Teresa became one of the mistresses of José I. Her daughter, the voluptuous María de las Mercedes Santa Cruz y Montalvo (1789-1852), followed in her footsteps. She acquired the title of Condesa de Merlin upon her marriage to the French general Antoine-Christophe de Merlin. When José developed an interest in her, he kept her husband busy with tasks outside Madrid. She stayed at the Spanish court until the French evacuation of Spain in 1813. In Paris she became a noted feminist and literary figure.[7]

Europe had been at war for many years before Casa-Calvo's arrival in Spain. After the naval disaster at Trafalgar, Napoleon attempted to cripple his most potent rival—Great Britain—by denying the "nation of shop-keepers" trade through a blockade in the countries he controlled. Independent Portugal, however, defied him because of its cen-

7. Kuethe, "Havana in the Eighteenth Century," 31; Kuethe, *Cuba, 1753-1815*, 148-49, 152-54, 159, 164-65; Prieto Benavent, "Mercedes de Santa Cruz y Montalvo," 83-96. In his book *Spanish Bourbons*, 140, Bergamini refers to the Condesa de Mopox as "the complaisant countess." Many years after the French invasion, the Condesa de Merlin, who became a celebrated writer, recalled aspects of life in José's Madrid in her work, *Mis doce primeros años e historia de Sor Inés*, edited by Francisco Calcagno (Havana: Imprenta El Siglo XX, 1922). See also Ciro Bianchi Ross, "The Mysteries of Two Havana Women," in *The Digital Magazine of Cuban Arts and Culture* (Cuba/Now.net), which is based on Elizabeth Vassal Fox (Lady Holland), *The Spanish Journal of Elizabeth, Lady Holland* (London: Longmans, 1910); and Adriana Méndez Rodenas, *Gender and Nationalism in Colonial Cuba: The Travels of Santa Cruz y Montalvo, Condesa de Merlin* (Nashville: Vanderbilt University Press, 1998).

tury-old commercial alliance with Great Britain. That decision led the French emperor to plot the invasion of the defiant kingdom in 1807 and its partition into three segments: one for Spain, another for Godoy, and a third yet undetermined. The Portuguese colonies, meanwhile, would be divided between Spain and France. To carry out the overland invasion of Portugal, Carlos IV and Godoy agreed to the Treaty of Fontainebleau that allowed French soldiers to pass through Spanish territory. That decision, however, made peninsular realists predict an ominous future for Spain.[8]

Late in 1807, Casa-Calvo received the recognition he sought for his work overseeing the transfer of Louisiana and surveying the eastern boundary of Texas. The king appointed him *mariscal de campo* (field marshal) at a ceremony held at El Escorial on December 9, 1807. Casa-Calvo had spent most of the year near the government in Madrid waiting for it to resolve matters relative to Louisiana. Only several days before Casa-Calvo's promotion, his son Ignacio became a sublieutenant after spending four years as a cadet but not one day in a cadet school. He was still listed as part of the Havana infantry regiment as was his father. Notes in his service record stated that the Conde de Mopox, who was the Cuban inspector general, had permitted him to enroll as a cadet.[9] Like many things among the Havana elite, it was all a family affair.

As time progressed, Casa-Calvo gradually abandoned thoughts of returning to Cuba as he cast his fate on staying in Spain in imitation of his cousin and other Cuban expatriates. It was a decision O'Farrill most likely would have encouraged. Casa-Calvo's familiarity with Cuban agriculture had long ago made him an advocate for change and development. Possibly he felt that he could provide Cuban planters with another voice, perhaps even an influential one, at court. His decision, however, changed the course of his life. Had he left Spain in early 1808, he would have avoided unseen twists and turns that filled

8. Smith, *Spain*, 263.

9. Service sheets of Casa-Calvo and Ignacio Calvo de la Puerta, both of December 31, 1807, both in, AGM, ES.

his final years. These events evolved slowly and without warnings of the tortuous road that lay ahead.

Soon stability in Spain began to vanish. In late 1807, Napoleon and his advisers resolved to seize the kingdom, with Godoy initially providing help. Perhaps Napoleon realized the weaknesses in the Spanish monarchy such as the sharply divided royal family, its feeble military establishment, and its underdeveloped economy. They all appeared as invitations to be taken. Soon, with Godoy's connivance, French troops poured into the kingdom, with one hundred thousand present by early 1808. Only then did the court Lothario recognize his gross miscalculation, but it was too late. Moreover, Godoy battled Prince Fernando over direction of the government. Napoleon demanded lands in Spain north of the Ebro River, in Catalonia, while the royal family found it impossible to agree on a solution. Meanwhile, the Spanish masses loathed both Godoy and the French. One day in March they moved into Madrid's principal avenues and rioted inasmuch as they detested the chief minister's collusion with France and sacked the houses of the principal government officials. At the same time, another mob of ten thousand, including frenzied French soldiers guarding the town, destroyed Godoy's palatial residence in Aranjuez. Discontent with the king and the government, which was nurtured in good part by Fernando's scheming with the lower classes, forced the weak Carlos IV to abdicate on March 19, 1808, in favor of his son. When that happened, Godoy fled into hiding although he was later discovered and jailed. The wretched monarchy of Carlos IV had collapsed due to the king's frail character, the queen's injudicious intervention in politics, Fernando's unrestrained ambitions, and Godoy's egotistic and dim-witted plotting.[10] But there were weightier reasons, too, such as the pen-

10. Smith, *Spain*, 264-65; Corona Baratech, *Revolución y reacción en el reinado de Carlos IV*, 364-79. There has been disagreement among the people involved in the uprising against the French. Corona Baratech argues in his *Precedentes ideológicos de la Guerra de Independencia* (Zaragoza: Institución Fernando El Católico, 1959), that the revolt was led by people implicated in the conspiracy against Godoy. Rioters directed most of their fury against persons in Carlos IV's government who exercised the most influence. Raymond Carr, however, insists in his *Spain, 1808-1975*, 2nd ed.

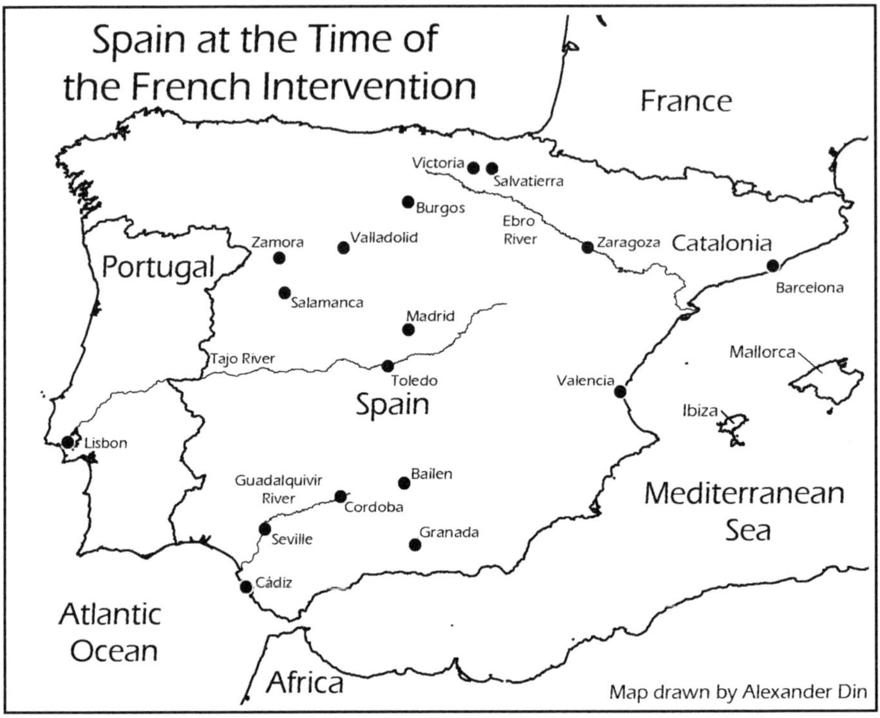

insula's scant development and reluctance to alter its medieval-like society and economy, dependence on New World wealth, and repeated European wars that devoured the kingdom's scarce resources.

In the struggle that was beginning, Fernando VII initially had the support of the common Spanish people as well as many of the kingdom's oldest aristocrats. Seeing an opportunity, however, Napoleon soon revealed his own plans. He used the rioting in Madrid and Aranjuez to annul Carlos IV's abdication and declare the throne vacant despite Fernando's claims to it. Privately, the emperor planned to install one of his brothers as king, although much had to be arranged first. French troops soon entered Madrid under Marshal Joachim Murat while Napoleon arrived at Bayonne on the Franco-Spanish border in

(Clarendon Press: Oxford, U.K., 1982), 1-30, that the origins of the uprising were diverse. See also Gabriel H. Lovett, *Napoleon and the Birth of Modern Spain*, 2 vols. (New York: New York University Press, 1965), 2: 843-50.

April and summoned Fernando to meet him. French power-brokers wanted at least a quasi-legal transition to authority through a second abdication by Carlos IV. Soon French soldiers conducted members of the royal family to meet Napoleon in Bayonne, where even Godoy, who was released from jail, went. With French soldiers doing as they pleased in Madrid, the anger of the common people grew until together with units of Spanish soldiers they exploded. Incensed at Fernando's "kidnapping," they stormed the foreign troops found on the streets of Madrid on May 2 and perpetrated a bloodbath. The French, nonetheless, quickly retaliated, overpowered the rioters, and the next day began shooting prisoners and persons found with weapons (they numbered fewer than eighty), events that Francisco Goya commemorated in his famous paintings of *Dos de Mayo* and *Tres de Mayo*.[11]

While French soldiers quickly pacified Madrid, they did not endear themselves to the Spanish people. Napoleon attempted to smooth the coming transition of the Spanish monarchy to his older brother José (Joseph) by getting Fernando to recognize his father as the legitimate king after which Carlos IV would relinquish the throne in favor of Napoleon. Following these events, on May 12, 1808, the Spanish royal family moved to a luxurious French chateau and began a captivity that lasted several years. On June 6, Napoleon reassigned the Spanish crown to José, who was still in Italy and did not arrive in Madrid until July. Although ambitious, José lacked the wisdom and behavior needed to win over the Spanish people because they knew the convoluted manner by which he had achieved power. More important, at Bayonne Napoleon dictated a liberal constitution, Spain's first that the aristo-

11. Smith, *Spain*, 267-68. According to one story, Gonzalo O'Farrill went into the streets of Madrid late at night on May 2, waving a white handkerchief as he tried to stop the fighting. Charles M. Wilson, *Liberty or Death! The Life and Times of Asencio Nabot—Franciscan Friar, Guerrilla Leader, Secret Agent and Exile* (Victoria, B.C.: Trofford Publishing, 2008), 43. A description of the rioting in Madrid on May 2, by the French marshal Joachim Murat is in Fernando Díaz-Plaja, *Historia de España en sus documentos* (Madrid: Siglo XIX, 1983), 41-42. Goya's paintings are in Madrid's El Prado Art Museum. Although Goya died in 1828 in Bordeaux, France, his remains were to returned to Madrid in 1919, and are today at the Hermitage de San Antonio de la Florida. Wilson, *Liberty or Death!,* 453.

crats reluctantly ratified. Casa-Calvo was there as a substitute delegate in June and July 1808, since only a small number of nobles initially showed up, and he voted to approve the constitution. His cousin Gonzalo, a collaborator in the change of government, had encouraged him to travel to Bayonne, and his participation established him as a supporter of José.[12]

With new political groups then forming in Spain, Gonzalo O'Farrill understood the upheavals raging at court. A friend described him glowingly as a "great military man, able politician, a person of wealth, well-educated and multi-talented, who unites the refined and urbane manners of a subject of the world with the serious and austere customs of a philosopher."[13] He and others in government, including older politicians who had served prior to Godoy's takeover as first minister in 1792, regarded the French as a better choice than Fernando and his minions. They recognized that France was still at the center of the Enlightenment. Consequently, O'Farrill quickly accepted José as king. Casa-Calvo, on the other hand, was buffeted by the confusion of the time with numerous events occurring that exceeded his comprehension. He leaned on his cousin's persuasiveness and high government position to choose sides since he well understood the politics underlying the shifts in power and the personnel involved. Besides favoring alterations that the country desperately needed, O'Farrill had personal reasons for welcoming a change in government. He had become minister of war during Fernando's brief reign, and he wanted to retain his position despite the king's ouster. He wrote to Napoleon Bonaparte who assured him indirectly that he had no cause to worry about his situation. O'Farrill probably neither anticipated nor welcomed the war that soon broke out since he did not regard military action as a harbinger of change, only a generator of destruction. Moreover, he

12. Smith, *Spain*, 268-70; Miguel Artola, *Afrancesados* (Madrid: Ediciones Altaya, 1957), 313-14; Carlos Sanz Cid, *La constitución de Bayona* (Madrid: Editorial Reus, 1922), 149, 152, 442; Michael Glover, *Legacy of Glory: The Bonaparte Kingdom of Spain, 1808-1813* (New York: Charles Scribner's Sons, 1971), 37-38.

13. Cited in Albert Derozier, *Manuel José Quintana y el nacimiento del liberalismo en España*, trans. Manuel Moya (Madrid: Ediciones Turner, 1978), 367.

looked upon Napoleon as more committed to reform than the decadent Spanish Bourbons who now dwelled on the past, especially power-hungry Fernando and his self-centered group of noble advisers.[14]

In his effort to help create a regime devoted to advancing Spain, O'Farrill became an *afrancesado* even before José arrived in the kingdom. Afrancesados were Spanish bureaucrats who cooperated or empathized with Napoleon's reforms, sentiments that were widespread among government functionaries interested in change and in safeguarding their employment. They included noblemen, clergy, and middle class bureaucrats and technocrats, in short followers of both the Enlightenment and the 1789 French Revolution. Deeper-rooted reasons, however, included their loathing for the Spanish royal family—the king, queen, and Godoy, and their lack of affection for the British, a tie Fernando promoted. O'Farrill's house in the fashionable San Bernardo district of Madrid was a meeting-place for like-minded individuals and filled with progressive French literature. He worked tirelessly to recruit as many top officials to the French cause as he could. While many afrancesados objected to having a foreigner on the throne, they preferred a smooth transition in power over a calamitous lower-class upheaval that would not bring desperately needed development. They desired improvement from the top, including a reduction of the church's power that widespread groups in traditional society resisted, especially the untutored lower-classes. In time more than two million Spaniards took the oath of loyalty to José, but genuine afrancesados made up a far smaller number.[15]

14. (Napoleon) to Joachim, Grand Duke of Berg, Bayonne, May 10, 1808, *Correspondance de Napoleon*, 32 vols. (Paris: H. Plon, 1858-70), vol. 17, letter 13839, pp. 82-83; Charles Esdaile, *The Peninsular War* (London: Penguin Books, 2002), 236-37. The British have written much about their soldiers in the Iberian Peninsula fighting the French, but often ignoring Spanish participation.

15. Artola, *Afrancesados*, 23-42 and 54-55; Dérozier, *José Quintana*, 128. Much in Spain has been published on the *afrancesados*. Besides works already cited, see Juan López Tabar, *Los famosos traidores: los afrancesados durante la crisis del Antiguo Régimen (1808-1833)* (Madrid: Biblioteca Nueva, 2002), 46-49; and María Teresa Regueiro García, *Relaciones Iglesia-Estado: afrancesados y doceañistas* (Valencia: Tirant lo Blanch,

The transition to a new and non-Spanish king, however, did not proceed well. Soon Spaniards in opposition throughout the peninsula rose up in armed resistance. They established local governments hostile to José, the French, and their Spanish allies. *Fernandistas* and antagonistic provincial governments instigated these juntas. Some of them appealed to England for military equipment and assistance. The English had already sent an expeditionary force to help the Portuguese army defend their kingdom against the French. Spanish fighters also battled José's forces wherever they appeared. A "flying column" of the French army soon went south to try to help their fleet at Cádiz, but its disorderliness due largely to their unfitness succeeded only in plundering Córdoba. Near the upper Guadalquivir River, the *Grande Armée* ran into a Spanish force at Bailén that trounced it in July 1808, a defeat that rattled Gallic convictions about their invincibility. After losing more than 2,000 dead and 400 wounded, 17,365 more Frenchmen (many of them Swiss and German auxiliaries and poorly trained French conscripts) surrendered. Spanish casualties numbered under a thousand. The triumph caused the French position in Madrid to collapse and José I to withdraw temporarily—and no doubt O'Farrill and Casa-Calvo joined him. Meanwhile, the British army in Portugal also scored successes that cleared the French from the kingdom. The struggle, however, was far from over as lands frequently changed hands. In addition, the victory at Bailén induced many functionaries still in government as well as nobles to join the mounting opposition to the intruder José.[16]

Bonaparte had initially anticipated the Spanish nation to accept the new king as life would continue with negligible disturbances. French soldiers would be needed only to garrison the principal fortresses. But as fighting intensified through the summer of 1808, and the public

---

2012).

16. Smith, *Spain*, 271-72; Bergamini, *Spanish Bourbons*, 141; Geoffrey Bruun, *Europe and the French Imperium, 1799-1814* (New York: Harper and Row, 1963), 162. See also Juan Mercader Riba, *José Bonaparte, Rey de España, (1808-1813): Estructura del estado español bonapartista* (Madrid: Consejo Superior de Investigaciones Científicas, 1983).

turned against the French, and what initially had been described as a civil war became a struggle of patriotic Spaniards against the French interlopers and their Spanish followers. French military reversals finally forced Napoleon to march into Spain with an army of three hundred thousand soldiers in November 1808 to finish its subjugation. He was unstoppable as he moved south to Madrid and declared Spanish nobles who had deserted the French faction traitors and confiscated their lands. When he arrived at the capital on December 1, the city resisted only briefly. On entering Madrid, the hostile people greeted him sullenly. Without consulting José, Napoleon reorganized the French government, demonstrated his liberal proclivities by abolishing the Inquisition and many monasteries, and confiscated their wealth. He also eliminated Spain's internal customs and feudal taxes that had long burdened commercial transactions.[17]

Since both were members of the new royal government, Casa-Calvo and O'Farrill spent most of the period of the French intervention in Madrid. Casa-Calvo presumably continued to mingle with other Cubans who remained in the city and participated in social gatherings with people of similar persuasion. In the midst of the war that engulfed many places, Madrid turned into a lively hub for several years as King José enjoyed carousing with the local population and available women. Whether Casa-Calvo approved of or joined in all the war-time dissipation is unknown, but as a widower and parent of adolescent Ignacio, he seems to have avoided the excesses of the pleasure-seeking monarch.

Despite the recapture of Madrid, it was the French seizure of Zaragoza on February 21, 1809, that threw momentum in the war in their favor. Notwithstanding this, more noblemen, who had early shown José deference, deserted and joined the patriot forces. José bravely declared Spaniards who forsook his regime public enemies, invalidated their titles, and seized their property. The Marqués de Casa-Calvo found himself caught in the turmoil on titles. He was among the still loyal members of José's Spanish aristocracy. In early 1809, José

17. Smith, *Spain*, 272-73; Mercader Riba, *José Bonaparte*, 320; Bruun, *Europe and the French Imperium*, 166-67.

started to organize a government over the areas he controlled. Possibly through O'Farrill's intervention, the new king appointed Casa-Calvo to his council of state that consisted of high ranking officials who served as advisers; perhaps Casa-Calvo inadvertently became a representative for the New World colonies. Furthermore, it was from these noblemen that José appointed regal commissioners to govern the new territorial divisions he created in Spain. The Marqués de Caballero was the first person chosen for the post of Salamanca and Zamora, but he resigned upon learning that subversives filled the region. In February, José named Casa-Calvo the regal commissioner to the vacated post, and he accepted it despite its unreliable inhabitants. While during daylight hours the people acted unobtrusively, at night they brought the insurgency to life. With widespread unrest disturbing the countryside, Casa-Calvo became one of the few regal commissioners who actually traveled to his region, but he did so only once. Nevertheless, some commissioners in quiet areas managed to govern from1809 until the French evacuated Spain in 1813. Casa-Calvo relished joining the French party as long as he had a significant role in government. Possibly he initially believed that the French in Spain would be successful and his tie to the new monarch could be exploited to earn him and Cuba new favors. As it was, José compensated the commissioners with mortgages that paid dividends for their service inasmuch as he did not have metallic currency, and his representatives sent to assume charge of the overseas colonies were rejected and at times even killed.[18]

Casa-Calvo's position as a regal commissioner involved a plethora of duties. He was to see that the inhabitants of his district remained loyal and peaceful; ensure that subordinate officials faithfully carried out their assignments; administer oaths of obedience to José I and implemented his decrees; maintain order; and suppress defamatory literature, especially that coming from the *Junta Central de Sevilla* that purported to rule in Fernando's name. Casa-Calvo was to make certain that parish priests and provincial intendants received and implemented the royal orders published in the court newspaper, the *Gaceta de*

18. Mercader Riba, *Los afrancesados*, 323-24; Glover, *Legacy of Glory*, 167.

Madrid, the same gazette used by earlier monarchs. To guarantee an efficient-functioning administration, all regal commissioners had to submit frequent reports to Madrid recounting events in their districts.[19] Casa-Calvo probably handled few if any of these duties personally since he spent negligible time at his post and delegated responsibilities to subordinates. His obligations on the council of state required his presence in Madrid.

Another aspect of José Bonaparte's rule in Spain affected Casa-Calvo. A large number of *grandes*—the highest aristocrats of the land—and other titled nobles were *fernandistas* and not amenable to the entreaties of José. On August 18, 1809, he retaliated by dictating the need to reconfirm all aristocratic titles. It involved 119 Spanish *grandes*, 535 titles of Castile (one of which was Casa-Calvo's), and approximately 500,000 hidalgos who prided themselves on their purity of blood. A three-member commission chosen from José's council of state received the task of reviewing and reissuing titles.[20]

Going farther, on September 18, 1809, José abolished all military orders of knighthood except for two honorary auxiliaries. Casa-Calvo's own Order of Santiago numbered among the titles eliminated. Henceforth, income from the abolished orders would go to fill José's coffers. Immediately after terminating the orders, José created a new title that he called the Spanish Royal Order and opened it to both churchmen and nobles. Twenty-eight religious numbered among the first appointees. Casa-Calvo was one of the first fifty-six aristocrats inducted into the order, and it reflected his favorable standing with the new monarch. Among the eighty-four military persons named were generals and officers of lesser rank. Minister of War Gonzalo O'Farrill, similar to his family in Havana, had never sought a title of nobility, but he figured among the recipients of this decoration inasmuch as he was a lieutenant general.[21]

19. Mercader Riba, *José Bonaparte*, 179-83. José divided Spain into districts headed by regal commissaries. Their duties are outlined in ibid., 236-37.

20. Ibid., 320-21.

21. Ibid., 328-29. Among the persons who received titles from José I was the painter

José punished government employees who did not renew their oaths of allegiance to him, a practice employed by the *fernandistas* as well. He ended their employment, cancelled their state bonds, and confiscated their property. To ensure the loyalty of his employees, José granted large sums of money in state bonds to his ministers, such as the Duque de Campo Alange who received two million reales, his twelve aide-de-camps one million each, and O'Farrill four million. The minister of war, however, declined the grant for himself and asked that his niece, the Condesa de Jaruco, receive it instead as funds from Havana had dried up and she needed money. The state bonds that José dispensed, however, were not effective currency, and turning them into cash meant accepting huge discounts. Casa-Calvo received 500,000 reales in bonds as a state counselor, a welcomed amount because he, too, was without funds. He brought only a limited sum of money from Havana since nothing suggests that on his departure he intended to remain in Spain. Moreover, once the war began in the peninsula, it was difficult or impossible for his children in Havana to provide him with funds.[22]

The year 1810 appeared to be the summit of José's reign as king of Spain. In 1809 French marshals who commanded the armies overran much of the kingdom. They took their orders from Napoleon, not José who despaired that he had no control in Spain. Furthermore, he was chronically out of money and complained bitterly to his brother, who ignored most of his letters. By early 1810, the French marshals drove the patriot soldiers back to Cádiz, the southern-most edge of Spain, and it forced the *Junta Central de Sevilla* to disband. In late January José visited Andalusia in a victorious procession designed to demonstrate his prowess in subduing the rebellious kingdom. He took as many high-ranking government officials, roughly a dozen, as were willing to go, and they included both O'Farrill as minister of war and Casa-Calvo as a member of the regal council. The tour lasted until May of 1810. Nevertheless, it was a well-protected entourage since guerrilla

---

Francisco Goya. Ibid., 330.

22. Glover, *Legacy of Glory*, 167 and note. One estimate of a million reales was $70,000. Ibid., p. 37 note.

bands operated almost everywhere.[23]

Furthermore, success empowered José to leave Spain for three months in 1811, and he did not return from France until July. He visited both his wife, who never joined him in Spain or complained about his extra-marital activities, and his brother Napoleon.[24] In that same year, the emperor began planning the invasion of Russia and withdrawing soldiers from Spain.

The loss of troops changed the course of the war in Spain as it turned in favor of the anti-French forces by 1812. Moreover, José could no longer summon fresh troops to combat the energized armies of Spaniards and Britons. Propaganda pamphlets from the patriot camp calling a meeting of the Spanish *Cortes* (parliament) appeared plastered to walls throughout the nation in the spring of 1812, even in French-held cities such as Granada, Córdoba, Sevilla, Valencia, Salamanca, Valladolid, Burgos, and still others. The subversive literature demonstrated the extent of anti-José sentiment. In addition, by mid-1812 food carts from the countryside around Madrid stopped coming in unless the city's soldiers brought them, and the city's inhabitants labeled it "the year of hunger." That year, Arthur Wellesley, who was subsequently ennobled as the Duke of Wellington and had been fighting the French in Portugal and Spain, again entered Spanish territory and scored victories. The capture of Salamanca on July 22 drove José from Madrid along with thousands of afrancesados three weeks later, and both Spanish and British forces entered the city late that month. No doubt Casa-Calvo and O'Farrill fled Madrid as well. More than two thousand carts, carriages, and wagons conveyed ten thousand refugees and their possessions eastward to Valencia where they were welcomed. Several French marshals united their armies there to help the displaced king. The troops enabled José and his government to return to Madrid

23. Artola, *Afrancesados*, 149-57; Corona, *Revolución y reacción*, 611. See also Francisco Luis Días Torrejón, *José Napoleón I en el sur de España: un viaje regio por Andalucía (enero-mayo 1810)* (Córdoba, España: Publicaciones Obra Social y Cultural, 2008).

24. Corona, *Revolución y reacción*, 512.

one last time for several additional months. But the embattled kingdom under his control soon began to disintegrate.[25]

As conditions worsened, in March 1813 José traveled north to Valladolid, where he planned to either direct the war or flee to France. Insurgents wandered about undercover, and in early 1813 in Madrid they surreptitiously clapped posters on walls designed to rouse the public to arms, threatened police commissioners who arrested and shot subversives, and proclaimed members of José's judiciary criminals. Seeing his regime crumbling, José turned severe, apprehended more defectors, sent some of the arrested to Bayonne, and confiscated the property of wealthy people.[26]

While the combatants ravaged the peninsula in 1808 and 1809, Spaniards opposed to the French took steps to form a government to rule the areas they held for Fernando. It led to the creation of a dominant junta, the *Junta Central de Sevilla*, which enlisted officials from the old regime to fill offices. But when the French swept through Andalusia in 1810, the *Junta* collapsed, and its members fled to the island of León off the coast of Cadiz. Their lack of courage angered the populace. Later that year, a regency of top officials summoned a Cortes to meet in September 1810. The deputies swore loyalty to King Fernando VII, but inasmuch as he was a prisoner in France, they retained executive and legislative power for the present. Two principal parties, the *liberales* and the *serviles*, emerged among the delegates to the Cortes. The Serviles unquestioningly supported the king's absolutism while the Liberals favored a constitutional monarch and a government that participated in law-making and reined in the powers of the king, clergy, and aristocrats. Many of their goals bore similarities with those of the afrancesados, differing principally on whether they supported Fernando. In fact, when Napoleon saw their finished work, he declared in astonishment that it was the Constitution of Bayonne. The *Junta*'s document of 1812

25. Artola, *Afrancesados*, 240-45; Smith, *Spain*, 273-74; Prieto Benavent, "Mercedes de Santa Cruz," 88; López Tabar, *Famosos traidores*, 62.

26. Corona, *Revolución y reacción,* 97, 515-16, 519; Bergamini, *Spanish Bourbons*, 151.

decreed equality for Spaniards everywhere and even permitted colonials token representation, but the Cortes granted the concessions only after the American possessions had initiated movements for independence. The new government under the Cortes was to have a one-house legislature and a forty-member council of state as a consultative body beneath the monarch. The king would rule through ministers who had charge of different areas of government, while he personally conducted foreign relations and commanded the armed forces. The royal children succeeded to the throne according to birth, with females having equality with males. In 1813 the Cortes abolished the Inquisition, a step that earned the enmity of the clergy, and the feisty Cortes responded with more anticlerical legislation.[27]

The struggle against the French in Spain produced a new type of warfare, or at least added a new word to the vocabulary. War had usually been waged only by army soldiers with civilians not taking sides. But that changed in Spain because of the weakness of its military forces. Early in the war, the common people—few of whom had military training—gathered in bands to battle the French, and their style of fighting gave rise to the word *guerrilla* or "little war." Small groups of warriors gathered together to catch the enemy off-guard by using hit and run tactics, operating in sparsely populated areas, and often fighting at night. Guerrillas harassed the enemy by attacking small convoys and detachments, frequently in isolated regions, and by cutting lines of communications. The French did not have sufficient soldiery to police every nook and cranny even in lands they allegedly controlled, as they preferred dominating cities. In Catalonia a corps of volunteers resisted the French from mountain hideouts. Banditry, an often common phenomenon in impoverished nations, had been widespread in Spain before the French invasion, and many of the highwaymen or criminal element looked upon the foreign soldiers as prime targets on whom to ply their trade. Signs of the grim fighting were everywhere with the frequent shooting of prisoners and slaughter of innocents. Goya again familiarized the public on the war's brutality with his sketches, *Los de-*

27. Smith, *Spain*, 275-76.

sastres de la guerra (The Disasters of War).[28]

By early 1813, the patriot forces were winning everywhere. As noted, José fled Madrid to Valladolid in March, after which he continued to Burgos in June. A large baggage train and thousands of afrancesados, who realized that the Napoleonic regime in Spain was ending and feared reprisals, accompanied him. Among the refugees were Spanish women who had become attached to their French lovers. José had left Madrid with persons who had held important government positions and countless wagons crammed with his ill-gotten art works. Nevertheless, some of his Spanish supporters temporarily remained in the capital. The Napoleonic soldiers fought a pitched battle against the patriot army north of Valladolid at Vitoria, which was the last significant contest in Spain. French losses numbered in dead, wounded, and prisoners more than eight thousand, while casualties among the patriots surpassed five thousand. Meanwhile French losses in military equipment totaled 151 cannons mounted on carriages, nearly 2,000,000 musket cartridges, 20 tons of gunpowder, and an uncounted mélange of wagons. The defeat unmistakably advised the French that abandoning Spain was the wiser course to take.[29]

Both Calvos de la Puerta in Spain served the Bonapartist regime. While Sebastián had a role in José's regal administration, Ignacio, who joined José's cavalry, took part in the battle at Vitoria. Sometime after the intervention began in Spain, he entered French service. He was soon promoted to captain of cavalry, and after reaching the age of twenty-one in 1811, he became a colonel. He allegedly participated in other battles besides the clash at Vitoria, but nothing is known about them. Because of wartime, promotions came quickly, perhaps helped by his father's close connection to the king. In contrast, Casa-Calvo was over forty before he became a brevet colonel in an infantry regiment. What is also notable was that José designated Casa-Calvo a *capitaine général* during the war; the title signified an administrative post with military authority rather

28. Ibid., 276-77.

29. Smith, *Spain*, 277; David Gates, *The Spanish Ulcer: A History of the Peninsular War* (London: De Capo Press, 1986), 386-90.

than a rank in the French army. In Spain, however, a *capitán general* meant the rank above lieutenant general and a person in charge militarily of a portion of the kingdom while in the Spanish colonies a captain general signified a political-military post that was below a viceroy.[30]

Exactly when Casa-Calvo and O'Farrill exited Spain is not certain, but perhaps it occurred in the fall of 1813 with other afrancesados. Possibly they were somewhat close to José in the retreat northeast toward France in 1813. When José arrived at a town named Salvatierra immediately after the defeat at Vitoria, he dined on meager fare with O'Farrill and several other members of the royal party. The rout at Vitoria classically symbolized the fate of the war in Spain, and there was no reason to suffer more casualties. Before long, units of the French army were on the Bidassoa, a stream that for ten kilometers marks the boundary in the Pyrenees. Meanwhile, Gen. Maximilien Sébastien Foy brought his troops that had been retreating along the eastern coast and picking up French garrisons at forts that still flew the tri-color. Foy avoided the British by traveling to Zaragoza and crossing the Pyrenees through Roncesvalles Pass. Approximately twelve thousand afrancesados, a number often used but probably a low estimate, sought asylum in France when the struggle concluded in Spain.[31]

The refugees fled into France, where safety was not assured until early the next year when Paris fell to the victorious allies and Napoleon abdicated on April 11, 1814. These acts concluded the war except for Napoleon's hundred-day foray from Elba to Waterloo in 1815 as he tried to reclaim his former position. His quest for additional glory, however, ended dismally with his definitive defeat on June 18, 1815, and his imprisonment soon afterwards on Saint Helena, a desolate island in the south Atlantic.[32]

Several reasons contributed to Bonaparte's failure in Spain. Perhaps chief among them was his belief in his invincibility and talent to oper-

30. Calcagno, *Diccionario biográfico cubano*, 150.

31. Glover, *Legacy of Glory*, 306-7; Gates, *Spanish Ulcer*, 390-91.

32. Bergamini, *Spanish Bourbons*, 151; Jules Moiroux, *Le cimetière du Père Lachaise* (Paris: A. Maréchal, [1922]), 96.

ate in several theaters of war simultaneously. Even as his victory in the peninsula remained incomplete, he withdrew significant numbers of troops for the invasion of Russia. In the tsarist kingdom, he unexpectedly met the same popular resistance that characterized the struggle in Spain as he lost four hundred thousand of his five hundred thousand man invasion force, many of whom succumbed to a brutal winter. His imprudent incursion into Russia devastated his army while the war in the peninsula worsened as its people, particularly the lower classes and soldiers, fought on. They sacrificed themselves in what they called their War of Independence. The British helped the Spanish patriot forces with the training of their soldiers and providing military equipment not produced in Spain in the struggle they named the Peninsular War.[33]

In late 1813 as the fighting was ending, Fernando, who was detained at Valençay in France, and Napoleon held conversations. Napoleon was then facing defeat in Europe after his Russian fiasco, and he offered to pull his troops out of Spain if the British abandoned the Iberian Peninsula. He wanted the French soldiers posted there for battles in other arenas, and he intimated to Fernando that the British presence menaced the Spanish throne, religion, and social order. Fernando protested in reply that he owed Great Britain a debt for its help in the war. To speed his release, Fernando signed the Treaty of Valençay on December 11, 1813. Among its terms, he agreed not to prosecute the afrancesados after the war. A French delegation soon traveled to Spain to gain the treaty's ratification from the regency, but surprisingly it refused because of claims that duress had compelled Fernando to sign the treaty. With clear signs that Napoleon's power was collapsing everywhere, Fernando gained his freedom on March 7, 1814. Before the month ended, he crossed the border into Spain.[34]

As the peninsular war closed, the constituent Cortes that represented Fernando dissolved in October 1813, and a new Cortes of elected deputies met in Madrid in January 1814. Conservatives made up most of the assemblage as right-wing extremism gripped the public that re-

33. Smith, *Spain*, 277-78.

34. Bergamini, *Bourbon Spain*, 162.

acted against the left-leaning French. At assemblies, Spanish supporters chanted "Long Live the Absolute King" and "Down with Liberty," sloganeering that delighted the masses who did not fully comprehend the implications of the words. The demonstrations emboldened Fernando upon his return to claim his traditional rights that meant a return to the past. Fernando started by undoing the enlightened reforms of the eighteenth century as he welcomed back the Jesuits, returned seized ecclesiastical and feudal properties, and restored the Inquisition. By May he had repudiated all the Cortes's work to diminish traditional authority in Spain. Furthermore, Fernando expropriated lands and properties that had belonged to José's adherents, banished the afrancesados, prohibited foreign books, and abolished freedom of the press.[35]

Meanwhile, many Spanish refugees soon found life in exile difficult due to money shortages and cultural differences such as language and customs. In Paris, O'Farrill seemed to have eluded the financial exigencies that plagued many refugees, including his cousin Casa-Calvo. Money, perhaps supplied by his well-heeled wife, permitted O'Farrill to enjoy life in a comfortable apartment located in an upscale Parisian neighborhood. One of his first thoughts after reaching Paris was to refute the unfounded charges that emanated from Madrid on behalf of Fernando who was determined to destroy the reforms of the past century. Fernando's obsession with obliterating his erstwhile rivals disappointed the more liberal-minded Spaniards who had supported him in the war while those in exile felt that the conflict had served no purpose but to return Spain to a more dismal time. Among the prominent exiles were persons who wanted reconciliation, and they tried to explain their reasons for siding with José. Pardons would enable them to return to Spain, recover their property, and resume their lives. For example, no sooner were Miguel José de Azanza, who had been the minister of the treasury, and Gonzalo O'Farrill ensconced in Paris than they put pen to paper to refute charges that Fernando's lackeys hurled at them. Many afrancesados used this ploy to inveigle the king to grant them amnesty. Azanza and O'Farrill claimed that they were not in gov-

35. Smith, *Spain*, 166-67; Chapman, *Spain*, 494-95.

ernment service when events unfolded that brought José to power in Spain. Azanza had been at home in Granada for several years while O'Farrill had been commanding troops in Tuscany, Italy, until illness forced his return in March 1808. Azanza traveled to Madrid to take charge of the ministry of the treasury in Fernando's government, which he did on March 28, 1808, and O'Farrill was named director of the army's school of artillery before he began service as the minister of war on April 5. Called by Napoleon, King Fernando journeyed to Bayonne five days later. Azanza and O'Farrill pointed out that Carlos IV, under the guidance of Godoy, had signed the Treaty of Fontainebleau of October 27, 1807, that allowed French troops to enter Spain, and worse yet another treaty that gave them control of Spanish fortresses along the border. The ministries of the treasury and war, Azanza and O'Farrill argued, had no part in those nefarious agreements. Moreover, they denied they gave authority to place Spanish soldiers under the command of French generals, said they had not granted French troops permission to enter Madrid in 1808, and stated they had not written friendly letters to Napoleon.[36] These excuses, however, fell on deaf ears in Spain inasmuch as the petitioners had labored in the alien French government between 1808 and 1813.

While Spain quickly relapsed into absolutism in the postwar era, the restless Spanish American colonies had already begun their move in a contrary direction. Change had begun in 1810, when colonial leaders learned that no Spanish government existed as the *Junta Central* had dissolved when French troops seized much of the kingdom. Communications with the overseas possessions had already deteriorated due to British supremacy on the Atlantic Ocean. In short order, the more intrepid colonies started seizing governing authority from peninsular officials and ruling themselves through the Cabildos of capital cities. They claimed to govern for Fernando, but it was a temporary

36. Miguel José de Azanza and Gonzalo O'Farrill, *Memoria de D. Miguel José de Azanza y D. Gonzalo O-Farrill, sobre los hechos que justifican su conducta política, Desde marzo de 1808 hasta abril de 1814* (Paris: P. N. Rougeron, 1815), 12-16. Bonaparte's correspondence, however, shows that O'Farrill had written at least one letter to the emperor.

ruse before they declared independence. In doing so, they followed the recent examples of the United States in 1776, France in 1789, and Haiti in 1804. The chronic instability stirred up by prolonged fighting in the Atlantic world had enabled the colonies to do so. They had wearied of the home government's taxes and political, economic, and social restrictions because the colonies were seen primarily as revenue producers, and the Bourbon reforms that the crown slowly introduced never quenched colonial expectations. Nevertheless, independence did not come easily as the mainland possessions battled for fifteen years before they shook off the peninsular yoke.[37]

Insular Cuba and Puerto Rico, however, had not joined in the rebellions that consumed the mainland colonies, largely because of their close relations with the mother country and the large numbers of Spaniards in them. A growing slave population also raised concern among the islands' leaders. Meanwhile, Spain perennially needed money inasmuch as it was a poorly developed nation with a gigantic empire. Upon his release from detention, Fernando labored to return not only the peninsula but his American colonies to their former obedience. The Cuban upper classes, among whom the sugar barons were the wealthiest in the island's society and who called themselves Spaniards, dominated what little politics there was and regarded the king's urgent need for money as an opportunity to wrestle concessions from him. In fact, they obtained virtually everything in the years after 1814 that they had been lobbying for. Shortly after Fernando reassumed the throne, he lifted restrictions on Cuban land usage. In 1815 he consented to the unlimited cutting of timber in Cuba's hardwood forests that had been reserved for ship construction. Cubans could now use forests freely to build sugar boxes and burn as fuel for sugar boilers. Furthermore, Fernando ended the tobacco monopoly in 1817, and thereafter he did not protect tobacco fields from the grasping hands of sugar growers. Finally, Fernando went beyond Carlos III's 1776 decree that made

37. Lester D. Langley, *The Americas in the Age of Revolution, 1750-1850* (New Haven: Yale University Press, 1996),166-211; Manuela Albertone and Antonino De Francesco, eds., *Rethinking the Atlantic World: Europe and America in the Age of Democratic Revolution* (New York: Palgrave Macmillan, 2009); Liss, *Atlantic Empires*, 193-221.

Havana a free port, and in 1818 he allowed Cuba unlimited trade with all nations. Planters had long yearned for these concessions, and the king granted them because he desperately needed funds to battle the insurgents on the American mainland. Once they achieved their victories, the Cuban planters embarked on the path that turned the island into the major sugar producer in the Caribbean.[38]

At the time of Napoleon's hundred-day return to France in 1815, Fernando worried that his opponents in exile might start scheming to overthrow his regime. Surprisingly, however, the afrancesados in France were too disorganized to take action against him. Consequently, they either remained neutral or sided with the new French Bourbon king, Louis XVIII. Spanish exiles in France had increased in number between 1814 and 1820 as the Liberals among Fernando's supporters found their presence no longer tolerated in his repressive regime. In addition, military insurrections headed by liberal generals occurred each year between 1814 and 1817, and were suppressed harshly. While some of these Liberals conspired against Fernando in Spain and in adjacent lands, others preferred life in the New World Spanish colonies where they joined the insurgents and fought against the mother country. Although suspicion marred relations between the afrancesados and Liberals in France and prevented them from uniting forces, Fernando's government requested Louis to eradicate their presence from the Franco-Spanish border. The uncooperative French king, however, merely removed the most vocal Spanish dissidents in the four cities of Tarbes, Toulouse, Pau, and Bayonne.[39]

The afrancesados had no reason to remain neutral toward the Spanish autocrat. At the Congress of Vienna (1814-15), ambassadors from the major kingdoms met to establish a lasting peace through a "balance of power" among them. Fernando's representative, Wenceslao Ramírez de Villa-Urrutia, Marqués de Villa-Urrutia, demanded that all afrancesados in France be returned to Spain without pardons.

38. Kuethe, "Havana in the Eighteenth Century," 33-4; Knight, "Origins of Wealth," 242. Segre et al., *Havana*, 30.

39. Artola, *Afrancesados*, 271-73; Chapman, *Spain*, 495.

Spanish royalists believed that Louis XVIII treated the exiles too leniently, and Fernando feared they might plot against him since they moved about freely in exile. Charles Maurice de Talleyrand-Périgord, who was known simply as Talleyrand and was the French delegate to the Congress, resented Villa-Urrutia's attempt to encroach on French law enforcement and emphatically rejected his demand. Furthermore, Talleyrand refused to restore the multitude of paintings, sculptures, tapestries, and other objects d'art stolen during the French occupation. The looted items filled hundreds of wagons that José and his generals carefully conducted back to France.[40]

Unexpectedly, a major change of fortune began in early 1820 in Cádiz. It started when Spanish soldiers slated for duty in the colonies refused to embark. Their insurgency echoed a widespread complaint among the common soldiers, many of them draftees, who refused to be sacrificed on New World battlefields, and they soon gathered the support of the entire Spanish military establishment. They embraced the Liberal dissidents where the officer class in particular was filled with adherents of the Freemasons, and acting together they effortlessly overthrew Fernando's repressive regime. The Liberal politicians soon imposed the Constitution of 1812 on the nation and allowed Fernando to retain the throne but with restricted authority. He became a reluctant constitutional monarch in a reform-minded government that ruled Spain for three years.[41]

Casa-Calvo soon heard the news in far-off Paris. But at that time in the spring of 1820, he was clinging precariously to life. The significant changes sweeping through Spain gave him a modicum of consolation,

40. Artola, *Afrancesados*, 273; Wenceslao Ramírez de Villa-Urrutia, *España en el Congreso de Viena según la correspondencia de D. Pedro Gómez Labrador, Marqués de Labrador*, 2nd ed., (Madrid: Francisco Beltrán, 1928), 61-62. On the Congress of Vienna, see David King, *Vienna 1814: How the Conquerors of Napoleon Made Love, War, and Peace at the Congress of Vienna* (New York: Harmony Books, 2008); and Harold Nicolson, *The Congress of Vienna: A Study in Allied Unity, 1812-1822* (New York: Harcourt, Brace, and Company, 1946).

41. Chapman, *Spain*, 495-96; José Deleito y Piñuela, *Congreso de Cádiz: El regreso de los afrancesados a España en 1820* (Madrid: Talleres Poligráficos, 1927).

The final resting place of Casa-Calvo in Père-Lachaise cemetery, Paris, France
Photo courtesy of Pierre-Yves Beaudouin / Wikimedia Commons

and perhaps even convinced him that he had not chosen the wrong side in the recent war after all. Events of his past six years in Spain and seven in France, along with his children in distant Cuba, must have filled his last thoughts. Luckily, he had Ignacio near him during his time of troubles when money was short; however, his daughters in Havana finally were able to send funds that enabled him to live more comfortably. Nothing is known about Casa-Calvo's final malady or how long he had suffered from it. Throughout his life, medical problems had periodically troubled him. Although pardons and return of property came with the new Liberal government in Spain, the news arrived too late to help Casa-Calvo. He died on May 27, 1820, less than three months short of his sixty-ninth birthday.[42]

Ignacio most likely made the funeral arrangements for his father. Sebastián was buried in what eventually became the prestigious Parisian cemetery of Père-Lachaise, the final resting place of many French and foreign celebrities of the last two centuries. Possibly it was Ignacio who set up the the monument in which Casa-Calvo's remains rest in a sarcophagus. On the outside, the monument has marble pillars and a roof, under which is the interior chamber. His epitaph is inscribed on a pillar that faces the front. Ignacio, and perhaps his sisters in Havana, footed the costs for the burial plot and monument. It still stands today despite the passage of almost two hundred years since his demise, and it appears to be in reasonably good shape since it looks refurbished. The brief inscription reads in Spanish:[43]

> Sebastián Calvo, / Marqués de Casa-Calvo. / Born in Havana / and died in Paris / On May 27, 1820. /
> He served in the army of Spain, / his country. /

42. Mallén, *Historia de familias cubanas*, 121.

43. Moiroux, *Le cimetière du Père-Lachaise*, 96. Among the well-known foreigners buried in this cemetery was Manuel Godoy (May 12, 1767-October 4, 1851), who had been in exile from Spain since 1808. Chastenet, *Godoy*, 253. Upon his death, his body spent a year at the Church Saint Roch before a banker bought a small plot for him at the Père-Lachaise cemetery. Although talk has circulated of returning his remains to his native province in Spain, it has not yet happened.

> He was Captain General of his commands. / He protected the helpless, / And always treated the unfortunate well. / His children and his friends / Consoled him in his adversities, / and they sobbed for him upon his death.[44]

When Fernando's absolutism terminated in 1820, many of the exiles returned to their homeland. Unfortunately, the Spanish Liberals in power were not overly generous in allowing the afrancesados into the nation and decreed that they could only reside in the Basque region of northern Spain and in the province of Burgos. Perhaps this was a compromise chiseled by reluctant Conservative politicians. Thus the returnees crowded into tiny Basque towns with only limited economic opportunities, and it forced most of them to depend on relatives in the rest of Spain for their sustenance. Some of the former exiles, however, dissatisfied with the miserable conditions they encountered, daringly slipped back to their hometowns where they lived more comfortably. Perhaps they were not disturbed, then or later. After eighteen months, however, Spanish consuls on the French border stopped issuing the former afrancesados passports they needed to enter Spain. Thereafter, amnesty and restoration of properties were only gradually extended to them in the late 1820s. Spaniards who served in the highest posts of José's government, and they included O'Farrill, were the last to be pardoned. Many, however, did not return home. Among them was O'Farrill, possibly because he did not trust Fernando and knew that he could not revive his career in the army since the victors in the recent war now filled its ranks. Moreover, age had overtaken O'Farrill as he entered his seventies by the mid-1820s.[45]

The Liberal interlude in Spain ended in 1823 when the conservative European kingdoms took action in keeping with agreements made at the Congress of Vienna. Fernando secretly appealed to the conservative monarchs about his incarceration and the miserable conditions he and his regal followers lived in. That inspired the reactionary mon-

44. Information provided by Jorge Aúñon. While the French title of *capitaine-général* was administrative, in Spain it was both a military rank and a high administrative post that had a military function.

45. Deleito y Piñuela, *El regreso de los afrancesados a España en 1820*, 125-38.

archies to turn against Spain's Liberal government, perhaps fearful that similar dissidents might instigate uprisings in their nations, and they designated France under Louis XVIII to send troops to overthrow the despicable regime since his was the only powerful nation possessing a contiguous border with Spain. Once French soldiers entered Spain, the Liberal regime quickly collapsed. This time there was no protracted war, just the rapid restoration of Fernando and his minions to their earlier positions of authority.[46]

Similar with many other afrancesados, Gonzalo O'Farrill had remained in Paris throughout the political changes of the early 1820s. His wife had relocated to Paris, and her fortune allowed them to live well. When he died on July 19, 1831, she buried him in a pantheon in the Père-Lachaise Cemetery, where in time she joined him. It was ironic that O'Farrill and Casa-Calvo, two cousins who were born in Havana two and a half years apart, pursued army careers and traveled individually to many places in both the New World and Old, spent considerable time in Spain, died eleven years apart in the same city, and were both buried in the same French cemetery. Unlike Casa-Calvo, however, O'Farrill's epitaph lists his rank of lieutenant general in the Spanish army and not his post of minister of war during the French intervention.[47] Unfortunately, his grave site has deteriorated and today appears in a state of collapse.

After Casa-Calvo's death and the Liberal pardons, the government returned his properties in Cuba to his children. Their sequester had never troubled his two daughters, María Catalina and María Antonia, since both their husbands belonged to the Cuban affluent. Casa-Calvo relied on them, and not on his older son Pedro, to see him through his last difficult years.[48] Pedro became the second Marqués de Casa-Calvo,

46. Chapman, *Spain*, 496-97.

47. Moiroux, *Le cimetière de Père Lachaise*, 96, 265.

48. In Havana on December 2, 1798, Casa-Calvo's oldest child, María Catalina, married Francisco de Paula Chacón y O'Farrill, the oldest offspring of the Conde de Casa-Bayona, who held titles in the royal army and positions in the Havana Cabildo. María Catalina died in Madrid on August 21, 1857, at age seventy-five. On August 3,

and had married María Catalina de Cárdenas y Zayas from a wealthy family, on June 29, 1803, when his father was in New Orleans. Her father was the second Marqués de Cárdenas de Montehermoso. Pedro had at least two daughters, María Matilda and María Luisa, who both married into the sugar autocracy, before he separated from his wife in the 1820s or early 1830s.[49] Earlier, he had held military positions during the colonial wars as a captain of dragoons and a militia cavalry colonel and relinquished his service after the conflicts ended. Pedro had grown up with little parental supervision or discipline as his mother died when he was nine years old and his father was often absent. As a consequence, he fell into the vices that troubled many maturing Cuban males: gambling, carousing, and alcoholism. He inherited much of his father's estate and, despite his money squandering, still possessed a sizable fortune in the 1830s. Upon abandoning his wife, he moved into a sleazy neighborhood outside the walls of Havana called Horcón that was inhabited by lowlifes who adored the egalitarian nobleman for his unpretentiousness. There he opened his bachelor's residence to card players, especially to persons addicted to the popular game of chance called Monte, and to lower class delinquents and even criminals. In a letter of October 26, 1835, Felipe Martínez, an investigator, enumerated the many failings of Pedro's debauched lifestyle to the strait-laced Capt. Gen. Miguel Tacón y Rosique, the governor of Cuba. Tacón disliked Cuban Creoles and surrounded himself with Peninsulars. He excluded Cubans from government. Furthermore, Pedro seemed addicted to the folk medicine of a group of Africans called ñáñiguismo that had a following among some wealthy Cubans. Upon assuming his post as captain general (1834-36), Tacón determined to cleanse Havana of its vices such as gambling, thievery, and vagrancy. He sized up Pedro as an embarrassment and a disgraceful example to Havana's aristocrats, among whom there were too many already behaving deplorably. To

1803, Casa-Calvo's younger daughter (and third child), María Antonia, married Juan Montalvo y O'Farrill, who rose to the rank of field marshal in the royal army and held many military titles and decorations. Mallén, *Historia de familias cubanas*, 121.

49. Ibid., 122.

Tacón, Pedro's alleged mistreatment of judges and the law made him one of the worst delinquents, and Tacón exiled him to Puerto Rico, much to the annoyance of Pedro's supporters of all classes who vigorously protested his ouster. If the captain general thought that it would mend Pedro's errant ways, it was a mistaken notion since Pedro remained unrepentant. He escaped from Tacón's control in Puerto Rico and traveled to Madrid to implore the crown now under Queen María Christina, the deceased King Fernando's daughter, to override the Cuban captain general and permit his return to Havana. Also in Madrid he became the darling of the Cuban ex-patriots who showered him with attention inasmuch as they detested Tacón. Before Pedro secured his return to Cuba, he succumbed to a pulmonary disease on October 24, 1837. He was buried in Madrid, the city where his father had spent many years. Twenty years later his older sister, María Catalina, who had journeyed to Spain under happier circumstances, also died in Madrid and was buried there. In Havana the sugar oligarchy regarded Pedro a victim of Tacón's vicious persecution of their members.[50]

Pedro's disreputable life gave rise to defamatory literature about him, including a book that was published in New Orleans. It was entitled "Biography of D. Pedro Calvo, called Marqués de Casa-Calvo." Documents and letters about his life sent from Havana to New Orleans aided in the book's composition. In New Orleans an advertising pamphlet for the scandalous biography described Pedro as "a man filled with vices and a character that was violent and perverse."[51] How accurately it portrayed him, however, is open to ques-

50. Juan Pérez de la Rosa, ed., *Correspondencia reservada del Capitán General don Miguel Tacón, con el Gobierno de Madrid, 1834-1838* (La Habana: Biblioteca Nacional José Martí, 1963), 38, 52-53, 182-85, 192-93, 314-15; Arango, *La Sacarocracía*, 139, 273-76. Pérez de la Rosa is sympathetic to the second Casa-Calvo despite his vices since he disapproved of Tacón. See also Segre et al., *Havana*, 32-33. On gambling in Havana, see María Dolores Gonzáles-Ripoll Navarro, *Cuba, la isla de los ensayos, cultura y sociedad (1790-1815)* (Madrid: Consejo Superior de Investigaciones científicas, Centro de Humanidades Instituto de Historia, 1999), 95.

51. Calcagno, *Diccionario biográfico cubano*, 150. It is possible that some of the vitriol used to describe Pedro Calvo de la Puerta in his biography was later directed

tion as the book's publisher undoubtedly employed lurid descriptions to boost sales.

In contrast, Casa-Calvo's second son Ignacio, after his early years in Havana, had grown up under his father's supervision. As a consequence, his childhood differed significantly from Pedro's. Ignacio, who never knew his mother to any degree since he was only two when she died, was thirty years old when his father Sebastián passed away after spending twenty years with him as he was maturing. With no reason for remaining in Paris after his father's demise, Ignacio returned to Havana in the early 1820s. Upon the restoration of the family's properties, he likely received a share as he seems to have lived reasonably well in the city. In the 1820s, he was included in a painting made of his sister María Antonia's family—the only known portrayal of two members of the Casa-Calvo children. She, her husband who was Juan Montalvo y O'Farrill and a field marshal in the royal army, and their eight young children take up most of the picture (one or two of the children had already died but were pictured nevertheless). Off to one side of the painting was Ignacio, who appeared almost a marginal figure. Upon his return to Havana after an absence of a decade and a half in Europe, he was possibly then living with his sister. He briefly lent his services as a colonel to a Cuban cavalry unit composed of the elite gentlemen of Havana. But soon after his 1824 marriage, he retired from public life and never entered politics. He married twice, first to Dolores Herrera y de la Barrera (1805-1846), who was the daughter of the Condes de Gibacoa and needless to say wealthy. With Dolores, Ignacio had four children. After her death and at fifty-eight years of age, Ignacio married again on November 11, 1848. His second wife was Rafaela, the daughter of attorney Antonio del Monte y Tejada. Ignacio died in Havana on New Year's Day, 1857.[52]

Ignacio had acquired upon his father's death his military papers. They traced Casa-Calvo's army career. Career officers typically kept im-

---

against his father, Sebastián Calvo de la Puerta.

52. Mallén, *Historia de familias cubanas*, 4: 122. See also Vallellano, *Nobiliario Cubano*, 251; Calcagno, *Diccionario biográfico cubano*, 150.

The lady seated on the chair is doña María Antonia Calvo de la Puerta y Peñalver, daughter of Sebastian Calvo de la Puerta and wife of don Juan Montalvo y O'Farrill, standing at the left. The children are theirs. Seated at the right is Ignacio Calvo de la Puerta y Peñalver, brother of doña María Antonia Calvo de la Puerta and younger son of Sebastian Calvo de la Puerta. Courtesy of Jorge Auñón.

portant military papers that noted their service, correspondence, and important events. Casa-Calvo appears not to have taken these documents to Louisiana in 1803 or to Spain in 1806 because they had grown into a bulky collection. From these papers, the only documents known to have survived are those published in Antonio del Monte y Tejada's study, *Historia de Santo Domingo.*[53] They shed light on Casa-Calvo's military service on Hispaniola (and selected letters were used in chapter five of this study) between 1793 and 1796. Monte y Tejada, who was Ignacio's father-in-law, acknowledged that with Ignacio's per-

53. Monte y Tejada, *Historia de Santo Domingo*, 3: 159.

mission he made copies of items in the collection to provide morsels of knowledge on Dominican history. Speculating, it is possible the original documents somehow survived Ignacio's death and with luck were bequeathed to an archive or library or perhaps placed in the attic of a Casa-Calvo descendant where they still lay unidentified and awaiting the proper person to rescue them.

During Sebastián Calvo de la Puerta y O'Farrill's lifetime, Cuba seems to have produced few native sons who had as many adventures in diverse places as he experienced. Two exceptions were, of course, Gonzalo O'Farrill who went to Europe as a teenager and never returned to Cuba and Francisco Montalvo who in time rose to become viceroy of New Granada. In most respects, O'Farrill became a Spaniard.

Casa-Calvo, on the other hand, never forgot his Cuban heritage. He was born into a wealthy family of ability that was enriched by cattle, tobacco, sugar, and other agricultural products. It also became aristocratic during his lifetime as it obtained two titles of nobility. The story of the rise of his ancestors from near obscurity in the sixteenth century illustrates how his forebears, and indeed many early Cuban families, achieved their prominent positions two or three centuries later. Casa-Calvo was only one of perhaps a hundred or so Cuban males who was born to wealth and status and lived through the second half of the eighteenth and early nineteenth centuries. Not many of them, however, rose to distinction for their services in either civilian or military life inasmuch they entered neither the army, church, militia, nor government service, or made notable contributions to society. They were content to pass their lives as planters or dependents on family estates. Gonzalo O'Farrill's brothers who stayed in Cuba, for example, did not achieve his rank of lieutenant general in the regular army, although they fared reasonably well in wealth and rank in Cuban society.[54]

Casa-Calvo's military service, on the other hand, took him to many locations. Important among them were his two lengthy tours of duty

54. Of Gonzalo O'Farrill's younger brothers, Ignacio (1757-1838) became a priest while Juan Manuel (1756-?) became first a dragoon captain and later a lieutenant colonel of the Matanzas militia cavalry. Mallén, *Historia de familias cubanas*, 338.

in Spain. Even so, he spent a large part of his time in the colonies. He fought in a peninsular regiment against Great Britain between 1779 and 1783 in and near the Gulf of Mexico and saw action against revolutionary France in Santo Domingo and Saint-Domingue, where he first commanded a battalion and later a regiment. In addition, he had a prominent role in the formation of the Fixed Infantry Regiment of Cuba in the 1780s, served as interim governor of Louisiana and West Florida for two years (1799-1801), rose through ability and experience—and not through purchase—to command the Fixed Infantry Regiment of Havana, and participated in the transfer of Louisiana to France and the United States. On his last journey to Louisiana, he stayed on to oversee the Spanish evacuation of Louisiana and to head the survey of the boundary line along the Sabine River. This last work gave rise to his belief that he needed to present vital information about the boundary and the defense of Texas directly to the government in Madrid. He momentarily thought that Louisiana could be regained through the introduction of Irish settlers. This plan, however, had flaws that made its realization highly improbable: It was incredibly expensive to fulfill since it entailed transporting immigrants across the Atlantic and maintaining them until they became self-supporting. Furthermore, as the Irish were British subjects, Spain did not want to annoy Great Britain by removing large numbers of them. These problems made his designs for the defense of Texas and the recovery of Louisiana unfeasible. Finally, his third and final sojourn in Spain was the least documented part of his life. Nothing is known of his discussions about the borderlands with Spanish officials or what effect they had. But it seems likely that his report and map made during the survey helped to fix the boundary between Spain and the United States along the Sabine River, where it continues today to divide the present-day states of Louisiana and Texas. His name, however, is seldom mentioned whenever the establishment of the boundary is cited.[55]

55. An exception to Casa-Calvo not receiving recognition for the boundary along the Sabine River is Jack D. L. Holmes's "The Marqués de Casa-Calvo, Nicolas de Finiels, and the 1805 Spanish Expedition through East Texas and Louisiana," *Southwestern Historical Quarterly* 69 (January 1966): 324-39. This work first brought at-

His last years in Spain came during a chaotic time, when the royal family under Carlos IV, his wife María Luisa, his son Fernando, and his first minister Godoy who must not be excluded, forfeited responsibilities in sound government. Collectively, they illustrate the flaws in the institution of absolute monarchy, especially since none of them was trained in government or cared about it, except for Fernando and Godoy who both reveled in exercising power however unwisely they did so. The powerful Napoleon Bonaparte soon appeared wanting to incorporate Spain and Portugal in his political orbit as he strove to make himself emperor of Europe. These events introduced an unexpected final adventure in Casa-Calvo's life.

He likely followed the guidance of O'Farrill in joining the afrancesados, José Napoleon, and the French in Spain. Hindsight—that seldom if ever fails—tells us that it was an ill-fated decision inasmuch as the reformers under José were unsuccessful in bringing meaningful change to Spain, and their work, plus that of their eighteenth-century predecessors, quickly vanished when Fernando VII came to the throne in 1814. Only a year after returning to Europe in 1806, Casa-Calvo found himself caught in a vise between a traditional absolutist government and a new dynastic line of reformers that swerved far more to the left than the agricultural improvements he sought for Cuba.

In a recent study, *The Marquis: Lafayette Reconsidered*, Laura Auricchio describes her subject, Marie-Joseph Paul Yves Roche Gilbert du Motier de Lafayette, better known by his last name, who tried to bring liberal reforms to benefit the neglected segments of French society. After his experiences as a general in the American Revolution, Lafayette tried to become a reformer at home, and he bears some comparison with the fate of the afrancesados. In his case, Lafayette stood between the monarchy and aristocrats on one side and the downtrod-

---

tention to Casa-Calvo's contribution in designating the boundary between Louisiana and Texas. José Antonio Pichardo, in *Pichardo' Treatise on the Limits of Louisiana and Texas*, ed. Charles Wilson Hackett, 4 vols. (1931; repr. Freeport, N.Y.: Books for Libraries Press, 1971), mentions Casa-Calvo but does not discuss his work on the Sabine River because he did not live to finish his treatise to disprove that Texas was a part of Louisiana inasmuch as he died in 1812.

den on the other who badly needed a lessening of absolutist powers in government, economy, and society. Without seeking to overthrow the monarchy which he, in fact, strove to preserve, Lafayette championed reforms for the exploited that allowed an improvement in their lives. But similar to the way Casa-Calvo and the afrancesados were treated in Spain, believers in the French *ancien régime* considered Lafayette as too radical while true reformers regarded him as a conservative.[56]

If Fernando had indeed owed a debt to England as he once told Napoleon, his obligation to the conservatives—aristocrats, churchmen, and the unlettered common religious folk—was greater. Spain under Fernando and much of Spanish society turned their backs on the developments of the early nineteenth century that in ensuing decades in Western Europe saw the gradual rise of constitutional monarchies and industrialized societies that slowly, and not without additional upheaval, improved the rights of lesser privileged individuals at least to some degree. For the most part, however, Spain was not among those nations. A return to the past, with the exile of the afrancesados and Liberals and the eradication of reforms, pleased the restored power groups, but those attainments did not advance political, economic, or social conditions within the poverty-stricken kingdom, at least not immediately. Change came to Spain slowly through the nineteenth century as it experienced military coups d'états, internal wars, religious conservatism despite the abolition of the Inquisition, and a scant effort to initiate meaningful change to the worn-out rut that Spain was stuck in.[57]

Casa-Calvo had the misfortune of being born at a time when Spanish imperial supremacy was in sharp decline. And, indeed, his death coincided with the loss of many of Spain's overseas possessions. Had the empire been in its formative stage or at its pinnacle during

56. Laura Auricchio, *The Marquis: Lafayette Reconsidered* (New York: Alfred A. Knopf, 2014), 222-303. It should be noted that President Jefferson once offered Lafayette the post of governor of Louisiana and added to his offer a large land grant. However, Lafayette was unable to accept because he was then imprisoned by the French authorities. Hatfield, *Claiborne*, 120-21.

57. See Carr, *Spain, 1808-1975*; and Corona, *Revolución y reacción*, 355-67.

his life, possibly he would have reaped the glory of victories and sidestepped the failures that seemed to hound him as he journeyed from one troubled colony (Santo Domingo) to another (Louisiana) and finally to tradition-bound Spain. Although he would have preferred that both colonies remained within the Spanish realm, they slipped its grasp. Moreover, Casa-Calvo's education seems to have failed him as late in his military career he appeared unacquainted about Spain's financial straits and the aspirations of colonials who sought to free themselves from peninsular repression. Quite likely it was because he did not share their sentiments. While he was cognizant of the quest by Cuba's upper class for economic freedom, he seemed not to understand the hopes of all the island's inhabitants and social groups. Instead, he was a man of his class and of his times, and he believed that the leaders of his status were solely responsible for Cuba's prosperity. Certainly this was the thinking of his younger brother Nicolás while he lived. As an elitist Cuban, Casa-Calvo believed in the expansion and development of wealth in his home colony but largely, if not solely, for the benefit of his class. He appeared disinclined to promote greater freedom or opportunity for the larger number of Cuba's inhabitants. He clearly did not support Cuban independence from Spain or alterations to the social and economic orders as he understood them. The Cuban upper class, he judged, had arrived at their position due to their own efforts, and he felt no desire to initiate change. As it turned out, several more generations of privileged Cubans would enjoy these advantages before a revolutionary transformation occurred in the mid-twentieth century. All the same, an examination of Casa-Calvo's life and his world on both sides of the Atlantic Ocean raises an awareness of the *Sturm und Drang* (Storm and Stress) or social upheavals as he experienced them in the late eighteenth and early nineteenth centuries.

Bibliography

Archives, Documentary Collections, and Manuscripts

Archivo General de Indias, Seville

Casa de Contratación, legajo 5533

Estado, legajos 2, 5A, 17

Indiferente General, legajos 1, 2, 27, 527

Papeles Procedentes de la Isla de Cuba

Legajos 44, 69, 70B, 71A, 72, 73, 76, 77B, 78, 106A, 154B, 155B, 156AB, 179B, 1304, 1550, 1551, 1552, 1573, 1771A, 2355

Pasajeros de Indias, legajo 3, expediente 2383

Títulos de Castilla

Archivo General Militar, Segovia

Expedientes de Servicio

Hojas militares de Sebastián Calvo de la Puerta y O'Farrill

Hojas militares de Ignacio Calvo de la Puerta y Peñalver

Archivo General de Simancas

Guerra Moderna, legajos 6840, 6842, 6843, 6851, 6855, 6880, 6881, 6912, 6926, 7161

Archivo Histórico Nacional, Madrid

Estado, legajos: 3407, 3888, 3892*bis*, 3900, 3901

Órdenes Militares, expediente 8114

Biblioteca Nacional, Madrid

Sección de Manuscritos

Colección de Documentos de la Luisiana, 1767 a 1792, 3 vols.

Cathedral of Havana, Cuba

Sacrarium, Baptismal Books of White Persons, Book 19

Mississippi State Department of Archives and History, Jackson, Mississippi

Mississippi Provincial Archives

Spanish Dominion. 9 vols. Microfilm in Spanish

New Orleans Public Library

Actas del Cabildo, 1769-1803. 10 vols. Microfilm of WPA transcripts in Spanish

Books, Articles, Dissertations, and Unpublished Papers

Abbey, Katherine Trimmer. "Efforts of Spain to Maintain Sources of Information in the British Colonies before 1779." *Mississippi Valley Historical Review* 15 (1928): 56-68.

Acosta Rodríguez, Antonio. *La población de Luisiana española, 1763-1803*. Madrid: Gráficas Condor, 1979.

Aimes, Hubert H. S. *A History of Slavery in Cuba, 1511 to 1868*. New York: Knickerbocher Press, 1907.

Aiton, Arthur S. "Spanish Colonial Reorganization under the Family Compact." *Hispanic American Historical Review* 12 (1932): 269-80.

Albertone, Manuela, and Antonino De Francesco, eds. *Rethinking the Atlantic World: Europe and America in the Age of Democratic Revolution*. New York: Palgrave Macmillan, 2009.

Altman, Ida. *Emigrants and Society: Extremadura and America in the Sixteenth Century*. Berkeley: University of California Press, 1989.

Andújar Castillo, Francisco. *Necesidad y venalidad: España e Indias, 1704-1711*. Madrid: Centro de Estudios Políticos y Constitucionales, 2008.

———. *El sonido del dinero: Monarquía, ejército y venalidad en la Espa-*

ña del siglo XVIII. Madrid: Marcial Pons, 2004.

Arango, Ruben C. *La Sacarocracía: Historia de la Aristocracia Azucarera Cubana*. Miami: Eco Group, Inc., 2006.

Arthur, Stanley Clisby. *The Story of the West Florida Rebellion*. St. Francisville, La.: St. Francisville Democrat, 1935.

Arthur, Stanley Clisby, and George Campbell Huchet de Kernion. *Old Families of Louisiana*. Reprint. Baton Rouge: Claitor's Publishing Division, 1971.

Artola, Miguel. *Los Afrancesados*. Madrid: Ediciones Altaya, 1997.

Auricchio, Laura. *The Marquis: Lafayette Reconsidered*. New York: Alfred A. Knopf, 2014.

Azanza, Miguel José de, and Gonzalo O'Farrill. *Memoria de D. Miguel José de Azanza y D. Gonzalo O-Farrill, sobre los hechos que justifican su conducta política, desde marzo de 1808 hasta abril de 1814*. Paris: P.N. Rougenow, 1815.

Baade, Hans W. "The Law of Slavery in Spanish Luisiana, 1769-1803." In *Louisiana's Legal Heritage*, edited by Edward F. Haas, 43-86. Pensacola: Perdido Bay Press for the Louisiana State Museum, 1983.

Baily, Francis. *Journal of a Tour in the Unsettled Parts of North America, in 1796 and 1797*. Edited by Jack D. L. Holmes. Carbondale: Southern Illinois University Press, 1969.

Barbé-Marbois, François. *The History of Louisiana*. Edited by E. Wilson Lyon. Baton Rouge: Louisiana State University Press, 1977.

Baudier, Roger. *The Catholic Church in Louisiana*. New Orleans: [A. W. Hyatt], 1939.

Bayle, Constantino. *Los cabildos seculares en la América española*. Madrid: Sapientia, 1952.

Beerman, Eric. *España y la independencia de los Estados Unidos*. Madrid: MAPRE, 1993.

Bergamini, John D. *The Spanish Bourbons: The History of a Tenacious Dynasty*. New York: G. P. Putnam's Sons, 1974.

Bishko, Charles Julian. "The Spanish and Portuguese Reconquest, 1095-1492." In *The Fourteenth and Fifteenth Centuries*, 396-456. Vol. 3 of *A History of the Crusades*, edited by Harry W. Hazard. Madison: University of Wisconsin Press, 1975.

Berry, Trey, Jeanne Clements, and William Dunbar. *The Forgotten Expedition, 1804-1805: The Louisiana Journals of Dunbar and Hunter*. Baton Rouge: Louisiana State University Press, 2006.

Bjork, David K. "Alejandro O'Reilly and the Spanish Occupation of Louisiana, 1769-1770." In *New Spain and the Anglo-American West*, 1: 165-82. 2 vols. in 1. New York: Kraus Reprint Co., 1969.

Bonaparte, Napoleon, Emperor of the French. *Correspondance de Napoleon*. 32 vols. Paris: H. Plon, 1858-70.

Borah, Woodrow. *New Spain's Century of Depression*. Berkeley and Los Angeles: University of California Press, 1951.

Boyd-Bowman, Peter. *Índice geobiográfico de cuarenta mil pobladores de América en el siglo XVI*. Bogotá: Instituto Caro y Cuervo, 1964.

———. "Patterns of Spanish Emigration to the Indies until 1600." *Hispanic American Historical Review* 56 (November 1976): 580-604.

Boyer, Richard. "Mexico in the Seventeenth Century: Transition of a Colonial Society." *Hispanic American Historical Review* 57 (August 1977): 455-78.

Bradley, Jared William, ed. *Interim Appointment: W. C. C. Claiborne Letter Book, 1804-1805, edited with Biographical Sketches*. Baton Rouge: Louisiana State University Press, 2002.

———. "W. C. C. Claiborne and Spain: Foreign Affairs under Jefferson and Madison, 1801-1811." In *The Louisiana Purchase and Its Aftermath, 1800-1830*, edited by Dolores Egger Labbe, 110-37. Vol. 3 of *The Louisiana Purchase Bicentennial Series in Louisiana History*. Lafayette: Center for Louisiana Studies at the University of Southwestern Louisiana, 1998.

Brooks, Philip Coolidge. *Diplomacy and the Borderlands: The Ad-*

ams-Onis Treaty of 1819. Berkeley: University of California Press, 1939.

———. "Spain's Farewell to Louisiana, 1803-1821." *Mississippi Valley Historical Review* 21 (June 1940): 29-42.

Bruun, Geoffrey. *Europe and the French Imperium, 1799-1814*. New York: Harper and Row, 1963.

Caballero, José Agustín. "Elogio del señor Nicolás Calvo y O'Farrill." In *Escritos varios*, 179-96. Havana: Editoriales de la Universidad de La Habana, 1954.

Calcagno, Francisco. *Diccionario Biográfico Cubano*, 1878, Reprint, Miami: Editorial Cubana, 1996.

Carr, Raymond. *Spain, 1808-1975*. 2nd ed. Oxford, U.K.: Clarendon Press: 1982.

Carrera Montero, Fernando. *Las complejas relaciones de España con La Española: El Caribe hispano frente a Santo Domingo y Saint Domingue, 1789-1803*. Santo Domingo: Fundación García Arévalo, 2004.

Céspedes del Castillo, Guillermo. *América hispánica (1498-1898)*. Barcelona: Editorial Labor, 1983.

Chambers, Henry E. *Mississippi Valley Beginnings: An Outline of the Early History of the Earlier West*. New York: Knickerbocker Press, 1922.

Chapman, Charles E. *Colonial Hispanic America: A History*. New York: MacMillan, 1933.

———. *A History of Spain*. New York: Macmillan, 1918.

Chapman, Carl H. "The Indomitable Osage in the Spanish Illinois (Upper Louisiana), 1763-1804." In *The Spanish in the Mississippi Valley, 1762-1804*, edited by John Francis McDermott, 287-308. Urbana: University of Illinois Press, 1974.

———. *Origin of the Osage Tribe*. New York: Garland, 1974.

Chastenet, Jacques. *Godoy: Master of Spain, 1792-1808*. London:

Batchworth Press, 1953.

Chávez, Thomas. *Spain and the Independence of the United States: An Intrinsic Gift*. Albuquerque, University of New Mexico Press, 2002.

Claiborne, W. C. C. *Official Letter Books of W. C. C. Claiborne, 1801-1816*. Edited by Dunbar Rowlands. 6 vols. Jackson, Miss.: Mississippi Department of Archives and History, 1917.

Clark, John G. *New Orleans, 1718-1812: An Economic History*. Baton Rouge: Louisiana State University Press, 1970.

Coker, William S., and Hazel P. Coker. *The Siege of Mobile, 1780, in Maps, with Data on Troop Strength, Military Units, Ships, Casualties, and Prisoners of War Including a Brief History of Fort Charlotte (Conde)*. Pensacola: By the authors, 1982.

Coker, William S., and Thomas D. Watson. *Indian Traders of the Southeastern Spanish Borderlands: Panton, Leslie and Company and John Forbes and Company, 1783-1847*. Pensacola: University of West Florida Press, 1986.

Conover, Bettie Jones. "British West Florida's Mississippi Frontier Posts, 1763-1779." *Alabama Review* 29 (1976): 177-207.

Cook, Noble David. *Born to Die: Disease and New World Conquest, 1492-1650*. Cambridge, U.K.: Press Syndicate of the University of Cambridge, 1998.

Corona Baratech, Carlos E. *Revolución y reacción en el reinado de Carlos IV*. Madrid: Ediciones Rialp, 1957.

———. *Precedentes ideológicos de la Guerra de Independencia y su época*. Zaragoza: Institución Fernando El Católico, 1959.

Conrad, Glenn R., gen. ed. *A Dictionary of Louisiana Biography*, 2 vols. [Lafayette, La.]: Louisiana Historical Association in cooperation with the Center for Louisiana Studies of the University of Southwestern Louisiana, 1988.

Cox, Isaac Joslin. "The American Intervention in West Florida." *American Historical Review* 17 (January 1912): 290-311.

———. *The Early Explorations of Louisiana*. Cincinnati, Ohio: University of Cincinnati Press, 1906.

———. "General Wilkinson and His Later Intrigues with the Spaniards." *American Historical Review* 19 (July 1914): 794-812.

———. *The Louisiana-Texas Frontier.* 2 vols. Austin: University of Texas Press, 1906.

———. "The Louisiana-Texas Frontier during the Burr Conspiracy." *Mississippi Valley Historical Review* 10 (December 1923): 275-84.

———. *The West Florida Controversy, 1798-1813: A Study in American Diplomacy*. Baltimore: Johns Hopkins University Press, 1918.

Cummins, Light Townsend. *Spanish Agents in the American Revolutionary War*. Baton Rouge: Louisiana State University Press, 1992.

Dalrymple, Margaret, ed. *The Merchant of Manchac: The Letterbooks of John Fitzpatrick, 1768-1790*. Baton Rouge: Louisiana State University Press, 1976.

Davis, William C. *The Rogue Republic: How Would-Be Patriots Waged the Shortest Revolution in American History*. Boston: Houghton, Mifflin, Harcourt, 2011.

Dawdy, Shannon Lee. *Building the Devil's Empire: French Colonial New Orleans*. Chicago: University of Chicago Press, 2009.

DeConde, Alexander. *This Affair of Louisiana*. New York: Scribners, 1976.

De la Fuente, Alejandro. *Havana and the Atlantic in the Sixteenth-Century*. Chapel Hill: University of North Carolina Press, 2008.

———. "Sugar and Slavery in Early Colonial Cuba." In *Tropical Babylons: Sugar and the Making of the Atlantic World, 1415-1680*, edited by Stuart Schwartz, 115-57. Chapel Hill: University of North Carolina Press, 2004.

Deleito y Piñuela, José. *Congreso de Cádiz: El regreso de los afrancesados a España en 1820*. Madrid: Talleres Poligráficos, 1927.

Delgado, Jaime. "El Conde de Ricla, Capitán General de Cuba." *Re-*

vista de Historia de América 55/56 (January-December 1963): 41-138.

Dérozier, Albert. *José Quintana y el nacimiento del liberalismo en España*. Translated by Manuel Moya. Madrid: Ediciones Turner, 1978.

DeVille, Winston. "Charivari at Pointe Coupée in 1800." *Louisiana Genealogical Register* 40, no. 4 (December 1993): 356-58.

———, ed. *The Louisiana Manifesto of 1769*. Ville Platte, La.: Provincial Press, 2004.

Díaz-Plaja, Fernando. *Historia de España en sus documentos*. Madrid: Siglo XIX, 1983.

Diccionario de Autoridades. Madrid: Editorial Gredos, 1979.

Din, Gilbert C. "Carondelet, the Cabildo, and Slaves: Louisiana in 1795." *Louisiana History* 38 (Winter 1997): 5-28.

———. "'For Defense of Country and the Glory of Arms': Army Officers in Spanish Louisiana, 1766-1803." *Louisiana History* 43 (Winter 2002): 5-40.

———. *Francisco Bouligny: A Bourbon Soldier in Spanish Louisiana*. Baton Rouge: Louisiana State University Press, 1993.

———. "Francisco Bouligny; Marqués de Casa-Calvo; Manuel Juan de Salcedo; Pierre Clement, Baron de Laussat; Colonial Governors, 1799-1803," In *The Louisiana Governors: From Iberville to Edwards*, edited by Joseph G. Dawson III, 74-79. Louisiana State University Press: Baton Rouge, 1990.

———. "In Defense of Capt. Tomás Portell: An Episode in the History of Spanish West Florida." *Revista Española de Estudios Norteamericanos* 12, nos. 21-22 (2001): 143-58.

———. "Lieutenant Raimundo DuBreüil, Commandant of San Gabriel de Manchac, and Bernardo de Galvez's 1779 Campaign on the Mississippi River." *Military History of the West* 29 (Spring 1999): 1-30.

———. *Louisiana in 1776: A Memoria of Francisco Bouligny*. New Orleans: Louisiana Collections Series, 1977.

———. "Marqués de Casa-Calvo." In *Dictionary of Louisiana Biography*. 2 vols. New Orleans: Center of Louisiana Studies, 1988.

———. "Mississippi River Gunboats on the Gulf Coast: The Spanish Naval Fight against William Augustus Bowles, 1799-1803." *Louisiana History* 47 (Summer 2006): 277-308.

———. *Populating the Barrera: Spain's Immigration Efforts in Colonial Louisiana*. Lafayette: University of Louisiana at Lafayette Press, 2014.

———. "Protecting the '*Barrera*': Spain's Defenses in Louisiana, 1763-1779." *Louisiana History* 18 (Spring 1978), 183-211.

———. *Spaniards, Planters, and Slaves: The Spanish Regulation of Slavery in Louisiana, 1763-1803*. College Station: Texas A&M University Press, 1999.

———. *War on the Gulf Coast: The Spanish Fight against William Augustus Bowles*. Gainesville: University Presses of Florida, 2012.

———. "William Augustus Bowles on the Gulf Coast, 1787-1803: Unraveling a Labyrinthine Conundrum." *Florida Historical Quarterly* 89 (Summer 2010): 1-26.

Din, Gilbert C., and John E. Harkins. *The New Orleans Cabildo: Colonial Louisiana's First City Government, 1769-1803*. Baton Rouge: Louisiana State University Press, 1996.

Din, Gilbert C., and A. P. Nasatir. *The Imperial Osages: Spanish-Indian Diplomacy in the Mississippi Valley*. Norman: University of Oklahoma Press, 1983.

Dorsey, James Owen. *An Account of the War Customs of the Osages*. Philadelphia: n.p., 1884.

Ekbert, Carl J. *French Roots in the Illinois Country: The Mississippi Frontier in Colonial Times*. Urbana: University of Illinois Press, 1998.

Ely, Roland T. "Cuba Emerges from Isolation: Economic and Social Changes between 1760 and 1839." In *Background to Revolution:*

The Development of Modern Cuba, edited by Robert Freeman Smith, 159-67, New York: Alfred A. Knopf, 1966.

Enciclopedia Espasa Calpe. Vol. 24: 1505-1506. Madrid: 1964.

Esdaile, Charles. *The Peninsular War: A New History*. London: Penguin Books, 2002.

Fagg, John Edwin. *Cuba, Haiti, and the Dominican Republic.* Englewood Cliffs, N.J.: Prentiss Hall, 1965.

Faber, Eberhard L. "The Passion of the Prefect: Pierre Clément De Laussat, 1803 New Orleans, and the Bonapartist Louisiana That Never Was." *Louisiana History* 54 (Summer 2013): 261-91.

Fernández, Mark F. *From Chaos to Continuity: The Evolution of Louisiana's Judicial System, 1712-1862*. Baton Rouge: Louisiana State University Press, 2001.

Fernández Moya, Rafael. "The Irish Presence in the History and Place Names of Cuba." *Irish Migration Studies in Latin America* 5 (November 2007): 189-97.

Fernández Santalices, Manuel. *Las calles de la Habana intramuros: Arte, historia y tradiciones en las calles y plazas de La Habana vieja*. Miami: Ediciones Saeta, 1989.

Ferrer, Ada. "Cuba en la Sombra de Haiti: Noticias, Sociedad, y Esclavitud." In *El Rumor de Haití en Cuba: Temor, Raza y Rebeldía, 1789-1844*, edited by Dolores González-Ripoll et al., 179-231. Madrid: Consejo Superior de Investigaciones Científicas, 2004.

———. "Noticias de Haiti en Cuba, 1791-1804." *Revista de Indias*, no. 229 (Madrid: CSIC, 2003): 675-94.

Fick, Carolyn E. *The Making of Haiti: The Saint Domingue Revolution from Below*. Knoxville: University of Tennessee Press, 1990.

Figueras, Francisco. *Cuba y su evolución colonial.* Havana: Imprenta Avisador Comercial, 1907.

Gagliardo, John G. *Enlightened Despotism*. New York: T. Y. Crowell, 1967.

García del Pino, César. *La Habana bajo el reinado de los Austria*. Havana: Ediciones Boloña, 2008.

Gayarré, Charles. *History of Louisiana: The French Domination*. 3rd ed. Vol. 2. 1885. Reprint. New York: AMS Press, 1972.

Geggus, David. "The Major Port Towns of Saint Domingue in the Later Eighteenth Century." In *Atlantic Port Cities: Economy, Culture, and Society in the Atlantic World, 1650-1850*, edited by Franklin W. Knight and Peggy K. Liss, 87-117. Knoxville: University of Tennessee Press, 1991.

———. *Slavery, War and Revolution: The British Occupation of Saint Domingue, 1793-1798*. Oxford, U.K.: Clarenden Press, 1982.

Gershoy, Leo. *The French Revolution and Napoleon*. New York: Appleton-Century-Crofts, 1964.

Glickstein, Don. *After Yorktown: The Final Struggle for American Independence*. Yardley, Penn.: Westholme, 2015.

Glover, Michael. *Legacy of Glory: The Bonaparte Kingdom of Spain, 1808-1813*. New York: Charles Scribner's Sons, 1971.

Gold, Robert L. "Governor Bernardo de Gálvez and Spanish Espionage in Pensacola, 1777." In *The Spanish in the Mississippi Valley, 1762-1804*, edited by John Francis McDermott, 87-99. Urbana: University of Illinois Press, 1974.

González-Ripoll Navarro, María Dolores. *Cuba, la isla de los ensayos: cultura y sociedad (1790-1815)*. Madrid: Consejo Superior de Investigaciones Científicas, Centro de Humanidades Instituto de Historia, Departamento de Historia de América, 1999.

González-Ripoll, Dolores, Consuelo Naranjo, Aida Ferrer, Gloria García, and Josef Opatrny. *El rumor de Haití en Cuba: Temor, raza y rebeldía*. Madrid: Consejo Superior de Investigaciones Científicas, 2004.

Grafe, Regina, and María Alejandra Irigoin. "The Spanish Empire and Its Legacy: Fiscal Re-Distribution and Political Conflict in Colonial and Post-Colonial Spanish America." *Journal of Global History* 1 (September 2005): 1-68.

———. “A Stakeholder Empire: The Political Economy of Spanish Imperial Rule in America,” *Working Papers*, no. 111 (November 2008): 32-33.

Greene, Jack P. and Philip D. Morgan, eds., *Atlantic History: A Critical Appraisal.* Oxford, U.K.: Oxford University Press, 2009.

Hanger, Kimberly S. “‘Almost All Have Callings’: Free Blacks at Work in Spanish New Orleans,” *Colonial Latin American Historical Review* 3 (Spring 1994): 141-64.

———. “Avenues to Freedom Open to New Orleans’ Black Population, 1769-1779.” *Louisiana History* 31 (1990): 236-64.

———. *Bonded Lives, Bonded Places: Free Black Society in Colonial New Orleans, 1769-1803.* Durham, N.C.: Duke University Press,1997.

Haring, Clarence H. *Buccaneers in the West Indies in the XVII Century.* New York: E. P. Dutton and Company, 1910.

———. *Trade and Navigation between Spain and the Indies in the Time of the Hapsburgs.* Cambridge, Mass.: Harvard University Press, 1918.

Hatfield, Joseph T. *William Claiborne: Jeffersonian Centurion in the American Southwest.* Lafayette, La.: Center for Louisiana Studies, 1976.

Herr, Richard. *The Eighteenth Century Revolution in Spain.* Princeton, N.J.: Princeton University Press, 1958.

Hilton, Sylvia L. “Movilidad y expansión en la construcción política de los Estados Unidos: ‘estos errantes colonos’ en las fronteras españolas del Misisipí.” *Revista Complutense de Historia de América* 28 (2002): 63-96.

Holland, Elizabeth Vassall Fox. *The Spanish Journal of Elizabeth Lady Holland (1791-1811).* Edited by the Earl of Ilchester. New York: Longman, 1910.

Holmes, Jack D. L. “*Dramatis Personae* in Spanish Louisiana.” *Louisiana Studies* 6 (1967): 149-85.

———. *Gayoso: The Life of a Spanish Governor in the Mississippi Valley, 1789-1799.* Baton Rouge: Louisiana State University Press for the Louisiana Historical Association, 1965.

———. "The Marqués de Casa-Calvo, Nicolas de Finiels, and the 1805 Spanish Expedition through East Texas and Louisiana." *Southwestern Historical Quarterly* 69 (January 1966): 324-39.

Humboldt, Alexander von. *Personal Narrative of Travels to the Equinoctial Regions of the New Continent During the Years 1799-1804.* Translated by Helen Maria Williams. London: Longman, Hurst, Rees, Orme, 1829.

Jacobs, Auke Pieter. "Pasajeros y polizones: Algunas observaciones sobre la emigración española a las Indias durante el siglo XVI." *Revista de Indias* 172 (1983): 437-79.

Jacobs, James Ripley. *Tarnished Warrior: Major-General James Wilkinson.* New York: Macmillan, 1938.

James, C.L.R. *The Black Jacobins: Toussaint L'Ouverture and the San Domingo Revolution.* New York: Vintage Books, 1963.

Johnson, Sherry. *Social Transformation of Eighteenth-Century Cuba.* Gainesville: University Press of Florida, 2001.

Kamen, Henry. *Philip V: The King who Reigned Twice.* New Haven: Yale University Press, 2001.

———. *Spain, 1469-1714: A Society of Conflict.* London and New York: Longman, 1983.

———. *The War of the Spanish Succession, 1700-1715.* Bloomington: Indiana University Press, 1969.

King, David. *Vienna 1814: How the Conquerors of Napoleon Made Love, War, and Peace at the Congress of Vienna.* New York: Harmony Books, 2008.

King, Grace. *Creole Families of New Orleans.* 1921. Reprint. Baton Rouge: Claitors, 1971.

King, Grace Elizabeth. *New Orleans, The Place and the People.* New

York: Macmillan: 1895.

King, Grace, and John R. Ficklen. *A History of Louisiana*. Rev. ed. New York-New Orleans: University Publishing Company, [1893].

Kinnaird, Lawrence, ed. *Spain in the Mississippi Valley, 1765-1794*. 3 Pts. Washington, D.C.: Government Printing Office, 1949.

Knight, Franklin W. *The Caribbean: The Genesis of a Fragmented Nationalism*. 2nd ed. New York: Oxford University Press, 1990.

———. "Origins of Wealth and the Sugar Revolution in Cuba, 1750-1850," *Hispanic American Historical Review* 57 (1977): 231-53.

Korngold, Ralph. *Citizen Toussaint*. New York: Hill and Wang, 1965.

Kuethe, Allan, J. *Cuba, 1753-1815: Crown, Military, and Society*. Knoxville: University of Tennessee Press, 1986.

———. "Havana in the Eighteenth Century." In *Atlantic Port Cities: Economy, Culture, and Society in the Atlantic World, 1650-1850*, edited by Franklin W. Knight and Peggy K. Liss, 13-39. Knoxville: University of Tennessee Press, 1991.

Kukla, Jon, ed. *A Guide to the Papers of Pierre Clement Laussat*. New Orleans: Historic New Orleans Collection, 1993.

———. *A Wilderness So Immense: The Louisiana Purchase and the Destiny of America*. New York: Anchor Books, 2004.

Landers, Jane G. *Atlantic Creoles in the Age of Revolutions*. Cambridge, Mass.: Harvard University Press, 2010.

Langley, Lester D. *The Americas in the Age of Revolution, 1750-1850*. New Haven: Yale University Press, 1996.

Laussat, Pierre-Clément de. *Memoirs of My Life*. Baton Rouge: Published for the Historic New Orleans Collection by the Louisiana State University Press, 1978.

Lawson, Katherine S. "Luciano de Herrera, Spanish Spy in British St. Augustine," *Florida Historical Quarterly* 23 (1945): 170-76.

Le Gardeur, René J. Jr. *The First New Orleans Theatre, 1792-1803*. New Orleans: Leeward Books, 1963.

Lewis, James A. *The Final Campaign of the American Revolution: Rise and Fall of the Spanish Bahamas.* Columbia: University of South Carolina Press, 1991.

Linklater, Andro. *An Artist in Treason: The Extraordinary Double Life of General James Wilkinson.* New York: Walker Publishing Company, 2009.

Liss, Peggy K. *Atlantic Empires: The Network of Trade and Revolution, 1917-1826.* Baltimore: Johns Hopkins University Press, 1983.

Loomis, Noel. "Philip Nolan's Entry into Texas in 1800." In *The Spanish in the Mississippi Valley, 1762-1804*, edited by John Francis McDermott, 120-32. Urbana: University of Illinois Press, 1974.

López Tabar, Juan. *Famosos Traidores: los afrancesados durante la crisis del Antiguo Régimen (1808-1833).* Madrid: Publicaciones Nuevas, 2001.

Lovett, Gabriel H. *Napoleon and the Birth of Modern Spain*, 2 vols. New York: New York University Press, 1965.

Lynch, John. *Spain under the Habsburgs.* 2 vols. Oxford, U.K.: Basil Blackwell, 1964.

Lyon, E. Wilson. *Louisiana in French Diplomacy, 1759-1804.* Reprint. Norman: Oklahoma University Press, 1974.

Mallén, Francisco Javier de Santa Cruz y Conde de San Juan de Jaruco y de Santa Cruz de Mopox. *Historia de Familias Cubanas.* Vol. 4. La Habana: Editorial Hércules, 1943.

Marchena Fernández, Juan. *Oficiales y soldados en el ejército de América.* Sevilla: Escuela de Estudios Hispano-Americanos, 1983.

Marichal, Carlos. *Bankruptcy of Empire: Mexican Silver and the Wars between Spain, Britain and France, 1760-1810.* Cambridge, U.K.: Cambridge University Press, 2007.

McAlister, Lyle N. *The "Fuero Militar" in New Spain, 1766-1800.* Gainesville: University of Florida Press, 1957.

———. "The Reorganization of the Army of New Spain, 1763-1766."

Hispanic American Historical Review 33 (1953), 1-32.

———. *Spain and Portugal in the New World, 1492-1700.* Minneapolis: University of Minnesota Press, 1984.

McGinty, Garnie William. *A History of Louisiana.* New York: Exposition Press, 1951.

McMichael, Andrew. "The Kemper 'Rebellion': Filibustering and Resident Anglo American Loyalty in Spanish West Florida." *Louisiana History* 43 (Spring 2002): 133-65.

———. "Maintaining Loyalty in the West Florida Borderlands: Land as Cause and Effect in the West Florida Revolution of 1810." In *Coastal Encounters: The Transformation of the Gulf South in the Eighteenth Century*, edited by Richmond F. Brown, 210-30. Lincoln: University of Nebraska Press, 2007.

———. "William Dunbar, William Claiborne, and Daniel Clark: Intersections of Loyalty and National Identity on the Florida Frontier." In *Nexus of Empire: Negotiating Loyalty and Identity in the Revolutionary Borderlands, 1760s-1820s*, edited by Gene Allen Smith and Sylvia L. Hilton, 285-89. Gainesville: University Press of Florida, 2010.

Méndez Rodenas, Adriana. *Gender and Nationalism in Colonial Cuba: The Travels of Santa Cruz y Montalvo, Condesa de Merlin.* Nashville: Vanderbilt University Press, 1998.

Mercader Riba, Juan. *José Napoleón, rey de España (1808-1813): estructura del estado español bonapartista.* Madrid: Consejo Superior de Investigaciones Científicas, Instituto de Historia "Jerónimo Zorita," 1983.

Merlin, Condesa de. *Mis doce primeros años e historia de Sor Inés.* Edited by Francisco Calcagno. Havana: Imprenta El Siglo XX, 1922.

Moiroux, Jules. *Le cimetière du Père Lachaise.* Paris: A. Maréchal, [1922].

Monte y Tejada, Antonio del. *Historia de Santo Domingo.* 4 vols. Santo Domingo: Imprenta de García Hermanos, 1890-92.

Montero de Pedro, José (Marqués de Casa Mena). *Españoles en Nueva Orleans y Luisiana*. Madrid: Talleres Prensa Española, 1979.

Moore, John Preston. *The Cabildo in Peru under the Bourbons: A Study in the Decline and Resurgence of Local Government in the Audiencia of Lima, 1700-1824*. Durham, N.C.: Duke University Press, 1966.

———. *The Cabildo in Peru under the Habsburgs: a study in the origins and powers of the town council in the viceroyalty of Peru, 1530-1700*. Durham, N.C.: Duke University Press, 1954.

———. *Revolt in Louisiana: The Spanish Occupation, 1766-1770*. Baton Rouge: Louisiana State University Press, 1976.

Morazán, Ronald Rafael, editor and translator. "Letters, Petitions, and Decrees of the Cabildo of New Orleans, 1800-1803." PhD diss. Louisiana State University, 1972.

Moreno Fraginals, Manuel. *Ingenio: el complejo económico social cultural del azúcar*. Tomo 1, 1760-1860. La Habana: Comisión cultural de la UNESCO, 1964.

Morison, Samuel Eliot. *Admiral of the Ocean Sea: A Life of Christopher Columbus*. Boston: Little, Brown, and Company, 1942.

Morison, Samuel Eliot. *Christopher Columbus, Mariner*. Boston: New American Library, 1942.

Moya Pons, Frank. *The Dominican Republic: A National History*. Princeton, N.J.: Markus Wiener Publishers, 1998.

———. "The Haitian Revolution in Santo Domingo (1789-1809)." *Yarbuch für Geschichte: Latainamerikas* 28 (1991): 125-62.

———. *Manuel de la historia dominicana*. Santo Domingo: Editorial UCMM, 1981.

Narrett, David E. "Geopolitics and Intrigue: James Wilkinson, The Spanish Borderlands, and Mexican Independence." *William and Mary Quarterly*, 3rd ser., 69 (January 2012), 101-46.

Nasatir, Abraham P. "Anglo-Spanish Rivalry on the Upper Missouri River." *Mississippi Valley Historical Review* 16 (December 1929-March

1930): no. 3, 359-82, and no. 4, 420-39.

———, ed. *Before Lewis and Clark: Documents Illustrating the History of the Missouri, 1785-1804.* 2 vols. St. Louis: St. Louis Historical Documents Foundation, 1952.

———, ed. *Spanish War Vessels on the Mississippi, 1792-1796.* New Haven: Yale University Press, 1968.

Navarro Latorre, Juan, and Francisco Solano Costa, *¿Conspiración española?1787-1789: Contribución al estudio de las primeras relaciones históricas entre España y los Estados Unidos de Norteamérica.* Zaragoza, España: Editoriales Librería General, 1949.

Nicolson, Harold. *The Congress of Vienna: A Study in Allied Unity, 1812-1822.* New York: Harcourt, Brace, and Company, 1946.

Nugent, Walter. *Habits of Empire: A History of American Expansion.* New York: Vintage Books, 2009.

Ojeda, Jorge Victoria. *Las tropas auxiliares de Carlos IV: de Saint-Domingue al mundo hispano.* Castellón de la Plana, Spain: Universitat Jaume, 2011.

———. *Tropas auxiliares del Rey en Centroamérica: historia de negros súbditos de la monarquía española.* San José, Costa Rica: Editorial UCR, 2009.

Oliveira, A. Ramos. *Politics, Economics, and Men of Modern Spain, 1808-1946.* Translated by Teener Hall. London: Victor Gollancz, Ltd., 1946.

O'Neal, Charles Edward. "'A Quarter Marked by Sundry Peculiarities': New Orleans, Lay Trustees, and Père Antoine." In *The Louisiana Purchase and Its Aftermath, 1800-1830*, edited by Dolores Egger Labbe, 421-55. Vol. 3 of *The Louisiana Purchase Bicentennial Series in Louisiana History.* Lafayette: Center for Louisiana Studies, University of Southwestern Louisiana, 1998.

Onís, Luis de. *Negociaciones entre España y los Estados Unidos de América.* 3rd ed.; Madrid: Ediciones J. Porrúa Turanza, 1969.

Oudard, Georges. *Four Cents an Acre: The Story of Louisiana under the French*. New York: Brewer and Warren, 1931.

Palacio Atard, Vicente. *Los españoles de la Ilustración*. Madrid: Ediciones Guadarrama, 1964.

Palmer, Robert R. *The Age of Democratic Revolution: A Political History of Europe and America, 1760-1820*. 2 vols. Princeton: Princeton University Press, 1959-1961.

Parry, J(ohn) H. *The Sale of Public Office in the Spanish Indies under the Hapsburgs*. Berkeley and Los Angeles: University of California Press, 1953.

Partington, Charles Frederick. *British Cyclopedia of Biography: Containing the Lives of Distinguished Men of All Ages and Countries*. London: W. Orr, 1837.

Payne, Stanley G. *A History of Spain and Portugal.* 2 vols. Madison: University of Wisconsin Press, 1973.

Pérez, Louis A., Jr. *Cuba: Between Reform and Revolution*. New York: Oxford University Press, 1988.

Pérez, Samantha. *The Isleños of Louisiana: On the Water's Edge*. Charleston, S.C.: The History Press, 2011.

Perry, Mary Elizabeth. *Crime and Society in Early Modern Spain*. Hanover, N.H.: University Press of New England, 1980.

Pezuela, Jacobo de la. *Crónica de la las Antillas*. Madrid: Rubio, Grilo y Vitturi, 1871.

———. *Diccionario geográfico, estadístico, histórico, de la isla de Cuba.* 4 vols. Madrid: Imprenta del Banco Industrial y Mercantil, 1866.

Pichardo, Jose Antonio. *Pichardo's Treatise on the Limits of Louisiana and Texas*. Edited by Charles Wilson Hackett. 4 vols. Reprint. 1931. Freeport, N.Y.: Books for Libraries Press, 1971.

Pierson, J. W. "Francisco de Arango y Parreño." *Hispanic American Historical Review* 16, no. 4 (November 1936): 451-78.

Pike, Frederick B. "The Municipality and the System of Checks and

Balances in Spanish American Colonial Administration." *Americas* 15 (1958-59): 139-58.

Pike, Ruth. *Aristocrats and Traders: Sevillian Society in the Sixteenth Century*. Ithaca: Cornell University Press, 1972.

———. "Sevillian Society in the Sixteenth Century: Slaves and Freedmen." *Hispanic American Historical Review* 47 (1967), 344-69.

Pike, Zebulon Montgomery. *The Southwestern Expedition of Zebulon M. Pike*. Edited by Milo Milton Quaife. Chicago: R. R. Donnelly and Sons, 1925.

Pitot, James. *Observations on the Colony of Louisiana from 1796 to 1802*. Translation and introduction by Henry C. Pitot. Baton Rouge: Louisiana State University Press for the Historic New Orleans Collection, 1979.

Posey, John Thornton. "Rascality Revisited: In Defense of General James Wilkinson," *Filson Club History Quarterly* 74 (Fall 2000): 309-51.

Powell, Lawrence N. *The Accidental City: Improvising New Orleans*. Cambridge, Mass.: Harvard University Press, 2012.

Prieto Benavent, José Luis. "Mercedes de Santa Cruz y Montalvo, Condesa de Merlin: 'une femme du monde.'" *Revista Hispano Cubana* 13 (Madrid: May-September, 2002): 83-96.

Ramírez de Villa-Urrutia, Wenceslao. *España en el Congreso de Viena según la correspondencia de D. Pedro Gómez Labrador, Marqués de Labrador*. 2nd ed. Madrid: Francisco Beltrán, 1928.

Ramos Oliveira, A. *Politics, Economics, and Men of Modern Spain, 1808-1946*. Translated by Teener Hall. London: Victor Gollancz, Ltd., 1946.

Recio Morales, Oscar. "When Merit is Not Enough: Money as a 'Parallel Route' for Irish Advancement in Spain. "*Irish Migration Studies in Latin America* 5 (July 2007): 121-24.

Regueiro García, María Teresa. *Relaciones Iglesia-Estado: afrancesados y doceañistas*. Valencia: Tirant lo Blanch, 2012.

Rivero Muñiz, José. *Tabaco, su historia en Cuba*. 2 vols. La Habana: Instituto de Historia, Comisión Nacional de la Academia de Ciencia de la República de Cuba, 1964/65.

Robertson, James Alexander, ed. *Louisiana under the Rule of Spain, France, and the United States, 1785-1807*. 2 vols. Cleveland: Arthur H. Clark, 1911.

Rodríguez Casado, Vicente. *Primeros años de dominación española en la Luisiana*. Madrid: Seminario Superior de Estudios Científicos, 1942.

Rojas, María Teresa de. *Índice y extractos del Archivo de Protocolos de la Habana, 1578-1585*. 3 vols. La Habana: Ucar, García y Cía., 1997.

Rollings, Willard H. *The Osages: An Ethno-historical Study of Hegemony on the Prairie-Plains*. Columbia: University of Missouri Press, 1992.

Rowland, Dunbar, comp. and ed. *The Mississippi Territorial Archives, 1798-1803: Executive Journals of Governor Winthrop Sargent and Governor William Charles Cole Claiborne*. Nashville: Brandon Printing Company, 1905.

Schoenrich, Otto. *Santo Domingo, A Country with a Future*. New York: Macmillan, 1918.

Scroggs, William O. *The Story of Louisiana*. Indianapolis and New York: Bobbs-Merrill, 1943.

Segre, Roberto, Mario Coyula, and Joseph L. Scarpaci. *Havana: Two Faces of the Antillan Metropolis*. Chichester, U.K.: John Wiley and Sons, 1997.

Serrano Álvarez, José Manuel, and Allan J. Kuethe. "La Familia O'Farrill y La Élite Habanera." In *Élites Urbanas en Hispanoamérica*, edited by Luis Navarro García, 203-10. Sevilla: Universidad de Sevilla, Secretariado de Publicaciones, 2005.

Serrano y Sanz, Manuel. *Documentos históricos de la Florida y la Luisia-*

na, siglos XVI al XVIII. Madrid: V. Sánchez, 1912.

Sevilla Soler, María Rosario. *Santo Domingo: Tierra de Frontera (1750-1800)*. Sevilla: Escuela de Estudios Hispano-Americanos de Sevilla, 1980.

Smith, Rhea Marsh. *Spain, A Modern History*. Ann Arbor: University of Michigan Press, 1965.

Smith, Robert Freeman, ed. *Background to Revolution: The Development of Modern Cuba*. New York: Alfred A. Knopf, 1966.

Smith, Ronald D. "Napoleon and Louisiana: Failure of the Proposed Expedition to Occupy and Defend Louisiana, 1801-1803." *Louisiana History* 12 (Winter 1971): 21-40.

Sorber, Edna C., and Joseph Velo. "A Sketch of the Marquis of Casa Calvo, Governor of Louisiana (1751-1820)." *Revista: Cuban Genealogical Society* 4 (July 1991): 1-6.

Stoddard, T. Lothrop. *The French Revolution in San* [sic] *Domingo*. Boston: Houghton Mifflin, 1914.

Stoltz III, Joseph F. "'The Preservation of Good Order': William C. C. Claiborne and the Militia of Louisiana Provisional Government, 1803-1805." *Louisiana History* 54 (Fall 2013): 424-47.

Suchlicki, Jaime. *Cuba, from Columbus to* Castro. New York: Pergamon Press, 1986.

Texada, David Ker. *Alejandro O'Reilly and the New Orleans Rebels*. Lafayette: Center for Louisiana Studies, 1970.

———, ed. "An Account of Governor Alejandro O'Reilly's Voyage from Havana to New Orleans in July, 1769." *Louisiana History* 10 (Spring 1981): 199-207.

Thomas, Hugh. *Cuba: The Pursuit of Freedom*. New York: Harper and Row, 1971.

Thornton, John. *Africa and Africans in the Making of the Atlantic World, 1499-1500*. Cambridge, U.K.: Cambridge University Press, 1992.

Tornero, Pablo. "Hacendados y desarrollo azucarero cubano (1763-

1818)." *Revista de Indias* 38, nos. 153-54 (July-December 1978): 715-37.

Torres Ramírez, Bibiano. *Alejandro O'Reilly en las Indias*. Sevilla: Escuela de Estudios Superiores, 1969.

Treudley, Mary. "The United States and Santo Domingo [*sic*], 1789-1866." *The Journal of Race Development* 7, no. 1 (July 1916): 98-145.

Turnball, David. *Travels in the West: Cuba, with notes of Porto Rico* [*sic*], *and the Slave Trade*. London: Longman, Orne, Browne, Green, and Longmans, 1840.

Turner, Frederick Jackson. "The Policy of France toward the Mississippi Valley in the Period of Washington and Adams." *American Historical Review* 10 (January 1905): 249-79.

Vallellano, Conde de (Fernando Suárez de Tangil y de Angulo). *Nobiliario cubano: Las grandes familias isleñas*. 2 vols. Madrid: F. Beltrán, [1929].

Veira, Alberto. "Sugar Islands: The Sugar Economy of Madeira and the Canaries, 1450-1650." In *Tropical Babylons*: *Sugar and the Making of the Atlantic World, 1450-1650*, edited by Stuart B. Schwartz. Chapel Hill: University of North Carolina Press, 2004.

Weber, David J. *The Spanish Frontier in North America*. New Haven: Yale University Press, 1992.

Wallerstein, Immanuel Maurice. *Geopolitics and Geoculture: Essays in the Changing World-System*. Cambridge, U.K.: Cambridge University Press, 1991.

Walton, William. *Present State of the Spanish Colonies*. London: Longman, et al., 1810.

Webre, Stephen Andrew. "The Social and Economic Bases of Cabildo Membership in Seventeenth-Century Santiago de Guatemala," PhD diss. Tulane University, 1980.

Weems, John Edward. *Men without Countries*. Boston: Houghton Mifflin, 1969.

Whitaker, Arthur Preston. *The Mississippi Question, 1795-1803: A Study in Trade, Politics, and Diplomacy*. Reprint. Gloucester, Mass: Peter Smith, 1962.

———. "The Retrocession of Louisiana in Spanish Policy." *American Historical Review* 39 (April 1934): 454-70.

White, David Hart. "The Indian Policy of Vicente Folch, Governor of Spanish Mobile, 1787-1792." *Alabama Review* 28 (July 1975): 145-55.

———. *Vicente Folch, Governor in West Florida, 1787-1811*. Washington, D.C.: American Academic Press, 1981.

Wilson, Charles M. *Liberty or Death! The Life and Times of Asencio Nabot—Franciscan Friar, Guerrilla Leader, Secret Agent and Exile*. Victoria, B.C.: Trofford Publishing, 2008.

Wilson, Maurine, and Jack Jackson. *Philip Nolan and Texas: Expeditions to the Unknown Land, 1791-1801*. Waco: Texian Press, 1987.

Wilson, Jr., Samuel. "Almonester: Philanthropist and Builder in New Orleans." In *The Spanish in the Mississippi Valley, 1762-1804*, edited by John Francis McDermott, 183-47. Urbana: University of Illinois Press, 1974.

Winston, James. "The Causes and Results of the Revolution of 1768 in Louisiana." *Louisiana Historical Quarterly* 15 (April 1932): 181-213.

Worcester, Donald E., and Wendell G. Schaeffer. *The Growth and Culture of Latin America*. New York: Oxford University Press, 1956.

Wright, Irene A., ed. "The Commencement of the Cane Sugar Industry in America, 1519-1538 (1563)." *American Historical Review* 21 (July 1916): 755-80.

———. "The Dutch and Cuba, 1609-1643." *Hispanic American Historical Review* 4 (November 1921): 597-634.

———. *Early History of Cuba, 1492-1586, written from original sources*. New York, Macmillan, 1916.

Index

N

O

P

Q

R

T